ANCIENT EPISTOLARY FICTIONS

This book offers the first comprehensive look at fictive letters in Greek literature from Homer to Philostratus. It includes both embedded epistolary narratives in a variety of genres (epic, historiography, tragedy, the novel), and works consisting solely of letters, such as the pseudonymous letter collections and the invented letters of the Second Sophistic. The book challenges the notion that Ovid "invented" the fictional letter form in his *Heroides*, and considers a wealth of Greek antecedents for the later European epistolary novel tradition. Epistolary technique always problematizes the boundaries between fictionality and reality. Based on a process of selection and self-censorship, the letter is a construction, not a reflection, of reality. Thus the author bypasses the slippery question of sincerity for a close look at epistolary self-representation, the function of the letter form, and the nature of the relationship between writer and reader in a wide range of ancient Greek texts.

PATRICIA A. ROSENMEYER is Associate Professor of Classics at the University of Wisconsin, Madison. She is the author of *The Poetics of Imitation: Anacreon and the Anacreontic Tradition* (1992).

ANCIENT EPISTOLARY FICTIONS

FICTIONS

The letter in Greek literature

PATRICIA A. ROSENMEYER

University of Wisconsin, Madison

CAMBRIDGE
UNIVERSITY PRESS

PUBLISHED BY THE PRESS SYNDICATE OF THE UNIVERSITY OF CAMBRIDGE
The Pitt Building, Trumpington Street, Cambridge, United Kingdom

CAMBRIDGE UNIVERSITY PRESS
The Edinburgh Building, Cambridge CB2 2RU, UK   www.cup.cam.ac.uk
40 West 20th Street, New York, NY 10011–4211, USA   www.cup.org
10 Stamford Road, Oakleigh, Melbourne 3166, Australia
Ruiz de Alarcón 13, 28014 Madrid, Spain

First published 2001

Printed in the United Kingdom at the University Press, Cambridge

Typeset in Baskerville and New Hellenic Greek [AO]

A catalogue record for this book is available from the British Library

Library of Congress Cataloguing in Publication data
Rosenmeyer, Patricia A.
Ancient epistolary fictions : the letter in Greek literature / Patricia A. Rosenmeyer.
p.   cm.
Includes bibliographical references and index.
ISBN 0 521 80004 8 (hardback)
1. Greek literature–History and criticism. 2. Letters in literature. 3. Epistolary fiction,
Greek–History and criticism. 4. Epistolary poetry, Greek–History and criticism. 5. Letter
writing, Greek–History. 1. Title.
PA3014.L37 R67 2001
883′.0109–dc21   00–041454

ISBN 0 521 80004 8 hardback

For Peter and Daniel

Contents

Acknowledgments   *page* ix

Prologue   1

I   EPISTOLARITY: AN INTRODUCTION

1   A culture of letter writing   19

II EPISTOLARY FICTIONS

2   Homer: the father of letters   39

3   Letters in the historians   45

4   Staging letters: embedded letters in Euripides   61

5   Letters in Hellenistic poetry   98

III THE EPISTOLARY NOVEL

6   Embedded letters in the Greek novel   133

7   The *Alexander Romance*   169

8   Pseudonymous letter collections   193

9   *Chion of Heraclea*: an epistolary novel   234

IV EPISTOLOGRAPHY IN THE SECOND SOPHISTIC

10 The *Letters* of Alciphron   255

11 Aelian's *Rustic Letters*   308

12 The *Erotic Epistles* of Philostratus   322

Afterword   339

Bibliography   347
Index   363

Acknowledgments

This book is the result of many years of writing and revising, and it has transformed itself with each step of my own academic odyssey. The project was conceptualized in Ann Arbor, matured in New Haven and Providence, and finally declared itself complete in Madison. I have many individuals and institutions to thank for their support, both financial and moral, along the way. I am grateful to the National Endowment for the Humanities for a fellowship during the academic year 1992–93, during which time I took leave from my teaching duties at Yale University to work on the book. I also taught a graduate seminar on the subject at Yale, which challenged me to think more profoundly about the literary and theoretical issues surrounding epistolarity, and I thank the students in that seminar for their participation. The Department of Classics at Yale generously allowed further leave time for research, which was invaluable in completing a first draft. During much of that time, I enjoyed the hospitality of the Department of Classics at Brown University, where I was a Visiting Scholar. In the final stages of the project, I acknowledge the assistance of the Graduate School and the Institute for Research in the Humanities at the University of Wisconsin–Madison; as a Fellow of the Institute for one semester in 1998, I found an ideal forum for the exchange of ideas.

While institutional support is an absolute necessity, my most sincere thanks go to friends and colleagues who read this project at various stages and suggested improvements. In particular, I am grateful to Alessandro Barchiesi, Victor Bers, S. Marie Flaherty Jones, Simon Goldhill, Stephen Hinds, Richard Hunter, David Konstan, Sara Lindheim, Nellie Oliensis, Tom Rosenmeyer, Debbie Steiner, and Froma Zeitlin. S. Marie Flaherty Jones patiently read multiple drafts with consummate editorial skill; her comments on both style and general focus led me to rethink critical points and helped me immensely in my revisions. I am fortunate to have Pauline Hire as my editor, and thank her for her continued support. She found readers for the typescript who engaged with my material both critically and constructively. Without her gentle direction, and the readers' excellent and detailed recommendations, this project never would have seen the light of day. I also benefitted greatly from the careful copy-editing skills of Linda Woodward at the Press. In the last stages of revision in Madison, Holly Sypniewski worked as my editorial assistant, and my colleague Laura McClure assisted with matters both practical and professional. Let me express my heartfelt thanks to three long-distance friends who have sustained me emotionally in the last few years: Sara Lindheim, Rosina Lippi-Green, and S. Marie Flaherty Jones. Finally, I acknowledge the pleasant distraction of family; in the midst of the stresses of academic life, Peter and Daniel provide a much-needed sense of balance.

Earlier versions of parts of chapters 5 and 9 appeared originally as articles: "Love Letters in Callimachus, Ovid, and Aristaenetus, or, the Sad Fate of a Mail-order Bride," *MD* 36 (1996) 9–31, and "The Epistolary Novel," in J. R. Morgan and R. Stoneman, eds., *Greek Fiction: the Greek Novel in Context* (London 1994) 146–65.

Prologue

The following passage in Plutarch's *Lives* neatly evokes the special status of letters, particularly personal letters, in the ancient world. In 305 BCE the inhabitants of Rhodes were under siege by Demetrius Poliorcetes, son of Antigonus I; Demetrius followed his father in trying, in vain, to reunite Alexander's empire by waging war against the divided rule of Ptolemy in Egypt and Seleucus in the East. In this instance, the Rhodians, who will eventually be victorious, intercept a ship containing things sent from Demetrius' wife (Plut. *Life of Demetrius* 22.2):[1]

When Phila his wife sent him letters, bedding, and clothing, the Rhodians had captured the vessel containing them, and sent it, just as it was, to Ptolemy. In this they did not imitate the considerate kindness of the Athenians, who, having captured Philip's letter-carriers when he was making war on them, read all the other letters, but one of them, which was from Olympias [his wife], they would not open; instead, they sent it back to the king with its seal unbroken. However, although Demetrius was exceedingly exasperated by this, when the Rhodians soon after gave him a chance to retaliate, he would not allow himself to do so.

The Rhodians intercept Demetrius' personal letters and reroute them to his rival Ptolemy I, but do not treat the documents in any way differently from the rest of the ship's contents: the whole vessel is sent to Ptolemy "just as it was," for inspection by the enemy. The letters here are treated as booty, and the Rhodians ignore the potentially private nature of the correspondence between husband and wife. By contrast, in similar circumstances two generations earlier, the Athenians open all their enemy's letters except the one from his wife, hoping to discover, one assumes, secret campaign plans, news of supplies coming from Macedonia, or other military

---

[1] Text and translation from B. Perrin, *Plutarch's Lives* (London 1920).

I

information from Philip's allies. They also may hope to learn something more about the man himself, his character and thoughts, from his own letters or those addressed to him: anything that could help them outwit and conquer their attacker. But they treat the personal letter differently: even in war the Athenians respect the private nature of a written message from wife to husband, and they forward Olympias' letter to the king with its seal unbroken.

The passage in Plutarch raises a number of issues around Olympias' letter. Plutarch seems to imply that the Athenians act decently by scrupulously declining to eavesdrop on a private conversation. But further issues arise. Olympias' letter is singled out from "all the other letters" in the possession of the letter-carrier presumably because it is written by a woman, in this case Philip's wife. Do the Athenians assume that this is a love letter, a private message between a married couple that could refer only to their relationship, their family, and other purely personal matters? Or do they suppose that the purportedly innocent cover of a wife's letter might possibly hide within itself military or political information, but are nevertheless restricted by some universal code of behavior to respect the privacy of the couple's mail? Plutarch, by mentioning the letter but not reporting its contents (which realistically he could not do, since the letter was sent straight on to Philip), exploits the tension between his readers' desire to open and read someone else's mail, and their knowledge that it is a gross violation of privacy to do so.

The issue of epistolary decorum seems as relevant today as it did in Philip's fourth-century Macedonia. Is a private letter meant for the eye of its addressee alone or written with a sense of a larger readership? Do all letters become public property once out of the hands of their original correspondents? What is so intriguing about a person's private thoughts expressed on paper? The Athenians in Plutarch's example treated such a letter as taboo, and honored its privacy by sending it on to its intended addressee without breaking its seal. In modern times, the commercial appeal of the confessional or romantic epistolary mode seems too great for publishers to resist. Thus Ted Hughes defines his last collection of poems as "letters" addressed to his famous wife, and the jacket blurb of *Birthday Letters* (New York 1998) claims that, "[i]ntimate and candid in manner, they are largely concerned with the psychological drama that led both to the writing of her [Sylvia

Plath's] greatest poems and to her death." Hughes' poetic letter form incorporates formal verse and "psychological drama," intimacy with a careful editorial hand.

An even more striking example is a group of fourteen letters actually sent from J. D. Salinger to his lover during a brief but intense romance in 1972–73. When, more than twenty-five years later, the former lover announced plans to auction the letters in the public arena of Sotheby's New York, *The New York Times* published a story on the controversy about the ownership of the documents, teasing its readership by printing a photograph of the letters, some typed and others handwritten but all partially legible, spread out as if someone had just begun reading them, and topped by a stamped and postmarked envelope with Salinger's return address:[2]

> On the one hand, the letters, like a high-intensity flashlight beamed into a musty attic, are a startlingly intimate glimpse of the most private and reclusive of American authors. Because Mr. Salinger, now 80, has so zealously guarded his private life and last wrote for publication in 1965, the letters will surely intrigue scholars and others interested in his work.
>
> On the other hand, they are as private as correspondence can be, essentially love letters to someone he describes almost from the start as a kindred soul. As such they will no doubt strike many as a grievous invasion of Mr. Salinger's consistently and insistently stated desire to maintain his privacy.

For Mr. Salinger, the question of epistolary decorum is frighteningly real, but for most of the letters treated in this book, the issue is less of reality than of literary or fictional effect. Of course, the distinction between "real" and fictive letters is often unclear, both in antiquity and now. For example, can we count as "real" the letters of Cicero, although they were quasi-public compositions, clearly written with a view to eventual publication? In most cases, we are dealing with two sets of readers: the actual addressee, the first reader who expects some glimpse at intimacy, and the wider public, secondary readers, reading over the shoulder, who may expect and achieve something entirely different from their reading experience. But the epistolary mode encourages both sets of readers and critics towards the misguided assumption that let-

---

[2] P. Applebome, "Love Letters in the Wind," in *The New York Times*, Wednesday, May 12, 1999, B1.

ters necessarily reveal a kind of "pure" emotion, the depths of the writer's soul. Thus the critic Demetrius of Phalerum, whose work is dated between 100 BCE and 100 CE, tells us that "one writes a kind of image of one's soul when one writes a letter" (*On Style* 227), and Basil, the fourth-century bishop of Caesarea agrees: "words are truly the images of the soul" (*Letter* 9).[3]

The image of epistolary immediacy persists through the ages. Heloise turns to letters to communicate with her beloved Abelard because "they have soul, they can speak, they have in them all the force which expresses the transports of the heart."[4] Much later Dr. Johnson echoes her words:[5]

A man's letters ... are only the mirror of his breast, whatever passes within him is shown undisguised in its natural process. Nothing is inverted, nothing distorted, you see systems in their elements, you discover actions in their motives.

So, too, Samuel Richardson, in the preface to *Clarissa*, describes his idea of "writing to the moment," in which letters are used to embody an emotional situation still in process, revealing a character in the middle of a crisis. Letters represent the ongoing experience of the present as a critical moment, seized and recorded by the letter writer:[6]

... the letters on both sides are written while the hearts of the writers must be supposed to be wholly engaged in their subjects: the events at the time generally dubious – so that they abound not only with critical situations, but with what may be called *instantaneous* descriptions and reflections, which may be brought home to the breast of the youthful reader; as also, with affecting conversations, many of them written in the dialogue or dramatic way.[7]

The letter has always seemed a particularly personal and immediate mode of expression, as if its very form encouraged intimacy and directness.

My approach in this study will be to attempt to challenge

---

[3] The image is discussed in H. Koskenniemi, *Studien zur Idee und Phraseologie des griechischen Briefes bis 400n. Chr.* (Helsinki, 1956) 40–42.

[4] Quoted in C. M. Gillis, *The Paradox of Privacy: Epistolary Form in "Clarissa"* (Gainesville FL 1984) 129.

[5] Quoted in I. P. Watt, *The Rise of the Novel* (Berkeley CA 1957) 191.

[6] See J. Preston, *The Created Self: The Reader's Role in Eighteenth-Century Fiction* (New York 1970) 39.

[7] Samuel Richardson, *Clarissa*, ed. A. Ross (London 1985) 35.

these assumptions of epistolary "honesty." Epistolary technique always problematizes the boundaries between fiction and reality. While this issue is not limited to the epistolary genre – lyric poetry, for example, creates a different *ego* upon each occasion of reperformance – it has a huge impact on our reading of letters, whether literary or practical (i.e., actually sent). Whenever one writes a letter, one automatically constructs a self, an occasion, a version of the truth. Based on a process of selection and self-censorship, the letter is a construction, not a reflection, of reality. Thus the slippery question of sincerity may be bypassed for a closer look at epistolary self-representation, the function of the letter form, and the nature of the relationship between writer(s) and reader(s).

The very word "letter" encompasses a huge variety of epistolary forms in antiquity. There are no ancient Greek words to distinguish government from private letters, business contracts in letter form from love letters, St. Paul's epistolary sermons from Alciphron's sophistic epistolary fictions. Even when epistolary theorists in antiquity did attempt to categorize letter writing, they restricted themselves to descriptions of practical and functional forms: letters of recommendation, letters to a superior, and so on. It was the discovery of large numbers of non-literary papyrus letters at Oxyrhynchus in Egypt at the turn of the last century that precipitated the first real crisis in classical scholarship about the nature of letters. At stake was not just an issue of classification and historical accuracy. These scholars turned to the papyrus letters as keys to the past, documents they hoped would allow them unmediated and direct access to classical antiquity. But not all the letters answered their intellectual needs or fitted their images of the past they had previously inherited, and the ensuing debate raised issues of continuing relevance.

Adolf Deissmann, a biblical scholar working in the early 1900s, felt that a distinction needed to be made between such rudimentary "documents of life" as were being uncovered at Oxyrhynchus, and the related but very different "products of literary art" that had become canonical reading for generations of schoolboys.[8] The former he labelled a true "letter" ("Brief"), while the latter he

---

[8] A. Deissmann, *Light from the Ancient East*, 4th edn., trans. L. Strachan (New York 1927) 227, originally published as *Licht vom Osten* (Tübingen 1923).

termed an "epistle" ("Epistel"). His main goal was a reevaluation of the epistolary writings of Paul in the New Testament (which he argued were true letters), but his views strongly influenced contemporary classical scholarship.[9] He identified spontaneity as the defining characteristic of the true ancient letter, and created a Paul who was a champion of the lower classes, passionately arguing directly from the heart, his reported speech untouched by literary or rhetorical conventions.[10] In his zeal to recover the "true" Paul, he molded the evidence to suit contemporary German tastes.

According to Deissmann, a letter ("Brief") is first and foremost non-literary. It is confidential, personal in nature, intended for a specific addressee, and concerning only the writer and the reader, not a wider public; its message is private, yet essentially ephemeral, not meant to last beyond the moment of comprehension. He goes on to state that "there is no essential difference between the letter and an oral dialogue," and, since "its contents may be as various as life itself," letters may be seen as the "liveliest instantaneous photographs of ancient life."[11] The image of the instant photograph elicits two critical observations: first, Deissmann avers that, just as a photograph can capture a scene straight out of lived experience, so a letter directly reflects "real life," not retouched, colorized, or edited in any way. Second, the composed nature of the letter is ignored and its ephemerality underscored in order to emphasize the contrast between a letter and a literary epistle.

Meanwhile, an epistle "differs from a letter as the [Platonic] dialogue from a conversation."[12] An epistle resembles an oration, or a drama, or a variety of other artistic literary forms. It is precisely this dichotomy between natural and artistic, lifelike and artificial, that Deissmann sees as the decisive factor separating the two modes.[13] The epistle thus may have the *form* of a letter, but otherwise it is completely the opposite: it is public, its address functions merely as external ornament or pretext, and its message may be

---

[9] For an excellent assessment of the theological and scholarly positions against which Deissmann directed his arguments, see W. G. Doty, "The Classification of Epistolary Literature," *Catholic Biblical Quarterly* 31 (1969) 183–99.

[10] S. Stowers, *Letter Writing in Greco-Roman Antiquity* (Philadelphia 1986) 18.

[11] Deissmann (1927) 228.

[12] Deissmann (1927) 230.

[13] Deissmann (1923) 194–96: "Die Epistel unterscheidet sich vom Brief ... wie die Kunst von der Natur. Der Brief ist ein Stück Leben, die Epistel ein Erzeugnis literarischer Kunst."

understood by a wider audience without any knowledge of the author or the nominal addressee. Deissmann thus divides letter and epistle by intent of the author (private vs. public), style (artless vs. sophisticated), and occasion (ephemeral vs. permanent). The letters of Paul are valued precisely for their privacy (we are merely the lucky eavesdroppers), for their artlessness (as if Paul had written directly from the heart), and their historical occasion; it is a fortunate accident that they survived to influence later generations. The idea that Paul's letters were written with a wider public in mind, that they followed strict epistolary conventions and formulations, or that they were specifically written to outlast their author, was untenable to scholars of Deissmann's generation.

When he acknowledges the existence of letters that fall in between his strict categories, Deissmann reveals the full extent of his assumptions about epistolary style and content: "letters ... more than half intended for publication, are bad letters; with their frigidity, affectation, and vain insincerity they show us what a real letter should not be."[14] But it is not enough to admit that *some* letters straddle the categories; in fact, *no* letters fall neatly into separate categories of wholly literary constructions or wholly natural and unedited outpourings of the heart.[15] The most personal and intimate letter depends on highly stylized epistolary conventions for its form, while the more literary productions are still inevitably connected to an individual, his addressee, and his society. Deissmann's distinction between what is natural and what is conventional, and the high ethical value he placed on "nature," were typical of his Victorian era, but are, in the end, misleading. It is counterproductive to define the letter so narrowly that we miss the larger phenomenon of what people actually did with letters in antiquity.[16]

---

[14] Deissmann (1927) 230.

[15] For objections to Deissmann, see Koskenniemi (1956) 88–95; K. Thraede, *Grundzüge griechisch-römischer Brieftopik* (Munich 1970) 1–4; and Stowers (1986) 18–20.

[16] Stowers (1986) 20. G. Luck, "Brief und Epistel in der Antike," *Das Altertum* 7 (1961) 77–84, while criticizing the inflexibility of Deissmann's formulation, remains firmly under his influence, comparing a "real" letter with its "einfache Nachricht eines unbekannten Mannes an seine Frau" favorably with the "künstlerische Objektivität" of one of Pliny's epistles to his wife (80–81). He also unquestioningly retains the idea of the superiority of nature over art: "Überhaupt soll der Briefstil möglichst anspruchslos und natürlich sein" (82).

As Deissmann's theories were debated by new generations of scholars, the impulse to categorize did not disappear. We intuitively feel some substantive difference between letters that are actually exchanged between historical persons, and letters that are written as more self-consciously "literary" products for an audience not limited to that particular place and time, but we are hard pressed to explain which particular aspect of the letter determines its affiliation to one group or the other. Scholars turned to classification according to the writer's education,[17] to chronology, or to content or substance.[18] In his authoritative entry on epistolography, written for Pauly-Wissowa in 1931, J. Sykutris retained the distinction between private (i.e. "real") and literary letter, but went on to offer five separate letter types: official, literary-private, the letter as formal "disguise" for philosophical musing or other didactic purposes, the letter-in-verse, and the fictive letter.[19] In the 1950s, Heikki Koskenniemi investigated epistolary content and the writers' relationship as criteria for his typology.[20] He divided "real" letters into three types: (1) the impersonal letter containing news (2) the letter combining news and personal information and (3) the purely personal letter motivated by friendship rather than by the need to communicate specific information. Positing the relationship of the writer to the reader as a guideline, he differentiated between letters sent among friends and family, and those written by superiors to inferiors, or vice versa.[21]

In the late 1960s, pursuing Deissmann's interest in the Pauline letters but abandoning the letter/epistle opposition, W. G. Doty concluded that the basic differentiation between epistolary types is that some are primarily more private and others primarily less private in nature. He then established a classificatory system straight out of the ancient rhetorical handbooks: less private letters may be official (administrative, commercial), public (news, propaganda), "non-real" (pseudonymous, fictive), discursive (sci-

---

[17] See S. Witowski's (1906) division of papyrus letters as "epistulae hominum eruditorum," "modice eruditorum," and "non eruditorum"; his theories (*Epistulae privatae Graecae* xiii–xv) are discussed in Koskenniemi (1956) 12.

[18] See the analysis in Doty (1969) 195 and note 14.

[19] J. Sykutris, "Epistolographie," in *RE* suppl. 5 (1931) 185–220.

[20] Koskenniemi (1956) 88–95.

[21] This system recalls Cicero's divisions between public and private letters (*Pro Flacco* 37), and his argument for different writing styles according to category and addressee (*Ad Fam.* 15.21.4).

entific, literary-critical), or other special types (erotic, poetic, inserted, dedicatory, etc.).[22]

The most recent attempt at epistolary classification rejects issues of content and privacy as defining criteria, and instead bases its division on the occasion or setting of the letter writing: according to Luther Stirewalt's *Studies in Ancient Greek Epistolography* (1993), "letter-settings are either normative, extended, or fictitious. They differ according to the degree to which the correspondents and the contexts move from reality to imaginary construct."[23] Thus, both official and personal letters are defined as "normative" because they are developed in actual correspondence between real people, and act as basic models for "derivative" uses of the form. Stirewalt emphasizes that this sort of letter writing is a social or political act, a communicative exchange conducted in both the private and the public sectors. Extended letters are characterized by an extension of both the audience – a personal letter may be passed around to a wider group, publicized in some fashion, or permanently displayed in the community – and the subject matter: "extended settings provide the contexts in which writers publicize non-epistolary topics for a group of people, identified or unidentified, and known or assumed to be interested. Such activity is represented by letters on technical and professional subjects and for propaganda."[24]

Stirewalt is quick to remind his readers that normative and extended letter settings do not by definition exclude acts of imagination or visualization: "Even in these settings the writer models the letter's reception, feels the presence of the recipients, anticipates their reaction ... he is engaged in creative activity through the medium of a letter."[25] But the shift from extended to fictitious hinges on the degree of imagination involved: "Imagination apart from reality, and conscious creativity move the letter from the normative settings into fictitious settings."[26] A fictitious letter is one in which the writer invents a persona or impersonates another writer, and may even manipulate responses; the actual sending of the letter is not required, and the audience may be a classroom (in the case of a fictional letter written as a school assignment) or a reading public.

[22] Doty (1969) 196–99.   [23] Stirewalt (1993) 1.   [24] Stirewalt (1993) 3.
[25] Stirewalt (1993) 3.   [26] Stirewalt (1993) 3.

There are several aspects of Stirewalt's classification that strike me as problematic. First, the labels "normative" and "derivative" inevitably carry with them a value judgment, just as a social or political agenda is to be understood as somehow more serious than a letter whose main role is entertainment (as if entertainment did not depend equally on a shared social or political context). This classification is as strictly hierarchical as Deissmann's distinction between the "real" letter and the literary epistle. A related problem is that Stirewalt's definitions are closely tied to the sender's intentions and the occasion of the first reading, but the recipient's reactions and potential second or third readings will blur some of his boundaries. Thus a "normative" letter can shift into the "extended" category when a spatially or temporally removed second reader chooses to use the letter as a window into the world of the sender and first reader, or if either sender or recipient decides to publish the letter in a collection. Second, Stirewalt acknowledges the workings of imagination in even his so-called "normative" and "extended" settings; he speaks of a difference according to degree, as the correspondents and contexts move from reality to imaginary construct. But the point is, if imagination and creativity function at the very root of the epistolary experience, and surface in even the most "normative" official correspondence – as, for instance, when the junior officer decides what to tell and what to hide from his superior – can they be used as reliable, objective criteria in distinguishing between epistolary types? When Stirewalt tries to differentiate between conscious and unconscious creativity ("conscious creativity move[s] the letter from normative settings into fictitious settings ... He consciously invents a persona ..."),[27] his categories begin to self-destruct. All letter writers consciously participate in the invention of their personas; there is no such thing as an unself-censored, "natural" letter, because letters depend for their very existence on specific, culturally constructed conventions of form, style, and content.

A letter precludes any sense of objective truth such as might be produced by the presence of an external commentator who establishes "reality," such as the narrating poet in epic, or by the interaction of voices, found in choral response or dialogue in drama. The letter writer thus is free to present himself in whatever light

---

[27] Stirewalt (1993) 3.

he wishes (within the limits of probability or believability), and he is most likely to offer a picture which will have a specific targeted effect, whether negative or positive on his reader, in the same manner as an orator such as Lysias creates a plausible courtroom character for his client. Letter writing is inherently "fictional" in that the writer can create himself anew every time he writes. Epistolary discourse entails the construction of a self based on an assumption of what might interest the intended addressee, not on some unchanging vision of one's "true" self. Every letter is also an artifact purporting to be historically authentic, striving for chronological accuracy. But better to ask not whether Ovid's Sappho writing to Phaon (*Heroides* 15) represents the "real," historical poet of Lesbos, but rather what rhetorical effect Ovid achieves by representing her voice through the medium of a letter.

I suspect that a great part of the problem with modern epistolary classifications is their debt to Deissmann's original division, which was invented specifically for the interpretation of the historical Pauline letters. For our purposes in this study of ancient literary fictions in letter form, the most useful approach may still be that of J. Sykutris, mentioned above, whose categories encompass a large variety of letters types, both real and fictive.[28] He divides official letters from literary private letters, for example, the letters of Cicero. Next he treats the letter as a screen ("Einkleidung") or mask with specific goals that reach beyond the bounds of the format, such as a speech in the shape of a letter to the general public, a didactic treatise or scholarly tract (e.g. Epicurus' letters), a dedication, magical spell or curse (found mostly on papyri). His fourth division, that of the verse letter, shifts partially into the world of fiction, and contains a number of different types: invitation letters in the *Greek Anthology*, Ovid's *Tristia*, *Epistulae ex Ponto*, and *Heroides*, Propertius' epistolary poems 1.11, and 3.22, and so on. Sykutris' fifth and last division is defined primarily by its fictiveness: the fictive prose letter ("der fingierte Brief"), letters whose writers or receivers are inventions, but who use the standard prose of a "real" letter. This includes embedded letters (in, for example, historical prose, drama, or the novel), pseudonymous letters composed in the names of famous people, epistolary novels, imaginative love letters, and mimetic letters, such as those of Alci-

---

[28] Sykutris (1931) 185.

phron, in which the writer represents the life and times of invented characters, complete with the dialect and local color of a particular period.

I will be concerned in this book with Sykutris' final two divisions: verse and prose fictive letters. While there is obvious formal similarity between the supposedly autobiographical and the purely fictive verse letters in Ovid's "exile" poems, the *Tristia, Epistulae ex Ponto*, and *Heroides*, I would argue against Sykutris' lumping together of these poems under the rubric of "verse letter."[29] The difference between verse and prose, to my mind, is less crucial in an epistolary context than the difference between fictive or imaginative letters and letters whose writers or receivers are not invented. Ovid may have invented various details in his letters home from Tomis, but his whole programme depended on Augustus' belief in the veracity of his representation of himself as miserable in exile. His heroines were also meant to convince their readers of their misery, but both writers and intended readers are inventions from myth and literature: these are believable fictions, and the reader reads with an awareness of their untruth.[30]

Let me conclude this prologue by offering a brief outline of the chapters to follow. Some of the epistolary material from antiquity discussed in this book will be familiar to most readers: Phaedra's suicide note, for example, or the embedded letters in the Greek novelists. Other works will be less well known, especially the later epistolographers of the Second Sophistic: Alciphron, Aelian, and Philostratus. Until now, scholars of epistolography have focused on individual authors and texts; several have found Ovid's *Heroides* to be fertile ground for critical comment.[31] By contrast, in spite of Ovid's huge influence on the European epistolary novel, I have chosen to emphasize the role of fictive letters in Greek literature. No comprehensive study of epistolography in ancient Greek literature from Homer to the Second Sophistic exists. This project attempts to fill that gap, to pull out of obscurity both the writers and

---

[29] P. A. Rosenmeyer, "Ovid's *Heroides* and *Tristia*: Voices from Exile," *Ramus* 26 (1997) 29–56.

[30] J. R. Morgan, "Make-Believe and Make Believe," in C. Gill and T. P. Wiseman, eds., *Lies and Fiction in the Ancient World* (Austin TX 1993) 226.

[31] D. F. Kennedy, "The Epistolary Mode and the First of Ovid's *Heroides*," *CQ* 34 (1984) 413–22; R. A. Smith, "Fantasy, Myth, and Love Letters: Text and Tale in Ovid's *Heroides*," *Arethusa* 27 (1994) 247–73.

the genre of epistolary fiction, and to argue for the "special status" of letters in literature. There may not be a Samuel Richardson in the Greek past, but I hope to convince the reader of the merits of the lesser known epistolary authors, and to appreciate the special qualities of epistolary passages in more familiar authors. Euripides' Phaedra and Alciphron's Glaucippe (*Letter* 1.11) both write letters about sex and suicide; studying them together in the context of epistolography will help us better understand how each author interprets the power of a letter, and how each in turn manipulates his audience or readership through the choice of epistolary form. One word of caution is appropriate at this point: I am obviously unable in the context of one book to treat every example of epistolary narrative from antiquity, and have had to limit myself accordingly; some will be disappointed not to read more about Plato's *Letters*, the pseudepigraphic letters of the Pauline corpus, or the letters of the Apostolic Fathers. There may even be some hardy souls who miss references to the works of the later antique epistolographers Aristaenetus and Theophylactus of Simocatta. To those I apologize in advance, and hope that the material I do cover here will inspire others to read and consider the missing texts in a new light.

Questions about epistolary form and convention, as well as the pleasures and pitfalls of reading "private" letters, will resurface throughout the book, which is divided into four main sections: an introduction to the culture of letters in Greek antiquity, epistolary fictions from the archaic period to the Hellenistic era, the epistolary novel, and epistolography in the Second Sophistic. In the first section (chapter 1), I consider briefly the earliest evidence that we have for an actual letter in the Greek-speaking world, and the cultural context of writing letters.

The second section (chapters 2–5) turns to the epistolary fictions themselves, starting with the earliest references to fictional letters in archaic and classical Greek texts. I use as examples the embedded letters in the poets Homer (*Iliad* 6.160–80) and Euripides (*Hippolytus, Iphigenia in Tauris,* and *Iphigenia in Aulis*), as well as documentary letters found in the historians. My focus here is on the role of letters in a culture that is gradually moving from primary orality to general familiarity with writing. The texts that mention letters seem fascinated with the connections between epistolary writing and deception. In Homer, we read of Bellerophon, accused unjustly by his host's wife of improper behavior, who is sent away with letters of introduction to another household. In reality, these are "murderous symbols ... inscribed on a folding tablet, enough to destroy life," a death sentence in disguise. The power over life and death in the form of a letter, set against a backdrop of erotic tension, resurfaces in Euripides' *Hippolytus*, when a similar story is played out by Phaedra: her letter is given even more authority by her subsequent suicide, so that the recipient, Theseus, finds himself unable to question its truth value, and the letter achieves its writer's goal of complete destruction of the family. In other passages, anxiety about the fragility of writing and the danger of failed communication is foregrounded. In the *IT*, Iphigenia not only writes a letter to her brother but reads it aloud on stage to the messenger, so that even if the actual letter-tablet is lost, the message will have a chance of reaching its intended addressee (also, of course, allowing both Orestes and the audience to overhear). In the *IA*, Agamemnon tries to undo the damage of his earlier, deceitful letter to his wife by writing another, truthful version; but the letter fails to reach its addressee, and the tragedy unfolds around Agamemnon's inability to take back his words once sealed and delivered. The Homeric paradigm sustained in tragedy also affects the status of letters in Herodotus and Thucydides, who continue to explore, although in a less overtly fictional format, the relationship between letter writing, political authority, and deception.

Chapter 5 will discuss developments in Hellenistic verse epistolography, looking at the role of writing in a well-read world. It discusses several epistolary poems from the *Greek Anthology*, and then offers a close reading of Callimachus' Acontius and Cydippe episode (*Aetia* book 3), in which a lover sends his unsuspecting beloved a message carved on a love token. Since he has inscribed an oath on it, her act of reading aloud binds her to obey. The moment of reading a letter marks the success of the communicative effort on one level, but also opens up numerous possibilities for misunderstandings and misreadings. Here the lover uses epistolary convention to trap his (internal) reader into a performative utterance (in J. L. Austin's terminology[32]), and she falls dangerously ill until she can "answer" his letter by marrying him. Ovid later picks

---

[32] J. L. Austin, *How To Do Things with Words* (Oxford 1962).

up their story in his paired epistolary *Heroides* 20 and 21, in which Cydippe's response to Acontius' second letter begins with an expression of her anxiety about yet another trap: she makes sure this time to read silently so as to avoid further complications. The fifth-century CE epistolographer Aristaenetus in turn reports his own version of their courtship in letters.

The third section of the book (chapters 6–9) looks at a group of epistolary collections that have been associated with the generic label "novel." Some are loose collections of related epistolary texts that recall a jumbled pile of old letters in someone's attic, others reveal an epistolary core beneath a larger narrative pattern, and yet another has unanimously earned the appellation "epistolary novel" from modern critics. Greek prose fiction uses the imaginative letter in two very different ways: as embedded narrative and as a structural determinant. In Xenophon of Ephesus (*An Ephesian Tale*) and Chariton (*Chaereas and Callirhoe*), discussed in chapter 6, we find embedded letters primarily in erotic contexts: a married woman propositions the hero by letter, and he writes back a rejection, setting off a chain of disasters; or love letters fall into the wrong hands with dire consequences for all concerned. Pseudo-Callisthenes' *Alexander Romance* (chapter 7) includes the mutual correspondence of Alexander the Great and his numerous adversaries, descriptions of marvels in letters sent home to his family, and his deathbed speech, carefully transcribed by a secretary. Scholars suspect the presence of an earlier epistolary novel embedded in part of the narrative.

Chapter 8 addresses the extremely complex issue of pseudonymous letter writers, "those little pedants that have stalked about so long in the apparel of heroes," as Richard Bentley wrote in his influential *Dissertation upon the Epistles of Phalaris* (London, 1697). Most of the pseudonymous letter collections are later literary inventions, even if they may include some original material or may be based on genuine collections no longer extant. I investigate several of the collections as representatives of free-standing epistolary fiction that, in hindsight, may be seen as moving in the direction of the epistolary novel. Here we have shifted from embedded letters to letters acting as structural determinants, shaping the plot and divulging information through their exchange. Finally, chapter 9 looks at our sole surviving example of the epistolary novel, *Chion of Heraclea*, a carefully plotted set of seventeen letters written in the first century CE, reflecting the spurious authorship of the historical figure Chion of *ca.* 350 BCE. Chion writes to his father and friends, evoking the political situation in Athens at the time of Plato, and the epistolary structure allows for numerous variations on a theme, including letters of introduction, philosophical musings, and a farewell letter before dying.

The fourth and final section deals with the flourishing genre of epistolary fiction in the second and third centuries CE, including the so-called Second Sophistic. The epistolographers of this period experimented freely with forms, and we find letter collections unlike any that have come before. Alciphron (chapter 10) and Aelian (chapter 11), for example, wrote free-standing collections of letters in the voices of fishermen, farmers, parasites, and courtesans – all fictional writers addressing fictional readers. These narratives construct a window into the past by imitating the language and manners of fourth-century BCE Athenian society. Although most of the letters are unidirectional, several pairs develop a miniplot or story (e.g. Alciphron *Letter* 4.18–19: an exchange between Menander and Glycera), often heavily dependent on Greek New Comedy. Another epistolographer of this period, Philostratus (chapter 12), wrote a collection of first-person narratives to women and boys on erotic themes; his "discourses of desire"[33] may be read as an erotic autobiography in letters.

The letter form appears and reappears in ancient Greek literature from the earliest references to written language to Byzantine practitioners of rhetorical display. In some contexts the letter form may seem incidental or artificial, but in others it structurally determines the entire work. In considering examples of the letter as a literary device in ancient Greek literature, and in asking how the ancient authors' attitudes towards fictive letters changed over time as the literary culture developed, I hope to address both classical scholars, who have often ignored the imaginative epistolary genres of later antiquity, and scholars of modern epistolary fiction. By combining a philological approach with insights gained from modern literary theory, the book will ask questions about genre and voice that should be of interest to scholars in many fields of Western literature.

---

[33] This phrase is borrowed from L. S. Kauffman, *Discourses of Desire: Gender, Genre, and Epistolary Fictions* (Ithaca 1986).

I

Epistolarity: an introduction

CHAPTER I

A culture of letter writing

Nature, pleased with the customs of friendship,
invented tools so that those absent could be united:
the reed-pen, paper, ink, a person's handwriting,
tokens of the soul that grieves far away.

Anth. Pal. 9.401 Palladas

This first chapter will touch briefly on two issues of epistolary
practice in ancient Greece: first, a working definition of a "letter,"
including some practicalities of writing and sending in antiquity;
second, a consideration of the cultural context of ancient Greek
letter writing: its origins in myth and history, and its changing
status over time.

PRACTICAL ASPECTS OF THE LETTER

A logical starting place for our definition is an exploration of the
ancient terminology for "letter." Centuries of Greek practice reveal a number of terms, including βύβλος or βυβλίον (papyrus)
and δέλτος (tablet), which are used metonymically and thus emphasize the materials used for writing, and γράμματα (alphabetic
letters) and other derivatives of γράφειν (to write), which refer to
the act of writing itself.[1] The word ἐπιστολή,[2] derived from the
verb ἐπιστέλλειν, refers to the necessity of sending a communication over a certain distance: an ἐπιστολή is anything sent by a
messenger, whether oral or in writing. While Thucydides, for example, uses the word for both oral and written messages, Xen-

---

[1] For the historical development of the individual terms, and their usage by specific authors, see Stirewalt (1993) 67–87: "Greek Terms for Letter and Letter-Writing."
[2] Stirewalt (1993) discusses the difference in meaning between the singular and the plural
form (84–85).

ophon and the orators limit its definition to a written form; by Hellenistic times, ἐπιστολή or ἐπιστολαί are the common terms found in papyri for both private letters and official documents.[3] The early history of ἐπιστολή in Greek usage points to an association of letter writing with official or military oral communication;[4] the extension of the word to the writings of private citizens came later. The ancient definition of "letter" thus remains closely connected to its original context: a written message, usually private, sent to accompany or replace an oral injunction or private conversation between two persons geographically removed from one another.

In our own culture, we should have no trouble defining the object: a letter is a message, written and signed by its author, sealed, addressed, and finally delivered (by hand, airmail, or pony express) to an addressee. The situation calls for a letter either because the addressee is absent and could not have been communicated with otherwise, or because the writer prefers the medium of writing to communicate matters of secrecy, formality, or emotional delicacy. The letter contains an epistolary greeting, a conventional closing, and perhaps a postscript; the body of the letter may be handwritten, dictated, or typed, but the final signature is usually in the writer's own hand.

Since the advent of such modern technologies as electronic mail and faxes, however, these definitive characteristics have become slightly more varied. Perhaps the biggest change is that the new forms of mail are disconnected from their sources: there is no "signature," only standardized fonts; there is no contact with a physical object previously handled by another person. The privacy of a sealed communication and the suspense of unfolding an envelope or a page have been replaced by codes and passwords, or commands to "scroll down" (a wonderfully anachronistic image). The envelope and stamp have disappeared, although the return address remains on the cover page of a fax and in the screen headings of an e-mail. The conventional format of greetings, paragraphs, and closing formulas has been abandoned for the more casual style of electronic transmission, which no longer demands capitalization or formal punctuation. Certain documents,

---

[3] Stirewalt (1993) 82–83. The earliest use of ἐπιστολαί for letter appears in Thucydides (e.g. 1.129) and Euripides (*IT* 589).
[4] See J. L. White, *Light from Ancient Letters* (Philadelphia 1986) 191–93.

however, remain unsuitable for electronic delivery: the highly formal genre of the wedding invitation, for example, or (at the time of writing), a text with the power to bind its signatory legally.

Electronic mail has also redefined the audience, and what it means to publish a letter: a computerized "list" allows a letter to be read by numerous unknown readers with a common interest, although such a list focuses primarily on the distribution of information, and lacks the aesthetic dimension of the epistolary collections of a Horace or a Cicero, for example, who published their epistolary poetry books for a wide audience, but obviously using slower mechanisms of publication and dissemination. The modern public's "access" is instantaneous, and their responses are equally quick. Speed and convenience are critical features of this new epistolary mode: a "regular" letter delivered through the postal service is no longer the unmarked term, as avid users of electronic mail now condescendingly label it "snail mail." In a final postmodern twist, a company in California (of course) now offers a service called Letterpost for those who are "too technologically absorbed to put paper to envelope" but still want to communicate with non-computer literate friends and family: for a small fee, it prints out e-mail, puts it in an envelope, and drops it in the nearest mailbox, thus converting e-mail back to snail mail.[5]

The definition of a letter may continue to change along with the technology invented for its production and transmission, or perhaps these changes will be so radical that new forms of communication will arise, which are not letters, but which may share some characteristics with letters. The rapid change in the practice of letter writing that has overtaken our society may not be comparable to the events of any one era in antiquity, but it does provide us with an appreciation of the interconnectedness of letter writing and other social and cultural practices. Starting as a token of power and authority in the hands of the few, letter writing in the classical period remained a relatively unusual activity. Letters flourished as literacy slowly developed, and at the more educated social levels, letter writing became part of everyday life in Hellenistic Egypt, both in administrative affairs and in private households.[6] The gradual development of a culture of letters also

---

[5] *The New York Times*, Thursday, May 27, 1999, D8.
[6] W. V. Harris, *Ancient Literacy* (Cambridge MA 1989) 127–28.

presumably effected a change in education, as the curricula adapted to the requirements of "modern" life; so, too, schools in today's society have introduced classes in computer skills.

The written nature of the letter may be seen as the only defining feature to survive the massive changes in epistolary technology from antiquity until now. What were some of the actual physical circumstances of writing and sending a letter in ancient Greece? Epistolary fictions frequently allude to the physical nature of the letter itself, and the difficulties of ensuring a safe delivery, as if such references could invest their letters with the sort of concreteness found only in the material world. Thus writers of fictional letters apologize for their shaky handwriting, mention tears shed on the page, or worry about the next boat leaving for Athens. An understanding of the situation of "real" letters will deepen our appreciation of the fictional recreations of these circumstances.

The materials used for letter writing changed over time as new supplies were developed or became more readily available. One of the earliest forms used was the folded, hinged tablet (δέλτος, πίναξ), which could be of clay (tablets found at Knossos and Pylos),[7] wood with a waxed surface (Homer *Iliad* 6.168–70; Hdt. 7.239.3; Plautus *Curc.* 410), metal (the late sixth-century BCE lead letter from Berezan), or ivory (Augustine, *Letters* 15.1).[8] The tablets were inscribed with a sharp-pointed pen, then folded, secured with thread or bands, and finally sealed with wax and a signet ring. The malleability of the waxed surface allowed for multiple reuse (Propertius 3.23.3). The use of ivory tablets is uncommon, as we learn from Augustine's apologies to a friend:[9]

Does this letter not show that, if we are short of papyrus, we have at least an abundance of parchment? The ivory tablets I possess I have sent to your uncle with a letter; you will the more easily forgive this bit of skin, since my message to him could not be postponed, and I considered it very impolite not to write to you. If you have any tablets of mine beside you, please send them back for such emergencies as this.

---

[7] L. H. Jeffery, "Writing," in A. J. B. Wace and F. H. Stubbings, eds., *A Companion to Homer* (London 1962) 555.

[8] See R. G. Ussher, "Letter-Writing," in M. Grant and R. Kitzinger, eds., *Civilization of the Ancient Mediterranean*, vol. III (New York 1988) 1575–76.

[9] Augustine to Romanianus, *Ep.* 15, as translated by J. H. Baxter, *St. Augustine: Select Letters* (Cambridge MA 1980) 13–16.

Augustine grumbles that the shortage of papyrus forces him to use his highly valuable ivory tablets as well as the less desirable (but still fairly high-grade) parchment for his correspondence. His letter also reveals that, in a lapse in an exchange, tablets might stop circulating in the addressee's house, rather than being returned empty to their owners. He requests the return of any tablets stored at his friend's house. We may also read between the lines of this request a gentle reprimand to a friend who has not written back.

Returning to archaic times, an unusual variation on the flat surfaces used for letter writing is the Spartan method of sending coded messages into the field. The message itself, usually some sort of military command, was written on a strip of leather rolled at an angle around a particular stick called a σκυτάλη. When it was taken off the stick, the words were unintelligible, but the addressee had an identically shaped stick, and when he rewound the leather strip around it, the message would become readable again.[10]

The preferred medium for letters, however, as Augustine suggested above, was papyrus, imported from Egypt, and written on with an inked reed pen. The papyrus fibers were treated, pasted together and polished to form a smooth writing surface, and then folded, rolled, tied up and sealed to ensure privacy. Papyrus letters carried an address on the outside, and occasionally the date of the sending. Papyrus is known to have been used in Athens as early as 490 BCE, although it was probably still fairly expensive in the late fifth and early fourth centuries.[11] Hundreds of letter papyri, the earliest dating from the third century BCE, have been excavated in Greco-Roman Egypt, and more continue to be unearthed.[12]

The actual delivery of letters could be a complicated affair. Official letters had their own channels: military dispatches went by courier – soldier or slave – and government documents went by

---

[10] The σκυτάλη is discussed by F. D. Harvey, "Literacy in the Athenian Democracy," *REG* 79 (1966) 585–635, esp. 625, who refers the reader to the chapter in Aeneas Tacticus (31) on secret codes. Ancient references include Thuc. 1.131; Xen. *HG* 3.3.8; Ar. *Lys.* 991 (with an obscene allusion to its similarity to an erect penis); Plu. *Lys.* 19.

[11] Harris (1989) 95: "the expensiveness of papyrus, the only material which could be used for long private messages, limited the usefulness of writing and so indirectly put a brake on literacy." Hdt. 5.58 mentions papyrus; see Hdt. 5.35 for his "living" parchment.

[12] Ussher (1988) 1576.

government messengers. But private letters were excluded from this system, and a letter writer without the financial means to dispatch his own slave depended primarily on travellers going in the right direction, or merchants plying a regular route on land or sea. Delivery was by no means guaranteed: a letter writer could expect delays on account of bad weather, accidents, or untrustworthy couriers. The situation in both classical and Hellenistic Greece contrasts remarkably with the long-standing organized postal system of the Persian empire described by Herodotus in book 8: a relay system was set up to carry royal dispatches to the far reaches of the kingdom; riders equal in number to the days of the journey were posted at regular intervals along the roads, and the messages were then passed from rider to rider, producing a postal system unparalleled in speed and efficiency (8.98). But again, the system was in place for official government business, not for private citizens.[13] Similarly, the Roman postal service ("cursus publicus") was devised by Augustus for military and official transport, involving messengers and relay stations providing a change of horse and carriage.

Now that we have briefly explored the physical nature of a letter and the systems for its delivery, let us remind ourselves of the larger cultural context of letters in Greek antiquity. I will approach letters as a cultural phenomenon in two ways: first, by asking questions about their place in the general Greek imagination, and in particular their myths of origin; and second, by looking at actual examples which may offer insights into the function and role of letters at that particular moment in history.

A CULTURE OF LETTERS

Greek antiquity was fascinated by the progress of society through individual inventions, and it therefore comes as no surprise to find the "invention" of letters attributed to a specific individual. Clement of Alexandria, a Christian well educated in pagan Greek literature who was active in the late second century CE, provides us

---

[13] See D. T. Steiner, *The Tyrant's Writ* (Princeton 1994) 150, for a stimulating discussion of the monarch's monopoly over the systems of communication in his kingdom, and his power to block all attempts by others to write or circumvent his system, which in turn produced elaborate stratagems for the secret delivery of subversive mail.

with a list of inventions the Greeks borrowed from barbarians: musical instruments, styles of warfare, metal smelting, and so forth. The inventions attributed to women are limited to cosmetic improvements – Medea is said to have been the first to color her hair, for example, while Semiramis is remembered for introducing purple cloth – until Atossa enters the list. Clement quotes the fifth-century historian Hellanicus of Lesbos: "Hellanicus says that the first person to compose a letter was Atossa, queen of the Persians" (πρώτην ἐπιστολὰς συντάξαι Ἄτοσσαν τὴν Περσῶν βασιλεύσασάν φησιν Ἑλλάνικος).[14]

Clement's statement is tantalizingly brief, and we are left to wonder under what specific circumstances Atossa is believed to have "invented" the letter. We have no details of the materials used or the system of sending. Did she invent letter writing as a totally new form of communication, or did she improve and codify an already existing method? Did she replace a face-to-face court encounter with a written message, in an attempt to formalize the protocol of addressing a royal personage, or was she just trying to communicate with a family member abroad? Was the letter a military or political document, and if so, did she merely devise the medium or did she also write the actual message? I am tempted to interpret this moment of invention as a public rather than a private matter. If Atossa had been trying to reach a friend or relative, she could have sent a trusted slave with an oral message. The information for which she invented the letter must have been secret, political, and with potentially serious ramifications. These requirements were also true for what we usually think of as the first instance in literature of letter writing, namely the scene with Bellerophon and Proetus in *Iliad* 6.168ff., to which we will have occasion to return.

It is hard to say what Hellanicus really meant by making Atossa the first inventor. The Persians were famous in antiquity for their

---

[14] The Greek text is O. Stählin, *Clemens Alexandrinus Stromata Buch I–VI*, vol II, 3rd edn. (Berlin 1960) 50 (= *Strom.* 1.16.76.10). See also the version in Hellanicus (Jacoby *FGrH* 4 fr. 178). The word used for composing is not "to write" (γράφειν), but rather "to organize or compose in an orderly fashion" (συντάξαι, or συντάσσειν in Hellanicus), which Jacoby in Hellanicus glosses as εὗρεν. See also the discussion in W. Roberts, *History of Letter Writing from the Earliest Period to the 5th Century* (London 1843) 1–2, and M. van den Hout, "Studies in Early Greek Letter Writing," *Mnemosyne* 2 (1949) 23–24. On the use of letters rather than personal interview to communicate with a king, see Hdt 1.99 (Deioces).

professional postal system described above, and the Persian monarchs carefully controlled the systems of communication within
their kingdom. In this regard it may have seemed logical to assign
epistolary skill to this particular cultural group. But equally nota-
ble is that the invention of letter writing is ascribed here not just
to a foreigner, but to a female foreigner. We may contrast this
with the attribution of the origins of alphabetic writing to Palamedes, a legendary culture hero. Euripides mentions the benefits
of writing in the context of letters, as Palamedes boasts of the
usefulness of his invention; the origins of alphabetic writing are
tied to the need to communicate at a distance (*Palamedes* fr. 578.3–
5):[15]

I invented the art of writing for mankind,
so that someone who has not crossed over the surface of the sea
may still learn clearly, in his own house, about all the things out there.

Diodorus Siculus writes in similar terms of the legendary lawgiver
Charondas (*ca.* sixth century BCE), who campaigned for general
literacy, emphasizing the ability of alphabetic letters to allow
(12.13.2)

... men widely separated in space [to] have conversations through written
communication with those who are at the furthest distance from them, as
if they were standing nearby.

Later we learn of the supposed invention of the imaginary letter
in Greek prose by Lesbonax, a rhetorician named by Lucian.[16] In
these three instances, letter writing is "naturalized": it is Greek,
male, and put to practical or artistic uses. A sophist in Synesius
Letter 138c takes the argument even further: the letter is clearly so
indispensable to human life that no mere mortal man could have

---

[15] For the Greek tragic fragments, I use Nauck's 2nd edition. The Euripides fragment is
discussed in Harvey (1966) 616. Evidence for Palamedes as the inventor appears also in
Stesichorus *PMG* 213, Gorgias 82B 11a30 DK. Cf. Aeschylus *PV* 460–61, who says that
Prometheus is the πρῶτος εὑρετής. Hecataeus (*FGrH* 1F20) says Danaus brought writing
from Egypt, while Herodotus (5.58–61) champions the view that Cadmus brought it from
the Phoenicians. For further discussion, see P. E. Easterling, "Anachronism in Greek
Tragedy," *JHS* 105 (1985b) 1–10, esp. 5.

[16] The Roman tradition also favored a male inventor of writing (and therefore letters):
"Primus litteras Mercurius enarraverit: necessarias confitebor et commerciis rerum et
nostris erga Deum studiis" (Tertullian, *De Corona* 8.2). Mercury inherited many of the
gifts attributed to the Egyptian god Thoth. Notice the (typically Roman?) emphasis on
the practicality of writing for business affairs.

been the inventor, but only a god.[17] It seems to me that Hellanicus' association of letter writing with the quintessential "other," female and barbarian, reflects a certain uneasiness with its possible other functions. By connecting the letter's origin with a powerful Persian queen (and at that time Persia was still very much the "enemy" in the minds of the Greeks), Hellanicus suggests that there may be something exotic, effeminate, and potentially explosive about letters in general.

As we look at more examples of letters in Greek society and literature, it becomes clearer that letter writing was often viewed with some suspicion. The act of writing was an act of power, separating those who could read and understand from those who could not. Often this division worked along lines of class or gender: an example of the latter is a distich from the comic poet Menander:[18]

> He who teaches a woman letters (γράμματα) well,
> provides a frightening snake with additional venom.

Men can be trusted with literacy and letter-writing skills since they can be relied upon to put their skills to good use; women, on the other hand, Menander seems to imply, would turn their knowledge into venom, write deceitful letters, and plot and conspire against men and society. Learning letters also means learning to read, and reading tragedies, for example, could give women nasty ideas. This, of course, is the customary sexist paranoia familiar from Old and New Comedy alike. But letters seem to intensify the possibilities for danger and deceit: particularly in a military or political correspondence, the bond between the writer and his addressee is usually at someone else's expense. Letters frequently transmit secret or harmful information, and communicate information designed for a restricted audience.[19] D. Steiner argues that in Herodotus, for example, writing itself is never a neutral activity: "It rapidly gathers both sinister and pejorative associations, and appears within a complex of activities designed to illustrate

---

[17] R. Hercher, *Epistolographi Graeci* (Paris 1873) 723; cf. H. Rabe, "Aus Rhetoren-Handschriften: Griechische Briefsteller," *RhM* 64 (1909) 284–309, esp. 293ff.

[18] The lines are emended variously, and remain corrupt; I have taken the text from S. Jackel, *Menandrii Sententiae* (Leipzig 1964) 114: Menandri et Philistionis Disticha Parisina 1–2 = Kock fr. 702.

[19] Steiner (1994) 107.

the despotism of the Oriental monarchs ... [in] contrast with the "normative" behavior of fifth-century Greek communities," which consists of open discussions, debates, and other oral communications in the context of governing the city-state.[20] Much of her thesis, which goes far beyond letter writing to include all forms of inscription and writing, rests on the assumption, with which I fully agree, that no writing is an "unloaded tool" whose purpose and function are merely to inform: it is always more widely referential, a reflection of the culture and the purpose which produce it. Thus, Steiner argues that in Herodotus' Persia or Egypt, the king is the ultimate author and reader of all letters, the controller of all information which travels efficiently along his carefully planned postal routes.[21] Athens, by contrast, is defined by the public nature and availability of its texts, as public writing ("open" letters) covers the city walls in the form of decrees and laws; inscribed altars, grave monuments, and sculptures meet the eye at every turn. The multiplicity of hands and voices that decorates the public spaces of Athens stands in strong contrast to the despotic presence of an all-powerful Persian king. We will return to this issue when considering the embedded letters in Herodotus. But Steiner's point that the historian emphasizes the foreign nature of private writing, its essentially undemocratic nature, sits well with the myth of Atossa's invention.

It is unlikely that we will ever be able to pinpoint the exact moment of the discovery of letter writing, but we can connect historical letters with the general spread of literacy in antiquity. In Greek poetry, the first reference to writing is a reference to a letter: Bellerophon carries horrible signs (Hom. *Il.* 6.168: σήματα λυγρά), written by Proetus on a folded tablet. It is unclear whether these signs were actual alphabetic signs, some sort of pictograph, or a code known only to the writer and his addressee. Whatever the case may be for Proetus and his addressee, it is unlikely that large numbers of the population were literate at that time.

One might expect to find some letters written in the lively environment of colonization and trade during the eighth and seventh centuries BCE, as people traveled widely and settled in new lands; but the evidence, if it ever existed, has not survived.[22] The earliest

---

[20] Steiner (1994) 127.   [21] Steiner (1994) 228–29.
[22] The following section on letters and literacy owes much to Harris (1989), esp. 56–57.

historical letters we have are those of Polycrates of Samos and King Amasis, dated to the early 520s (Hdt. 3.40–43). The earliest letter that actually survives (late sixth or early fifth century BCE) is a private letter written on lead by a not very well educated Greek, found at Berezan on the Black Sea; the letter was presumably sent to or from the colony of Olbia, founded by Miletus.[23] The letter was found rolled up, probably undelivered, with the addressees' names written on the outside: "The lead (τὸ μολίβδιον) of Achillodorus to his son and Anaxagoras." Since he names his message after the material on which it was written, the writer presumably knew of no other word for letter. A number of errors, as well as the use of the third person in the body of the letter, suggest that it was written for the sender by another person, who was not himself particularly competent as a scribe.[24]

O Protagoras, your father [Achillodorus] sends [this] to you. He is being wronged by Matysas, for he [M] enslaves him and deprives him of his job as carrier. Go to Anaxagoras to explain this, for he [M] says that he [Ach] is the slave of Anaxagoras, claiming "Anaxagoras has all my things: male and female slaves and houses." But he [Ach] disputes it and says that there is nothing between himself and Matysas, and says that he is free, and that there is nothing between himself and Matysas. As for what is between Anaxagoras and Matysas, only they themselves know. Tell these things to Anaxagoras and to [Ach's] wife. [Your father] sends you other orders: take your mother and your brothers who are at Arbinatai into the city, and Euneuros himself will come to him [Ach] and go straight down there.

The letter opens with what will become the conventional greeting, including the names of writer and addressee: "O Protagoras, your father sends this to you." The Greek is ὁ πατήρ τοι ἐπισ-τέλλε (sic),[25] an interesting formulation that means that the father "sends a message" or even "sends a command." The text consists of approximately twelve lines from a father to his son, explaining that he, the father, is in grave danger of being enslaved because of a rather confusing transfer of property. He orders his son to inform the appropriate magistrate (Anaxagoras) that he is being wronged,

[23] On the lead letter, see J. Chadwick, "The Berezan Lead Letter," *PCPS* 199 (1973) 35–37; and the discussion, with further bibliography, in Harris (1989) 56–57.
[24] Chadwick (1973) 35. My translation is based on Chadwick's text. The use of third person alone does not necessarily point to a scribe, since epistolary convention often dictated it.
[25] In this letter, ε is used for the diphthong ει, and psilosis is a normal east Ionic feature of the Milesian dialect.

and to arrange the removal of his family to a safe place so that they will not suffer the same fate. Achillodorus quotes his opponents' actual words, perhaps to underline the legal context of their affairs. He also retains the third person form throughout when talking about himself, again perhaps suggesting a legalistic mindset as well as the intervention of a scribe. The second part of the letter, which contains the command to shift the family to the city, is introduced by a formula parallel to that of the opening: ἕτερα δέ τοι ἐπιστέλλε. This suggests to me that the initial greeting may reflect the early epistolary context of an injunction or command; thus what the father sends his son is not just the lead tablet itself, but more importantly the orders of action described inside.[26]

The Berezan lead letter may disappoint in its apparent triviality: a minor legal squabble between two men, expanding to affect their immediate families and business partners. But it serves us well as a model for later literary epistolary developments. Many conventions found here will reappear in fictional letters: the formal opening, the careful use of an identifiable third-person voice, the mixture of political and family affairs, the use of a letter in a time of crisis. Also, the drama of the lawsuit takes on greater urgency when we realize that this letter may never have reached its addressee; it was found still folded and sealed, and no return letter tells us how matters ended for Achillodorus and his family.

In spite of the curious letter from Berezan, which shows a man of little education, perhaps even illiterate, turning to letter writing in a time of crisis far from home, it is difficult to gauge the importance of letters in archaic society. Even in the classical era, as literacy and the functions of the written word began to expand, letters did not become commonplace. Some literary sources imply that letters were reserved for very serious occasions or for secret communications: letters quoted in Thucydides, Herodotus, and Euripides are closely connected with crises such as betrayal, deceit, and even death.[27] On the other hand, towards the end of the fifth century and after, letters are sometimes mentioned in a way which suggests that they are perfectly ordinary and normal methods of communicating. Thus in the writings of the Athenian orator Anti-

---

[26] Chadwick (1973) 37, translates "your father [Akhillodoros] sends you this command" and "A second command for you."

[27] Harris (1989) 88.

phon, we find a forged letter being used as key evidence in a murder case (5.53–56). The prosecution alleges that the accused murderer had written a note boasting of his deed to his accomplice. The accused claims that the note was planted in an effort to frame him; he argues that the forged letter should be dismissed in the face of a confession (elicited by torture) made by the slave who, he claims, committed the crime. He hopes that the court will believe the oral testimony rather than the suspicious letter. This example suggests that letters were acceptable evidence in court, and therefore must have been familiar to the general public.

By the late fourth century BCE, letter writing had developed beyond specialized circles to larger spheres of both private and official communications. In government affairs, the Ptolemaic bureaucracy frequently used letters to organize its vast administration. Official letter writing only increased after the death of Alexander, as the fragmented empire tried to consolidate its different centers of power.[28]

Private letter writing is also well documented in the Hellenistic period, and references in literature attest to it as common practice at various social levels.[29] Theophrastus, friend and pupil of Aristotle, paints a vivid picture of an arrogant fellow whose epistolary style reveals a major character flaw (*Char.* 24.13):

In his letters you do not find "You would oblige me," but "My desire is this," or "I have sent to you for that," or "Be sure that you do the other," and "Without the least delay."

Herodas, in the opening piece of his collection of literary mimes, depicts a middle-class woman who points out that her friend's traveling husband/lover (Mandris) has apparently forgotten all about his wife/girlfriend back home – she has not received even one letter in almost a year (1.23–25):

From the time when Mandris left for Egypt,
ten months have gone by, and yet he does not send even a letter to you,
but he has completely forgotten about you, and drinks from a new cup.

This passage suggests, then, that by the early to mid-third century, people expected a husband away on business to write home fairly

---

[28] For examples, see C. B. Welles, *Royal Correspondence in the Hellenistic Period* (London 1934).
[29] For examples of family letters, see *Select Papyri*, trans. A. S. Hunt and C. C. Edgar (Cambridge MA 1932), vol. I, 269–394.

frequently to his wife. In this period, we also find letters written by a wide range of people: women to their absent husbands, masters abroad writing to their slaves, soldiers on campaign to their families, parents and children, and private citizens announcing marriages, births, and deaths. Letters were written by writers of both high and low social classes, and by hired scribes of varying skill, during prolonged separations caused by various conditions, and in emergency situations not unlike that of Achillodorus of the Berezan letter some four centuries earlier. The backgrounds and situations of the writers vary as much as the material and intentions that the letters themselves convey: consoling, expressing thanks, praising someone, giving orders, reporting events, mediating a quarrel or a lawsuit, giving or requesting advice, maintaining a friendship, to name a few.[30] These epistolary habits continued uninterrupted into Roman and then Christian times. The popularity of letter writing was limited only by the pace of the spread of literacy, and the materials and means available for writing and sending letters. The means, of course, depended heavily on some form of education, where the letter writer, whether professional scribe or stumbling schoolboy, could learn the basics of epistolary composition.

There is good evidence that, for an "average" literate person in the Hellenistic period, letter writing was learned in the classroom. Schoolboys copied model letters along with their Homer and Plato, although perhaps with a more practical goal in mind. Because of our incomplete knowledge of the school systems in place in diverse regions of the Hellenized world, however, we cannot know for certain the extent to which letter writing was taught at the lower levels of schooling, or whether such training was reserved for more advanced students of rhetoric.[31] It is likely that basic epistolary composition was taught in some schools at an early stage, perhaps with the help of rudimentary collections of model letters, and presumably concentrating on grammar and

---

[30] Stowers (1986) 15–16, offers a list of examples of "things people could do with letters."

[31] For a convincing argument against the unquestioning acceptance of a three-tier model of schooling, in which a student progresses from primary to secondary school and then on to rhetorical training, see R. A. Kaster, "Notes on 'Primary' and 'Secondary' Schools in Late Antiquity," *TAPA* 113 (1983) 323–46, who argues tentatively for a socially segmented two-track pattern, in which the "school of letters" taught basic literacy to the lower classes, while the "liberal schools" offered the élite a more sophisticated education.

form rather than on niceties of style.[32] The main reason for this assumption is the uniformity of epistolary conventions (e.g. opening and closing formulas, wishes for the addressee's good health, requests for responses, etc.) in papyrus letters, written frequently by people of a low educational level; the formulas, unchanged over centuries, suggest a common influence from school instruction based on a limited number of handbooks.[33] An example of the low level of skill attained by someone receiving only a rudimentary education in epistolary form is the ungrammatical and awkward letter on papyrus of the schoolboy Theon to his father (*P Oxy.* 119), summarized by Deissmann as "a specimen of the most uncultivated form of popular speech," and dated to the second or third centuries CE.[34] This letter has been quoted by every scholar working on Hellenistic education since its publication over a century ago.

Theon to his father Theon, greetings.
You did a fine thing. You didn't take me with you into town. If you don't want to take me with you to Alexandria, then I won't write you a letter, and I won't speak one word to you or wish you good health. And if you go to Alexandria [without me], from now on I won't take your hand and I won't greet you. So if you won't take me along, these things [will] happen. Even my mother said to Archelaus [my brother] "he is driving me mad – take him away." You did a fine thing. You sent me fine gifts: locust beans! They deceived us there on the twelfth day, when you sailed. Finally, send for me, please, please. If you don't send for me, I won't eat and I won't drink. So there.
Farewell, I pray you. [dated] the 18th of Tybi [January].

The letter is written in a schoolboy's uncial hand, so presumably by Theon himself. It must have reached his father somewhere between their local town and Alexandria, when the traveller stopped long enough to pick up his mail at a prearranged spot. The writer's spelling, grammar, and language all testify to his youth and limited education. It appears that his father has tricked him, with a distracting bribe of delicious locust-beans, out of a trip to

---

[32] For this position, see A. J. Malherbe, *Ancient Epistolary Theorists* (Atlanta GA 1988) 6–7, and White (1986) 189–92. For further information on the shape of the school system, see now T. Morgan, *Literate Education in the Hellenistic and Roman Worlds* (Cambridge 1998).

[33] On the conservative nature of epistolary conventions, particularly the opening address, see Koskenniemi (1956) 14–15.

[34] Deissmann (1927) 201. I base my translation on B. P. Grenfell and A. S. Hunt, *The Oxyrhynchus Papyri* vol. 1 (London 1898) 185–86.

the big city, and his response is an epistolary tantrum, as it were, complete with threats of never speaking to his father again, and suicide by starvation. He rejects all the nice manners his parents have been trying to teach him: shaking hands, saying hello politely, wishing people good health, and writing letters. If his father proceeds on the trip without him, threatens Theon, he will never receive a letter from his son again.

Most commentators focus on the childish usages and bumpy syntax of Theon's Greek, and imagine the letter as a document of "popular speech," a transcription of a conversation. But even in this basic message, a piece of epistolary blackmail, the young Theon shows a startling familiarity with epistolary convention. He alludes to epistolary formulas by threatening to undermine them: it is customary to wish one's addressee good health, but Theon insists from the start that he won't wish his father good health; his father will expect a letter from his family while he is away in Alexandria, but Theon threatens angrily not to write. As peeved as he is, the child still knows the value of epistolary closing convention: thus the letter ends with a proper "farewell, I pray you," and on the verso the address states "deliver to Theon from his son Theonas," using a pet form of his own name that he may expect will elicit his father's affection.[35] The letter of this "uncultivated" child actually tells us a great deal about good epistolary manners in Hellenistic Egypt.

If Theon grew up and continued his education under a secondary school teacher (γραμματικός) or a teacher of rhetoric, he probably was assigned elementary exercises of literary composition (προγυμνάσματα), in particular the προσωποποιία, exercises in characterization or impersonation. By practicing to write in the voice of a certain mythical or historical person, and by representing a situation or opinion fitting for that person, the student learned to develop facility in adopting various literary styles; along the way he presumably also lost his ability to express himself as freely and imaginatively as young Theon did.[36] This practice was meant to train students in rhetoric, but it may also have offered inspiration for the forging of "letters from famous people," a topic which we will discuss in detail in a later chapter.

In presenting these details of "real" letters from Greek antiq-

---

[35] Deissmann (1927) 203, note 5.   [36] Malherbe (1988) 7 and White (1986) 189–90.

uity, I have attempted to lay the groundwork for the main focus of the remaining chapters, namely the use of letters as a literary device in almost every genre of ancient Greek literature. While each author will be shown to incorporate epistolarity in a way unique to his genre and period, all the letter fictions do share certain unchanging elements: an awareness of the stylistic conventions of "real" epistolary exchange; an appreciation of the tension between the first private reading and a secondary wider audience; and a concern with sustaining epistolary verisimilitude in the context of the fictional narrative. Now let us turn to the narratives themselves.

II

Epistolary fictions

CHAPTER 2

Homer: the father of letters

Ham.　　　Up from my cabin,
My sea-gown scarf'd about me, in the dark,
Grop'd I to find out them, had my desire,
Finger'd their packet, and in fine withdrew
To mine own room again, making so bold,
My fears fogetting manners, to [unseal]
Their grand commission; where I found, Horatio –
Ah, royal knavery! – an exact command . . .
My head should be strook off.

Shakespeare, *Hamlet* V.ii.12–24[1]

In the previous chapters we attempted to define the letter, described its form and function in antiquity, and explored its myths
of origin. The material discussed above will guide us now in closer
study of the fictive letters themselves: the topic of the following
four chapters will be epistolary fictions from the archaic to the
Hellenistic period in Greece. In tracing letters in literature from
Homer to Callimachus, we begin with yet another "myth" of origin. Homer, the undisputed "father of literature," reveals himself
also as the "father of letters," the site of the first epistolary exchange. Not only is the earliest reference to a letter in Greek literature found in Homer's *Iliad*, but the issues raised by that letter
recur repeatedly in later authors: Homer's epistolary passage will
define for us some critical characteristics of epistolary exchange
that function paradigmatically for later literature.

The earliest extant reference to a letter in Greek literature is
that of Homer in the sixth book of the *Iliad*. In a momentary
pause in the mass fighting on the plains of Troy, two heroes stand
ready to duel: Glaucus, second in command of the Lycian con-

---

[1] G. Blakemore Evans, ed., *The Riverside Shakespeare* (Boston 1974) 1181.

39

tingent defending Priam's city (*Il.* 2.876), and Diomedes, son of
Tydeus and friend of Odysseus. As they boast of their lineage and
bravery before the engagement, Glaucus discovers a connection
with his enemy Diomedes through an ancient act of hospitality,
which leads the two warriors to put down their weapons and exchange (famously unequal) gifts as hereditary guest-friends.

In the process of their encounter, Glaucus relates the story of
his ancestor, Bellerophon, who was once a guest in King Proetus'
house. Anteia, the wife of King Proetus, falls madly in love with
Bellerophon and confronts him with her desire. When he rejects
her advances, she goes to her husband with an invented story of
sexual assault, and demands that he kill their young guest. Proetus
responds with an epistolary deceit, sending Bellerophon away
carrying a false letter of introduction to Anteia's father (*Iliad*
6.167–70):

> He shunned the idea of killing him, since he had some sense
>   of honor in his heart,
> but he sent him to Lycia, and gave him baneful signs (σήματα
>   λυγρά),
> writing in a folded tablet many soul-destroying things,
> and ordered Bellerophon to show them to his wife's father,
>   that he might be killed.

Bellerophon takes the sealed message to the King of Lycia, who,
following custom, entertains him generously for nine days without
opening the tablets. On the tenth day he asks to see the token, but
when he discovers its evil message (6.177 σῆμα κακόν), he, too,
balks at polluting his own hands, and instead enrolls the young
man in a series of life-threatening tasks, counting on the deadly
chimaera or the fierce Amazons to carry out the murder.

Doublets and variations of this epistolary moment exist in
many traditions. Some emphasize the erotic component, such as
David's letter to Uriah in pursuit of Bathsheba (Sam. 2.11.14–17),
or Phaedra's vengeful suicide note in Euripides' play *Hippolytus*;
others, such as the foiled epistolary plot against Hamlet, foreground
the potentially murderous power of the letter. In the case of the
Homeric example, scholars continue to debate the nature of the
inscription on the tablet.[2] Some argue that the σήματα are

---

[2] See A. Heubeck, *Schrift* (Göttingen 1979) 128–46.

alphabetic signs, evidence of alphabetic writing systems in eighth-
century Greece.[3] Others interpret the word σῆμα as some kind of
pictograph or a secret code of symbols known only to Proetus and
the Lycian king. Most recently, D. Steiner differentiates between
the singular and plural forms of the word, pointing out that the
tablet itself is a σῆμα or token, regardless of what is written on it:
"the tablet functions inferentially and can deliver its message
even without the semiotic inscription;" consequently the symbols
inscribed on the tablet are the σήματα, linguistic signs.[4] She sees
two models of communication at work here: one of tokens and
one of written texts. But she goes on to argue that for Bellerophon, the sealed tablet is not even a token (σῆμα) because he
remains unaware throughout the episode that the letter contains
murderous signs directed against him, that he is a "vector between
the sender and recipient of the message."[5] I would phrase it somewhat differently. Bellerophon, ignorant of the plot against him,
misinterprets the σῆμα; he assumes that the tablets contain, in
addition to any other news that Proetus may wish to communicate
to his father-in-law, an introduction to his new host, and a recommendation for hospitality.

I do not mean to suggest that written letters of recommendation
were familiar items in Homeric epic, which is set in an era before
the invention of alphabetic writing as we know it. The scene of
drawing lots in the *Iliad* (*Il.* 7.183–89), in which each man recognizes only his own sign, argues forcefully against a common writing system. Even if Bellerophon's σήματα were an anachronism
that had crept in later in the eighth century, a date often assigned
to the "invention" of fully alphabetic writing and the transcription
of oral epic, general literacy did not proliferate until two centuries
later; as W. Harris states in his book on ancient literacy, "nothing
in the texts of Homer or Hesiod suggests that writing was at all
important in the everyday world in which the poets lived."[6] But
in spite of these chronological constraints, we can easily view the
tablets as some kind of σύμβολον, not necessarily alphabetic, of
guest-friendship ties. If such tokens sent with travelers were rare,
Bellerophon would no doubt become suspicious of his burden. But
instead, we might infer, he views the tablets as a conventional

---

[3] R. Bellamy, "Bellerophon's Tablet," *CJ* 84 (1989) 289–307.
[4] Steiner (1994) 15.   [5] Steiner (1994) 16.   [6] Harris (1989) 45–48.

symbol of hospitality and guest-recognition, and mistakenly assumes that the information within matches the external circumstances of his travel. Proetus deceptively exploits a familiar
situation, that of the token of hospitality or "letter of recommendation," to send an altogether different message, namely one of
guest-murder.[7]

Even after Bellerophon's arrival, Proetus' message takes some
time to reach its addressee. The conventions of guest friendship
are such that the guest is welcomed and entertained before he is
asked for any tokens of identification; we see this throughout the
Homeric epics, particularly during Odysseus' travels. In the case
of Bellerophon, the letter condemning him to death lies unopened
and ignored for nine days before his host turns to business: its
message can be activated only by the act of reading. Proetus' hostile words lie unseen and therefore powerless, while the Lycian
king treats his guest with honor and generosity. But the tension is
there for the reader, who wonders when the letter will be called
for, and how quickly it will be acted upon once read. The Lycian
king makes the same assumption as Bellerophon: that he is receiving a conventional letter of introduction from his son-in-law. Both
are victims of Anteia's deceit, but find temporary respite in the
social customs regulating behavior towards guests and strangers. If
Proetus had chosen to send the letter by another messenger, the
gap between the letter's writing and reading might have been
much smaller. The king would have interpreted the letter as a
potentially important communication, separate from and unrelated
to its courier. But the narrative takes advantage instead of the
dramatic impact of an unknowing victim carrying his own death
warrant.

It is not just the primacy of the Homeric passage, the fact that it
is the first appearance of a letter in Greek literature, that gives
it such importance to my project. Rather, the passage, early as it
is, contains within itself the seeds of epistolary fiction that will
develop over the next millennium and beyond. The Bellerophon
story in the *Iliad* introduces three major themes of epistolary
writing that will inform many of the questions and discussions to
follow. First, it establishes a connection between letter writing and

---

[7] See Steiner (1994) 30–31, and the dissenting opinion of G. Herman, *Ritualised Friendship
and the Greek City* (Cambridge 1987) 63 and note 65.

treachery that recurs throughout ancient Greek literature.[8] In
Euripides' *Palamedes*, for example, Odysseus forges a letter from
Priam to Palamedes that results in that hero's death.[9] Pliny the
Elder (*ca.* first century CE) teases us with a reference to a letter by
Sarpedon, the commander of the Lycians, also written at Troy,
but without giving us further context; Pliny is at a loss to explain
Sarpedon's apparent use of paper, since when Homer was writing,
Egypt (and therefore papyrus) did not yet "exist" (*NH* 13.27):

> otherwise, if paper was already in use, why is it known to have been the
> custom to write on lead folding tablets or linen sheets, or why did Homer
> assert that even in Lycia itself wooden tablets, and not paper letters,
> were given to Bellerophon?

Bellerophon carries a letter between the writer and the receiver,
but is not told the contents of his burden. The sealed and unread
text will haunt letter carriers in centuries to come; some will have
the courage to break open the document and avoid the death
planned for them at the hands of the receiver, whereas others, all
too obedient, will be killed as soon as they deliver the letter. The
motivations for murder may differ (jealousy, secrecy, wartime
precautions), but in this model, the letter carrier is always at risk,
the script potentially deceptive, and the sealed letter a probable
harbinger of death. This epistolary model will resurface in examples from history, tragedy, and the ancient novel. But the later
genres inevitably treat letters differently in that, unlike epic, they
flourish in a culture wholly familiar with writing.

   The Bellerophon passage introduces a second theme that is
picked up by later authors, namely that of women and letters.
Proetus may write the actual letter, but his rebuffed wife in essence dictates its contents. It is not accidental that women are
closely associated with dangerous or deceptive aspects of writing.
In ancient Greek literature, erotic interest in women usually trig-
gers suspicion. In epic, Clytemnestra neatly combines both seductive power and treachery in her murder of Agamemnon, and even
supposedly chaste Penelope is shown deceiving the suitors with her
weaving tricks. The Bellerophon passage introduces the dangerous
combination of a woman thwarted in love who turns to the power

[8] See W. Speyer, *Die literarische Fälschung im heidnischen und christlichen Altertum* (Munich, 1971)
126.
[9] This text will be dealt with in greater depth in the following chapter.

of writing to exact vengeance. Anteia pushes her husband to write the letter in this scenario, but later heroines, Euripides' Phaedra in particular, will take the power of writing into their own hands. The genres connected with treachery above – tragedy and the ancient novel – could equally well be listed in the category of "women and letters," as all their instances of treachery are linked to erotic misadventure or seduction. The imperial Greek writers develop these themes in their epistolary forms. Yet while Greek authors are intrigued by the extremely powerful effect of letter writing in the hands of women in love, it is only Ovid who takes Phaedra's legacy and makes it central to the genre, in his *Heroides*, the model for European epistolary novelists in the Renaissance and beyond.

The third theme of letter writing in antiquity is evident only in what Bellerophon's tablets do not – but are assumed to – contain: the friendly letter of recommendation or shared news. In this context, a letter transmits a friend's best wishes and functions as a symbol of friendship *in absentia*. This casual writing style, imitating intimate conversation, is markedly absent from the early periods, but surfaces in Hellenistic epigrams, in the epistolary novel *Chion of Heraclea*, in some of the pseudonymous writings, and again in the Second Sophistic, often in the name of epistolary "realism."

Homer thus sets the framework for the investigation to follow. As we explore fictive letters in classical, Hellenistic, and post-classical sources, the circumstances and effects of Bellerophon's letter will haunt the pages, cautioning both internal and external readers: "caveat lector."

CHAPTER 3

Letters in the historians

Ham. I had my father's signet in my purse,
Which was the model of that Danish seal;
Folded the writ up in the form of th' other,
[Subscrib'd] it, gave't th' impression, plac'd it safely,
The changeling never known.

Shakespeare *Hamlet* V.ii.49–53[1]

The relationship between letters and treachery will reveal itself in this chapter to be the strongest common thread between Homer and the historians of the fifth century. But with Herodotus and Thucydides, we have entered a world far different from that of Homer's epics. The existence of a writing culture by the fifth century BCE becomes evident when Herodotus claims that Homer and Hesiod made a theogony for the Greeks by assigning them names, titles, skills, and honors (Hdt. 2.53).[2] His statement implies that the *Iliad*, the *Odyssey*, and the *Theogony* had been written down and were well on their way to becoming canonical, whether in recitation at symposia or memorization in schools. Authors in the late fifth century thus begin to treat earlier texts as reliable sources for political, historical, and literary information from the past.

The historians themselves dealt with earlier texts in ways characteristic of their times. Herodotus probably consulted books, whether "local" histories or city archives, while preparing to write down his history; he also appears to understand the importance of epigraphic texts for an accurate reconstruction of the past.[3] But

---

[1] Blakemore Evans (1974) 1181.
[2] Harris (1989) 61–62.
[3] This paragraph owes much to Harris (1989) 80–81. See also C. Higbie, "Craterus and the Use of Inscriptions in Ancient Scholarship," *TAPA* 129 (1999) 43–83; S. West, "Herodotus' Epigraphical Interests," *CQ* 35 (1985) 278–305; and F. Hartog, *Le Miroir d'Hérodote* (Paris 1980) 282–97.

documentary research was not his main goal, and on occasion he freely invents texts: not only speeches which he could not possibly have heard, but even texts, such as letters, which had been written down and might still have been available for copying. In this latter case, the role of the author took precedence over that of the historian, the impact of the whole scene over the exact words. Writing several decades later, Thucydides treated documents with a slightly greater level of respect. He still preferred oral testimony to written, and, as A. Momigliano puts it, "it could never occur to him that written records were the primary source for history."[4] But in his search for more reliable information from the past than Herodotus had managed to gather, Thucydides did include on occasion careful transcriptions of critical texts.[5]

How do letters fit into this diligent search for accurate historical information? Both Thucydides and Herodotus insert letters into their histories, and for efficiency's sake I will limit myself to these two authors as representative of the genre.[6] Letters interrupt the direct narration of events in historical narrative in much the same manner as reported speeches, and in both cases we are asked to believe at some level that we are reading an accurate document transcribed word for word. At some times this belief is easier to sustain than at other times, depending on the circumstances of the writing and the likelihood that the author could have gained access to the particular letter. Sometimes the author declares the accuracy of the embedded letter with prefaces and postscripts: "it was written as follows ..." (ταῦτα, τάδε), or "such was the letter." At other times the author admits he is paraphrasing a letter's exact text, introducing the contents with the words "something like this" (τοιαῦτα, τοιάδε), or offers a summary of the contents of the letter, alerting the reader that the narration is in the author's own voice, not that of the letter writer. This allows the author to elaborate on a situation, to embroider the text of a letter if it will give

---

[4] A. Momigliano, *Studies in Historiography* (London 1966) 135.

[5] C. Meyer, *Die Urkunden im Geschichtswerk des Thukydides* (Munich 1955).

[6] Letters in the historians are mentioned in van den Hout (1949) 18–41; and O. Longo, *Techniche della communicazione nella Grecia antica* (Naples 1981) 58–86. Xenophon uses far fewer letters. He includes a reference to military officers writing home (*Cyrop.* 2.2.9), and occasionally inserts the text of a complete letter: thus at *Cyrop.* 4.5.26–34, Cyrus reads aloud a letter he has written to Cyaxeres, in order that the messenger "may understand and confirm its contents, if he [Cyaxeres] asks you anything about them."

the reader a better picture of the unfolding events, the characters involved, and the mood of the times.[7] In this view, history is often better served by approximation and paraphrase than by direct quotation.

The connection between deception and letter writing is sustained and developed in both historians, partly because political and military contexts invite the use and abuse of letters in precisely this way. Armies at war are obsessed with dispatches: how to keep them out of enemy hands, to ensure efficient delivery, and to invent unbreakable codes. Sometimes the deception is perpetrated within the letter itself, in which case the model is one of epistolary treachery. At other times the writer puts all his energy into the method of delivery, and the deception is simply a device to keep the message safe from prying eyes.

Letter writers solve the problem of delivery by disguising the letter as something other than it is, or by otherwise hiding its contents in an unremarkable "envelope." In Herodotus, the disguises are often quite ingenious. At 1.123, Harpagus wants to send a letter to Cyrus to urge a rebellion against Astyages, but since the roads are closely guarded, he contrives a way of sending word secretly.

He took a hare, and cutting open its gut without damaging the fur, he put in a letter containing what he wanted to say, and then carefully sewed up the stomach; he gave the hare to one of his most faithful slaves, disguising him as a hunter with nets, and sent him off to Persia to take the meat to Cyrus, ordering him tell Cyrus, by word of mouth, to cut open the animal himself, and to let no one else be present at that moment.

Not only is the letter "enveloped" in a carcass, but the courier is dressed up to match his commission. The safe delivery still depends on an oral message from the "hunter," who hints to Cyrus that this is no ordinary hare and suggests privacy for its reading. We can almost imagine a mock ritual of "haruspicium" as Cyrus "reads" the entrails of the animal. The message gets through, and Cyrus organizes his revolt. Interestingly, his first act of rebellion is to write a false letter from Astyages to himself, which he reads out to the Persians, claiming that he has been made their general by

[7] Speyer (1971) 21–25.

royal decree (1.125). They immediately obey Cyrus' orders, accepting his forged credentials without question.[8]

Two Herodotean variations on the hidden letter are equally successful in their delivery ploys. In 5.35, when Histiaeus desires to revolt from the king, he sends a letter to a potential ally, Aristagoras,

by taking the trustiest of his slaves, shaving all the hair off his head, and then inscribing letters on the skin, and waiting until the hair grew back again; . . . as soon as the hair was grown, he sent the slave to Miletus, giving him only this message: "When you arrive in Miletus, tell Aristagoras to shave your head and look at it."

This writer places the message where no enemy would think to look for it. The writing surface actually changes shape, from a smooth medium for tattooing, to a carpet of hair, the perfect camouflage.[9] The secrecy of the message is guaranteed by the placement of the tattoo: the messenger above could have cut up the hare himself and read the letter, but the inscribed slave cannot read his own head en route. Both hare and head are non-alphabetic tokens, and the writers depend on this fact to guarantee the safe arrival of their messages past suspicious guards on the lookout for written documents.[10]

The third example from Herodotus is much bolder in its disguise: it uses a wax tablet – a conventional writing surface – but in a highly unusual way. Demaratus, a Spartan king in exile in the Persian court, tries to warn his people of Xerxes' imminent invasion without attracting suspicion (7.239):

He took a pair of tablets, cleared the wax away, and wrote directly on the wooden surfaces what the king was planning to do; having done this, he spread more wax over the writing, and then sent the tablets. In this way, the guards placed to inspect the roads would see nothing but blank tablets, and would cause no trouble for the messenger.

In this instance, the writing surface is not only familiar but wholly alphabetic in nature; the wax tablet exists solely for the purpose

[8] Steiner (1994) 152, notes that Cyrus declares first the written commands of Astyages, and then reverts to his own voice to order the Persians to take up arms; she writes that the "would-be king Cyrus cleverly appropriates the royal writing before making his bid for the throne."

[9] Steiner (1994) 154–59, offers excellent observations on inscribing the body. The method chosen by Histiaeus is reported also in Aeneas Tacticus 31.17; cf. Ovid *Ars Am.* 3.625ff.

[10] This is perceptively stated by Steiner (1994) 151.

of transmitting written messages. But without its inscription, the vehicle appears a meaningless blank page. Again, the secretive writer takes advantage of the expectation that a text should be inscribed on top of the wax rather than under it, much as Proetus had used Bellerophon's expectations of epistolary convention to suppress any curiosity he might have felt about the tablets he carried. Of course the danger is that not just the guards will be deceived, but also the receiver, which is precisely what does happen. When the tablet reaches Sparta, the Spartans, just like the Persian guards, are unable to decipher the meaning of the empty wax; they suspect that the tablet is significant because of the oddity of a tablet arriving without an inscription, and they seem to realize that there is more to the token than meets the eye, but they can make no sense of it. Finally, Herodotus tells us (7.239),

... as I have been told, Gorgo, the daughter of Cleomenes and wife of Leonidas, discovered [the trick], and told the others. "If they would only scrape the wax off the tablet," she said, "they would be sure to find writing on the wood underneath."

We are not told precisely how Gorgo discovers the secret of the empty tablet. In fact, Herodotus takes care to qualify his narrative here by saying "as I have been told," thus implying some doubt about the details of the situation. But as in the case of Atossa, the purported "inventor" of letter writing, surely the gender of the discoverer is highly significant. The model of Hesiod's Pandora rears its symbolic head (*W&D* 60–105): Pandora appears beautiful and serene on the outside, but within she is mischievous and full of evil intentions toward man. So the tablet offers the Persian guards an innocuous surface of smooth, blank wax, but hides underneath its evil intentions: it betrays Xerxes and his kingdom to the Spartans. One could argue that it takes a woman, a representative of deceit and indirection by virtue of her gender, to discover that what seems empty is indeed full of signs, once she looks beneath the surface of the object.[11]

These three letters succeed in arriving at their destinations because of disguise: they either do not look at all like conventional

---

[11] Steiner (1994) 151, argues that "the Spartans, with their notorious mistrust of writing and rejection of *grammata* for all but the most restricted of uses, are ideally suited to discover the meaning of the *pinax*." But it seems to me that Herodotus says precisely the opposite, that the Spartan men are equally duped, and that only Gorgo can discern the true meaning of the tablets.

letters, or they look exactly like letters but appear to say nothing at all.[12] They manage not to be intercepted by defying epistolary conventions – the expectations people had at this time of what a letter should look like. The pattern is now firmly established: letters can be dangerous objects, carrying with them orders to revolt or execute someone, for example. They are potentially dangerous to the carrier, who risks death in his mission,[13] but also to the person from whom they are being hidden. In the following Herodotean case, letters actually bring about a man's murder.

The Persian soldier Bagaeus volunteers to help King Darius punish a rebellious but powerful official, Oroetes, governor of Phrygia, Lydia, and Ionia (3.127–28). Oroetes had been misbehaving toward his king for some time, as this anecdote reveals (3.126):

> Darius sent a courier to Oroetes whose message was not pleasing, so Oroetes ordered him to be ambushed and murdered on his way back to the king; the man and his horse both disappeared, and no traces were left of either.

But Bagaeus' and Darius' task is complicated by Oroetes' status and military power. Bagaeus devises the following ruse: he orders several letters to be written and seals them all with Darius' seal; he then goes to Oroetes' court, where the scribe reads each letter aloud to the assembled men and bodyguards. The first letter gently tests the men's loyalty to their king, Darius, while the second letter orders the guards to stop protecting Oroetes. When it is clear to Bagaeus that the audience respect Darius' letters and are willing to abandon their own ruler, he hands over the last letter, which calls for Oroetes' death. The guards slay their former master on the spot.

The recipients of the letters are so impressed by the royal seal that they never doubt for a minute the authenticity and implicit correctness of their contents. It makes no difference that the letters were actually written by a subject (Bagaeus) or read aloud by a

---

[12] One example of a failed delivery does not depend as much on disguise as it does on accident: (Hdt. 8.128) during the siege of Potidea, letters were sent from a traitor inside the city walls to the besiegers outside the city by being tied around an arrow-shaft which was then covered with feathers. Unfortunately for the traitor, one arrow hit a citizen in the shoulder, and the Potideans promptly uncovered the plot. This story is also recorded in Aeneas Tacticus 31.16.

[13] E.g. Hdt. 3.126, and 3.44–45, where the Samians, sent by Polycrates to Cambyses, realize the trap and save themselves.

scribe. The governor's men honor the words of the letter as if the king himself were speaking, acknowledging his proxy in the document that bears his seal. We are left to wonder at the power of the royal seal, which, disconnected from the body of its rightful owner, still represents to the soldiers an ultimate authority that must be blindly obeyed.[14] Oroetes' bodyguards are not bothered by the ethical constraints that hamper Proetus and the Lycian king in Homer. In both cases, the letter condemns a man to death; in Herodotus, the death sentence is carried out instantaneously.

There is a less successful (for the plotters, at least) variant of the Oroetes story at Herodotus 6.4: Histiaeus writes letters to the Persians in Sardis encouraging them to rebel against Artaphernes. His courier, instead of delivering the letters to Sardis, hands them over to Artaphernes himself. Artaphernes wisely tells the courier to deliver the letters as addressed, but to bring back all the responses to him. In this way he determines who is disloyal, and punishes them accordingly. Similarly misdelivered letters appear in Xenophon (*Anabasis* 1.6.3–5), where Orontas tries to send letters by a trusted courier to the king as part of a plot against Cyrus, but the courier delivers both letters and consequently Orontas himself into the hands of his enemy.[15]

All the Herodotean letters thus far have been written and sent in an aura of secrecy and urgency, involving matters of life and death. There are two more passages I would like to mention in which letters, while retaining the aspect of urgency, are of a very different nature from those mentioned above. The first example will become conventional in later epistolary literature: the letter of friendship or advice. The earliest known example of a "historical" letter is precisely this type, a friendly letter exchange between Amasis and Polycrates of Samos in the early 520s. In Herodotus 3.40, Amasis has become worried about Polycrates' sustained good fortune. He writes to Polycrates that he cannot be pleased at his friend's abundant prosperity, for the gods are jealous and will surely find ways of punishing him. He advises Polycrates to save himself by throwing away an object that is most dear to him, thus

---

[14] Steiner (1994) 152–53, has many excellent things to say on this passage. For another example of the immediate impact of royal letters, see Hdt. 5.14, when Darius writes to Megabazus and orders him to make war on the Paeonians.

[15] A variation on delivery to the wrong person is no delivery at all, as in Demosthenes *Against Phormio* 6.8.

balancing his happiness with sorrow. Polycrates reads the letter and follows Amasis' advice; but the precious ring he tosses into the sea returns to him in the belly of a fish on his dinner table (3.41–42). Polycrates recounts the miracle to Amasis by letter, who interprets the event to mean that his friend is doomed. He then breaks off all relations not by letter, but by herald, which must have been perceived as proper public protocol, perhaps because of the less personal and more official nature of the oral pronouncement (3.43). Herodotus explains Amasis' actions as follows: "This he did, that when the great and heavy misfortune came, he might escape the grief which he would have felt if the sufferer had been his bond-friend."[16] The correspondence between Polycrates and Amasis, which includes letters of friendship, advice, and news, recalls the kind of letter Proetus could have written to his father-in-law, in less unusual circumstances, upon discovering a traveler passing through his territory and heading towards Lycia.

The second example of an unusual type of letter in Herodotus is an epistolary document manufactured not by the Persians or other barbarians, as has been the rule so far, but by Greeks at war with the troops of Xerxes. Themistocles thought that if some of Xerxes' Greek allies could be encouraged to rebel, the united forces might be able to defeat the barbarians (8.19). Herodotus tells us that Themistocles wished to communicate with the Ionians before the Persians could discover his plan; he chose his words carefully so that, if the Persians did intercept the message, the Ionians would be suspected of treason and kept out of battle, which would serve Themistocles' ends equally well. His method of communication is unlike any other military dispatch yet encountered (8.22):

And now Themistocles selected the swiftest ships among the Athenian fleet, and, proceeding to the various harbors along the coast, cut inscriptions on the rocks, which were read by the Ionians the next day, on their arrival at Artemisium. The inscription read as follows (τὰ δὲ γράμματα τάδε ἔλεγε), "Ionian men (Ἄνδρες Ἴωνες), you do wrong to fight against your own fathers, and to help enslave Greece. We beg you therefore, if you can, to come over to our side ..."

According to epistolary convention, the τάδε, meaning "as follows," suggests that Herodotus reports what follows *verbatim*,

---

[16] Diodorus (1.95) reports the event slightly differently, and does include a letter as the means of dissolving the friendship.

rather than in paraphrase or probable reconstruction. But West argues that Herodotus was much less scrupulous than Thucydides in differentiating between τάδε and τοιάδε, thus confusing our categories of precise direct speech and paraphrase.[17] Did Herodotus have the opportunity to copy the actual inscription? The inscription was erected about fifty years before Herodotus wrote, and in an easily accessible area, so the possibility cannot be ruled out. Did the Ionians remember the words and report them later in local histories? In other passages in the history, readers are not as concerned about the likelihood of Herodotus' personal access to the materials discussed: he could not have overheard the words exchanged between Candaules and Gyges, for example (Hdt. 1.8–12). In most cases, the reader is willing to suspend disbelief for the sake of entertainment: direct speech offers dramatic liveliness and convincing characterization.[18] But the textual nature of an inscription or a letter complicates the matter, since Herodotus could be expected himself to see and copy down such a document, and the reader's expectations are therefore heightened.

There are, of course, serious doubts about the accuracy of Herodotus' description of this "letter," not the least of which is that the text Herodotus records is eighty-seven words long, rather inconvenient for inscribing on a cliff wall.[19] But doubts notwithstanding, this letter is highly unusual in that it is public, written on rocks which any passing sailor could see; the rocks are neither hidden nor sealed, but stand open to all eyes. The message is addressed to a collective rather than an individual, and its source is anonymous. It is as immutable as the stone it is inscribed on, in sharp contrast to the portable and recyclable materials ordinarily chosen for letters. After its initial reading, we can only conclude that the inscription will remain until worn away by the elements, a testimony to a brief chapter in the Persian Wars. Its function may be quite familiar – an attempt to encourage rebellion in the ranks and gain allies – but its medium and method of delivery are unique.[20] Still, it functions as a letter and should be read as one;

[17] West (1985) 286.
[18] West (1985) 286.
[19] See Harris (1989) 59–60; West (1985) 278–305.
[20] I disagree here with van den Hout (1949) 27–28, who rejects this message as "a letter in the strictest sense of the word." See also Steiner (1994) 153–54, who points out an interesting coda to the incident at 9.98, when a herald's oral appeal to the Ionians is compared to Themistocles' earlier written communication.

the idea of an open letter to a whole community is something that will recur in the context of philosophical treatises, such as Diogenes of Oenoanda's Epicurean letters inscribed on the walls of his stoa, and in the Pauline pastoral letters.[21]

Up to now we have looked at letters only in Herodotus. Herodotus includes especially those letters which are curious for the way in which they are written or delivered. His characters' letters are forged, hidden, misdelivered, intercepted, and surrounded by secrecy. In fact, only two epistolary communications are *not* the products of some unusual technique or falsification (Amasis and Polycrates at 3.40–42; Darius at 5.14).[22] For Herodotus, epistolary narratives offer an opportunity to examine the way a tale is recorded or transmitted, to contemplate in a moment of self-reflexivity the art of narration itself. The carefully explained details of sending and receiving remind the reader of the fragility of the physical letter, the many chances it has to go astray, perhaps even never to arrive. Throughout, letters embody the tension between successful and failed communication; the elaborate stratagems work toward the goal of verbal contact between separated individuals, even if the contents of the letters may glorify deceit and treachery, the destruction of human relations.[23] In most cases, Herodotus never saw the letters whose texts he presents, and he includes them not to explain a moment of historical crisis, or to transcribe an important document, but to make his overall story more lively, to bring "ancient history" to life.

Conversely, Thucydides includes letters in his work primarily because of their importance for the history itself, and not for the unusual circumstances of their execution or delivery.[24] In his *History of The Peloponnesian War*, we learn little about secret methods of writing, or precautions taken when sending letters across enemy lines. The document may be crucial for the next stage of campaigning, but the manner of its delivery is of less concern than

---

[21] See D. Clay, "A Lost Epicurean Community," *GRBS* 30 (1989) 313–35.

[22] Van den Hout (1949) 28.

[23] One could take this line of thought further and argue that Herodotus' use of letters challenges and undermines the very text in which they are embedded. The anxiety about the transmission of the letters affects our perception of the source of the historical information in the rest of the work. The inserted text, epistolary quotations from some "authentic" source, begins to change our reading of the frame, and we find ourselves asking more frequently for written proof and documentation.

[24] On letters in Thucydides, see Longo (1981) 67–69; Steiner (1994) 135–36, 221–22.

its safe arrival. Thucydides certainly offers his share of epistolary betrayals and lies, but even these letters travel undisguised by courier, and are therefore all the more easily intercepted.

Thucydides' letters seem more documentary in nature than those of Herodotus, since they are introduced primarily to illustrate the history rather than to enliven the narrative. But his characters do on occasion follow their literary model Proetus in writing treacherous letters to betray a former friend and ally. The epistolary mode allows them to keep their plan confidential and to communicate with a specific addressee. In the first epistolary passage of Thucydides' history, the Spartan general Pausanias sends a letter to accompany a group of prisoners of war to Xerxes, opening up a secret dialogue in which he promises to make Sparta and the rest of Hellas subject to the Persian king (1.128). Xerxes is pleased with the letter, and sends Pausanias a messenger with his response, accompanied by the royal seal as a guarantor of the letter's authenticity (1.129). The alliance thus formed through the epistolary exchange pushes Pausanias further in the direction of treachery, and makes him bolder in his behavior. He is called back several times by the Spartans to explain his intentions, the first time by a herald carrying a σκυτάλη, that uniquely Spartan message stick, with orders to return home or be declared a public enemy (1.130). But the ephors lack evidence to convict him until a letter from Pausanias to Xerxes falls into their hands, delivered by a courier turned informer (1.132–33). It seems that all the other letter-carriers traveling between the two plotters had disappeared, and this particular courier became concerned for his own safety (1.132):

Worried by the realization that no previous messenger had ever returned, and having counterfeited the seal, so that, if he found he was mistaken in his assumptions, or if Pausanias should ask to make some correction, he might not be discovered, he opened the letter, and found the postscript that he had suspected, namely, an order to put him to death.

In an effort to keep his correspondence secret, Pausanias had apparently been ordering his couriers to be killed upon arrival at Xerxes' court. We witness a repetition of the Bellerophon story, with a much more unpleasant outcome, since the Persians do not hesitate to murder innocent men. The passage also provides details about the basics of letter writing: a seal could be relatively easily reproduced, and it was not uncommon to send a corrected letter.[25] The courier then shows Pausanias' letter to the Spartan authorities, who delay acting on the information; they want to hear Pausanias incriminate himself in person. Their suspicion of written documents, which may be forgeries even when appropriately signed and sealed (after all, the courier had already counterfeited one seal), and their faith only in an oral pronouncement from the man himself, reflect an ongoing debate between oral and written authority. The ephors finally arrange to eavesdrop on Pausanias' conversation with the courier, just as they had "eavesdropped" earlier on his letter, and eventually take action against the traitor in their midst (1.133–34).

Letters appear elsewhere in Thucydides in secret negotiations between unlikely allies. Still in book 1, we meet Themistocles, fleeing the Spartan forces, writing to Xerxes' son Artaxerxes; he reminds the new king how much he had done for Persia during the previous war, and requests asylum in his court (1.136–37). Themistocles' letter, a mixture of introduction and supplication, achieves what he desired, as the king grants his request, and may in turn have played a part in inspiring an epistolary "novella" based on the life and letters of Themistocles, which we will consider in a later chapter.[26] Later, in book 4, we find a letter that is unusually frank in acknowledging the linguistic confusion that can occur during international hostilities (4.50): the Athenians intercept a letter from Artaxerxes to the Spartans that must be translated from the Assyrian.

In book 8, we come across a series of letters that lie, defame, and betray at every turn. None of these letters is reproduced directly, but we gather all we need to know from the narrator's description. One falsely reports a raid at Erythrae (8.33) in order to create a distraction so that troops can escape from Samos; another unfairly defames a man as a traitor for refusing to help his allies, and eventually causes his dismissal (8.38–39).[27] A longer

---

[25] Van den Hout (1949) 35 points out that corrected letters appear frequently among papyri fragments.

[26] Thucydides chooses to give part of the letter as a direct quotation, and part in summary; the summary is accompanied by the narrator's comment that it included false statements, which might not have been obvious to the external reader. The narrator's interruption is less intrusive than it could have been if he had quoted the letter in its entirety and then added a postscript to the reader that parts were untrue.

[27] Both these false letters are written by the same man, Pedaritus.

epistolary sequence occurs at 8.50–51, a complicated exchange between Alcibiades and the Persians which leads up to the oligarchic coup of 411.[28] Phrynichus, aware of Alcibiades' plot to weaken the Athenian and Spartan forces and betray his country to the Persians, writes a letter exposing him to the Spartan general Astyochus. Astyochus, however, betrays Phrynichus to Alcibiades and his Persian allies. Alcibiades responds in kind, writing a letter exposing Phrynichus for his betrayal of the Athenian cause. Phrynichus in desperation writes yet again to Astyochus, offering him a chance to destroy the Athenian fleet at Samos, which letter is duly passed on to Alcibiades. The final letter comes from Alcibiades to the authorities in Samos, informing them that they have been betrayed by Phrynichus. The entire exchange, characterized by broken confidences, character assassinations, betrayals, and denunciations, fulfils our expectations of the duplicity of letters observed thus far in Thucydides' writings. In time of crisis, the narrator seems to imply, people are unstable allies, and often turn to letters as weapons of war.

My final example of a letter in Thucydides is the so-called "letter of Nicias" (7.11–15), a lengthy message that has been compared to a speech both in form and function. In the summer of 414 BCE, the Athenian forces in Sicily were hard pressed, and Nicias debated with himself how best to inform the Athenian people of the crisis. Thucydides writes at some length about Nicias' concerns (7.8):

Fearing that his messengers might not report the facts, either through inability to speak, or through loss of memory, or because they wanted to say something pleasing to the crowd, Nicias wrote a letter (ἐπιστολήν), thinking that the Athenians would best learn his own viewpoint in this way, unobscured by anything the messenger might say, and they would then make plans about the true situation. So the messengers left, carrying the letter (τὰ γράμματα) which he had written and all the things he had ordered them to report.

The letter is delivered by messengers the following winter, and Thucydides elaborates on the double system of written and oral message: the messengers had been instructed to give the information by word of mouth not just to reinforce the written message, but also so that they could answer any questions asked by their

---

[28] This exchange is discussed by Steiner (1994) 221–22.

audience (7.10). This is something that the letter itself, obviously, could not have done, and Nicias was worried that the Athenians, so far from the desperate situation in Sicily, might underestimate the magnitude of the disaster. Thus the oral message corroborates and reinforces the letter, which in turn acts as its physical "proof."

After the messengers have delivered their speeches, they hand over Nicias' letter, and Thucydides relates the manner of its presentation (7.10):

And the clerk (ὁ γραμματεύς) of the city came forward and read the letter to the Athenians as follows (τοιάδε): "What has happened before, O Athenians, you have learned in many other letters (ἐπιστολαῖς); but now it is even more critical for you to learn in what condition we are, and to make plans ..."

Looking back over these passages, we are told that Nicias had sent oral messages home in the past, but now no longer trusts his messengers to report what he commands. He turns to letters as a more secure method of communication in a moment of military crisis, but still sends messengers along to answer direct questions which the letters cannot. At 7.11, Nicias' letter begins with reference to numerous letters sent previously during the campaign. His letter continues to emphasize its "writtenness": "you to whom I write understand ..."; and "I could have written other things more pleasant than these" (7.14).[29] Thucydides closes the recitation of the letter with the formula "such things the letter (ἐπιστολή) of Nicias revealed, and when the Athenians heard it [read aloud] ..." (7.16).

The debate continues whether to view the passages from 7.11–15 as a letter or a speech. Jebb argued that the introductory words τοιάδε (7.10) strongly suggested a speech, and Wilamowitz insisted that the rhetorical opening address ὦ Ἀθηναῖοι (7.11) could not have stood at the head of a real letter.[30] Others claim that the abnormal length of the text prevents it from being read as a letter, since generally a letter takes up only one sheet of papyrus; the letters of Herodotus average about 98 words compared to Nicias' 735.[31] If we look to ancient sources for help, we find little clarifica-

---

[29] Although cf. "you prefer to *hear* what is most pleasant" (7.14).
[30] R. Jebb, *Essays and Addresses* (Cambridge 1907) 403 note 4; U. von Wilamowitz, *Aristoteles und Athen* (Berlin 1893) vol I, 130 note 12. Quoted in van den Hout (1949) 37.
[31] Van den Hout (1949) 37–38.

tion: Dionysius of Halicarnassus (*On Thuc.* 42) calls the piece a letter (ἐπιστολή), yet categorizes it with Nicias' other great speeches (λόγοι) in books 6 and 7, while "Demetrius" (*On Style* 228) seems to include it in his condemnation of the letters in Thucydides that are too long, moving in the direction of treatises rather than letters.

I choose to read Nicias' letter as an epistle for reasons that, I hope, in the context of this study, have become clear. Jebb's objection has more to do with issues of accuracy rather than genre: Thucydides uses τοιάδε to hint that the letter is not a direct transcription but rather an approximation of the exact words of the original document. Wilamowitz's concern about the opening formula is also misguided: this letter is written from an individual to a group, namely the Athenian citizens who are in charge of relieving Nicias of his command or sending him reinforcements. The plural address highlights the democratic nature of Athenian government, in which no single man makes decisions. We can point to the comparable case in Herodotus, Themistocles' letter to the Ionians (8.22), which is similarly addressed to a multitude. The particular situation determines the singularity or plurality of address; while the plural address comes to dominate oral style among rhetoricians and politicians, it is not necessarily here a marker of epistolary inauthenticity. As to unusual length, my response would be that the crisis in Sicily is unusually severe, and Nicias needs to present enough detail to convince his audience of the seriousness of the moment. Again, the particular situation justifies what may be interpreted as epistolary "abnormalities."

Finally, I would argue strongly that Nicias' letter is a letter because of Thucydides' constant references to the written nature of the document. As stated above, we are told that Nicias turns to letter writing rather than oral messages for security and accuracy, that he had sent letters before during his campaign, and that the clerk read his letter out loud to the assembled Athenian people. Within the letter itself, Nicias refers to his audience as "those to whom I write," and insists that he could have written more pleasant news, but felt they deserved to hear the truth. The line between letter and speech may blur when the clerk reads the letter out loud, but he still is reading a document, not reciting a speech. Thucydides uses this letter as he had used others in his narrative: to clarify a historical moment, to document a stage in a military endeavor, and to record the details of a specific request for troop support. It also functions in a manner characteristic of all letters, explaining the perspective of a general away on campaign to his compatriots home in Athens: a sharing of information between people geographically separated. The epistolary nature of the text offers a change from an impersonal narration of events and creates a scene of colorful individuality, as Thucydides recreates the direct "speech" of Nicias, captured on papyrus in Sicily and re-performed in Athens. Interestingly, it is the last letter in direct speech reported in Thucydides' history.

It is not the documentary status of the "historical" letters that has interested me most here, nor the accuracy of each epistolary insertion. Rather, both Herodotus and Thucydides, by including letters in their historical narratives, reveal the affinity of letters with other forms of fictional narration: letters, whether documentary, freely invented, or something in between, reflect the invention of a self, a story, a plot in both senses of the word. Herodotus uses letters to enliven his narrative, Thucydides to bolster his historical arguments; both include letters as a kind of external reassurance, to persuade their readers of the quality of their work. Whatever their difference in approach, many of the historians' letters follow the pattern of epistolary treachery established by Homer. It is easy to forget that in the case of Glaucus, the σήματα λυγρά given to Bellerophon by his host provide a model of what *not* to do in his own exchange of words and gifts with Diomedes. But the fateful letter itself retains the stigma of its original use, and serves as a paradigm for letters yet to be written, in genres yet to be developed.

CHAPTER 4

Staging letters: embedded letters in Euripides

> Granted then, that all of literature is one long letter to an
> invisible other, a present, a possible, or a future passion that
> we rid ourselves of, feed, or seek.
>
> *The Three Marias: New Portuguese Letters* (Letter 1)[1]

The fifth and early fourth centuries in Athens reveal a gradual
increase in the functions of the written word in all its manifes-
tations.[2] Epic was still flourishing in oral recitation, but the reperformance of choral and monodic poetry, composed for but
outlasting a particular occasion, implies a gradual shift from traditional oral methods of transmission to written "master texts";[3]
similarly, the performance of tragedy on stage, while perceived as
oral/aural and visual to its audience, was already a reenactment
of a script in the hands of the author. The tragic poets praise
writing as an aid to memory (*PV* 460–61) and a general benefit to
mankind: a mark of civilization. Euripides (*Palamedes* 578 Nauck)
presents an encomium on the written word, praising its ability to
settle disputes and create inventories which in turn can be used
to assign inheritances.[4] In the same passage, the written word is
exalted as a method of permitting a person to learn everything
that goes on abroad; in this last case, the author must be referring
to letters.

Of the three surviving tragedians, Euripides alone appears to
have given letters serious attention on the tragic stage. He introduced letters in his *Hippolytus* (performed in 428 BCE), *Iphigenia*

---

[1] Maria Isabel Barreno, Maria Teresa Horta, and Maria Velho da Costa, *The Three Marias: New Portuguese Letters* (New York 1975) 15.

[2] Harris (1989) 66.

[3] I have investigated this in "Her Master's Voice: Sappho's Dialogue with Homer," *MD* 39 (1998) 123–49.

[4] In referring to the tragic fragments, I use Nauck's second edition: A. Nauck, *Tragicorum Graecorum Fragmenta*, 2nd edn. (Leipzig 1889).

in Tauris (*ca.* 412) and *Iphigenia in Aulis* (*ca.* 405). These are the plays that will occupy this chapter. Fragments of Euripides' lost play *Palamedes* (*ca.* 415 BCE, fr. 578.1–9 Nauck) also reveal an epistolary scene that may have been crucial to the plot. Written documents are certainly alluded to earlier by Aeschylus and Sophocles, but usually with reference to books or tablets (e.g. of written laws), lists or records, and other inscriptions on stone or bronze.[5] We also find early metaphors of writing suggestive of letters, such as the phrases "to inscribe in the heart," to write "on the tablets of the mind," or "on the folds of the tablet of Zeus."[6] Terms used in tragedy for the act of writing or the written text include γραφή, γράμμα(τα), δέλτος, τεκμήρια, and variations on the verb "to write" (e.g. τὰ ἐγγεγραμμένα). The word ἐπιστολή, by contrast, which later becomes the accepted term for letter, is applied by Aeschylus and Sophocles in its plural form solely to instructions or spoken commands, not letters.[7]

There is, however, one instance of the word in Sophocles' *Trachiniae* which does seem to point towards an epistolary use of the term. Trying to regain her husband's love, Deianeira sends λόγον ... ἐπιστολῆς, a message through Lichas (492–96), but also a gift for Heracles: the fateful robe locked up in a casket which she seals with the stamp of her signet ring (614–15). Thus, while the actual message sent through Lichas is still oral, Deianeira adds a concrete token of her love. The robe sealed in its casket functions almost as a letter would: it attempts to bridge the distance between the separated lovers, defends its authenticity by way of a signet ring, and metaphorically transfers Deianeira's love with it to its recipient, Heracles.[8]

---

[5] E.g. Aesch. *Suppl.* 946–47; Soph. *Trach.* 47, 157; fr. 144 (Nauck). See B. M. W. Knox, *Word and Action: Essays on the Ancient Theater* (Baltimore 1979) 284.

[6] E.g. Aesch. *PV* 789; *Choe.* 450; *Eumen.* 275; *Suppl.* 178–79, 991–92; Soph. *Phil.* 1325; *Trach.* 680–83; *Ant.* 707–9; fr. 540 (Nauck); Eur. *Hipp.* 985; *Trojan Women* 661; fr. 506.2–3 (Nauck). The metaphors appear also in Pindar *Ol.* 10.1–3; Plato *Phil.* 38e–39a, *Phaedr.* 275d–276a, and Gorgias *Helen* 17. For further discussion, see J. Svenbro, *Phrasikleia* (Paris 1988) 201; C. Segal, *Interpreting Greek Tragedy: Myth, Poetry, Text* (Ithaca, NY 1986) 81; R. Pfeiffer, *A History of Classical Scholarship* I (Oxford 1968) 25ff.; and Easterling (1985) 1–10.

[7] E.g. Aesch. fr. 293 (Nauck); Soph. *OC* 1601; *Trach.* 493; *Aj.* 781; fr.124 (Nauck). F. Ellendt writes of ἐπιστολή in Sophocles that "de litteris non exstat" (*Lexicon Sophocleum* [Berlin 1872] 266).

[8] On *Trach.*, see C. Segal, *Tragedy and Civilization* (Cambridge MA 1981) 94ff.; Page duBois, *Sowing the Body* (Chicago 1988) 130–66, esp. 153ff.; and F. Zeitlin, "Playing the Other: Theater, Theatricality, and the Feminine in Greek Drama," in F. I. Zeitlin, *Playing the Other* (Chicago 1996) 341–74.

By the time ἐπιστολαί meaning "letters" appears in Euripides, we may assume that writing and reading had become familiar enough concepts in everyday urban life that the introduction and recitation of a letter on stage would not confuse most members of the audience. But the use of the letter specifically as a stage device was still a distinct novelty. Like similar theatrical devices, such as the *ekkyklema* or *deus ex machina*, or props such as Electra's urn, letters were introduced presumably to liven up a scene, to support an argument with a visual aid, or to impart critical information that could not, according to dramatic conventions, otherwise be revealed. Euripides used letters in his dramas primarily as a means to vary the conventions of tragic narrative. In the *Hippolytus*, as Theseus reads his dead wife's accusations, a letter replaces what might, in different circumstances, have been a stock messenger scene: in other words, it is a device for bringing a past event onto stage in narrative rather than in acted form. In the *Iphigenia in Aulis*, a letter adds vividness to an interior monologue of vacillation, as Agamemnon writes, erases, seals, and unseals his fateful message to Clytemnestra; and the letter in the *Iphigenia in Tauris* infuses the recognition scene between Orestes and Iphigenia with extreme tension and irony.

The letter as a dramatic device works only in certain specialized contexts. There must be an element of distance between correspondents, a staging problem that was, before Euripides, normally corrected by a messenger scene. Euripides offers a variation on this theme in his *Theseus* (fr. 382 Nauck), when a shepherd, "unskilled at letters," attempts to describe alphabetic characters on a ship sailing toward him; as he painstakingly reads out Theseus' name, the audience learns that the hero is about to arrive.[9] In this case the signs on the ship's sail function as a letter bearing news of the identity of the traveler.

Tragic letters may identify their bearer or offer a guarantee, as in the conventional letter of recommendation; but in the complex ethical context of tragic drama, they may also disseminate mis-

---

[9] For a brief discussion of this fragment, which is preserved in Athenaeus 10.454b, see F. D. Harvey, "Literacy in the Athenian Democracy," *REG* 79 (1966) 603–4; also Segal (1986) 96. The scene was later imitated by both Agathon (fr. 4 Nauck) and Theodectes (fr. 6 Nauck). Svenbro (1988) 377, offers an interesting parallel of spelling aloud on stage in the tragic poet Achaeus' *Omphale* (fr. 33 Nauck = Athen. 11.466ff.), where a satyr tries to decipher the letters on a "speaking object," a σκύφος dedicated to Dionysus.

information as readily as information. Two such letters appear in Euripides' *Palamedes*. Palamedes is killed at Troy by the Greeks after they find "evidence" of treachery in his tent. The evidence consists of gold, planted there by his arch-enemy Odysseus, and a letter, forged by Odysseus, purporting to be from Priam to Palamedes. Euripides shows Odysseus, the master of trickiness, taking advantage of the ease with which letters can be forged and misattributed. At the same time as Odysseus uses the medium of a letter to dishonor Palamedes, the hero's brother in desperation writes a plea for help on oar-blades which he then tosses out to sea. Aristophanes parodies the latter scene in his *Thesmophoriazousae* (768–84), where the Relative, held hostage by female celebrants, sends a distress signal to his cousin Euripides: for lack of oars, he turns to wooden votive tablets.[10] His reference to oar-blades provides both a direct allusion to his tragic model and a spot of humor; after all, his model uses oars because he has no writing tablets, not because they are the ideal writing surfaces.

In spite of these passages, as far as we can tell from extant literature, the letter never became a stock element in fifth-century drama. The comic dramatist Cratinus, an older contemporary of Aristophanes', may have included a scene in a play in which a letter is publicly declaimed: one extant line reads "listen now also to this letter!" (ἄκουε νῦν καὶ τήνδε τὴν ἐπιστολήν) (Kassel–Austin 316). There is some evidence that New Comedy adopted letters for its own purposes in the fourth century, perhaps as writing and receiving letters became even more common in the Hellenistic world.[11] There are possible letters or written tokens in Menander's *Epitrepontes* (389 τὰ γράμματα), *Misoumenos* (417–25), and *Sikyonios* (141–44). It may be that the bourgeois world of Middle and New Comedy invited such communication based on private intrigue and secrecy, which in the heroic world of tragedy,

---

[10] It is worth noting that these messages are in effect palimpsests, since the votive tablets already had vows to Demeter etched on their surfaces which the Relative presumably writes over. I am not wholly convinced by duBois' (1988) suggestion that these tablets are actually images of the goddesses, and that inscription here "mimics the act of possession" (157).

[11] Note lost comedies by Alexis, Euthycles, and Machon (Kassel–Austin fr. 2) with the title Ἐπιστολή and Timocles' (Kassel–Austin frs. 9–10) Ἐπιστολαί; see Koskenniemi (1956) 185 note 1. The interest in letters in Greek New Comedy may have influenced Plautus' use of letters on stage for the purpose of intrigue (e.g. the opening scenes of the *Pseudolus*).

emphasizing the direct encounter of irreconcilable forces, seemed inappropriate or out of place; its unconventionality explains precisely why Euripides, ahead of his time in so many ways, decided to champion the device.

LETTERS ON STAGE: NECESSARY ADAPTATIONS

When a letter is used on stage, its formal and functional characteristics, far from being merely ornamental, significantly influence the way meaning is consciously and unconsciously constructed by the epistolary writers and readers. The Euripidean letters we will discuss do not just report events or carry information between characters; rather they function as agents in the plot, provoking reactions and directing events kinetically.[12]

Let us pause here a moment to mention the difference between action described in a letter and one developed through or by means of letters.[13] In "communicative" letters, the letters report events to correspondents who are otherwise uninvolved in the events that are narrated, playing a passive or static role: for example, in Richardson's *Clarissa*, letters narrate and describe present action but are not themselves part of that action, as the heroine writes to her confidante Miss Howe about the events that have occurred between herself and the antagonist, Lovelace. By contrast, in the active or "kinetic" method, the action progresses through the letters themselves, as they provoke reactions or function as actual agents in the plot: in Laclos' *Dangerous Liaisons*, the protagonist writes directly and provocatively to the antagonist, who responds in kind. In the latter case, the letters themselves are the actions that make up the plot, or, put another way, the action or event is the writing itself, the manner in which things are written and interpreted, the order in which the letters are presented, and so forth. Epistolary form itself creates and manipulates meaning.[14]

---

[12] References to the terminology may be found in F. Jost, "L'Evolution d'un genre: le roman épistolaire dans les lettres occidentales," in his *Essais de littérature comparée* (Fribourg 1968), vol. II, 89–179, and in Altman (1982).

[13] This distinction was first formalized by F. Jost, "Le roman épistolaire et la technique narrative au XVIIIe siècle," *Comparative Literature Studies* 3 (1966) 397–427, and amplified in Jost (1968) 89–179, 380–402. The distinction is also discussed in Altman (1982) 7–8, 203–4.

[14] See J. Rousset, *Forme et Signification* (Paris 1962) 74.

The "kinetic" method is what is found in Euripides' staging of
letters.

In order for a letter to be presented on stage, certain epistolary
elements which would be problematic in a dramatic context must
be confronted or resolved. Tensions and contradictions arise when
a letter is used in the primarily oral/aural and visual environment
of a play. The authority of the letter on stage is highlighted by its
oral surroundings; when a character "reads" a letter, the visible
script, frozen in time from the moment of its recording, is brought
into focus in a way that the memorized and thus invisible lines of
the rest of the tragedy are not.[15]

One of the most important points of conflict in the transition
from epistolary private exchange to dramatic presentation is that a
written letter is actually an obstacle to communication on stage. In
order for it to function effectively, it must be passed around to the
rest of the characters on stage (in which case the audience remains
in the dark), "overheard" by other characters and the audience, or
read out loud for all (onstage and offstage) to hear. A modern
example of the last case is Alan Gurney's play *Love Letters*, which
sacrifices dramatic illusion to communicative directness by having
each character sit at a writing table on stage and read aloud each
letter in turn to the audience.

There are, of course, dramatic contexts in which the contents of
the letter are never revealed to anyone, on stage or off, but its
mere presence fuels the action. A prime example outside the realm
of drama is Edgar Allen Poe's short story, "The Purloined Letter,"
in which a letter never arrives at its destination yet directs the entire narrative proceedings.[16] Todorov has pointed out that every

---

[15] Both epistolary and non-epistolary dramatic passages are based on written texts, but in
one case the written nature of the text is emphasized by its physical presence on stage.
The fact that an author's written script lies behind an entire play is forgotten by the audience in performance; these are two different degrees of writing. See Svenbro (1988)
188–89, and T. M. Lentz, *Orality and Literacy in Hellenic Greece* (Carbondale IL 1989) 145–
64. There is also a difference in "reading" if a character reads his/her own words (e.g.
Agamemnon, Iphigenia) or the words of another (Theseus). In the case of Iphigenia
in the *IT*, discussed below, her recitation allows her to interrupt herself and answer her
listeners' questions, which would not have been possible had they themselves read her
letter in her absence.

[16] This story spawned a famous debate in *Yale French Studies* among modern theorists:
J. Lacan, "Seminar on 'The Purloined Letter'," trans. J. Mehlman, *YFS* 48 (1972) 38–72
(originally written in 1956); J. Derrida, "The Purveyor of Truth," trans. W. Domingo
et al., *YFS* 52 (1975) 31–113; B. Johnson, "The Frame of Reference: Poe, Lacan, Derrida," *YFS* 55/56 (1977) 457–505.

epistolary message has a double meaning: first, what the sentences that compose the message mean, that is, the literal meaning; second, the connotations of the letter as a social phenomenon, whether as a mark of intimacy, a proof of authenticity, a change in situation, or other related information.[17] Sometimes the presence of the letter is far more important to the story than its contents: "that the letter is can be far more weighty than what it means, and the letter's very itinerary can generate action."[18] Merely accepting a letter marks a person in some way, establishing, for example, the beginnings of a love affair. In *Dangerous Liaisons*, Valmont sends to his intended beloved the same letter four times in a different envelope, because he knows she will return it unread; she believes that by refusing to read and respond to his letters, she can protect her virtue. When she finally does answer, she writes that he must stop the correspondence. The very act of writing back reveals feelings of involvement and attachment, in spite of the contents stating a desire to break off the connection.[19] Sending a letter is a powerful signal in its own right, and can be a form of manipulation; accepting or refusing to accept a letter is equally significant.[20] We will see in the *IT* that when Pylades "accepts" the letter from Iphigenia's hands, the action signals to the audience the beginning of the play's resolution.

But the reception of the letter is rarely limited to a single reader; in fact, on stage, as stated above, a single silent reader would be an obstacle to the dramatic function of the letter. Instead, we may find ourselves confronting a crowd of interpreters: the letter's intended recipient, an interceptor who reads a letter not meant for his or her eyes, an eavesdropping chorus, the external reader.[21] Each reader offers yet another perspective on the events: in the *IA*, Agamemnon, his trusty servant, and Menelaus,

[17] T. Todorov, "The Discovery of Language: *Les Liaisons dangereuses* and *Adolphe*," *Yale French Studies* 45 (1970) 113–26, esp. 115.

[18] F. Meltzer, "Laclos' Purloined Letters," *Critical Inquiry* 8 (1982) 515–29, esp. 519.

[19] See further T. Todorov, *Littérature et signification* (Paris 1967) 32.

[20] Altman (1982), ch. 1, has an interesting discussion of the letter as metaphor or metonym. A metaphor of the lover is generated by the epistolary situation, which conjures up interiorized images and comparisons (the beloved can experience disappointment, if the lover does not match up to the illusion created by his letters). The letter can act metonymically for the lover, through physical contact; cf. Straton's image of a book roll lying suggestively in his beloved's lap (*Anth. Pal.* 12.208), discussed in P. Bing, *The Well-Read Muse* (Göttingen 1988) 30–31.

[21] Meltzer (1982) 517.

all read the same letter ordering Iphigenia not to come to Aulis with very different emotions and reactions, while the external audience reads along with the added perspective of omniscience: we know that the letter will be contradicted by the tradition in which Iphigenia is indeed sacrificed for the sake of the fleet.

External readers, from their privileged status, may have a view of the complete story which the internal readers cannot share.[22] But they also imitate internal readers in dealing with apparent contradictions while trying to make sense of the situation. The Euripidean audience eagerly awaited new twists and turns in the conventional plot: the inserted letters answered that need, offering a temporary diversion as the plot worked its way to the expected conclusion. Agamemnon's letter delays the inevitable, while Phaedra's and Iphigenia's speed it up. The effect of the external audience's continuous double reading process, one within and the other outside the epistolary text, is a hermeneutic overlay or palimpsest.[23] In an epistolary novel, an external reading may agree or disagree with a prior reading or interpretation which is displayed within the fiction. In some way it always recapitulates the fictionalized, internal process of interpretation. This double or palimpsestic reading can also make the reader self-consciously aware of the reading process itself. Within the epistolary fiction, the act of seeking meaning is exposed as problematic or hazardous; letters are ambiguous linguistic artifacts in that they symbolize communication but do not necessarily embody it. If external readers follow the pattern of internal readers, they too must be aware of potential dangers and misunderstandings in their own search for meaning. The active participation of the external reader in the creation of meaning is characteristic of the epistolary novel. The more voices there are in a polyphonic epistolary fiction, the more work there is for the external reader, who takes on a role usually filled by a narrator: that of organizing and sifting out the abundance of data (both information and emotional responses to that information) in the search for a clear "story."[24] In this way the reader "writes" the text into being.

---

[22] This is referred to by Rousset (1962) 98.

[23] See T. Castle *Clarissa's Ciphers: Meaning and Disruption in Richardson's "Clarissa"* (Ithaca 1982) 43, who compares the reading going on inside the text to "histoire" and the external reading to "discours."

[24] Castle (1982) 167.

In the context of epistolarity, we must remember that a writer can at any time become a reader; a writer, for example, may reread her letter before sending it. Rereading one's own letter entails a switch in perspective from writer to reader, and a consequent distancing that may lead to self-discovery or self-disclosure. This will occur in two of our Euripidean examples: Agamemnon "rereads" his letter for the benefit of his messenger, and thereby reassures himself that this second letter is the one that reflects his true feelings, while Iphigenia recites her letter before sending it and discloses herself to the very person to whom she was writing. A reader becomes a writer when he or she decides to answer the letter received. The act of writing a letter is not only an opportunity to define oneself in a relationship to the other person, but it is also an opportunity to draw that other into becoming the subject of another text. This is especially true in a fiction based on the exchange of love letters; the epistolary lover demands a reciprocal emotion, but this emotion is to be represented by an answering letter. The difficult task of the author is to sustain a believable relationship between the alternating writer(s) and reader(s) while at the same time making the narrative accessible to external readers.

This last issue is a critical one for all epistolary discourse, not just that on the tragic stage: the need for "realism" may interfere with the amount of information available to be transmitted by letters to the external reader. J. Altman summarizes this problem neatly in the context of the modern epistolary novel:

The writer of epistolary fiction has a fundamental problem: the letter novelist (A) must make his letter writer (B) speak to an addressee (C) in order to communicate with a reader (D) who overhears; how does he reconcile the exigencies of story (communication between novelist and reader) with the exigencies of interpersonal discourse (communication between correspondents)?[25]

Different authors find a variety of ways to circumvent this basic problem of the genre. Let me rephrase Altman for our discussion of letters on stage. In an "ideal" non-dramatic epistolary exchange, A writes to B; in a dramatic epistolary context, however, the author (A) creates a character (B) writing to another character (C) but must also ensure that D, whether an internal audience

---

[25] Altman (1982) 210.

(another character) or an external one (viewers or readers), also learns the import of the written message. Thus, for the letter on stage to have an impact on its "readers," its secrecy must be violated and its contents made public. It is no surprise, then, that two of the three extant Euripidean letter scenes involve some sort of interception or revelation before the letter can be delivered to its correct addressee.

Because the letter is a physical object that must be transferred from one person to another, it can take on an additional dimension of authority and power in this primarily oral context. The letter-tablet is backed with an apparently incontestable seal of authenticity, namely the mark of the writer's signet ring. A letter becomes a token or sign similar to a piece of cloth or a footprint, representing or identifying the writer or owner.[26] Iphigenia keeps her letter, a cry for help, in the sanctuary of the temple of Artemis, out of sight of the local Taurian king, but surely also because of its "holy" nature: she treasures it as her only hope for survival, even if she has been as yet unable to send it. Letters can also be used powerfully yet unethically. Agamemnon abuses both his royal and paternal authority when he sends a deceitful letter to his wife and child, who promptly obey the written orders. Phaedra's false accusation goes against all sense of justice, yet Theseus unwaveringly grants its text authority against Hippolytus' sworn oaths.

All three cases in Euripides also highlight the temporal complexities of letters on stage. Phaedra's letter is doubly powerful because its writer is now dead, leaving its text incontrovertible, impossible to question or doubt; the removal of the author gives an aura of truth to her words. Iphigenia's letter was written in the past but never sent, and the frozen words continue to describe her unchanging misery. Agamemnon frantically tries to undo an earlier letter by penning a separate postscript, but cannot escape his own prior words once they have reached their addressee; the second letter is intercepted and fought over until it is too late to undo the damage of the first.

The act of interception on stage interferes with the basic purpose of letter writing, namely to bridge the gap between a specific

---

[26] O. Taplin does not say much about letters in his chapter on "Objects and Tokens" in *Greek Tragedy in Action* (Berkeley 1978) 77–100, although he briefly mentions Phaedra's letter (95), calling it "an unusually small and naturalistic prop for Greek tragedy."

writer and an exclusive addressee. In both cases where messengers are used (in the *IT* and the *IA*), the delivery of the letters is compromised: Agamemnon's letter fails to reach its addressee off stage; Iphigenia's letter succeeds only because its loss is anticipated, the letter is read out loud in advance, and its addressee is not absent but very much present on stage. When no messenger is used, as in the unusual case of Phaedra's letter, the message is received without further complication, but here the gap between present reader and absent writer is widened rather than bridged, as Phaedra "speaks" from the dead through her last testament.

Letters, on stage and off, are particularly susceptible to forgery, deceit, and misinformation. Of the letters considered in this chapter, two communicate true information (Agamemnon's second letter, Iphigenia's) and two promulgate lies (Agamemnon's first letter, Phaedra's). If we remind ourselves of Proetus' murderous epistolary deceit, we may wonder whether letters in literary or fictional contexts contain within themselves a seed of suspicion sown by an earlier oral culture; are letters more often villains or heroes on the tragic stage?

I would suggest that the public perception of the letter's role on stage gradually shifts as the culture becomes more fully literate. Aeschylus puts these words in the mouth of the Argive king in his *Suppliants* (946–49):

These things are not written down on tablets or sealed up in the folds of scrolls; you hear the clear words of a tongue and a mouth that speaks in freedom.

One generation later, Cratinus (Kassel–Austin 128) sustains that archaic mindset for his contrast of honesty and alphabetic literacy:

By Zeus I do not know letters (γράμματα), nor do I understand them, but I speak to you instead through my tongue.

Euripides and the Middle and New Comic writers, however, fully embrace the role of letters on stage, much as they incorporate other objects and tokens such as rings, swaddling clothes, and locks of hair.

But while letters on the Euripidean and later comic stage may be usefully compared to other props, they are still often presented as slightly "different." Even in these more literate times, we recognize the tension articulated in Aeschylus' passage between sealed

words and a clear, free tongue. This is most obvious in the epistolary terminology employed. The text of the letter itself is "nor-
malized" into a context more appropriate to an oral culture: it is
personified as a voice or an active agent, whether speaking,
hiding, signifying, or desiring to act in some way. In the *Hippolytus*,
before Theseus reads the letter, he concludes from its presence
that it wishes to speak out a message to him (865 λέξαι δέλτος ἥδε
μοι θέλει). After reading it silently on stage, he cries out in anguish
that the letter shrieks aloud (877 βοᾷ βοᾷ δέλτος), and gives forth
a voice (880 φθεγγόμενον) through its writings. The image of the
letter here is that of a desiring subject, a speaking voice. In the
two Iphigenia plays, the letter is portrayed in a similarly active
manner, as it alternately hides and reveals its message: in the *IA*,
Agamemnon offers to share with his servant what the letter has
hidden in its folds (112 κέκευθε δέλτος ἐν πτυχαῖς), by translating
the writings into speech; in the *IT*, the letter itself seems to be
given the power of unmediated speech, as Iphigenia imagines that
the words written on the tablet, although silent, will speak out of
their own accord (641–42 δέλτος ... λέγουσα ... ἀπαγγέλλει; 763
αὐτὴ φράσει σιγῶσα τἀγγεγραμμένα). Euripides seems fascinated by the same paradoxes that will catch the attention of the
fourth-century BCE comic writer Antiphanes, to be discussed at the
end of this chapter: how is it that letters can be both silent and
speaking, inaudible yet understood, desiring yet inanimate, privately hoarded and publicly exposed? Let us turn to the individual
Euripidean plays to try to respond to this riddle.

IPHIGENIA IN TAURIS

When Euripides decided to dramatize Iphigenia's story, he had
many models to follow among his literary predecessors, but the
introduction of letters into the plot was his own contribution. It is
a testament to Euripides' skill that once the letter did appear on
stage, Aristotle could interpret it as a "wholly probable device."

Aristotle (*Poetics* 16.11) praises the recognition scene in the *IT*
because it is brought about directly by the incidents themselves;
the fact that the incidents are probable occurrences under the circumstances makes the resulting recognition all the more astonish-
ing to the audience. His statement that it is likely that Iphigenia
would send a letter under the circumstances reflects the function

of a letter as bridge, through which one can speak to an absent friend or relative. He presumes that in her state of powerlessness, Iphigenia's only option would be to write a plea for help to her brother. Now that the opportunity of sending the message has arrived, it is indeed likely that she should act as she does. Aristotle discusses the same scene as a type of recognition which occurs together with a reversal, and which involves two sets of recognitions to effect that reversal. "Thus Iphigenia was revealed to Orestes through the sending of the letter, but a separate discovery was needed to make him known to Iphigenia" (*Poetics* 11.8). Aristotle acknowledges the effectiveness of the epistolary device in these scenes, but focuses on the sending of the letter rather than on its spoken revelation. He does not mention that the letter, previously written and sealed, is really an obstacle to immediate recognition, and that Euripides must provide strong motivation for its message to be made public.

When we first see Iphigenia, she has been exiled in Tauris for many years, acting as the priestess of a local cult which demands the death of any stranger that arrives at its temple. She still hopes for rescue, and to this end she carefully guards a letter, a plea for help, which she dreams someday will find its way to her brother Orestes. The letter itself was prepared long ago, dictated to a prisoner who felt pity for Iphigenia in spite of his impending death at her hands (*IT* 582–90). Only now, when Orestes and Pylades arrive together, does Iphigenia, who does not recognize them, have the option of letting one go free to act as her messenger. Iphigenia's letter exists simultaneously on two temporal levels: it is both a testament to her emotions at an earlier time, prior to the opening scene of the play, and a document of her present intent.

Burnett interprets the letter as "a material witness to a principal quality of Iphigeneia's spirit, her faithful confidence, reminding us that she had never quite ceased to hope for rescue and return."[27] One could also see the previously written and sealed message more corporeally as (metonymically) representing the heroine herself, body as well as soul, trapped in the temple of Taurian Artemis. The proper delivery of that letter is a prerequisite for the deliverance of both Orestes and his sister. As Iphigenia tries to hand over

---

[27] A. P. Burnett, *Catastrophe Survived* (Oxford, 1971) 54–55.

the letter which she thinks will eventually bring about her rescue, she effectively hands herself over to the protection of her brother. The letter thus reflects the personality of its writer to such a degree that it comes to represent or embody that writer.[28]

The question of the double time frame emphasizes how complicated the issue of temporality can be in the context of letter writing. In a conventional exchange of letters across any physical distance, the built-in time gap between the acts of writing and reading endows all epistolary verbs with potential multivalence. What was immediate and critical at the moment of writing may be entirely resolved by the time the addressee receives the letter. The epistolary "now" may refer to the actual performance time of the event described, the moment it is written down, the time the letter is sent, received, read, reread, and answered. There are four different levels of narrative time in any epistolary fiction: (1) erzählte Zeit, the time of the narrated action (2) Erzählzeit, the time of narration, the temporal frame of the internal correspondents (3) the time of the editor of the letters, or the dramatist, in which he organizes the text, effectively reordering the correspondents' time (4) reading or performance time, our time frame as an external audience.[29] At any given moment in the epistolary fiction, the narrated time may relate to the time of narration as past to present (e.g. "yesterday I met x"), present to present ("I am writing this while listening to music"), or future to present ("I will meet x tomorrow").[30] Thus the epistolary present tense figures as a pivot for the past and future. When Samuel Richardson represents Clarissa writing "to the moment," he tries to reduce the difference between narrated time and time of narration, aiming to approximate immediacy and spontaneity, in order to draw the external reader into the ongoing events of the story.[31] When the Ovidian heroines write in the present, their narration, full of emotion and anxiety, oscillating between memory and hope, becomes more important

---

[28] The idea that a letter reflects the personality of its writer occurs in numerous epistolary theorists: "Demetrius"*On Style* 227 (text in Malherbe [1988]); Cic. *Ad Fam.* 16.16.2; Sen. *Ep.* 40.1. On the parallelism between letters and women, see duBois (1988) 152ff., and F. I. Zeitlin, "The Power of Aphrodite: Eros and the Boundaries of the Self in *Hippolytus*," in P. Burian, ed., *Directions in Euripidean Criticism* (Durham NC 1985) 52–111.

[29] R. C. Rosbottom "Motifs in Epistolary Fiction: Analysis of a Narrative Subgenre," *L'esprit créateur* 17 (1977) 286, and Altman (1982) 123.

[30] Altman (1982) 123.

[31] Rosbottom (1977) 286.

than any remembered past or anticipated future event: "the memory is less important than the experience of remembering."[32]

Epistolary discourse tries to create an impossible present, a collapsing of Erzählzeit and erzählte Zeit, by shifting between recent past and future, memory and expectation. But the epistolary present is ultimately caught up in the impossibility of seizing itself, since the narrative present must necessarily postdate or anticipate the events narrated (unless the event is the act of writing itself). Altman lists three impossibilities that entrap the epistolary present, which are paraphrased below:[33]

1 Narrative time (Erzählzeit) can never be simultaneous with the event it is narrating (erzählte Zeit), unless the event is the act of writing the letter. The writer is restricted to writing what she has just done or will soon do.
2 The written present cannot remain valid; when a writer records an emotion, that emotion is valid for only that moment, and will inevitably be modified or contradicted by the next sentence.
3 The present time of the writer is not the same as the present time of the internal reader; there can be no epistolary dialogue in a shared present. If the writer writes "I feel," the reader must interpret it as "you felt when you wrote the letter."

Thus the epistolary writer and reader find themselves on either side of a temporal and spatial gap. Unlike participants in a conversation, they cannot interrupt each other, rephrase unclear sentences, or receive immediate answers. As soon as the writer becomes aware of this gap that separates him from his reader, however, he tries to bridge it. Because epistolary communication is the product of so many kinds of "absence," it is preoccupied with immediacy and presence. The comparison of a letter to an imaginary conversation which puts the writer in the presence of his reader, something which ancient theorists accepted as a basic tenet of epistolarity, is just one way in which the writer tries to overcome the insurmountable gap between present and future, here and over there.[34]

In Iphigenia's case, the misery which she describes in her letter has remained the same for an indefinite amount of time, so that

---

[32] Altman (1982) 128, with reference to the Portuguese Nun's letters.
[33] Altman (1982) 129.   [34] Altman (1982) 135.

the previously written letter retains its full impact of sustained grief and desperation. Iphigenia's message waiting for its messenger is an unusual case of the usual epistolary paradox described above: "the *I* can address only a *you* who is an image persisting from the past; likewise, the *you* who receives the message exists in yet another time, which was future to the *I* sending the message."[35] Iphigenia attempts to circumvent the image of Orestes past (she last saw him as a very young child) by creating a stronger image of Orestes in the future, one who will take responsibility for his sister and lead her back home. The vocalization of the written text, as Iphigenia recites it aloud unwittingly to her brother, appears to collapse the paradox, as Orestes benefits from the immediacy of speech; but this speech is still a reconstruction or repetition of words recorded earlier, and so the paradox remains.

Iphigenia stands in front of Orestes and Pylades with the letter in hand. At the crucial moment, spurred on by Pylades' wish not to perjure himself if the letter were to be lost, she repeats its contents from memory. She does not read the actual letter, for the simple reason that, unlike Phaedra, she appears unable to read or write.[36] If she had been able to, she would not have needed to dictate her earlier message. Iphigenia carefully justifies her recitation to the men on stage as well as to her wider audience (760–65):

> The things within that are written on the folds of the tablet
> I will recite to you, and you will report it all to my family.
> For thus the outcome is sure: if you save my writings,
> the words themselves, although silent, will speak;
> but if these letters perish in the sea,
> by saving your body, you will also save my message.

---

[35] Altman (1982) 132.

[36] A point ignored by most critics who claim that Iphigenia "reads" her letter aloud, e.g. Segal (1986) 103, and *La Musique du Sphinx: poésie et structure dans la tragédie grecque* (Paris 1987) 263–98; Knox (1979) 287 (although he acknowledges the problem at 293, note 52), and "Silent Reading in Antiquity," *GRBS* 9 (1968) 421–35; Burnett (1971) 54. In their descriptions of Iphigenia's actions, M. Platnauer, *Euripides Iphigenia in Tauris* (Oxford 1938) 125, C. Whitman, *Euripides and the Full Circle of Myth* (Cambridge MA 1974) 22, and G. M. A. Grube, *The Drama of Euripides* (London 1941) 325, prevaricate with "recites" and "tell contents." In contrast, E. B. England *The Iphigeneia Among the Tauri of Euripides* (London 1886) 192 (and note on line 765), G. Monaco, "L'epistola nel teatro antico," *Dioniso* 39 (1965) 334–51, esp. 347, Harvey (1966) 622, and duBois (1988) 160–61, make clear that she is unable to read or write, and therefore repeats the contents of the letter from memory. In this connection, see also S. G. Cole, "Could Greek Women Read and Write?," in H. Foley, ed., *Reflections of Women in Antiquity* (London 1981) 219–45.

In an ideal situation, Pylades will be able to confirm the contents of the letter, but in the event of disaster, if the letter is lost, human memory will suffice. Iphigenia's statement reflects the idea that text is silent until a reader can animate it; she hopes the letter will survive to be read by its intended addressee, to speak to the person who reads.[37]

The shift on stage from written text to speech is swift and irreversible, and as the contents become public the letter itself becomes obsolete, because Orestes is standing within earshot. It is ironic that the revelation of the written words depends on the imagined loss of the physical letter,[38] but once the oral message has been delivered, the delivery of the letter is reduced to a pantomime, an empty gesture rejected by Orestes as he tosses the text aside to embrace his sister. Speech reduces text to something already in the past, and transforms the imaginary loss of the tablets into a real one.

What are the words that Iphigenia recites? Can we reconstruct the conventional form and outline of a letter, or is this really nothing more than a carefully justified overheard soliloquy? Iphigenia begins her speech by answering Pylades, who had asked to whom he should carry the letter, and what news to announce. Iphigenia responds in epistolary format by providing crucial information at the start: the name of the addressee, complete with patronymic, followed by the writer's identity and current location (769–71):

> Announce "to Orestes, the son of Agamemnon,
> she who was sacrificed in Aulis sends the following message,
> Iphigenia who still lives, yet is no longer alive for those at
> home."

The opening address of an ancient Greek letter is one of its most conventional and unchanging facets. Iphigenia's choice of words, "sends the following message" (ἐπιστέλλει τάδε), echoes the τοι ἐπιστέλλε of the lead letter from Berezan, as both writers omit the standard χαίρειν in the urgency of their situation. We

---

[37] See the ramifications of lending one's voice to a text in Svenbro (1988) 53–73, the chapter entitled "Le lecteur et la voix lectrice."

[38] As Burnett (1971) 53, puts it, "only when the tablets have been in fancy left at the bottom of the sea can the situation shape itself as it should, for it is speech that must be obtained, if this scene is to succeed."

find the same formula – "x greets/speaks/sends to y" – in papyri, in letters reported in the histories of Herodotus, and in literary letters from Lucian, Alciphron, and the Greek novelists.[39] But what is conventional in an epistolary context becomes critical in this dramatic situation, as the identity of both sender and addressee must be made explicit for the recognition to follow. Epistolary convention also helps us with an issue of punctuation in the modern text. I would read the words "to Orestes son of Agamemnon" as both an address on the tablet's exterior, and also as the first words of the actual letter, thus functioning as the indirect object of the next phrase, "she who was sacrificed in Aulis sends the following message . . ." The recitation of the body of the letter then begins at line 769, and not, as most editors would have it, at line 770.

Iphigenia presents herself as still living and yet not alive for her family, present in Tauris yet absent for her brother whom she supposes to be in Argos. This curious situation is almost a prerequisite for letter writing – one writes to turn absence into presence, to make someone come alive through words. Seneca writes "I never receive a letter from you without being in your company forthwith" (*Ep.* 40.1 "numquam epistulam tuam accipio, ut non protinus una simus"). For Orestes and Iphigenia, the commonplace is amazingly true: through the recitation and reception of the letter, he and his sister suddenly come face-to-face. The address reveals to Orestes her identity, and Iphigenia's assertion that she is indeed "she whom you see right here" confirms it. But Iphigenia recites the rest of her letter, allowing Orestes to understand what has happened since he last saw his sister.[40] Orestes' startled interruptions during her revelations are presented as asides. Since dramatic convention encourages lengthy messages and allows for a delayed response on the part of the listener that should realistically come after the first few lines of speech, this epistolary scene fits well within the customs of the stage.

[39] For discussions of epistolary openings, see Koskenniemi (1956) 155–67; Stowers (1986) 20. Examples include Hdt. 3.40: "Amasis speaks thus to Polycrates"; Lucian *Ver. Hist.* 2.35: "Odysseus sends greetings to Calypso"; all the prescripts of Alciphron's corpus; and, as an example of the formula in the novel, Chariton 8.4: "From Challirhoe: greetings to Dionysius, my benefactor."

[40] Cf. Burnett (1971) 54: "They have known her through the last fifteen lines . . . but they have chosen to keep their faces straight in order that Pylades might formally take custody of the precious letter, turn, and with mock solemnity present it to his friend."

In her letter, Iphigenia writes a scenario for the future: just as she expects Pylades to carry the letter to Argos, so should Orestes eventually carry her back home to Argos. She then turns to threats: when he reads the letter, he will be bound to reply, but if he fails to "answer," her curse will track him down just as the messenger has tracked him down. She demands not the customary return letter, but immediate action.

As Iphigenia recites her letter, she interjects words presumably not in the original document, whether in response to her interlocutors' reactions, or to emphasize a particular point in the letter. She tells Pylades to pay attention and remember the name of the addressee (779), and addresses Orestes twice when he interrupts (773, 780). After the last interruption, Iphigenia returns to her recitation in indirect speech, asking Pylades to "tell him [i.e. Orestes] that Artemis ... transported me to this country" (783–86). The letter seems to contain no conventional farewell, as the recitation ends abruptly here in the middle of a line. Iphigenia confirms this with her own words of conclusion spoken to the two men in front of her: "That is my letter, and those are the words inscribed on the tablets" (786–87). Such syntactical variation within the frame of her recitation should remind us that she is not reading a script, but rather recalling the sealed contents.

Once Iphigenia has spoken, she expects Pylades to leave with the letter. Instead, Pylades hands the tablets directly to Orestes, who is standing beside him. He describes his exaggerated movements with solemn emphasis: "I receive and I give over" (791–92). In an instant, the letter is "sent" by Iphigenia through Pylades to Orestes. Orestes answers "I receive it" (793), but then quickly drops the letter and embraces his sister. The oral presentation of Iphigenia has made the written token obsolete once its message has come across.[41] Through recitation, word has superceded text, and now action will supercede word as the characters move to the next crisis in the drama. The all-important letter, the object of Aristotle's praise, becomes just another stage prop.

In Tauris, the letter functions as rescuer, reuniting Iphigenia

[41] The message comes through for Orestes, but Iphigenia requires more proof, which comes in the shape of an embroidered piece of cloth that she had given her brother long ago. Steiner (1994) 36, points out that the illiterate Iphigenia puts her trust in a typical product of female industry (weaving), while Orestes accepts the sign of the written word (or, more precisely, the oral presentation of the written word).

with her brother and saving her from perpetual exile. When Euripides returns to the same myth later in his career, focusing on the earlier events at Aulis, he represents the letter as a message of destruction rather than of hope, one which fatally divides rather than reunites the family. But Euripides is not content with just one letter in the *Iphigenia at Aulis*; he complicates the plot by imagining two letters, one written before the action begins, and another being written before our eyes on stage, just as the play opens.

IPHIGENIA IN AULIS

The play opens with the Greek fleet becalmed at Aulis, and with Agamemnon desperate to appease Artemis who has stopped the winds from blowing favorably. The Greeks are confronted with an impossible situation: the oracles tell them to sacrifice Agamemnon's daughter Iphigenia or abandon the Trojan campaign. Agamemnon had made his decision and written a letter to Clytemnestra, asking her to send Iphigenia to Aulis but hiding the real reason for his request. The first scene of the *IA* unfolds in the quiet of the night.[42] Agamemnon's faithful servant observes the king writing a letter (34–40):

> But you, lighting the flame of your lamp,
> are writing a letter,
> that one which you still hold in your hands,
> and those same words you erase again;
> then you seal it up, only to open it once more,
> and you hurl the pine tablets to the ground,
> weeping copious tears.

The servant's words emphasize the immediacy and emotional intensity of the situation, and recreate for the audience a vivid scenario of action inside the tent from which we are presumably excluded.[43] Precisely because the king's troubles seem to be centered on the writing of a letter, the old man is unable to eavesdrop

---

[42] There are some textual questions about this opening scene; the arguments are summarized in Knox (1979) 284–87.

[43] One alternative to the old servant's report of his master's actions would have been to present Agamemnon miming the scene at the entrance to his tent during the opening of the play, but without detailed stage instructions, we cannot determine the details of performance.

or overhear. The letter is inaccessible to him on two levels: it is private, and it is written; possibly, as a servant, he cannot read or write.[44] The subject of the letter is unknown also to the audience, and the servant's request for an explanation spurs Agamemnon to reveal its contents to the "eavesdropping" audience as well.[45] As in the previous play, the letter's text must be presented orally before the action can continue.

In answering the servant's concerned questions, Agamemnon recalls his original letter sent earlier to Clytemnestra in response to the oracle's demand for Iphigenia's sacrifice; the present letter is a revocation of his instructions for Clytemnestra to send their daughter to him. The motivation for the writing of the first letter is described twice in the opening section of the play, first by Agamemnon and then by Menelaus, and their perspectives on its invention are, not surprisingly, diametrically opposed. Agamemnon claims that his brother persuaded him with words to "dare the terrible deeds" (97–98):[46] "writing in the folds of the tablet (κἂν δέλτου πτυχαῖς γράψας), I sent it to my wife so that she should send (our) daughter to marry Achilles" (98–100). In the same breath (104–5), Agamemnon calls his letter a means of persuasion (πειθώ) and an outright lie (ψευδῆ). We find out slightly later (124–26) that not only has Agamemnon invented the whole idea of a marriage between Iphigenia and Achilles, but that he has not even informed Achilles of his role in the plot. Agamemnon pretends to be speaking on behalf of the hero, inventing reasons that seem consistent with Achilles' character. The command that Iphigenia be brought to the camp seems genuine because the writer is clever enough to invent a reasonable scenario, to transmit demands which are in character for a well-known hero, and to swear those involved in the deceit to secrecy.

After Agamemnon has revealed to his solicitous servant the nature of the deceit, he immediately admits a change of heart. His current distress revolves around how to override the former command (107–10):

---

[44] Contrast Plautus' *Pseudolus*, where, in a reversal of customary social relations, the master hands over a letter written to him by his beloved to a clever servant, who then reads aloud for the benefit of the audience.

[45] For a brief discussion of the motivation behind Agamemnon's reading of the letter aloud, see Knox (1979) 285–86.

[46] It is unclear whether this refers to the sacrifice or to the deceitful letter.

The things which I decided badly then,
now I am rewriting into something good again,
on this tablet which you saw me, old man,
opening and resealing during the darkness of the night.

Agamemnon's change of heart is presented as an act of rewriting: "not well" done (107 οὐ καλῶς) becomes "well" done (108 καλῶς); "send" Iphigenia (100 πέμπειν) becomes "do not send her" (119 μὴ στέλλειν) – the simple addition or removal of a negative. The verb for rewriting is μεταγράφω (108), which suggests a change in the text of a letter, an emendation;[47] but in this case, since the first letter has already been delivered, it refers to the writing of a second letter. Agamemnon asks his servant to take the new letter to Argos and tells him precisely what the letter says: "what the tablet has hidden in its folds, all that is written on it, I will tell you, for you are loyal to my wife and to my household" (112–14).

Obviously, Agamemnon must read the letter out loud for the audience to understand the plot, but he also offers some justification for his actions.[48] Agamemnon wants his letter to be verified by the oral testimony of his servant; the illiterate servant remarks in turn how important it is for his words to be supported by physical evidence. Unlike Iphigenia's letter in the *IT*, in this case neither written nor oral message seems capable of standing alone. The old man wishes his tongue to be σύντονα (118), "wholly matching" or "tightly strained to fit" with the written words.[49] Given the precedent of the first, deceitful letter, which may or may not have had an oral message to support it, Agamemnon is rightly concerned

---

[47] This word was used by D. L. Page, *Actor's Interpolations in Greek Tragedy* (Oxford 1934) 138, to argue for a rejection of *IA* 106–14, as μεταγράφειν appears elsewhere in Greek literature only in prose passages. Knox (1979) 287–88, dismisses Page's objections and defends the verb in question as "a good fifth-century word" used by Thucydides (1.132.5) to mean a change in a letter text, by Xenophon (*HG* 6.3.19) in the context of changing the text of a treaty, and by Demosthenes (21.85) to mean an alteration in the records of a judicial verdict.

[48] See Knox (1979) 285–86.

[49] There is a textual problem in the placement of the lines 117–18: does the old man interrupt Agamemnon to press for an explanation after he has already begun to read the letter? Some editors (e.g. Günther's 1988 Teubner, Jouan's 1983 Budé) suggest that Agamemnon hesitates at this point, thus making further urging from the servant dramatically necessary; others (e.g. England 1891), following Reiske, argue for the transposition of lines 117–18 and 115–16.

about the potential reception of the second, in spite of its honesty. So he chooses a trustworthy family servant, and ensures that his message will match the written text of a letter and be verified by his signet ring. We can imagine the oral and written versions functioning together as a kind of *symbolon*, the two parts fitting together at the break. The oral and written messages coexist on stage and are represented as ideally mutually reinforcing, although, as will be suggested below, the written message does appear to carry more weight in a crisis, perhaps because of its physical nature: it can be produced as proof when needed, whereas a spoken message depends on witnesses who may have differing accounts of the same event.

When Agamemnon reports the contents of the letter, he presents the whole message as a postscript, as it were, an addendum to the previous missive (115–16, 119–23):[50]

> "I send this to you in addition to the previous
> tablets, daughter of Leda ...
> do not bring your child to
> the curved shoreline of Euboea,
> Aulis, unwashed by waves.
> For indeed some other time
> we will celebrate the child's wedding."

There is no listing of sender and addressee for informational purposes. Instead we read the verb "I send to you"; the pronoun is further explained in the next line by a matronymic, "the offspring of Leda." The sending is done "in addition to the previous tablets" (115–16 πρὸς ταῖς πρόσθεν/δέλτοις), with the idea of replacing them, especially as the contents are contradictory and mutually exclusive. All epistolary interaction presumes prior communication of some sort, but this case makes it explicit. The informality of the message, its lack of a conventional opening salute and closing farewell, is based on its direct connection with the first

---

50 Either Agamemnon hands over the letter at this point, recites its contents from memory as the old man holds it, and urges him to leave as soon as their discussion comes to an end (138 "but go now, hurry up, do not give in to your age"), or the letter stays in Agamemnon's hands, unsealed, until line 155–56, when the king says "guard this seal which you carry on the tablet," enacting his words by sealing the letter on stage. Depending on when the letter is handed over, Agamemnon may either read from the tablets or recite from memory; the contents of the letter, at any rate, are remarkably short.

letter, and on Agamemnon's haste to send it in time.[51] His recitation locates the present letter in relation to the previous one,
drawing a direct connection between them.

The message is quite short, beginning with the crucial words
"do not send your daughter." The possessive "your" instead of
"our" at line 119 suggests that Agamemnon is trying to distance
himself from his paternal identity, as if he could make the sacrifice
easier to accomplish if indeed the letter fails to achieve its goal.
He adds a brief, somewhat autocratic statement, that "we will celebrate the marriage of that child some other time" – not much of
a reason for changing his mind, compared to the carefully detailed
fictions about Achilles' motivation in the first letter.

The old man responds by thinking first of Achilles' feelings
rather than of Clytemnestra's or Iphigenia's; anticipating Achilles'
reaction to the loss of Briseis at Troy, he wonders if the hero will
become angry at Agamemnon's sudden change of mind. He makes
two assumptions here: first, that Achilles has indeed been offered
Iphigenia in marriage, and will be upset at the change of plans,
and second, that Agamemnon has not yet told any of the conspirators about his change of heart, much less Achilles. The truth
is that Achilles is totally unaware of both letters, as Agamemnon's
words at 128 explain: "Achilles provides us with his name, not any
other involvement." The first letter is thus in spirit a forgery,
Agamemnon's words deceptively claiming to represent accurately
the words and opinions of another man; this is corrected by the
second letter, written in Agamemnon's own paternal voice.

Agamemnon evinces great anxiety about the speed of his messenger and the safe delivery of the letter. But the servant is more
concerned about his reception once he arrives at his destination.
He asks "but tell me, how will I be believed when I say these
things to your child and your wife?" (153–54). Agamemnon responds "guard that seal which you carry on the letter" (155–56).[52]

---

[51] Some support for this interpretation is given by the general observations of White (1986)
217–18, who speaks about a first-century BCE papyrus from Egypt: "Letters were abbreviated or modified as a result of being quoted in, or appended to, another letter." There
may be additional reasons for the letter's informality; this letter has been assimilated to
the conventions of lyric dialogue, and the text of the *IA* remains problematic in spots.

[52] duBois (1988) 163 assumes that Agamemnon hands over not only the sealed letter, but
the signet ring itself, as further proof of authenticity. Although the Greek could be read
either way, I question the action of entrusting the royal seal to a servant, no matter how
trustworthy.

The final authority rests with the royal seal, unbroken, the letter closed and unaltered until it reaches its destination. The reliance on a seal to guarantee authenticity and to represent the power behind the words recalls the almost magical qualities attributed to writing, particularly by those who are illiterate.[53]

As the servant hastens to complete his task, the chorus offers the audience a convenient pause (164–302); we imagine a certain amount of time passing as the old servant makes his way out of the camp. The choral interlude gives the impression of temporal and spatial verisimilitude during the servant's departure and return, as he is intercepted with letter in hand and forced to turn back by Menelaus, who had been standing guard at the camp borders, anticipating just such an event.

During the hostile interchange between the messenger and Menelaus, we realize that the sanctity of a private letter is indeed a fragile thing. The violent tug-of-war over the letter emphasizes the importance of the physical nature of the document: both sides refuse to let go, and Menelaus threatens violence. It is clear that Menelaus already knows or has guessed the contents of the letter – he calls the message "evil" (308).[54] The letter continues to play a central role as Menelaus and Agamemnon confront one another (318ff.). At 322, Menelaus, in good courtroom style, asks if Agamemnon recognizes the letter, "messenger of the vilest words." Agamemnon acknowledges the letter and quickly asks for it to be returned to its owner, but Menelaus says that he wishes to make its contents known to all the Greeks. In horror, Agamemnon realizes from his brother's words that he knows all, and that he has already broken the seal to get this information (325). Menelaus admits the deed, having seen what was meant to be secret (326). The situation is represented repeatedly by both men as an issue of private versus public right; in terms of knowledge – whether the army has a right to know all of their leader's actions; and in terms of survival – the welfare of the leader's daughter clashes with that of his troops and allies.

---

[53] It would be interesting to know if Euripides imagined his Clytemnestra to be literate. Agamemnon's statements about the second letter could imply that the sight of the unbroken seal itself, rather than the contents of the sealed letter, would be enough to convince Clytemnestra of the truth of the servant's words.

[54] That he knows the contents seems rather dramatically improbable, since it is unlikely that Menelaus was able to read the letter during the argument with the messenger.

During their confrontation, Menelaus tells his own version of the first letter, which differs critically from his brother's. At 360ff., he claims that Agamemnon was delighted to learn from the oracle that Artemis could be appeased, and cheerfully prepared to slay his own daughter for the cause. Menelaus insists that the letter writing was voluntary and in no way forced, even if, in retrospect, Agamemnon would like to claim coercion (360–62):

> And so you sent a message to your wife, on your own accord,
> not forced to do it – you cannot claim that –,
> telling her to bring your child here,
> pretending that she will marry Achilles.

Menelaus emphasizes his brother's deception of his own family by using the possessive pronoun with reference to Iphigenia three times within seven lines (358–64): he calls her "your girl," "your child," "your daughter," varying the noun but retaining the modifier, which comes to be almost accusatory in tone. He claims to have caught Agamemnon in the act of sending another message (363), trying to worm his way out of his previous promise to Artemis and the Greek army. The brothers' dialogue degenerates into accusation and insult, and the letter lies forgotten, presumably still in Menelaus' hands as he exits at line 375, making room for the herald to announce the arrival of Clytemnestra and Iphigenia. From this point on, once all the main characters are in the camp, letter writing becomes superfluous, and the tragedy is free to proceed.

In the *IT* and the *Hippolytus*, which we turn to next, the different circumstances of the heroines prevent them from communicating orally or directly with their addressees. But Agamemnon's situation at Aulis is one that could have been handled purely through oral communication: the king could have realistically sent messengers to Clytemnestra in both cases without a supporting letter. Modeling his story on the Trojan cycle of epic, Euripides' choice of letters is in direct confrontation with the epic convention of heralds and messengers, whether mortal or divine, who repeat the exact words of their commands and are believed and obeyed instantly. Do these letters on stage suggest a deeper reflection on the part of the protagonists, and allow them to reveal second thoughts about their actions? If so, this would be quite unusual in Greek tragedy, which often deals with a larger-than-life hero:

strong-hearted Achilles rather than vacillating Aeneas, or unbending Antigone rather than Hamlet torn by self-doubt. If so, an additional value of the device of a letter on stage is that the same person can express two opposing opinions: either simultaneously and deceptively, as he or she reveals one state of mind in speech and another in writing, or consecutively, as the protagonist changes his or her mind as the play progresses.

In both Iphigenia plays, I have argued that while letters occupy a central role in the drama, once the epistolary device has played its part, the plot continues with direct confrontation and action. On another level, however, the letter remains on stage in a different form, namely that of Iphigenia herself. I suggested above that the letter written by the desperate Iphigenia among the Taurians reflects the personality of its writer to such a degree that it comes to embody that writer. Thus, the letter hidden in the temple represents the exile, isolated from the rest of humanity, and Iphigenia's handing over of the letter to Pylades foreshadows her own "delivery" at the hands of Orestes. We can see the same sort of identification in the present scene.[55] Agamemnon writes and rewrites, throws down and picks up again the wooden tablet, just as in his mind he repeatedly rewrites Iphigenia's fate, abandons his daughter and saves her again. He holds her life in his hands, and attempts to write a future that will keep her far away from his world of war and bloodshed. But Menelaus intercepts this version of the future, and the physical struggle over the letter itself foreshadows the violent end that threatens the still unknowing Iphigenia, whose actual death will be marked by a remarkable absence of physical struggle, a voluntary self-sacrifice. The failure of the second letter to arrive in time is underscored by the immediate arrival in the camp of its addressee. Just as the message in the undelivered letter now becomes useless, so the life of Iphigenia herself suddenly loses all meaning, becomes dispensable, without value except as a scapegoat. This identification of letter with a female character who writes or is written about will resurface in

---

[55] duBois (1988) 162–65, discusses this issue at length, and equates Agamemnon's sealing and unsealing of the letter with control of his daughter's sexuality: "he has sealed up her virginity, breaks it with the promise of marriage, but seals it up again as she is sacrificed as a virgin" (162). She argues that "all the language associated with this δέλτος is sexually charged" (163).

the *Hippolytus*, the last of the Euripidean examples of epistolary fiction in this chapter.

HIPPOLYTUS

Iphigenia's letter is never sent because its message successfully reaches its addressee orally; Agamemnon's two letters are designed to cancel each other out, but the letter we see on stage is intercepted and never arrives at its destination. Only Phaedra's letter both reaches its addressee and influences the dramatic action in unforeseen ways, embodying all of Phaedra's power and anger, yet functioning even more effectively than the character herself could have while alive.[56] One could not ask for a better example of Jost's category of kinetic letters, as Phaedra's letter instigates violent action and reaction, links suicide with homicide, and requires divine intervention to "rewrite" its contents.

The first half of the play focuses on the anxieties of Phaedra, who has fallen in love with her stepson Hippolytus, but knows she can never consummate her passion. After revealing her feelings to her nurse, she kills herself, but only after writing a suicide note intended to forestall any stain on her reputation: better to accuse the young man of desiring her, and destroy the house of her husband, than reveal her own incestuous love. The first we hear of the letter in the play is from Theseus, as he contemplates the body of his dead wife. The corpse is revealed to Theseus and the audience at lines 811, yet the grief-stricken husband does not notice the letter until forty-five lines later (856–59):

> Alas, alas – what is this tablet hanging from her dear hand?
> does it wish to announce some news?
> Or did that poor soul write a letter to make a request of me
> concerning our marriage bed and our children?

Theseus first assumes that the tablet must be a suicide note, an explanation of the gruesome tableau in front of him. His next

---

[56] The almost magical power of Phaedra's suicide letter is discussed by E. Garrison, "Suicide Notes in Euripides' *Hippolytus*," in K. Hartigan, ed., *Text and Presentation*, vol. IX (Lanham MD 1989) 73–85, esp. 77–78. C. Segal, "Signs, Magic, and Letters in Euripides' *Hippolytus*," in R. Hexter and D. Selden, eds., *Innovations in Antiquity* (New York 1992) 420–56, esp. 433, 436–37 discusses how Euripides here connects a primitive kind of love magic with the magical power of writing to evoke desire.

thought is that perhaps Phaedra has written a final request, asking him to take no other wife into his house but rather honor their marriage bond even in death.[57] In the end, the letter will reveal yet a third function: it is essentially a legal deposition, a document that Theseus will use to convict his son of a crime for which the letter (apart from Phaedra's corpse) is the only real evidence.[58]

As Theseus looks a little closer, he recognizes the familiar imprint of his wife's signet ring which seals the cords wrapped around the tablet (862–65):

> Truly the imprint of that golden seal ring –
> for it is hers, who is no longer alive – pleases me.
> Come, unrolling the covering of the seal,
> let me see what this tablet wishes to say to me.

The imprint of Phaedra's seal and the writing protected by that seal are the only traces left of a now stilled voice, and it testifies to the writer's absence in death. It pleases or "caresses" his eyes, either as a direct reminder of his beloved wife or as proof that the words it seals are indeed genuine, and that writing them was her last act before dying.[59] Death is central to the rhetorical power of her letter to persuade its reader.[60] What is so unusual about this epistolary situation is that the writer and receiver share the stage: Phaedra's dead body is very much present for Theseus, but the body itself can only offer one obvious message, the fact of her death. Further information about the circumstances of her death is lacking. Phaedra's voice, now silenced, has been transcribed by her own hand into the form of a letter, and her ring has endowed that letter with the seal of authenticity.[61] Now, instead of Phaedra wishing to speak or not to speak about her desire, the letter itself

---

[57] That this would have been considered a reasonable request may be inferred from Euripides' *Alcestis* (304ff.), when the husband swears loyalty even in death, but is forced to renege on his promise when Heracles rescues and returns Alcestis in disguise.

[58] There is a good analysis of these functions in B. E. Goff, *Noose of Words* (Cambridge 1990) 37–38.

[59] In addition, the letter may be perceived as making an ingratiating plea for attention, like a fawning animal. Segal (1992) 432–34, discusses the implications of the verb "caress" here, arguing that the word connects female speech with the animal sphere.

[60] Goff (1990) 101.

[61] Segal (1992) 432, states that the "language evokes the legality of testaments and other procedures to assure the veracity and genuineness of messages from the dead to the living."

is said to "wish to speak" in her place.[62] It is crucial to the success
of her plan that her accusation of Hippolytus not be questioned;
the letter, sent by an author now dead, effectively stops further
discussion. There is no messenger to question: the text is unanswerable and thus incontrovertible. But what the letter declares is,
of course, a complete perversion of the truth.

What caused Euripides to consider the use of a letter in this
context? Again, the story he inherited from myth and previous
literary productions surely did not include an epistolary device
integral to the plot; even the first version of Euripides' *Hippolytus*
probably had no such letter. But the negative reception of that
version by the Athenian public may offer us a clue. What shocked
and dismayed the spectators of the first *Hippolytus* was precisely the
face-to-face encounter of Phaedra and her beloved stepson, the
direct expression of her love for him that went beyond the bounds
of female decorum.[63] Euripides revised his plot to include the suicide of Phaedra before her confrontation with the young man, but
then was faced with the problem of revealing Phaedra's charges.
The letter was both a solution to the chronological impasse – how
to hear the voice of a person no longer present – and a convenient
medium of indirection, a way to mute, at least temporarily, the
disturbing implications of Phaedra's passion. The "confessional"
text removes some of the burning immediateness of an oral declaration. The letter is also a brilliant device for bringing out the
cruelty of the situation in which Hippolytus is placed. The victim
of a false accusation, he is prevented from exposing its falsity by
the death of his accuser. The accuser, in death, elicits sympathy
and credulity from those around her. Hippolytus cannot even attempt to refute the charge without endangering his relationship
even further with his father Theseus, who retains control over his
son's destiny.

---

[62] Segal (1986) 101, discusses the oral force of the letter as it intensifies throughout this
scene; see also his remarks in "Tragédie, oralité, écriture," *Poétique* 50 (1982) 131–54, esp.
148–49. The passage is also well treated by C. Calame, "Rythme, voix et mémoire de
l'écriture en Grèce classique," in R. Pretagostini, ed., *Tradizione e Innovazione nella cultura
greca da Omero all'età ellenistica: Scritti in onore di Bruno Gentili* (Rome 1993) 785–99, esp. 796–
98.

[63] According to its hypothesis, the second *Hippolytus* was meant to remove the morally ob-
jectionable features of the first; see also Aristophanes *Frogs* 1043ff. For a more detailed
discussion of the problem, see W. S. Barrett, *Euripides Hippolytos* (Oxford 1964) 10–45.

The moment of unsealing the letter has been compared to parallel acts of opening and revealing in the play: the opening of the palace doors to reveal the body; the sexual penetration that is Theseus' right but taboo to Hippolytus; and paradoxically the beginning of a "cover-up," a distortion of the facts that the unsealed letter, instead of revealing, serves to hide.[64] Euripides allows Theseus a brief amount of time in which to unseal and read the letter to himself, and as he stands on stage in silence, the chorus sing a short song (866–73).[65] Their presence is crucial for our understanding of the events. They are the last to speak before Theseus breaks his silence, and they predict some evil news (873), perhaps scanning Theseus' face as he reads. Upon reading, Theseus echoes their words, crying out that evil is piling up on evil (874); the letter contains something impossible to endure, incapable of being spoken aloud.[66] But in answer to the chorus leader's request, he does eventually reveal the horrible news within the tablet, at first somewhat obliquely (877–80):

> It shrieks, the tablet shrieks horrors. Where can I flee
> this weight of evils? I am utterly destroyed, finished,
> such a song, such a one I have seen, wretched one,
> speaking out in the writings.

Theseus' expression of horror reveals a curious use of terms which in turn reveals a clash between oral and written modes of communication. He sees (879 εἶδον), not hears, a song speaking

---

[64] These angles are explored by Segal (1992) 432–33, who speaks of "Phaedra's seal-ring, a synecdochic extension of her sexuality," and compares the scene with Deianeira's similarly sexualized gift to Heracles in the *Trachiniae*; duBois (1988) 151–56, with reference to the *Trachiniae*; Zeitlin (1985) 52–110, esp. 74–76, who associates folded tablets with the sexual secrets of the female body; and Goff (1990) 17. See also the wide-ranging discussion of Steiner (1994) 110–16, on metaphors of writing and the human body, and 108–9, on parallel acts of opening sealed objects in the *Hippolytus*.

[65] This appears to be the first reference to silent reading in antiquity; see Knox (1968) 421–35.

[66] Although λέγω meaning "to read" occurs only in compounds, in the simple form it can mean "to recite" something that is written. I wonder if the words οὐδέ λεκτόν (875) are meant to suggest "unreadable," "horrible to read"? A. Barchiesi, "Future Reflexive: Two Modes of Allusion and Ovid's *Heroides*," *HSCP* 95 (1993) 333–65, esp. 337, connects Theseus' horror and pain upon reading this letter with the softly seductive tone of Ovid's Phaedra, writing to Hippolytus at *Her.* 4.3: "quid epistula lecta nocebit?". The same woman can write a "harmless" love letter and a viciously defaming suicide note.

out in the writings (879–80 ἐν γραφαῖς μέλος/φθεγγόμενον).[67] The
tablet cries out horror and utters a song in its writings.[68] The
tablet is personified as a shrill voice, a singing voice, yet Theseus'
response to the voice is presented, in his words and by his actions
on stage, as an act of reading or seeing rather than hearing. Nor
do the chorus or the audience hear any words coming directly
from the tablet, until Theseus chooses to repeat its accusations out
loud for their benefit. The written nature of the news is emphasized over its oral nature, yet the latter is too strong a message to
be ignored by the author. The sequence of text begins with images
of sound, and ends firmly in the epistolary sphere of vision and
reading. The piling up and overlapping of sensory perceptions
here focus our attention on the overwhelming and drastic nature
of the evidence, the weight of evil from which Theseus sees no
escape.

Theseus goes on to speak the "unspeakable" evil in all its terrifying specificity, addressing not just the chorus on stage but the
whole city and its citizenry as a witness to the crime of his son. He
makes public the contents of Phaedra's letter, and turns a private
family scandal into a civic, religious crisis (885–86).[69]

> Hippolytus dared to touch my bed with force,
> dishonoring the sacred guardian eye of Zeus.

Should we consider these two lines (885–86) as epistolary text or
as speech?[70] They could very well represent the first two lines
of Phaedra's actual letter which Theseus presumably still holds,
particularly because the possessive adjective "my" applied to the
marriage bed may be understood as referring to either Phaedra or

---

[67] Although not citing this example, Svenbro (1988) 185–86, argues that with the invention
of silent reading, the written text no longer demands a vocal supplement, and the eye
can now "see" the sound; from now on, he claims, the eye alone will ensure the "recognition" of meaning. He cites Aeschylus *Seven* 103: κτύπον δέδορκα ("I behold the din").
In further discussion (198–99), he also points to the words of Theseus at *Hipp.* 877–80 as
proof of his argument. See also Calame (1993) 797–98, who speaks of this section of the
Hippolytus as revealing an "intégration de deux modes de communication et de deux
types de tradition" (797).

[68] Barrett (1964) 332–33, argues that γραφαῖς should be construed with φπεγγόμενον as an
instrumental dative, i.e "giving utterance by means of the writing"; the preposition ἐν is
then assumed to be a mistaken explanation inserted and recopied in the manuscripts.

[69] This is presumably what Phaedra wanted all along, but she used a private vehicle to
effect a public disgrace.

[70] Knox (1979) 287, briefly considers the possibility that Theseus may be quoting Phaedra's
letter here, but then rejects the idea with no explanation given.

Theseus.[71] If it is Phaedra's own bed, we hear the words as deceitful and manipulative; if Theseus does not read directly but comes to this conclusion from his prior silent reading of the written text, then the words strike us as a tragic and dangerous misinterpretation.

Theseus' immediate reaction to the evidence from the tablet is to curse his son, and when the two men finally meet on stage, the tablet continues to play an important role in the action. We gather from the dialogue of lines 959–61 that Theseus is thrusting the letter at his son as he speaks, emphasizing his actions with deictic pronouns. Hippolytus wishes that Phaedra were still alive in order to bear witness to his innocence (1022–23), as if he could somehow then convince her to retract her written accusation. But for Theseus, the letter says it all, and he presents it to Hippolytus as surer proof of his guilt than any prophecies or auguries (1057–59). Nothing Hippolytus says or does can change his father's mind, such are the power of Phaedra's letter and the certain proof of her dead body (958, 971ff.).[72] When the unhappy son calls on the house itself to find a voice and refute the false accusations (1074–75), Theseus mocks him for taking refuge in mute witnesses, (1076 ἀφώνους μάρτυρας), yet he himself could be charged with the same thing: he trusts in the silent text of the letter, which his voice alone has brought to life. Line 1077 sums up his specious logic: "the deed, although not speaking (οὐ λέγον), betrays you as an evil man." But there is no deed, only the deceptive text of the letter, and Artemis will confirm later how mistaken Theseus was to trust his dead wife's message.[73]

Towards the end of the play, after a messenger announces Hippolytus' death, another observation is made on the power of writing. The messenger says sorrowfully that he never believed the version of events described in Phaedra's fateful letter (1253ff.):

I will never be able to believe
that your son was guilty, even if the whole race of women
were hanged for it, not even if someone were to fill the pine
wood
of Ida with writings.

---

[71] Cf. 944, where the reference is unambiguously to Theseus' bed.
[72] This scene is well analyzed by Goff (1990) 17–18, 100–3.
[73] *Hipp.* 1320–23, 1336ff. There is a constant play between the written and spoken nature of the letter, which mirrors the tension between the true and false nature of its signs. See Steiner (1994) 39.

This hyperbole attempts to undo all the damage perpetrated earlier by Phaedra's deceitful letter.[74] In addition to polarizing the sexes and killing off the race of women so that father and son can be reconciled, the messenger's speech devalues writing by returning the wooden tablets to their natural origins. If someone were to fill all the wooden surfaces in the forest with accusations of Hippolytus, our messenger still would not believe them. Writing is reduced to "the materiality of the medium that holds the letters, in contrast to the figurative animation of things possessing a magical speech."[75] Writing, at the end of the play, no longer has the power to persuade: it has been defanged, numbing its reader by repetition. The multitude of imaginary texts are all lies; the trees of Ida repeat the (false) story of Hippolytus' guilt, and the writing thereby retains its deceitful nature. But readers and the messenger have learned by now to associate writing with deceit, and to question the authority of any epistolary text.[76]

Euripides constantly stretched the limits of the conventions of tragedy by introducing sudden reactions, changes of mind, or complete shifts in plot direction, attempting to achieve these effects without alienating his viewing public and without resorting to an improbable *deus ex machina* or one messenger scene too many. The device of the letter allowed the playwright to bring the mechanism for change on stage in an entirely believable and visually effective way. The letter itself may be understood as a miniature script within the larger context of the memorized lines of the whole tragedy; when brought on stage, it is as if the actor were coming forth with a newly written scene from the author, a fresh angle on a familiar story. As an authoritative written document, representing the voice of a particular character, it persuades its internal audience instantaneously: Theseus, Clytemnestra, and Orestes all respond to their respective letters without the shadow of a doubt as to their validity. The external audience, however, "reads" over the shoulder (or overhears) with overt skepticism, suspicious of the intrusive textual mechanism. Only in the *IT*, as Iphigenia reads to her brother who has recognized her as his sister, do the internal and the external audiences share a similar reaction.

---

[74] Segal (1992) 440.   [75] Segal (1992) 440–41.
[76] On this, see the comments of Goff (1990) 99.

This sense of peering over the shoulder of the epistolary reader may explain why we often jump to the conclusion that a character is reading the letter line by line. We want to know exactly who said what to whom, and paraphrase simply does not suffice. With a literate audience, one can imagine a surge forward in the front seats, as each person tries to decipher the message independently; our modern equivalent is a camera zooming in on a love letter, or a suicide note. Letters fascinate precisely because of their private and intimate nature. Accordingly, letters on stage are more often than not in the hands of women. In the plays discussed above, even when Agamemnon writes, he does not send military commands (although indirectly the affair is of important military consequences) but rather an invitation to a wedding, a supremely female concern. The entire arena of intrigue, for which letters provide the best means of communication, is one associated in tragedy more readily with female than male characters.

Letters on stage are prime couriers of intrigue because of the liberating lack of human interaction which might otherwise prevent the confusion in the first place, or alternatively separate fact from fiction. If Phaedra, Theseus, and Hippolytus had been able to meet in person, the case would have come down to the word of a woman against that of a man, and Theseus might not have been so quick to take action. If Agamemnon and Clytemnestra had been together at the time of his request for Iphigenia's presence, he might have been too indecisive to argue convincingly, and his wife would have asked some difficult questions. If Iphigenia had been able to speak intelligently with anyone among the Taurians, she might not have turned to letter writing in her miserable solitude. In all these cases, letters provide a means of communicating that bypasses, whether voluntarily or involuntarily, the usual directness of dramatic dialogue. In the process, the letters become more than just a means of passing on information: they become actors in their own right, personified as speaking voices for Theseus, representative of the actor herself for Iphigenia, and, in their doubleness, splendidly evoking the split personality of Agamemnon as leader and as father. Letters serve to further the plot by misdirection and misinformation, as well as by providing crucial information hitherto unknown. They are never mere devices in the hands of Euripides, but rather objects on stage with all the power and authority of a main character, agents of change, and a reminder that written text, not performed speech, often has the last word.

In this chapter, the last word belongs to Sappho as she is represented by Antiphanes' (fourth century BCE) play by that name (Antiphanes *Sappho*, Kassel–Austin fr. 194). Sphinx-like, she asks and answers her own riddle on the nature of letters (Athenaeus *Deipn.* 10.450e–51b):

There is a feminine being who keeps her babies safe under her breasts, and they, although without a voice, send forth a cry, heard loudly across the ocean waves and across all lands, which reaches those mortals they wish to reach, but others, even though present, are not permitted to hear. But they [the babies] have a dull sense of hearing ...

The feminine being, then, is a letter (ἐπιστολή), and the babies within her are the letters of the alphabet (γράμματα) she carries around. Although they are voiceless, they talk to people far away if they wish; yet if another person happens to be standing nearby, he will not hear when the letter is read.

In these lines we see encapsulated many of the themes discussed above.[77] Sappho views the letter and its text as a woman who keeps her babies safe at her breast. We have seen how Iphigenia and Phaedra are embodied in their letters to such an extent that the letters may be seen as representing them on stage. The letter is frequently aligned with the female rather than the male, or if the male, then a tricky or lying male voice: it is a document of secrecy and protection, in contrast to the conventionally direct, oral communicative mode associated with men and military command. As such, it can also be a document of deceit, another trait commonly connected with women; Phaedra takes full advantage of this aspect of epistolary discourse. Sappho delights in the ability of the text of a letter to speak to people far away, to act as a bridge over physical separation; thus Iphigenia dreams that her letter, once sent, will collapse the distance between herself and her brother. Finally, Sappho stresses the wonders of silent reading: even if

---

[77] The imagery of this passage is discussed by Svenbro (1988) 74–120, and Steiner (1994) 113–14, who quotes in passing the curious passage in the late Latin author Ausonius on the invention of the alphabet by Cadmus, in which alphabetic symbols are called "little black daughters of Cadmus" (*Ep.* 14.74). Women may be represented as nurturing and protective δέλτοι for their offspring γράμματα, but men are still assigned the more exalted role of having invented writing in the first place. Plato reverses the terms of the metaphor at *Phaedrus* 274e–275e, where letters turn to their "father" for help.

another person stands nearby, he will not hear the words of the letter unless the reader chooses to reveal them; we saw similar scenes as the old man questioned Agamemnon about his tablets, and as the chorus begged Theseus to read them the text of Phaedra's letter. The letter is typically intended for one addressee alone, and that addressee then has the option of exposing or protecting its contents. Without a voice of their own, the words of a letter can reach an audience far away yet paradoxically remain unheard by someone standing right next to the recipient. Both Antiphanes and Euripides have shown themselves to be utterly captivated by the challenge of staging the paradoxical nature of the letter.

CHAPTER 5

Letters in Hellenistic poetry

> Just as we used to spend long hours in talk
> Until the day ended with us still talking,
> So now our letters should carry forth and bring back our
> silent voices,
> And paper and hands perform the tasks of our tongues.
>
> Ovid *Tristia* 5.13.27–30

In classical Athens, as discussed in the last two chapters, letters in historical annals and in tragedy recall vividly the connections between letter writing and treachery introduced by Homer in the *Iliad*. In the Hellenistic period, however, as letters became more commonplace in personal and business transactions, we find correspondingly less interest among poets in particular in epistolarity as a fictional device.

The fourth-century BCE public of the Greek speaking world had become quite familiar with the practical letter in daily life. According to Plutarch (*Mor.* 790a–b), Seleucus I, who accompanied Alexander on his Asian campaign and then ruled his own territories in Syria and Asia Minor, complained that if people knew what hard work it was to read and respond to so many letters, they would not wish to pick up a crown if it had been thrown away. One hundred years later, by the mid-third century, government dependency on official documents and public records had only increased. Letters were a sign of "business as usual" in the large bureaucracy that was managing the royal economy of the Ptolemies: witness a document dated to 258/257 BCE that records that, in the span of one month, the accounting offices of the finance minister Apollonius received 434 papyrus rolls.[1]

The spread of political and administrative documents at court

---

[1] Harris (1989) 121, quoting *P. Col. Zen.* 3.4, and *P. Cair. Zen.* 4.59687.

was balanced by a comparable rise in interest in the written word among writers and scholars. Alexandria flourished as a cultural center, where philology and scholarship were supported by the financial patronage of the Ptolemies, who also built and staffed the monumental new library. This interest in scholarship filtered down to some degree even to the lower classes, if we can believe Herodas' complaints (*ca.* 270 BCE) of the mother of a lazy schoolboy (*mime* 3): she wastes time and energy smoothing wax on his writing tablets, while her son rarely uses them and can barely write at all.[2] But while Hellenistic culture has come to be synonymous with "book culture," as far as we can tell from extant evidence, this fascination with text does not carry over to the private epistolary sphere, or to an interest in experimenting with epistolary fictional forms.

In the private sector, the letter papyri that remain from this period concern mostly special events such as marriage announcements, complaints, or financial emergencies.[3] The sheer size of the Ptolemaic kingdoms must have influenced the private use of letters; we already mentioned in chapter one the passage in Herodas which implies that a wife or mistress could reasonably expect to receive letters from her absent partner more than once in ten months (Her. *mime* 1.23–25). Yet references to epistolarity in literature are surprisingly scarce. In historiography, Polybius seems to retain the suspicion of letters familiar from our discussion of Herodotus and Thucydides: he writes of treacherous forgeries (5.43.5–6; 5.50.11–12) and the misuse of authority through epistolary commands (5.57.5; 5.61.3).[4] Plutarch, although writing much later, tells two tales set in the Hellenistic period about the bravery of women, in which letters play an important role (*Mor.* 252a; 254d). In the latter passage, a Naxian woman Polycrite has been captured by Diognetus, an Erythraean general allied with the besieging Milesian forces (254d):[5]

Now when it was time for a festival which the Milesians celebrate in the army, and they all turned to drinking and partying, Polycrite asked Diognetus if there was any reason not to send some pieces of cake to her

---

[2] For the standard text of Herodas, see I. C. Cunningham, *Herodae Mimiambi* (Oxford 1971).
[3] Discussed by Harris (1989) 128, note 56, with numerous examples.
[4] Discussed by Harris (1989) 128.
[5] My translation is based on the Loeb text of F. C. Babbitt, tr., *Plutarch's Moralia*, vol. III (Cambridge MA 1931).

brothers. Since he allowed her and even urged her to do so, she placed inside the cake a note written on a strip of lead (μολίβδινον γραμματί-διον), and ordered the messenger to tell her brothers that they alone should eat what she had sent. The brothers discovered the lead and read the words (γράμματα) of Polycrite, advising them to attack the enemy that night, when they were all helpless because of drinking too much at the festival; her brothers took the message (προσήγγειλαν) to their generals and urged them to set forth, along with themselves.

The woman deceived her captor by hiding a letter in what appeared to be an innocent piece of pastry; to add insult to injury, the cake was in honor of a Milesian celebration, not a Naxian one, and Diognetus himself positively encouraged Polycrite to prepare it for her brothers, not knowing that he was "sending" more than he had bargained for. The ruse succeeds, the Naxians overcome their attackers, and Polycrite is freed by her brothers.

Turning to the poets, letters are not as prevalent as they will become in the prose works of fiction writers in the later Hellenistic and imperial periods. Letters played no part in Apollonius of Rhodes' reconstruction of epic society, and while Herodas could nod in the direction of a literate traveling man, Theocritus' rustics would look odd indeed in the company of a scribe.[6] The heavy use of letter documents in civic affairs seems not to have encouraged, and possibly even actively discouraged, creative use of the genre. Perhaps its very ubiquity in mundane matters took away from the awe-inspiring qualities we observed attributed to letters on the Athenian dramatic stage, for example.[7] It is certainly ironic that the Hellenistic age, famous for its writing culture, produced so few examples of verse epistolary fiction.

THEOCRITUS AND THE *GREEK ANTHOLOGY*

One kind of epistolary poem, however, was relatively popular in this period, namely the letter accompanying a gift, which exists in the corpus of Theocritus and the *Greek Anthology*. Theocritus'

---

[6] A. S. F. Gow considers three (6, 11, and 13) of Theocritus' idylls epistolary because they seem to be letter-poems addressed to a friend who is named in the poem's opening lines. But barring further connections with the genre, I am not convinced that any poem "addressed" to a specific individual should necessarily be read as a letter. See A. S. F. Gow, ed., *Theocritus* (Cambridge 1965), 2 vols., ad loc.

[7] This suggestion is put forward by Harris (1989) 123–24.

Idyll 28 is a poem written to accompany an ivory distaff which
Theocritus takes to Miletus to give to Theugenis, wife of Nicias
(28.1–3):

> Distaff, friend of the spinner, gift of grey-eyed Athena
> To women who have mastered the art of housekeeping,
> Accompany me cheerfully to the splendid city of Neileos ...

The speaker, presumably Theocritus himself, addresses not Theugenis or Nicias, as the recipients of the forthcoming gift, but the
gift itself, the distaff, praising its workmanship and predicting its
happy arrival in a new home. This is a curious rearrangement of
conventional epistolary roles: the addressee (the distaff) is currently
in the presence of the writer, so the absent person, Theugenis, for
whom the gift is destined, is not actually the recipient of the letter
accompanying the gift. Theocritus asks the distaff to accompany
him on the voyage to Miletus; if the giver of the gift will be present at its presentation, there is no real need for a letter. But in
typical Hellenistic fashion, Theocritus plays on the relationship
between the material artifact and his own poem: he tells the distaff
that its role is to remind Theugenis of her poet friend (28.23); it is
a material reminder, just as his accompanying poem enacts one
of the standard functions of a letter, namely to remind one of an
absent friend. The (letter-)poem and the distaff share the role of
reminding Nicias and Theugenis of Theocritus' friendship. But
the distaff succeeds better precisely because it is meant to be used
in public, seen by visitors, and appreciated by all; Theocritus ends
this poem by imagining the words of a future visitor (28.24–25):

> For seeing this [distaff] someone will say, "indeed great
>   affection
> exists in a small gift; and all that comes from friends is
>   precious."

The letter-poem remains in Miletus, but Theocritus' edited book
gives us the poem in its final incarnation, one that will outlast the
ephemeral fame of the material object itself.

In the *Greek Anthology*, we find epigrammatic letter-poems accompanying gifts. Epigrams, like letters, can be short, personal,
and specific to a particular occasion; again like letters, they can
exist independent of a larger context, but they may also be an-
thologized, the context and organization then adding to their
meaning. Epigrams had a strong appeal for readers in the Helle-

nistic period. Their archaic counterparts were inscriptions etched on funeral monuments or votive objects, intended for the private reading of casual observers or passers-by. Simonides, for example, active in the late sixth and the early fifth centuries BCE in Athens, was famous for his epitaphs for the victims of the Persian Wars.[8] These antecedents inform the compositional fiction of the *Greek Anthology*, a compilation of the Byzantine era based on selected collections formed in the Hellenistic period. The *Anthology* is presented as a collection of diverse epigrams, originally carved in stone, each written for a particular occasion, but later gathered into book form, organized primarily according to topic (symposiastic, erotic, dedicatory, etc.).[9] The reality is, of course, quite different. The Hellenistic epigram remained true to its form in that it was brief and concise, concerned with the personal or the particular. But these later epigrams never existed on stone; they were composed as sophisticated and allusive miniatures, intended for a book-reading audience. The passers-by became page-turners, and the epigrams gained new impact from their context within an anthology.

In the *Anthology*, letters accompany gifts of friendship (*Anth. Pal.* 5.90, 91, Anonymous = *FGE* 1088–89; 1090–91; 6.227, 229, 261 Crinagoras = *GP* 1781–86; 1787–92; 1793–96).[10] The letter-poems introduce the items in question, but also offer their author an opportunity to show off his literary skills. *Anth. Pal.* 5.90 and 91, anonymous variations on a theme, try to pack as much learning and style as possible into one couplet each, both exploiting parallelism and polyptoton, yet they neglect to fulfil the epistolary requirements of specific information about sender and addressee.

---

[8] Simonides' name was not attached to epitaphs or dedications until the late fifth century, so attribution remains doubtful for many of the elegiac couplets. See D. A. Campbell, *Greek Lyric Poetry* (London 1967) 380. Before Simonides, there are sepulchral epigrams dating as far back as the mid-sixth century in Attica (P. Friedländer *Epigrammata: Greek Inscriptions in Verse from the Beginnings to the Persian Wars* [Berkeley 1948] 135). Epitaphs could also be sources for biographical information on famous people, just as fictional letters were used to elaborate on a famous person's life; see K. J. Gutzwiller, *Poetic Garlands* (Berkeley 1998) 49–50. D. L. Page thinks that two epitaphs attributed to Simonides and preserved in the Anthology (*Anth. Pal.* 7.516, 7.77) were composed by some biographical source "to add colour and verisimilitude to an anecdote about a famous man"; see D. L. Page, *Further Greek Epigrams* (Cambridge 1981) 299.

[9] See Gutzwiller (1998) *passim*.

[10] See "Demetrius" *On Style* 223–35 in Malherbe (1988) 16–19: a letter itself is sent as a gift, representing friendly dialogue in writing (224); a letter is a brief expression of the heart's best wishes (231). For more on letters and love, see E. Gunderson, "Catullus, Pliny, and Love-Letters," *TAPA* 127 (1997) 201–31.

An anonymous "I" sends an unnamed beloved "you" the gift of perfume:[11]

> I send you sweet perfume, courting perfume with perfume,
>> Just as someone making a libation to Dionysus uses
>> Dionysus' own wine.
>>> *(Anth. Pal.* 5.90 = *FGE* 1088–89)*

> I send you sweet perfume, honoring not you but the perfume.
>> For you yourself can perfume the perfume.
>>> *(Anth. Pal.* 5.91 = *FGE* 1090–91)*

Here we find the unusual situation of anonymous "letters"; they function impersonally, almost as clichés, and anyone can use these "letters" to attach to his gift. The "I" and the "you" can suit any occasion – no need to worry if your sweetheart's name is unmetrical. Also, the lines are easily reused, so that the enterprising lover could even arrange for multiple simultaneous sendings. These couplets are the equivalent of mass-produced greeting cards or gift enclosures.

Two letter-poems written by Crinagoras to accompany gifts *(Anth. Pal.* 6.227, 229) include more customary epistolary details, that is, the name of the sender and the addressee, or rather the recipient of both letter and gift. In both examples, Crinagoras names himself as the writer, speaking in the third person to his second-person addressee. It would have been more "natural" to write in the first person, but the communication between author and external readers would then have been compromised, unless Crinagoras had found another way to identify himself to us. The first example celebrates a birthday gift of a pen-nib *(Anth. Pal.* 6.227 = *GP* 1781–86):[12]

> This pointed (spear-like) silver pen for you, on your birthday,
>> Proclus, newly polished,
> neatly carved, with well-divided tips,
>> and flowing well over the rapidly written page,
> Crinagoras sends you; it is a small gift, but one from a full
>> heart,
>> and one which works well with your recently acquired
>> eagerness to learn.

---

[11] The Greek texts on which I base my translations are from D. L. Page, ed., *Further Greek Epigrams* (rev. R. Dawe and J. Diggle, Cambridge 1981).

[12] The Greek texts of the next three Crinagoras' epigrams are from A. S. F. Gow and D. L. Page, *The Greek Anthology: the Garland of Philip*, 2 vols. (Cambridge 1968).

Crinagoras writes to Proclus that he is sending a silver pen-nib, one that "flow[s] well over the rapidly written page." Since the gift is itself a writing tool, we could read this letter as an invitation to write back, whether to send a simple letter of thanks, or to initiate a continuing correspondence. Proclus is depicted as having recently become enthusiastic about his studies; Crinagoras may hope that his "eagerness," as well as the newly polished and neatly carved pen-nib, will inspire his friend in turn to write him letters.[13]

The editorial placement of Crinagoras' second letter (*Anth. Pal.* 6.229 = *GP* 1787–92), and their equal length and shared vocabulary, suggest that the latter is meant to be read in conjunction with the former, but now the mood shifts from the (almost) sublime to the ridiculous: this letter-poem to one Lucius accompanies a toothpick (*Anth. Pal.* 6.229 = *GP* 1787–92):

> This quill of a crooked-beaked eagle, sharpened with steel,
>   and colored purple with dark dye,
> which knows how to remove discreetly, with its gentle point,
>   any remnants left behind after dinner between your
>   teeth,
> this humble token, not from a small heart, and a kind of
>   present for mealtimes,
>   your friend, Lucius, who is wholly yours, Crinagoras
>   sends to you.

The two poems differ in their allegiance to epistolary format in the opening lines. Epistolary convention demands an initial address of "X to Y, greetings." *Anth. Pal.* 6.227 chooses verisimilitude, and puts Proclus' name in the second line, even if it reserves Crinagoras' until the penultimate line (6.227.5), while 6.229 chooses poetic stylishness over epistolary practicality, putting the names in the last possible place in the line, neatly juxtaposed. When Crina-

---

[13] It is difficult to know whether to interpret Crinagoras' tone here as slightly condescending ("the boy can barely write and needs encouragement") or laudatory ("he is a quick study and is ready to tackle the complexities of epistolary style"). Another interpretation, based on Proclus' assumed youth, would be that the pen will inspire the young man to practice general writing exercises, not necessarily of the epistolary sort. Gow and Page (1968) 214 conclude that Proclus is "evidently a child who has recently learned to write." In this context, see the end of Gregory of Nazianzus' letter to Nicobulus (*Ep.* 51) in Malherbe (1988) 60–61: "with regard to the other aspects of letter writing, you will work hard at them yourself, since you are a quick learner, and also those who are skilled in such things will teach you."

goras calls the pen-nib a "small gift," we wonder if Proclus is expected politely to demur; but when he calls Lucius' toothpick "humble," we are hard pressed to disagree.

Crinagoras composed one other letter accompanying a gift in this book of epigrams, namely 6.261 (= *GP* 1793–96), with reference to a valuable bronze flask.

> A work of bronze just like silver, of Indian workmanship,
>> An oil flask, a gift to the house of his sweetest friend,
> Since this is your birthday, son of Simon,
>> Crinagoras sends me with his heart rejoicing.

The Greek text immediately indicates the difference in perspective with the third word in the first line: "me." The speaker identifies itself as "me" even before defining itself as a flask in the second line. It inscribes itself into the convention of speaking inanimate objects, but its concurrent allegiance to epistolary form reveals itself in the naming of both sender and addressee, Crinagoras and the "son of Simon." The question then arises whether the "me" is the flask or the letter? Since it is impossible to imagine the flask actually writing the letter, and therefore causing the pronoun to stand for both object and epistle, our only other option is to picture the letter inscribed on the flask, so that the "me" is simultaneously script and bronze object, a message *on* a bottle. We return to the anthology's fiction of original epigrammatic composition, in which the author inscribes an object with words to be read by another. But in this case, instead of the reader approaching the object in order to decipher its inscription, the object, letter-like, comes to him.[14]

Related to the letter accompanying a gift is the invitation letter. In book 11 of the *Greek Anthology*, a section devoted to symposiastic and satirical epigrams, we find a letter-poem sent by Philodemus inviting his friend Piso to a feast (*Anth. Pal.* 11.44 = *GP* 3302–09):[15]

---

[14] These verses may also hint at the epistolary game of "where the letter goes, so would I"; see Eur. *IT* 760–76, where Iphigenia hints that Pylades should "rescue" her letter and carry it to Orestes just as Orestes will then rescue her and return her to Argos. See also Ovid *Tristia* 1.1, on the letter *qua* book allowed to travel back to Rome and visit Augustus: "tu tamen i pro me, tu, cui licet, aspice Romam. / di facerent, possem nunc meus esse liber!" (*Tr.* 1.1.57–58). We will see this topos again in the epistolary conceit of Rufinus *Anth. Pal.* 5.9.

[15] The Greek text on which I base my translation is from Gow and Page (1968).

Tomorrow, dearest Piso, your friend whom the Muses love,
   and who celebrates the annual feast on the twentieth,
invites you to his simple hut, after the ninth hour;
   if you miss out on cow udders and toasts of Chian wine,
at least you will see honest friends,
   and you will hear things much sweeter than stories about
     the land of the Phaeacians.
But if you ever turn your eyes towards me in favor, Piso,
   we will celebrate the twentieth richly rather than simply.

Piso and Philodemus were followers of Epicurus, so the phrase "the annual feast on the twentieth" was wholly comprehensible to them. In this way, the poem sustains the illusion of a private letter by refusing to explain to an external audience obscure or private references; only the addressee, a fellow Epicurean, will understand the allusion to the master's birthday celebration. Equally obscure is "your friend, beloved of the Muses." Philodemus refuses to name himself as the letter writer, leaving Piso to guess which of his poet friends (μουσοφιλὴς ἔταρος) might be writing to him on this occasion; the external reader is saved by the editor's attribution. As if to compensate for this omission, Piso's name is written twice: once in the conventional position of the addressee in the opening line, but then again in the last couplet. I suspect that the repetition occurs because Philodemus shifts at the end of the letter to a different mode: what begins as an invitation to a feast finishes as an apparent request for patronage.[16]

Thus far we have considered epigrammatic letters (or epistolary epigrams) accompanying gifts and "invitation" letters. In book 5 of the *Greek Anthology*, which is classified as "amatory," one could hope to find verse love letters. Lovers are often separated, unhappy, or in crisis, and could be expected to turn to letter writing in their predicaments, in attempts to persuade, plead, or bridge an absence. But the original epigrammatic conceit, that of lines engraved on stone in a public place, may work against an amatory epistolary mode here, since the love letter is meant to be private, for the beloved's eyes only, and portable, sent directly to the ad-

---

[16] Horace, too, took advantage of this mode in his invitation-poem to Maecenas (*Ode* 1.20.1–2): "vile potabis modicis Sabinum/cantharis," as does Catullus 13.1–2: "cenabis bene, mi Fabulle, apud me/ paucis, si tibi di favent, diebus." Another possible interpretation of the "enrichment" of the meal would be that Piso's favor will make the originally planned simple meal "rich" in the spiritual or philosophical sense rather than materially more luxurious.

dressee rather than requiring the beloved to come to a particular place to read.[17] There are few love letters in book 5, but rather erotic monologues, dialogues, prayers to Aphrodite, and complaints. But book 5 does contain the only epigram composed explicitly as a love letter; its opening lines immediately and unmistakeably declare the poem's epistolary identity (*Anth. Pal.* 5.9 Rufinus):[18]

> I, Rufinus, send many greetings (πολλὰ χαίρειν) to my
>   sweetest Elpis,
>   if she is able to flourish (χαίρειν) apart from me.
> I swear by your eyes, I can no longer support this desolation,
>   nor separation from you in my lonely bed.
> But I visit the hill of Koressos or the shrine of great Artemis
>   always drenched in tears.
> But tomorrow my own city will receive me again, and I will
>   fly to your eyes,
>   praying a thousand best wishes for you (ἐρρῶσθαι).

Rufinus visits Ephesus, while his girlfriend, Elpis, waits back at home in his native city. He opens with epistolary convention of "x to y χαίρειν," but then plays on the convention by taking it literally: "if she is able to χαίρειν apart from me."[19] Both the sender, Rufinus, and the addressee, Elpis, are named in first line, as in a "real" letter. We also see the familiar awkwardness of the first-person presence defining itself with a name: "I, Rufinus." Even the addressee, Elpis, fluctuates in the letter between a third-person ("if *she* is able to flourish apart from me") and second-person address ("I will fly to *your* eyes"). The letter closes with a play on the customary closing formula ἔρρωσο, with no request for a response included, since Rufinus makes it clear that he intends to return immediately.

Rufinus offers us a love letter from a man who appears to be away from home on a trip, perhaps on a religious pilgrimage of sorts, since he refers to the temple of Artemis. He writes to his beloved to remind her of their love, but also to announce his return "tomorrow," as if he were returning early, unable to endure

---

[17] A gift letter is also on one level personal, but it is usually to the credit of all concerned, so therefore not as problematic as a love letter when made public.

[18] The Greek text on which I base my translation is from W. R. Paton, *The Greek Anthology, Books 1–6* (Loeb Classical Library, Cambridge MA 1916 repr. 1993).

[19] See Ovid's play with "salutem" in *Tr.* 5.13.2.

longer separation. The letter is the harbinger of the lover, as both letter and lover are imagined "flying" to Elpis' eyes: the letter to be read, and the lover to gaze and be gazed upon. The small word "tomorrow" fits perfectly as an erotic trope of immediacy, but could endanger the epistolary illusion, since it requires the letter to arrive "tomorrow" before its writer. We unfortunately have no idea where Rufinus' "native city" is.[20] If he leans toward sustaining the epistolary illusion, then his city must be within a day's journey of Ephesus; if he ignores epistolary verisimilitude for the sake of erotic urgency, then the location of his city is irrelevant.

Still in book 5, a writer identified as "Plato" offers a curious variation on the love letter. *Anth. Pal.* 5.80 (= *FGE* 594–95) is a two-line "letter" carved on an apple:[21]

> I am an apple. Someone who loves you throws me. But nod
>   your consent,
> Xanthippe, for both you and I are prone to decay.

The apple provides a convenient surface for the lover: it functions as a love gift, easily "delivered" with a toss of the hand. The lover remains within the realm of the imaginable by restricting his text to two lines, which could reasonably fit on the object. He does not request a return letter, since the surface of the apple must already be full, but merely a nod from the addressee. The apple also communicates with its "body" when it claims "for both you and I are prone to decay." The girl is told to look upon the fruit and think about their own shared vulnerability to old age and death.[22] This letter speaks in its own voice and identifies only the addressee, not the sender, which could complicate matters considerably. But we are free to imagine the sender not too far from his addressee, perhaps most likely a fellow dinner guest across the room: Xanthippe is meant to pick up the apple, read the message, and nod to her admirer across the room.

Let me pause briefly to consider more seriously the ramifica-

---

[20] D. L. Page, *The Epigrams of Rufinus* (Cambridge 1978) 71 suggests Samos, but also acknowledges that we have no information about the man himself beyond the thirty-seven amatory epigrams in *Anth. Pal.* 5. Page curiously concludes that in the case of this letter, the "occasion is more likely to be real than fictitious" (71), but offers no further explanation.

[21] The Greek text is from Page (1981).

[22] Cf. Theocritus 7.120–21: a beloved is "riper than a pear" and will soon lose his "bloom of beauty."

tions of including the apple of "Plato" in this study. Callimachus, in his *Aetia*, will use precisely the same device, as will Philostratus some four centuries later, and before discussing their particular narratives, it may be prudent to revisit the question of epistolary categorization. We have seen letters in disguise throughout this book: Herodotus' letter tucked into a rabbit skin, or the words written on the bare head of a slave. But even in these odd examples, the letter itself remained distinct from its medium: the head and the rabbit had no signification on their own, functioning merely as peculiar but practical surfaces or containers.

In the case of the apple, however, the object itself carries with it its own meaning: even without an inscription, it is a conventional love token, a symbol of seduction. As a non-verbal message, an erotic symbol in its own right, the apple has a long history in ancient Greek literature: Theocritus' rustic love gifts, the apples of Atalanta, and Sappho's Cydonian apple trees come to mind.[23] A further layer is revealed here as the apple itself speaks – "I am an apple" – imitating the speaking statues of the *Greek Anthology*, the self-identifying bronze flask mentioned above (*Anth. Pal.* 6.261), or the historical examples of memorial statues excavated in Athenian graveyards. The apple foregrounds itself more shamelessly than a statue, however: statues do not proclaim "I am a statue," but rather "I am the σῆμα of ..." In contrast, the apple boasts that it is indeed an apple, but this information turns out to be both self-evident and concealing a more important issue, namely that of the sender of the message. The apple proclaims its own identity but invents a riddle for its reader about the identity of its inscriber: "someone who loves you throws me." Here the "I" is effectively doubled, both apple and inscriber, but the recipient is asked to answer not the apple, but the inscriber: "nod your consent" to me, the one who throws. The apple functions as a letter, therefore, in that it is written, sent (thrown) in a situation of emotional delicacy (it circumvents open speaking in a public context which could compromise the lovers), and expects a response – here just a nod. As we will see in a later chapter, Philostratus, in his version (*Letter* 62), will ask that his beloved return the apple with her own brief inscription.

[23] There are several scholarly articles on the subject: J. Trumpf, "Kydonische Äpfel," *Hermes* 88 (1960) 14–22; A. R. Littlewood, "The Symbolism of the Apple in Greek and Roman Literature," *HSCP* 72 (1967) 147–81, with additional bibliography on 178–80.

The apple of *Anth. Pal.* 5.80 presses the question of epistolary and epigrammatic status in an interesting way. In that it is a piece of writing sent from one person to another, it is surely closely related to a normative letter. But in its physical form and vehicle – incision into the flesh of an apple – it recalls other forms of non-epistolary erotic activity, such as the suggestive gesture of throwing an apple at one's love object, or the carving of a beloved's name on a tree. The apple here also may be seen as recreating the fiction of the composition of an early epigram: it is an engraved object speaking directly to its "user." The apple as love letter/ epigram is also part of Callimachus' famous retelling of the love affair of Acontius and Cydippe in the *Aetia*, as well as Ovid's retelling in *Heroides* 20 and 21.[24] Let us now turn to Callimachus' narrative, keeping open the question of how appropriate the label "letter" may be for an inscribed apple.

CALLIMACHUS' LOVE LETTERS OF ACONTIUS AND CYDIPPE

To know that one does not write for the other, to know that these things I am going to write will never cause me to be loved by the one I love (the other), to know that writing compensates for nothing, sublimates nothing, that it is precisely *there where you are not* – this is the beginning of writing. (R. Barthes, *A Lover's Discourse*)[25]

Among the fragments of Callimachus' works, the apple in the myth of Acontius and Cydippe combines deception and *eros* in the same way we have seen letters connect *eros* with deception in Homer and Euripides. The tale of the lovers is told and retold by three authors whose works together span almost eight hundred years, and who write in both Greek and Latin.[26] Callimachus,

---

[24] See, e.g. E. J. Kenney, "Love and Legalism: Ovid, *Heroides* 20 and 21," *Arion* 9 (1970) 388–414; Barchiesi (1993) 333–65; P. A. Rosenmeyer, "Love Letters in Callimachus, Ovid, and Aristaenetus, or, The Sad Fate of a Mail-Order Bride," *MD* 36 (1996) 9–31.

[25] R. Barthes, *A Lover's Discourse: Fragments*, trans. R. Howard (New York 1978) 100.

[26] For general bibliography on Callimachus' Acontius and Cydippe story, see C. Dilthey, *De Callimachi Cydippa* (Leipzig, 1863); A. Dietzler, *Die Akontios-Elegie des Kallimachos* (Diss. Greifswald 1933); M. L. Coletti, "Aconzio e Cidippe in Callimaco e in Ovidio," *RCCM* 4 (1962) 294–303; N. Hopkinson, *A Hellenistic Anthology* (Cambridge, 1988), ad loc. For Aristaenetus' version, there is a translation into German by A. Lesky, *Aristaenetos: Erotische Briefe der griechischen Antike* (Munich 1967) 65–70, and a brief discussion by W. G. Arnott, "Imitation, Variation, Exploitation: A Study in Aristaenetus," *GRBS* 14 (1973) 197–211, esp. 207–8. The Ovidian material has a much larger bibliography, which will be touched on below, but two very useful pieces are Kenney (1970) 388–414, and Barchiesi (1993) 333–65, esp. 354–63.

writing in the third century BCE in Alexandria, inserts the story into his scholarly compendium on the origins of things (*Aetia*); Ovid, active in the late first century BCE in Rome, expands the format into an exchange of Latin erotic verse epistles (*Heroides*); and in the late antique author Aristaenetus (*ca.* fifth century CE), the chosen medium is a prose letter exhibiting a rich erotic and allusive texture (*Erotic Letters*). All three authors present the story of Acontius and Cydippe in such a way as to confirm and strengthen the literary connection among letters, deceit, and love.

In what follows, I attempt to read the different versions through the lens of epistolarity, exploring how the "apple as letter," used as an embedded device or an overall narrative structure, affects both the fictional characters' words and actions, and our own responses as external readers. In each of these "discourses of desire," a written message functions as an erotic trap in a game of sexual pursuit, as the lover/writer attempts to seduce and control his beloved/reader through a love letter. But the letter in this affair, as we have already hinted, will take the curious form of an inscribed apple.

The story of Acontius and Cydippe contains all the elements of an ancient Greek novel: a beautiful hero and heroine, their fateful meeting at a festival, the trials of their separation, and the final union assisted by a benevolent deity.[27] Both Acontius and Cydippe are young and surpassingly lovely, and are said to shine like two stars on their native islands of Ceos and Naxos (*Aet.* 67.8). Acontius meets Cydippe at a festival of Apollo on Delos, and is infatuated at first sight. At that moment, Eros inspires him to pick an apple and carve on it an oath intended to be read in Cydippe's own voice: "I swear by Artemis to marry Acontius"; he then rolls the apple in front of his beloved, who picks it up and reads it aloud, automatically but unintentionally binding herself to marry him. Unfortunately, Cydippe is already engaged to marry another. Acontius wanders in the solitude of the woods, carving his beloved's name in the trees for solace. As he continues to yearn for her, she is attacked by a sudden disease on the evening before her

---

[27] The reader may object that in the case of Greek novels, the love is usually mutual and reciprocated, while in Callimachus' version, Acontius is presented as the sole active lover and Cydippe merely his victim. But I would argue that other details overlap sufficiently to make the comparison a useful one. On the mutual love found in Greek novels, see D. Konstan, *Sexual Symmetry: Love in the Ancient Novel and Related Genres* (Princeton NJ 1994).

wedding. This happens three times before her father consults the Delphic oracle for an explanation. Apollo reveals the secret oath that Cydippe had sworn while on Delos, to marry no one other than Acontius, and the couple marry and live happily ever after.

What I have outlined above is a composite sketch drawn from three sources, each one adapting and presumably elaborating on its predecessor, and fitting the tale into the context of a different era and a distinct generic framework. Callimachus' *Aetia* is our earliest extant source, and in spite of the fragmentary nature of his text, we can assume with some certainty that Ovid and Aristaenetus based their versions directly on his.[28] Callimachus informs us that he found the account of the romance "mixed up" with the early history of Ceos in the works of a fifth-century historian, one Xenomedes (*Aet.* 75.54–55). The direct reference to the historical source supports his claim to scholarly authenticity, as he builds his text on the foundation of yet another text. Both Callimachus and Acontius seek to benefit from the putative authority of a written text. Callimachus' avowed dependence on a written document, rather than oral tradition, and his invocation of Xenomedes' voice to gain his readers' trust, duplicate Acontius' own procedure in using a written document, the letter, which is actually written in the voice of another, to persuade his reader, Cydippe, to believe his "story," namely that he loves her. But the two master writers base their actions on very different presumptions: Callimachus on the authenticity of written text, and Acontius on its tricky malleability.

---

[28] We cannot exclude the possibility of other intervening texts, of course, and scholars have argued both for and against Gallus' possible role in this particular poetic tradition. Several Latin poets chose to imitate Callimachus' poem. F. Cairns analyzes Propertius' indebtedness to Callimachus in his discussion of elegy 1.18: "Propertius 1.18 and Callimachus, *Acontius and Cydippe*," *CR* 19 (1969) 131–34; D. O. Ross, *Backgrounds to Augustan Poetry: Gallus, Elegy and Rome* (Cambridge 1975) 72–74, argues that Propertius also exploited Gallus' version of the story for his elegy. Others have written on the relationship between Virgil's *Eclogue* 2 and the Acontius story: A. La Penna, "La seconda Ecloga e la poesia bucolica di Virgilio," *Maia* 15 (1963) 484–92, esp. 488; I. M. Le M. DuQuesnay, "From Polyphemus to Corydon," in D. West and T. Woodman, eds., *Creative Imitation and Latin Literature* (Cambridge 1979) 48 and notes 127, 131; and E. J. Kenney, "Virgil and the Elegiac Sensibility," *ICS* 8 (1983) 44–59. See also R. Rosen and J. Farrell, "Acontius, Milanion, and Gallus: Vergil *Ecl.* 10.52–61," *TAPA* 116 (1986) 241–54. Finally, Catullus 65 has also been interpreted as referring to Callimachus' Acontius and Cydippe: see W. Kroll, *Catull* (Stuttgart 1923) 196–99; L. W. Daly, "Callimachus and Catullus," *CP* 47 (1952) 97–99; P. A. Johnston, "An Echo of Sappho in Catullus 65," *Latomus* 42 (1983) 388–94; R. Hunter, "Callimachean Echoes in Catullus 65," *ZPE* 96 (1993) 179–82.

When Ovid inherits the Callimachean retelling, he reshapes the story into elegiac epistolary form in his *Heroides*, a series of letters from famous lovers of myth and literature. The author (and there is some doubt as to the author of the last three pairs of letters, but I will assume it is Ovid) splits the love story into two distinct yet intersecting narratives: Acontius in *Her.* 20, and Cydippe's response in *Her.* 21.[29] Callimachus presented Acontius as letter writer and Cydippe as reader. Ovid expands the perspective so that both characters experience both sides of the epistolary exchange. The female character is given her own voice, a chance to be an active respondent as well as a passive reader, as the two trade roles. Ovid may even be tipping the scales in Cydippe's favor when he makes her letter slightly longer than Acontius'; we are certainly left with the impression that Ovid's Cydippe has a mind of her own.[30]

Aristaenetus includes the story of Acontius and Cydippe in a series of fifty prose letters which summarize love stories from various ancient sources. We do not know much about this author beyond an approximate date in the fifth century CE; even his name is suspect, taken from the first letter in his collection. His work may be compared to that of Parthenius, a Greek poet of the first century BCE, whose *Erotika pathemata*, dedicated to Cornelius Gallus, was a medley of sorrowful love stories claiming to provide Gallus' literary Roman friends with unusual subject matter in accessible form. Aristaenetus' text, so late in the ancient Greek literary tradition, proclaims its "authenticity" through frequent allusions to earlier authors, including Ovid and Callimachus. In *Letter* 10, the writer Eratokleia retells the story of Acontius and Cydippe to her addressee Dionysias: her name is composed of *eros* and *kleos*, perhaps someone who is "famous for love," and the receiver's name, Dionysias, is an obscure alternative name for Cydippe's island of Naxos, as Callimachus tells us in *Aetia* fr. 75.41. The whole letter is similarly encoded, offering all sorts of literary clues to be deciphered by the external reader.

Aristaenetus and Ovid allow us to reconstruct the message in-

---

[29] On the authenticity of last six letters, see e.g. E. Courtney, "Ovidian and non-Ovidian *Heroides*," *BICS* 12 (1965) 63–66; V. Tracy, "The Authenticity of *Heroides* 16–21," *CJ* 66 (1971) 328–30.

[30] Ovid acknowledges his debt to Callimachus in *Rem. Am.* 381–82: "Callimachi numeris non est dicendus Achilles, / Cydippe non est oris, Homere, tui." See also *Ars Am.* 1.457–58: "Littera Cydippen pomo perlata fefellit, / Insciaque est verbis capta puella suis."

scribed on the apple, since Callimachus' fragmentary text is silent just at the crucial moment. Even if there is no extant mention of letter writing in the *Aetia* episode, the fact that both Ovid and Aristaenetus retell the story in fully epistolary form argues strongly in favor of the inherently epistolary nature of the tale. Ovid interprets the apple-as-letter, the figurative letter as it were, in an unmetaphorical way, by turning the whole narrative into an extended epistolary moment, and Aristaenetus follows his lead. How the apple functions as a letter is precisely the focus of the following analysis.

THE APPLE AS LETTER

Let us investigate further this episode of the inscribed apple. What interests me most is the power of writing and reading in the context of *eros*: the apple itself is used as a letter, sent from the lover to his beloved. One could object that, in its verbal form and in its intended and performed mode of action, the apple more closely resembles the text of an oath, functioning as a script or prompt for its reader. "Normal" letters don't read quite like this, nor are they sent with the intention to provoke a legally binding utterance. In this way, the apple recalls a curse tablet or magical papyrus. This letter requests not a return letter but a performative speech act. But I would argue that the distinction is a matter of degree: all "normal" letters are written to persuade or affect their readers; Acontius' "letter" just takes the concept of persuasion to an extreme, forcing his reader to respond precisely in the way he desires. "Plato" requested a nod in answer, Philostratus a return message on the apple; Acontius demands a promise and ensures that Cydippe cannot wriggle out of it.

The epistolary power of this particular letter relies on the writer's ability to forge (in the sense of both "shape" and "compose fraudulently") a script for someone else, to write in the voice of another. Acontius as writer depends on Cydippe as reader to bring his words to life, so he cleverly arranges that *his* words actually become *her* words.[31] He writes the oath in the first person, anticipating her enunciation. Once he has enticed her to read, ensnared her in his plot, he never lets her go. Cydippe lends not just

---

[31] My approach here is heavily influenced by Svenbro (1988).

her voice to his text for a single reading, as Svenbro argues in the
case of a passer-by who reads a statue's inscription;[32] she is forced
to hand over her whole self, body and soul, betrayed by a voice
which is both hers and not hers. She functions as an echo of
Acontius' master voice. Acontius' awareness of his reader here
takes the form of textual entrapment and domination.

If we accept Callimachus' fragment 67 as a beginning, the
opening lines read as follows (67.1–4):[33]

> Eros himself taught Acontius the device (τέχνην), when
> the young man was on fire with love for the beautiful virgin
>   Cydippe –
> for he was not cunning – so that he might gain
> the name of lawful husband for the rest of his life.

We are introduced to Eros, Acontius, and Cydippe, and told that
Eros taught the youth a τέχνη, presumably a reference to writing
on the apple. The image of Eros as teacher is familiar from other
ancient sources, most frequently with reference to unhappy lovers
turning to poetic composition: thus Euripides writes in his *Sthene-
boea* that "Eros indeed teaches the poet, even if before he was
without inspiration."[34] Callimachus' Eros teaches Acontius a particularly powerful line of love poetry, a tricky phrase to be
scratched on an unusual writing surface. In Aristaenetus we read
correspondingly of a "most novel plan," a καινοτάτη βουλή
(1.10.23).[35] Aristaenetus then relates the initial encounter at Artemis' shrine, addressing Acontius directly in his narrative (1.10.24–
40):

As soon as you saw the girl sitting in the sanctuary of Artemis, you
picked a Cydonian apple [a quince] from the grove of Aphrodite, inscribed on it a speech of deception (ἀπάτης λόγον) and unseen, rolled it
in front of the feet of her maidservant. She took it up, admired its size
and color, wondering at the same time who of the girls there had
dropped it from the folds of her garment. She says to it "are you divine,

---

[32] Svenbro (1988) *passim*.

[33] Callimachus' text is found in R. Pfeiffer, *Callimachus*, 2 vols. (Oxford 1949) frs. 67–75.
The translation is my own.

[34] See S. Goldhill, *Foucault's Virginity* (Cambridge 1995) 77–78, who refers to the Euripides
passage as well as Nicias' response to Theocritus 11, Callimachus *Ep.* 46 Pf. (= *Anth. Pal.*
12.150), and Plato *Symp.* 203d7, where Diotima calls Eros a sophist. Goldhill also discusses
the role of Eros as teacher in Achilles Tatius' novel *Leucippe and Cleitophon*.

[35] The text used for Aristaenetus Letter 10 is the Teubner edition of O. Mazal, ed., *Aristaenetus, Epistularum libri II* (Stuttgart 1971); the translation is my own.

apple? what letters have been etched on your surface? and what do you wish to signify (καὶ τί σημαίνειν ἐθέλεις)? Mistress, take the apple – I have never before seen such a one, so overly large, so ruddy, with the color of roses; and what a sweet fragrance! Even from a distance it makes the senses rejoice. Tell me, dearest, what is that written around it?" And the girl, picking it up and letting her eyes run across the script, read as follows: "By Artemis I swear that Acontius is the one I shall marry" (μὰ τὴν Ἄρτεμιν Ἀκοντίῳ γαμοῦμαι). As she swore the oath – for it was an oath, even if an unwilling and unfair one – she threw the love charm (τὸν ἐρωτικὸν λόγον) away in shame, and left the last word only half spoken.

Aristaenetus, as did Ovid before him, explores the ethics of the lover's behavior and concludes that this is an unfair entrapment. The act of writing as trickery is contrasted implicitly (explicitly in Ovid *Her.* 21.128[36]) with the honest way to "catch" a girl, that is by asking her father for her hand in marriage, or by persuading her with tender words. So why does Acontius in his erotic predicament turn to writing? There are two parts to my question: (1) why writing as opposed to speaking and (2) why writing on an apple in particular?[37]

The impetus behind any sort of letter writing, even before it can attempt to persuade or affect its reader, is simply to create a bridge, to overcome distance or absence, and to sustain human contact.[38] Using the apple as a letter, Acontius tries to make contact with the beloved, because although he writes near her in the sanctuary, she is absent in spirit; there is no mutual awareness of love. Their distance is underscored symbolically by their associations with two opposing divinities: in Aristaenetus' version, Cydippe stands in the sanctuary of Artemis, virgin goddess, while Acontius lurks suggestively in a nearby grove of Aphrodite (1.10.24–26). An attempt at direct speech under these circumstances might have frightened off Cydippe. But a written message is both less intimidating, because it is disconnected from its

---

[36] *Her.* 21.128: "exoranda tibi, non capienda, fui."

[37] It is not entirely accurate to imply that writing is opposed to speaking in this encounter, since Acontius' written message is actually a prelude to Cydippe's own speaking of his words. But Acontius himself chooses to write to her rather than to address her orally, and in that way, he chooses writing over speech.

[38] R. Barthes, *Fragments d'un discours amoureux* (Paris 1977), trans. R. Howard, *A Lover's Discourse: Fragments* (New York 1978) 15, speaks of the other being absent as referent but present as allocutory.

writer's physical presence, and more lasting: one can read and reread a letter, and the reader retains a visual as well as an aural memory. It becomes "inscribed in the tablets of the mind," to use Aeschylus' terms.[39]

Acontius finds a channel for communication by rolling the inscribed apple in front of his beloved. Precisely because Cydippe is not in love, she does not understand the potential danger of the apple until it is too late. Acontius counts on Cydippe's innocent curiosity to get her to read its inscription, and this she promptly does, out loud for the benefit of her maid.[40] The inscription on the apple thus signifies Acontius' power through writing to fulfil his own desire, to manipulate Cydippe into reading, responding, and binding herself to him all in one performative utterance. It is as if a whole love story – first meeting, courtship, and final erotic union – were telescoped into one short phrase on the apple, which constitutes both a letter demanding an answer and, once read aloud, its own response. This is a controlling author's fantasy: to overcome his dependency on a reader by enslaving her. A further ironic twist to the self-responding letter is that Acontius' phrasing serves to make Cydippe appear the initiator, as if the whole idea of marriage were her idea rather than his, while simultaneously prohibiting her from any active response beyond an inadvertent echo of his words. Eros has indeed taught Acontius well.

Thus Acontius' "script" allows him to control the situation better than any face-to-face encounter would have, first because the impersonal letter allows him to avoid a potentially embarrassing or negative encounter in person, and second because the wording of his letter forces Cydippe to "answer" just as he wishes, in the affirmative. But we may also acknowledge that even if he had come into her presence in the grove, the lover really ceased "seeing" Cydippe after the first glance: the moment of falling in love blinded him to anything other than his desire, and Cydippe is seen only in her role as the object of that desire. Her image is frozen, already framed in his heart. Cydippe may try to return to Naxos and carry on with her future, but in Acontius' mind, she exists as an unchanging ideal, inscribed at that moment of falling in love

---

[39] Aesch. *Prom.* 789; *Choe.* 450; *Eum.* 275; *Suppl.* 178–79, 991–92. See Segal (1986) 81; Svenbro (1988) 201.

[40] This reading aloud is clearly motivated by the circumstances, but on the issue of reading silently or out loud in antiquity, see Knox (1968) 421–35.

that is reportable only in the past tense.[41] The act of giving the apple, that first attempt at contact, defines and constrains the participants by the problematic time lag that haunts all epistolary communication: the lover who writes can address only a beloved who is an image persisting from the past, while the beloved who receives and reads the message exists in yet another time, which was future to the lover sending the message.[42] Acontius' writing will not be powerful enough to drag Cydippe into his "present," but certainly strong enough to keep Cydippe from existing wholly in her own future; unable to proceed with her life, she is immobilized between the plans of her father and those of Acontius for her marriage.

STRANGE FRUIT: THE APPLE AS SIGNIFIER

Acontius chooses the apple as an apparently innocent yet potentially erotic gift. We may consider the aptness of a Cyd-onian apple for Cyd-ippe here.[43] Acontius plucks it from a grove of Aphrodite, and his action may be understood as a rehearsal for his eventual conquest of Cydippe. With this apple, he also attempts a metonymic transfer of his love: her acceptance of the apple prefigures and facilitates her eventual acceptance of him.[44] Cydippe's acceptance of the apple, even before she reads the inscription, is a telling moment in the story. Beyond its obvious symbolic appropriateness as a love-gift here, the apple is used as a medium for a written declaration of desire. Eros invites Acontius to inscribe himself into a larger literary tradition of scripted apples. The trick has been used before, and with disastrous results. I refer, of course, to the apple sent as a gift to Peleus and Thetis on their wedding day, which incited the Judgment of Paris, the abduction of Helen, and the ten-year Trojan campaign.[45]

A convenient summary of the events at the wedding may be found in the second-century writer Lucian, whose *Dialogues of the*

---

[41] Barthes (1978) 194: "Love at first sight is always spoken in the past tense: it might be called an anterior immediacy. The image is perfectly adapted to this temporal deception: distinct, abrupt, framed, it is already (again, always) a memory (the nature of the photograph is not to represent but to memorialize) . . ."

[42] I am paraphrasing the formulation of Altman (1982) 129–32.

[43] This pun was suggested to me by A. Barchiesi.

[44] See Barthes (1978) 74.

[45] This scene is attested in art much earlier than in literature: a relief on an ivory comb found in the sanctuary of Artemis Orthia at Sparta has been dated to *ca.* 700 BCE; see Plate 10 in R. D. Barnett, "Early Greek and Oriental Ivories," *JHS* 68 (1948) 1–25, esp. 14.

Sea Gods[46] reports the following: Discord tossed a beautiful golden apple among the wedding guests. Inscribed (ἐπεγέγραπτο) on the apple was, literally translated: "may the beautiful woman take me" (ἡ καλὴ λαβέτω). Hermes picked it up and read the inscription out loud. Again, as with Acontius and Cydippe, the precise wording of the inscription is crucial. The sender is anonymous – nobody would knowingly accept an apple offered by Discord; the message is an intentionally open address. Interestingly, epistolary message and address are one and the same thing in this instance; there is no "message" beyond the address itself "to the fairest." If a goddess were to pick it up first, she would immediately fulfil the wish of the inscription, and by reading the message aloud, she would only confirm her position as the most beautiful woman in the room. The myth plays with the idea of writing detached from its author being open to interpretation: another way to put it is that the author's intention (a dedication to the fairest) can be fulfilled only through an act of reader response (a goddess will read the words and conclude that she is the intended subject). But because there are too many eager readers present, Hermes must intercede to prohibit the direct enactment of the words; he can read the words without seeking to inscribe himself into the contest. Similarly, Cydippe's maid acts as an intermediary, although in her case illiteracy keeps her from direct involvement.

Another inscribed apple relevant to our discussion is found in Letter 62 of the *Love Letters* of Philostratus (*ca.* second century CE).[47] The letter writer recalls the Judgment of Paris and wishes to correct its outcome in favor of his own beloved. He writes (62.5–14):

Do not fight with one another, goddesses! For look here, I have the apple. Take it, fair one, conquer the goddesses, and read the inscription. For I have used the apple as a letter, too (καὶ ἐπιστολῇ τῷ μήλῳ κέχρημαι). The other was an apple of Eris, this one of Eros (ἐκεῖνο Ἔριδος, τοῦτο Ἔρωτος); the other was silent, but this one speaks. Don't throw it away, don't eat it. For not even in war is an ambassador abused. What, then, have I written on it? It speaks for itself: "Euippe, I love you." Read it and write underneath: "and I you." The apple has room to receive those letters too.

---

[46] Letter 7, the dialogue between Panope and Galene, in the Loeb edition of M. D. McLeod, tr., *Lucian* (Cambridge, MA 1961) 202–5.
[47] A. R. Benner and F. H. Fobes, *The Letters of Alciphron, Aelian, and Philostratus* (Cambridge, MA 1949).

Philostratus' apple comes from Love, and its inscription is
wholly unambiguous. Just as Acontius' apple becomes more than
an apple once it is used to carry a message, so Philostratus' apple
is certainly no longer meant to be eaten or thrown away. He
warns Euippe that it is not just any apple; rather, it is an object to
be treasured, and a letter to be answered. He hands the object to
his beloved, comparing it *explicitly* to a letter, and the apple speaks
both for itself and for him, with a direct address to Euippe. He
begs for an immediate response: she should write just underneath
his words "and I you" (κ'ἀγὼ σέ). Her words depend entirely on
his: he has supplied the name (Euippe) and the verb, the all-
important "I love" (φιλῶ). Her response requires the minimum of
effort, just a completion of the formula. The phrase "I love you" is
more directly emotional than "Euippe loves Philostratus," but it is
also a meaningless cliché without specific names; similarly, graffiti
are rarely seen without particularizing references.[48] Philostratus
tries to place one inscription close enough to the other that his
declaration can inspire and control hers, but Eros is a very slippery god, and I wonder if Euippe will not take advantage of the
loophole here.

All these examples suggest the dangerous consequences of writing detached from its source. Once the letter is sent it is beyond
the control of its author, and open to misinterpretation and abuse.
It may not reach its addressee, it may arrive safely but not be
read, or it may arrive and be read but its meaning decoded contrary to the intention of its author. The potential for failure is implicit in any letter, and Acontius is driven to strive against the
errors immanent in letter writing. That is why, to return to our main
plot, he must be so careful in his wording of the oath. A written
message must be more specific, more immediately understandable
than its spoken counterpart, because, as Socrates reminds Phaedrus, the reader has no way of asking questions of the text.[49] Acontius' letter must work on the first reading.[50]

---

[48] Consider the comparable situation of grafitti: "I love you" is nowhere to be found, while
specific phrases ("Jack loves Jill," or "I love Peter") abound.

[49] For ancient views on this quandary, see the discussion of writing vs. speech in Plato's
Phaedrus 274d–277a.

[50] This is not to deny that a letter could be reread, reinterpreted, or disputed. But for
Acontius, the apple has only one opportunity to bind his beloved to him; it barely gets a
complete first reading, and certainly will not get a second chance.

THE LETTER ARRIVES

Let us look closely at the moment of reading. First comes a scene of deferral: Cydippe's maid picks up the fruit and sees the letters running around its circumference. This is a very dangerous moment: Cydippe's name does not appear on the oath, so if the maidservant were to read the inscription, she would be equally at risk. But it is Cydippe's accuracy at deciphering the written text that will trap her. Acontius is guided in his actions by a god; he has been taught his cleverness by Eros. The female character's cleverness, specifically her literacy, condemns her to blind obedience. But for the moment, we are stuck with an empty message and deferred action: the sender has sent his letter, which has arrived intact, but the wrong receiver has picked it up, and the message remains unread.

The maid hands the apple to her mistress and begs for a reading. By itself the writing is silent and incomplete; only after the reader is provoked into a performance of it does it really "speak." Until then it remains just a trace of the absent writer, a jumble of alphabetic signs written around a spherical surface. In fact, there may not even be an obvious beginning and end to this circular text, given the lack of punctuation and word division in continuous prose. The inscription begins innocently enough, and the sting comes only in the tail. "By Artemis I swear that Acontius is the one I shall marry." Half-way through pronouncing the verb "I shall marry," Cydippe realizes the trick, and throws the apple from her sight, as if she could reject the message along with the medium.[51] Aristaenetus (1.10.40) tells us specifically that Cydippe "left the word placed at the very end only half-spoken" (ἡμίφωνον); there is no way to be sure whether this detail was also in Callimachus' text. So the reader initially submits herself to the writing, lending it her voice, but then pulls back from reading; in refusing to read further, she displays the only power she really has in this context.

On one level, leaving out any part of an oath should undermine its legality.[52] But the formulaic swearing by Artemis occurs at the beginning of the utterance, and this is presumably enough for the

---

[51] Dietzler (1933) 37 gives other examples of "throwing away" a *logon*: Plut. *Moral.* 367A, 801C; Pindar *Ol.* 9.35.

[52] For an interesting discussion of oaths in antiquity, see E. Benveniste, "L'expression du serment dans la Grèce ancienne," *RHR* 134 (1948) 81–94.

goddess. On another level, that of the half-spoken word itself, γαμοῦμαι, Cydippe utters the verb without its crucial personal or temporal markers.[53] Half the verb gives us its stem γαμ-, without the full ending -οῦμαι, and it thereby loses much of the impact of its signification; we may imagine her ending instead with an ambiguous vowel sound. At first sight, Acontius cannot possibly know Cydippe's name, so the oath is person specific only on the side of the sender, not the receiver.[54] That is why he must get the apple into her hands, and why she must utter the oath in the first person. Much of the cleverness of the trick lies precisely in Acontius' ability to prescribe Cydippe's own voice. By writing out her script for her and giving it to her to read aloud, he attempts to force her into his λόγος, to trap her into performing a speech act that will bind her forever. So what does it mean that she omits the crucial "I shall" of the verb "to marry?" And a related question, is it significant in this situation that the present and future tenses of the verb are identical?

I have two suggestions to offer, neither of which admittedly has any grounding in the Callimachean text itself. With regard to the double tense, I would like to think of Acontius as a super-writer, fully aware of the epistolary temporal paradox mentioned earlier, that the lover who writes can address only a beloved who is an image persisting from the past, while the beloved who reads the message exists in yet another time, which was future to the lover sending the message. We can imagine Acontius (with Eros' help) trying to collapse this paradox, knowingly putting the verb in the future at the moment of writing, planning for Cydippe's reading to transform the verb into its present tense. What is conceived of as a future event in Acontius' mind will be made dangerously present by Cydippe's voice. As she reads the performative verbs

---

[53] An alternative to this interpretation is the definition of "half-spoken" as not truncated, but rather whispered, spoken in a low voice. I would argue that Cydippe's eyes run ahead of her voice as she reads, and the meaning of the words enters her mind before she actually utters the full phrase, so that it would be more logical for her to break off as soon as the meaning sinks in, rather than completing the phrase in a lower voice.

[54] I am making the assumption here that Acontius does not know Cydippe's name, because otherwise he would have used it in the oath, but we are not told this explicitly in any of the sources. We are also uninformed about when and how exactly he does learn her name. Again, I assume that he has learned it in the Callimachean version by the time he wanders into the forest and inscribes her name on trees, but the circumstances are far from clear. On the inscribed trees, see more below.

(for both swearing and agreeing to marry are speech acts in their own right), she commits herself, is now "engaged," as the two time frames suddenly merge. The performative utterance "I swear that I shall marry you" refers simultaneously to a vivid present, the moment of swearing, and an equally vivid future, the promised day of marriage.

As to the second puzzle, the missing person marker, again making no claim that the ancient authors necessarily saw it this way, I would argue that its omission highlights its importance: Acontius' skill in writing an *ego* for Cydippe to animate is undermined by her own skill in avoiding the utterance of that significant personal ending, the *ego* which would collapse her identity into that of the writer/lover. On two levels, then, the personal and the temporal, we witness the desire for (on Acontius' part) and resistance to (on Cydippe's part) the collapsing of two identities into one.

Cydippe utters the oath and, although it is wholly unintentional (ἀκούσιον), unfinished, and thus illegitimate (νόθον), the words cannot be unsaid (Arist. 1.10.39). Cydippe does have some recourse, however. Just as she is intelligent enough to decipher the words, so she is clever enough to realize the only power she has left over her own *logos* is silence, silence not only in the middle of reading, but also afterwards, in the transmission of that reading. Cydippe swears her maid to secrecy and returns to Naxos. But the half-spoken oath remains to haunt her in the person of Artemis, who will not let her forswear herself.

OVID'S CYDIPPE

At this point I wish to consider briefly how Ovid explores the constant silent repetition of the oath inscribed in Cydippe's mind, and how its refrain gradually affects her emotions to such a degree that she finally hands herself over to Acontius.[55]

Ovid takes great delight in chronicling Acontius' manipulative efforts to get Cydippe to repeat the fateful words after her initial utterance. Acontius' letter, the first in the pair, tries to force the girl to respond, much as the original inscription had forced her to

---

[55] The text used for Ovid's *Heroides* is that of G. Showerman, trans., *Ovid, vol. 1: Heroides and Amores*, 2nd edn., rev. G. P. Goold (Cambridge, MA 1977). The reader may also wish to consult H. Dörrie, ed., *Epistulae Heroidum* (Berlin 1971).

commit herself to him. He asks for a response on two levels: in an epistolary sense, with a return letter, and in an erotic sense, to reveal her true feelings for him. He reassures her immediately that this letter is not another trick (20.1–3):

> Pone metum! nihil hic iterum iurabis amanti;
> > promissam satis est te semel esse mihi.
> Perlege!

> Put aside your fear! You will swear no second oath here to
> > your lover;
> > it is enough that you promised yourself once to me.
> Read through to the end!

But just six lines further (20.10–11) he writes: "verba licet repetas," "you may recall/reread the words" which were written on that apple, and remember your oath to Artemis. Twice more Acontius admonishes her to remember her oath, and finally he encourages her to "tell [her] mother all": (20.201: "matri licet omnia narres").

Acontius' rhetoric of persuasion begins with the idea of the binding oath, a κατάδεσμος in the technical vocabulary of Greek love charms, and then develops its imagery of binding in a more general erotic sense.[56] He claims that Amor has bound Cydippe to him with words (20.28: "adstrinxit verbis ingeniosus Amor"); in phrases dictated by Amor, Acontius wrote up the binding betrothal contract. Images of both physical and mental binding follow throughout his letter. At 20.39–40, Acontius asks the gods to help him place so many bonds ("nodos") on Cydippe that she can never get free of her original pledge. He commands her at 20.66: "insidiis esto capta puella meis," where his treacheries forcibly and visibly surround her, a "capta puella" caught in the middle of the line. He insists that his act of writing is not a "crimen," and that he is not to be compared to a rapist. Acontius presents himself as a victim as well, bound ("vinctus") not by chains but by passion for Cydippe. This is a familiar image from love poetry, but in Acontius' situation, I would argue, it is triggered specifically by the initial verbal binding mechanism of the oath.

Ovid's Cydippe is much too intelligent to fall into his trap again by repeating the oath. This time she does recognize the charged

---

[56] Barchiesi (1993) 356 uses the terminology of binding in the same way as I do to explain this passage.

erotic nature of the object, even before reading its message. She says the mere arrival of the letter into her hands pierced her like the tip of a dart (21.211–12): metonymically this is Acontius, whose very name means "dart" (ἀκόντιον), piercing her with fear.[57] She writes back (21.1–2):

> Pertimui, scriptumque tuum sine murmure legi,
> iuraret ne quos inscia lingua deos.

I was terrified, and I read through your letter without the slightest sound,
  so that my tongue might not unknowingly swear by some other gods.

Silent reading is her only salvation from a repetition of her first mistake. In a flashback to that first encounter, Cydippe relates how innocently she was admiring the wonders of Artemis' sanctuary, unaware that she had become a spectacle herself, when suddenly an apple appeared at her feet with the following verses on it. Just as she is about to repeat her mistake, she catches herself and stops (21.108): "ei mihi, iuravi nunc quoque paene tibi!" ("oh no, now once again I almost swore myself to you!"). The repetition of the oath would have bound her twice over, and since she is currently communicating by means of a letter, her second oath would have been in writing. Two lines later she carefully skirts the issue by saying "and so I read, great poet, your treacheries!" (21.110). Ovid teases the reader here, repeatedly leading up to a rereading/reciting/rewriting of the oath, but always stopping short of the actual formula.[58]

Cydippe challenges the legality of the oath by defining her action not as swearing but as simple reading without the benefit of intention (21.141–43):

> sed si nil dedimus praeter sine pectore vocem,
> verba suis frustra viribus orba tenes.
> non ego iuravi – legi iurantia verba . . .

If I have given you nothing but my voice without a heart,
  then you possess in vain words without their own force;
  I did not swear, rather I read words that swore . . .

---

[57] One could also interpret the "acumen" as a phallic threat to her emotional and physical integrity.

[58] Barchiesi (1993) 357 makes an interesting comparison here between Cydippe's and Ovid's actions: "If Ovid reproduces his model, he will be an imitator in the trap of repetition, one who swears according to the formula of his model."

She insists, responding to Acontius' images of binding, that no chains hold her unless they are legal and honest. Yet as Cydippe gradually realizes that she has no choice but to yield, she sees her capitulation as a direct result of Acontius' power of writing, and acknowledges that he has indeed trapped more than just her empty voice. She thinks Acontius has discovered some marvelous writing trick which ensnares even the gods when they read it (21.237–38). Otherwise, Artemis would not have taken his side in this matter. Since he holds the gods in his power, who is she to resist? Acontius is the stronger "writer," the author of texts approved by the highest authority, that of the gods.[59] She is forced to submit to his version of the events. Finally she confesses that she has indeed told her mother all, including the pledge in her own deceived voice (21.241): "fessaque sum matri deceptae foedera linguae." Thus she ends her letter with a repetition of the oath in the presence of a new witness, her mother. The words at 21.240 with which she describes her final action reflect images of bondage to the oath itself: she gives willingly ("do libens") her bound hands ("manus vinctas") into the power of Acontius' oath ("in tua vota").

ACONTIUS INSCRIPTOR

Ovid's depiction of Acontius and Cydippe is so vivid because he gives both of them their own epistolary voice. He also enlarges on the theme of the apple-as-letter by making the apple just the first in a series of letters between the two writers. But the Greek versions concentrate on Acontius alone – it is his love story, and the woman is merely a pawn in his game. Although she cannot avoid marrying him altogether, Cydippe's reticence can defer their union, and Acontius is made to suffer as well. Two fragments of Callimachus fill in the details: "therefore at every excuse he went into the countryside" (*Aet.* 72); "but on your bark may you bear carved letters, as many letters as will say that Cydippe is beautiful" (*Aet.* 73). Aristaenetus clarifies the matter by painting a portrait of an "exclusus amator," a man overwhelmed by *eros* who weeps all day and wastes away to a shadow. The great manipulator of writing can control his language but not his body; it betrays

---

[59] Again, Barchiesi (1993) 358 draws interesting parallels between the literary struggle between Acontius and Cydippe and that of Ovid and his model, Callimachus.

his emotions and exposes his obsession.[60] In his chapter entitled "Dark Glasses," Barthes writes in the voice of an unhappy lover: "I can do everything with my language, but not with my body. What I hide by my language, my body utters."[61] Acontius, without the benefit of dark glasses, is embarrassed to be seen in his condition and takes every excuse to retire into the countryside, where he speaks to the trees of his grief (Arist. 1.10.58–61):

Oh trees, if only you had minds and voices so that you could say just this – "Cydippe is beautiful." But at least you may bear these letters engraved upon your bark, as many as claim that Cydippe is beautiful.

The idea of wandering in the solitude of nature to assuage a broken heart is familiar from other sources. The custom of writing the name of the beloved on trees also appears to be widespread, as the Greek epigrammatists, Virgil, and the elegists testify.[62] The act of writing may be therapeutic, like writing a love letter that is never meant to be sent; or it may be a form of sympathetic magic: if you write it down and make it public, it will become true; or it may take the form of a monument to the durability of love: as the tree grows, so should your love grow.[63] But let us consider it in this particular tale, in the context of the initial frustrated message inscribed on an apple. After Acontius learns the first trick from Eros, he comes to realize the power of the written word. What does he imagine as he inscribes his beloved's name on trees? Presumably he has returned to Ceos, while Cydippe is home on Naxos. She cannot possibly walk by and read the inscription, so what is the point if no one reads the message? An apple can be sent as a symbolic love-gift, but a tree and its parts are by definition rooted and immobile – until cut up into tablets or harvested for its apples, of course. This may be part of the sympathetic magic here: Acontius turns nature into culture, makes the silent forest shout out Cydippe's name and beauty, as if the trees could metamorphose into nymphs singing hymns at their wedding, or compete with each other like symposiasts toasting their beloveds with wine-cups in-

---

[60] See Barthes (1978) 44.

[61] Barthes (1978) 44.

[62] Lucian *Amor.* 16; *Anth. Pal.* 9.341.3ff., 12.130.3; Prop. 1.18.22; Virgil *Ecl.* 10.53–54. There is also an unusual example in Theoc. 18.47, where a chorus of virgins singing in honor of Helen's marriage speak of a tree engraved with her name.

[63] Virg. *Ecl.* 10. 54: "crescent illae, crescetis amores."

scribed "so-and-so is *kalos*," as Kenney has suggested.[64] The presence of a name on the bark highlights the knowledge acquired since that initial encounter: the apple was inscribed with the names of Artemis and Acontius, but the trees now speak only of Cydippe.[65]

Acontius soon realizes that the oath may do them both more harm than good; in the *Heroides*, he prays that Cydippe may not be punished by Artemis for breaking her word, but in Callimachus fr. 75, three different illnesses seize the girl. Aristaenetus tells us that her parents were suddenly called upon to prepare a funeral rather than a marriage rite (1.10.84–86). Cydippe's father Ceyx appeals to the oracle of Apollo at Delphi, and Callimachus reports the god's direct words (Callimachus fr. 75.22–29):

> A solemn oath by Artemis frustrates the marriage of your
> daughter.
> For my sister ... was present on Delos when your daughter
> swore
> that she would have Acontius and no other as her bridegroom.
> Oh Ceyx, if you wish to accept my advice,
> you will fulfil now the oath of your daughter.

Ceyx duly returns to Naxos and questions his daughter; she reveals the whole matter truthfully, and is cured. In none of this do we see anything about Cydippe's state of mind, nor does the poet imply that her wishes are of any concern. The father is asked to fulfil the oath of his daughter, and it is in his power to do so, not hers. We will never know if Callimachus reported the actual words of the oath as Aristaenetus did, or if he preferred the indirect allusions of Ovid.[66] We are told simply that "faith was kept

---

[64] Kenney (1983) 49 cleverly suggests that Acontius got the idea of inscribing his beloved's name on trees from his own identity as a beloved *eromenos*, i.e. from the example of other men writing his name adoringly on cups, walls, etc. He also makes the interesting point that "the whole of *Heroides* 20, the epistle of Acontius, is in effect a much expanded version, though in a different (unspecified) setting, of Acontius' original expostulation to the trees" (58).

[65] As mentioned above, our sources do not mention how Acontius acquired knowledge of Cydippe's name, but I assume he had time to ask around before he left Delos. I do not read the inscribed trees as letters in the same way I do the apple; their text is not addressed to anyone particular, and is entirely in the third person, two aspects that contradict basic expectations of epistolary form and function.

[66] I will not speculate on an answer to the intriguing issue of the wording of the oath: as Aristaenetus reports it, the oath could not have appeared in the elegiac meters of Callimachus' version.

with the goddess," that Cydippe's friends sang her wedding hymn, and that Acontius would not have traded his wedding night for the speed of Iphicles or the wealth of Midas. The long-awaited night of love is typically not described, but rather deflected onto a list of masculine values (athletic skill, wealth), and Cydippe herself vanishes into a great future clan name, that of the Acontiadae, who still live on Ceos. With this Callimachus brings us into the realm of contemporary Cean history. Aristaenetus ends neatly with Callimachus' own beginning, comparing the two lovers to shining stars, each gazing in wonder on the other's beauty (1.10.121–23).

But I will conclude with Ovid's version. At the end of Acontius' letter, the young man utters an oath in his own voice, and vows an offering of thanksgiving to be dedicated on the day of his wedding to Cydippe. On that day (*Her.* 20.237–40):

> aurea ponetur mali felicis imago,
>   causaque versiculis scripta duobus erit:
> "effigie pomi testatur Acontius huius
>   quae fuerint in eo scripta fuisse rata."

> a golden image of the blessed apple will be built,
>   and the reason for its dedication will be inscribed in a
>   couplet:
> "by the statue of this apple Acontius declares
>   that what was written on it has been fulfilled."

Cydippe's name is still glaringly absent, but Acontius' declaration and his apple with its inscribed oath have been immortalized in gold. The Ovidian sculpture of the apple represents the ultimate victory of writing and its elevation to cult status.[67] The private apple-as-letter is now made public, an open letter to be read by all passers-by, both its original wording and the "completed" version etched onto the base. The inscribed lines function as a memorial and an epitaph of their love affair. It will stand there forever, a monument to Acontius the master inscriber, a reminder of his desire and the power of his writing to fulfil itself. But the writer fulfils his goal only through the silencing of the memory of Cydippe. Her name appears neither on the base of the statue nor on the golden apple itself. Acontius' scripts have all entailed violence against his reader: she is coerced, deceived, entrapped, and

---

[67] Barchiesi (1993) 355 perceptively suggests an allusion to Ovid's Callimachean model in the "causa" (*Aitia*) of *Her.* 20.238.

finally here erased. While his initial epistolary trick depended on the voice of the reader as a necessary supplement to his writing, once his power is unleashed, the writer can dispose of the specific reader and attract a wider audience, the universal readership of which we are a part. The question remains whether we, too, are victims or beneficiaries of Acontius' tale. It is only by reading these narratives self-consciously as epistolary that we can appreciate the dangers and delights of such "discourses of desire."

In this chapter, we have considered three disparate authors' renditions of the same story, in which the epistolary device takes the form of an inscribed apple. The apple in antiquity, I argued, is able to convey an erotic message even without bearing an inscription, but here Acontius personalizes the message by writing his own words on its surface. Callimachus presents the inscribed apple as an embedded letter in a larger verse narrative. Ovid develops the epistolary device further so that epistolarity comes to define his narrative's very form, and Aristaenetus imitates Ovid's stylistic innovation. As we turn to the next section of the book, exploring letters in prose narrative fictions and the Greek epistolary novel, the two approaches to using letters embodied by Callimachus and Ovid remain constant: authors choose either to insert letters into a larger prose narrative, or to structure the entire narrative around an epistolary format. The novel writers of the late Hellenistic and imperial periods, as was the case with Callimachus, will be shown to be deeply indebted to Homer's connection of letter writing with deception and *eros*; but their skill in narration, and their assumptions of sophistication on the part of their readers, take us into a world far from the plains of Troy.

III

The epistolary novel

CHAPTER 6

Embedded letters in the Greek novel

Le roman par lettres suppose toujours plus de sentiments que
de faits; jamais les anciens n'auroient imaginé de donner
cette form à leurs fictions.

Madame de Staël, *De l'Allemagne*[1]

... cette littérature du cardiogramme

J. Rousset, *Forme et Signification*[2]

Sometime in the mid-second century CE, the satirical writer Lucian
of Samosata in Roman Syria wrote a novella in Greek called *A
True Story* (*Vera Historia*), a tale of travels beyond the ends of the
earth. At one point in his adventures, the first-person narrator is
hosted by Odysseus and Penelope on the Isle of the Blessed (*Ver.
Hist.* 2.29). Odysseus secretly slips him a sealed letter and asks
him to take it to Calypso, still living in happy immortality on her
island. The traveler-turned-courier sets sail for Ogygia, but opens
and reads Calypso's letter before reaching his destination. We are
simply told that he opened the letter before delivering it, but are
given no specific reason for this action.

I would argue that the association of letters and erotic treachery, especially in the context of a married man writing to his mistress, is so strong that Lucian does not need to give an explicit
reason in order for his actions to be understood. The narrator
presumably recalls the example of Homer's Bellerophon and worries about his own fate at the hands of his hostess. Lucian playfully
rewrites Homer here. The famously uxorious Odysseus deceives
his unsuspecting wife with a "special delivery," but acts without
malice towards the courier; the courier, in contrast, may dwell on
Odysseus' epic reputation for many wiles, and suspect him of

---

[1] Madame de Staël, *De l'Allemagne*, part 2, chapter 28, "Des Romans."
[2] J. Rousset, *Forme et Signification* (Paris 1962) 78.

malice towards his fellow man; what he does not suspect is Odysseus' actual secret plot: to abandon Penelope, if he gets the chance, and return to Calypso. As it turns out, when the narrator opens the letter and quotes part of it for the sake of his own audience (i.e. the external reader), the letter is what it appears to be and no more: a love letter with a footnote, namely the hoped-for request for hospitality (*Ver. Hist.* 2.35):[3]

After three days we put in at Ogygia and landed, but first I opened Odysseus' letter. It read as follows.
Dear Calypso,
    This is to let you know what happened to me. As soon as I sailed away from you in the raft I built, I was shipwrecked. Thanks to Leucothea, I just managed to get ashore in Phaeacia. The Phaeacians sent me home, and I caught a lot of men trying to win my wife and having the time of their lives in my house; but I killed them all. Later, I was murdered by Telegonus, my son by Circe; now I am on the Island of the Blest, and very sorry that I left my life with you and the immortality you offered me. So if I get a chance, I'll slip away and come to you.
                                                    Odysseus
In addition to this, the letter said that we were to be entertained.

The letter's interception by the narrator allows us to peek at the private lives of characters we have come to know in a more heroic and less intimate context in Homeric epic. We read that Odysseus now regrets his decision to abandon Calypso and her offer of immortality, and promises to run away and join her the minute Penelope's back is turned. Lucian's narrator, relieved that the letter says nothing about his own fate but rather requests Calypso's hospitality, reseals the document and delivers it safely to its addressee. He becomes an epistolary go-between in this post-Homeric revisionist adventure among somewhat tarnished heroes and heroines. And we, the external readers, are treated to yet another chapter in Odysseus' wanderings. Homer represented Odysseus recounting his life story to Penelope upon his return, with the future obscurely foreshadowed in Teiresias' prophecy. Now, in Lucian's narrative, Odysseus can tell a still fuller story, including his adventures after death.

---

[3] For the novels quoted in this chapter, I use the translations of B. P. Reardon, *Collected Ancient Greek Novels* (Berkeley 1989). For this passage, see Reardon (1989) 645. For individual Greek texts, see ad loc. For Lucian, see M. D. Macleod, ed., *Luciani Opera* (Oxford 1872–87) vol. I.

Lucian's example shows what rich epistolary material emerges when we admit the category of "embedded letters" into our treatment of the genre.[4] We will see in the following chapters that a wholly epistolary novel is a relative rarity in ancient Greek literature: at most, we can point to *Chion of Heraclea*, the lost epistolary nucleus of the *Alexander Romance*, and perhaps a few of the pseudonymous collections. But if the category is expanded to admit novels which include some epistolary sections within their larger narrative framework, a larger corpus takes shape. Embedded letters turn up in a majority of the Greek novels that have survived complete, and in several of the fragments.[5] Letters play a small role in Xenophon's *Ephesian Tale* and the anonymous *Story of Apollonius King of Tyre*, as well as in the fragmentary *The Wonders Beyond Thule*, by Antonius Diogenes, and in Iamblichus' *Babyloniaka*, all of which we will discuss briefly below. In three other works, embedded letters are crucial to the workings of the plot: Chariton's *Chaereas and Callirhoe*, Achilles Tatius' *Leucippe and Clitophon*, and Heliodorus' *Ethiopian Story*; these three works will be considered in detail in this chapter.

If we accept an approximate date of the late first to early third century CE for the composition of most of these novels, we can read them against the background of the Second Sophistic, a time of renewed interest in rhetoric and the classical canon.[6] Later, in the last section of this book, I will turn to the free-standing epistolary collections of this period. The authors of the Second Sophistic were steeped in the literary traditions of an earlier age, and viewed themselves as heirs to a great intellectual and artistic culture. Their responses combined emulation with lively invention. In this and the following three chapters, I approach the novels as the products of sophisticated writers who are fascinated by writing itself, and its role in communication; their fascination is manifest

---

[4] Lucian also incorporated letters elsewhere in his works. His *Nigrinus* purports to be the record of a conversation between Lucian and the (possibly invented) Platonic philosopher Nigrinus. The conversation is framed by a dialogue and the entire work introduced by a letter, which opens in correct epistolary fashion "Lucian to Nigrinus, greetings" (εὖ πράττειν), and closes equally correctly with a conventional farewell (ἔρρωσο). See also Lucian's *How To Write History*, ostensibly a letter to Philo, and *Passing of Peregrinus*, which begins "Best wishes (εὖ πράττειν) from Lucian to Cronius."

[5] For a brief discussion of letters in the novels, see Koskenniemi (1956) 180–86.

[6] My comments agree with the chronology presented by E. L. Bowie, "The Readership of Greek Novels in the Ancient World," in J. Tatum, ed., *The Search for the Ancient Novel* (Baltimore 1994) 442–43.

in allusion, plot structure (including embedded stories and multiple narrators), and variation in narrative voice (e.g. in epistolary passages). This chapter will address the role of the explicitly epistolary passages and their function in guiding and misguiding both internal and external readers.

There is much scholarly debate about the readership of the ancient novel: its social class, gender, and level of literacy.[7] But whether or not the external audience was envisioned as literate, the internal audiences of most of the novels (with Longus' *Daphnis and Chloe* as an obvious exception[8]) spend a good deal of time engaged in literate activities: viewing inscriptions, sending and receiving letters, and interpreting the texts of oracles. The ability to read and write appears to be a requisite trait of the heroes and heroines, along with beauty and noble descent. We should not be surprised, then, at the abundance of letter types found in the narratives: declarations of mutual love, letters of seduction, military dispatches, ambassadorial messages, revelations of genealogy, farewell letters, death sentences, even an epistolary marriage proposal.[9] What may be of greater interest for this study than the sheer number of types is the way in which letters exemplify and illustrate a whole culture of writing in the novel.

There have been some superb narratological studies done in the last decade on the ancient novel, from J. Winkler's groundbreaking work on Apuleius to S. Bartsch's "decoding" of Heliodorus and Achilles Tatius, and the bibliography continues to expand.[10]

---

[7] See e.g. T. Hägg, *The Novel in Antiquity* (Oxford 1983) 81–108; B. Wesseling, "The Audience of the Ancient Novels," in H. Hofmann, ed., *Groningen Colloquia on the Novel*, vol. 1 (Groningen, 1988) 67–79; S. A. Stephens, "Who Read Ancient Novels?," in Tatum (1994) 405–418; Bowie (1994) 435–59. Looking at the characters of the novel, B. Egger, "Women and Marriage in the Greek Novels," in Tatum (1994) 264, notes that the "main female characters read and write as a matter of course, and with ease."

[8] The narrator of *Daphnis and Chloe* does inform the reader, however, that the children have been taught their alphabet (1.8.1); the lack of literate activity in the story has more to do with the general environment of innocence and rusticity than actual intellectual ability.

[9] B. Egger, "Zu den Frauenrollen im griechischen Roman. Die Frau als Heldin und Leserin," in Hofmann (1988) 43, underestimates the role(s) of letters in the novel when she states "Liebes-, Erkennungs-, Abschiedsbriefe werden im Aktionsroman nur verfasst und gelesen, um das Geschehen weiter zu treiben oder psychologische Einsichten zu vermitteln." But her comment does point out the inherent tension between static, descriptive, or informational letters and the novel of action; the category of kinetic letters, however, i.e. those which bring about action, dissolves that tension.

[10] J. J. Winkler, *Auctor et Actor: A Narratological Reading of Apuleius' Golden Ass* (Berkeley 1985; S. Bartsch, *Decoding the Ancient Novel: The Reader and The Role of Description in Heliodorus and Achilles Tatius* (Princeton 1989).

But no one has yet fully considered the implications of embedded letters as narrative devices in the ancient novel. Given the standard outline of the romantic novel, in which the lovers are separated during various trials and tribulations, the letter is a logical method of communication between the lovers themselves (if they know where their beloveds are at any given time) and those who either help or hinder their eventual reunion. But beyond the basic verisimilitude of a hero or heroine writing to an absent beloved, or a villain taking advantage of the beloved's absence to forge a letter, letters in the novel often provide a central impetus for movement in the narrative, in a genre that is characterized above all by action, movement, and revelation. The ancient novel, as we will see below, uses the embedded letter both as a kind of "littérature du cardiogramme," and also kinetically, as a prime instigator of action.

CHAEREAS AND CALLIRHOE

Chariton's *Chaereas and Callirhoe* has been acclaimed as the earliest extant work of Greek prose fiction, with an approximate date of the mid-first century CE.[11] Chariton sets his story in the fourth century BCE, and begins with an invaluable piece of information, as the author introduces himself: "My name is Chariton, of Aphrodisias, and I am clerk to the attorney Athenagoras. I am going to tell you the story of a love affair that took place in Syracuse" (1.1).[12]

The narrator here is imitating the mannerisms of the early historians who introduce themselves by name at the start of their enterprise: Hecataeus, writing in the mid-sixth to early fifth centuries BCE, is the first historian we have who puts his name to his work,

---

[11] Reardon (1989) 17. Evidence for Chariton's date is summarized in K. Plepelits, *Chariton von Aphrodisias: Kallirhoe* (Stuttgart 1976) 4–9.

[12] Critics assume that the novel itself does not begin until after this authorial declaration. See Reardon (1989) 17. Reardon also discusses narrative structure in "Theme, Structure, and Narrative in Chariton," *YCS* 27 (1982) 1–27, but does not mention the embedded letters. While I would question the assumption that the first two lines represent "fact" and the rest of the novel is "fiction," as if there were some sort of dividing line between the first- and third-person narration, and as if the "prologue" were not open to the same scrutiny as the rest of the work, I am more intrigued by the nature of the information the narrator chooses to reveal about himself. For the text of Chariton, see G. P. Goold, ed., *Chariton: Callirhoe* (Cambridge MA 1995).

while in the fifth century, Herodotus' name appears prominently as the first word of his *Histories*. Chariton represents himself as a clerk or secretary, in other words a person who makes his living by writing; the implication for the reader must be that he – the author or his persona – possesses both a wide knowledge of literature and a strong interest in forms of writing, including letters. No other novel begins with a purportedly authentic autobiographical note, a *sphragis* as it were. Achilles Tatius and Longus, by contrast, situate their tales within conversations between an unnamed *ego* (the narrator) and a stranger who meet in front of a temple painting, while Heliodorus and Xenophon open *in medias res* in the third person.[13] Heliodorus provides his autobiographical statement at the end of the novel (10.41 "So concludes the *Aithiopika*, the story of Theagenes and Charikleia, the work of a Phoenician from the city of Emesa, one of the clan of Descendants of the Sun, Theodosios' son, Heliodoros"), but to my mind the statement of authorship at the end of the work does not have the same impact as Chariton's initial claim. The assertion at the beginning is meant to control and direct our reading in a particular way; the concluding identification does not influence our reading unless we reread. The introduction of a literate, professional writer as the source for *Chaereas and Callirhoe* suggests that the author was trying to ally himself with historians, to justify the "truth" of his story by stating his credentials. But paradoxically, his words undermine his sincerity: who better than a professional writer, presumably someone who, day after day, writes uniform, highly conventional letters and documents for his employer, to experiment in his spare time with different narrative forms and fictional voices? The letters he creates in his novel, full of adventure, are of a nature wholly different from the ones he is paid to produce in his official capacity as a legal secretary.

Let us now look more closely at the story itself, and its use of letters as a narrative device. A great deal of action occurs before the first embedded letter, which appears almost halfway through the eight books. At the beginning of book 4, the married couple Chaereas and Callirhoe have been separated, each believing the

---

[13] J. J. Winkler, "The Mendacity of Kalasiris and the Narrative Strategy of Heliodorus' *Aithiopika*," *YCS* 27 (1982) 157, note 64, comments on the stylistic flourish of Heliodorus' "signature," far from a straightforward declaration of identity.

other dead, and Callirhoe, pregnant with Chareas' child, has been sold to Dionysius, the wealthiest man in Miletus, who wishes to marry her. Chaereas discovers she is still alive and seeks to contact her. But his letter to his wife becomes entangled in an elaborate web of love, confusion, and legal bureaucracy. The letter will completely change the direction of the narrative, although ironically Callirhoe herself will never actually receive the message: she will "read" the letter only once it is brought forward as evidence in a climactic courtroom scene. Precisely because the letter is read by almost all the novel's main characters *except* its intended addressee, it functions as the central engine of the second half of the novel, the impetus for all the action that follows.

When Chaereas is determined to confront his wife in person, his friend Mithridates, the governor of Caria, convinces him that, since love is a tricky business, it might be better to "try the woman out first by letter." He advises manipulation: "make her grieve, make her rejoice; make her search for you and call you to her" (4.4.5).

Chaereas' letter opens simply, with "From Chaereas to Callirhoe. I am alive ..." (4.4.7). Another reader might object that he is obviously alive if he has written the letter in question, but Chaereas addresses this letter solely to Callirhoe, who has assumed that he has been dead for some time. He anticipates his wife's reaction; his opening words answer her expected response ("but I thought you were dead!") before the words can even leave her mouth. His "I am alive" asks her to believe that the letter is not forged, and that he will present himself if she allows it. The letter also asks her to remember their love (4.4.8–10):

Death I expected – I am human; but I never thought to find you married. Change your mind, I beseech you – this letter of mine is drenched with the libation of my tears and kisses! I am your Chaereas – that Chaereas you saw when you went to Aphrodite's temple as a virgin, that Chaereas who caused you sleepless nights! Remember our bridal chamber ... You will say I showed jealousy. That is the mark of a man who loves you. Do not harbor malice against me ... Oh, if you should still remember me, my sufferings are nothing; but if you are minded otherwise, you will be passing sentence of death on me!

Chaereas seeks to regain his wife's heart by revealing his own, and the misery he experienced in solitude is represented in the letter as a physical mark of his emotional state. The tears and kisses on the page, however conventional or histrionic they may seem to us, are meant to convince her of his sincerity. Chaereas imagines how she might respond, and offers a rhetorically effective counter-argument: "jealousy" in her language means "love" in his. He hopes to cancel out their unhappiness with the vivid memories of their initial bliss. He closes with two alternatives: on the positive side, he hopes for a return letter expressing her love for him; but if she answers in the negative, or not at all, he is resolved to die (and write no more). Epistolary writing and responding are connected with all that is positive: mutual love and the continuation of a happy life together. Ironically, their happy reunion will obviate the necessity for further letter writing.

The letter for Callirhoe is entrusted to Hyginus, a servant of Mithridates, for delivery. But the epistolary adventure is just beginning. Mithridates, himself in love with Callirhoe, plans to use Chaereas as bait to attract her. So he, too, writes a letter to Callirhoe, deviously expressing goodwill, and promising to arrange the couple's reunion. Thinking to persuade her more easily, he sends along slaves with expensive gifts and gold, but in order to avoid suspicion, he tells them that all is destined for Dionysius. He confides the truth only to Hyginus, whom he orders to proceed carefully to Miletus, reconnoitering alone and in disguise, until he feels it is safe to bring along the rest of the group. So far, we have been informed of two letters to Callirhoe: one written in sincerity by Chaereas, begging her to leave Dionysius, and the other written by Mithridates with the same goal in mind, but out of self-interest and with intent to deceive.

Unforeseen circumstances prevent both letters from arriving at their intended destination, and Mithridates' attempt to avoid suspicion by "addressing" the whole entourage to Dionysius only complicates matters further. The slaves, caught in Hyginus' absence spending the money with which they were entrusted, are compelled to hand over the gifts and letters to a local magistrate, who forwards them, still sealed, along with a cover letter of his own, straight to Dionysius. Thus the false command and addressee are taken to be genuine by the interceptor of the letter (the magistrate), who thinks he is putting things right, when in fact he is setting the scene for an entirely unexpected reading by yet another interceptor or unintended reader (Dionysius). By this point, we are impatiently waiting for Dionysius' response to the intercepted letters; the author keeps us in suspense a moment longer, though, by reporting the full text of the magistrate's cover letter, a short factual description of his recovery of the booty (4.5.8). The unsuspecting Dionysius reads this letter at a public dinner, and assumes that the accompanying letters will also reflect the obedience of his subject Mithridates. In his eyes, the cover letter becomes the main letter, the text that presumably sets the tone for the two to follow. Accordingly, in great spirits, he orders the seals to be broken and begins to read.

He reads the letter from Chaereas first, and when he sees the words "From Chaereas to Callirhoe. I am alive," he faints. "But even as he fainted, he kept hold of the letters – he was afraid someone else might read them" (4.5.9). As he rereads the letters in private, he is gripped by emotions as strong as those Mithridates had predicted Callirhoe would feel upon reading Chaereas' letter: "anger, despair, fear, disbelief" (4.5.10). But after his dramatic initial response to Chaereas' opening line, Dionysius refuses to believe that his chief rival still lives; instead, he concludes that Mithridates has forged the one letter and lied in the other, in order to advance his own adulterous interests in Callirhoe and have her sent to him on the pretense of meeting Chaereas. While Dionysius, the unintended recipient, sees through the deceit of Mithridates' letter and unearths the truth of his subject's erotic obsession, he misinterprets Chaereas' true letter as a forgery. In other words, because the wrong person reads and constructs meaning, the truth value of each letter is temporarily reversed. The deceitful letter begins to mean something else when read side-by-side with the true one, especially since Dionysius assumes that the same man was the author of both.

Chaereas' love letter at this point is buried even deeper in layers of bureaucracy. Perhaps aware that he cannot be objective in this matter, Dionysius shows all the letters to his friend Pharnaces, governor of Lydia and Ionia, and begs his assistance. Chaereas' letter, originally intended for Callirhoe's eyes only, has now been read successively by Mithridates, Dionysius, and Pharnaces, and will eventually become a critical piece of evidence in a public trial. But first Pharnaces, acting as a mediator, writes a "confidential" letter (4.6.3–4) to King Artaxerxes of Persia, informing him of Mithridates' seduction plans; his letter is a good example of a message to a superior, obsequious in tone and subtly hinting that the king should take action lest the misbehavior of a minor local official discredit the whole government. Chaereas' original love letter has now been completely overshadowed and politicized by the convoluted epistolary machinery of the Persian empire and its bureaucracy. After the king reads the letter aloud to his friends and ponders with them a plan of action, he decides to settle the matter in court, and summons, in writing, both Pharnaces (on behalf of Dionysius and Callirhoe) and Mithridates.[14] Mithridates feels himself "betrayed by the letters" (4.7.1), as if the letters had a life of their own; Dionysius begins to wish he had never shown Pharnaces the letters in question, but had kept them to himself as instinct had first dictated. But the affair has grown beyond the confines of the original personal message from a husband to his wife, and the participants have no choice but to obey the command of their ruler.

The scene in book 5 now shifts to a courtroom in the Persian capital.[15] Pharnaces' letter and the king's response are read aloud so that the people can understand how the matter came to court (5.4.8). In addition, the king's letter is used to provide a rationale for calling Callirhoe as a material witness; an unspoken reason for her presence, of course, is that every participant in the case is desperately eager to view her famed beauty, including Artaxerxes himself. When all are finally assembled, Dionysius formally accuses Mithridates of forgery ("when Mithridates wants to commit adultery, he resuscitates the dead!"), explaining how the letters came into his hands by mistake (5.6.1–10).[16] He closes by giving Chaereas' letter to an official to read aloud to the court, following standard legal procedure with which Chariton would no doubt have been familiar. But while the reading does not appear in the

[14] Dionysius is shown reading the letter out loud to his friends and requesting their opinions on the issue; he is sensitive enough to their influence that when opinions prove to be evenly balanced, he makes no decision that day. This democratic behavior contradicts the usual portrayal of tyrants analyzed by Steiner (1994), discussed previously.

[15] Letters are mentioned twice in the narrative before the trial begins: 5.2.3, when Mithridates explains to Chaereas the situation brought about by the interception of their letters, and 5.4.3, when Dionysius trusts in the supposedly "forged" letter for an inevitable legal victory.

[16] Dionysius emphasizes the depravity of a man who capitalizes on another's death to achieve his ends: "what a shameless adulterer it is who even tells lies about a dead man" (5.6.10). The outrage lies in the fact that a dead man cannot defend himself in court.

narrative (after all, we already know the contents of the letter), Dionysius does repeat the opening line, omitting Callirhoe's name: "From Chaereas ... I am alive." He puts great emphasis on the patent absurdity of this line, the same line which caused him to faint at first reading; we may assume that his tone is now scornful, as he tries to persuade the court that the letter was written by Mithridates in Chaereas' voice. It may be a testament to Dionysius' basically good character that he censors the opening line in order to save the respectable Callirhoe the embarrassment of hearing her name spoken in public; the addressee is genuine, even if the sender is supposedly a mask for Mithridates, so there is nothing to be gained by stating her name. But his attempt at shielding his wife from public display is pathetic rather than effective, since the letter has already forced her to come in person, to open herself to scrutiny by all.

Mithridates responds to Dionysius' accusations by producing Chaereas, the real writer of the letter, and the court falls into an uproar at the unusual turn of events. The letters cease to play an active role in the narrative as all the participants confront each other in person. But Dionysius finally acknowledges the power that the letters had in setting off a chain of unexpected actions and reactions, and he wishes that he had stopped the affair before it began. He addresses himself (6.2.5–6):

"Miserable wretch," he said, "you will have to put up with this disaster – it is your own fault, it is you who are responsible for it happening. You could have kept Callirhoe even though Chaereas was alive. You were master in Miletus – the letter would never even have reached Callirhoe against your will."

If he had not shown the letter to Pharnaces, no one would have been the wiser, and he and his wife would still be living happily at home in Miletus. But his insistent misreading of Chaereas' letter has had exactly the opposite effect of the one he intended: since Callirhoe was in the courtroom, she too could "read" the letter during the public hearing, and its contents are now impossible to ignore. So in the end, Chaereas' letter has reached its intended addressee, and she believes wholeheartedly that he is indeed alive. The question that remains, however, is to which husband she will be loyal.

In yet another twist, a revolt in Egypt puts an end to the deliberations as the entire Babylonian court sets off on campaign. Chaereas sides with the pharaoh, and succeeds in winning Callirhoe back from Artaxerxes in battle. Loose ends are tied up by means of two letters, one from Chaereas to King Artaxerxes, and another from Callirhoe to Dionysius. In the first letter, Chaereas announces that as victor, he has magnanimously agreed to Callirhoe's request that he return Artaxerxes' captured wife unharmed. In response he asks that the king pardon all those Egyptians who chose to fight on Chaereas' side in the war. The letter is official, a military dispatch to a conquered enemy, establishing the terms for peace. Its tone is impersonal, except for one small dig at the king's lack of interest in his own wife (8.4.3 "I am restoring Statira to you rapidly, though you have not even asked for her return"), and his insistence that Callirhoe is responsible for his kind deed.

Callirhoe's letter, however, is another matter altogether. Even before we read her words, the way in which she writes and sends her message arouses suspicion. "This was the only thing she did independently of Chaereas; knowing his jealous nature, she was anxious to prevent him learning of it" (8.4.4). Since it was Chaereas' jealous nature that separated the lovers to begin with, it is not surprising that Callirhoe decides not to inform him of her actions here. After writing the letter, she seals it and hides it in a fold of her dress; then, as Artaxerxes' wife leaves to return to Babylon, Callirhoe secretly hands her the letter for Dionysius, blushing as she asks that it be delivered to her former husband. Callirhoe's blush may be interpreted in several ways. It may reveal feelings of guilt, either towards Chaereas, since she acts without his knowledge, or towards Dionysius, whom she abandons; it may also reveal a sense of shame in front of her courier, Artaxerxes' wife, who might suspect the secret letter of harboring words of passion, improper now that Callirhoe has been reunited with her first husband. All letters are "secret," of course, but the blush may hint that this letter is doubly so. Or perhaps the blush is a more straightforward acknowledgment that simply writing the letter is a bold act under these circumstances, no matter what its actual contents are. Perhaps the letter itself may give us some clues to Callirhoe's state of mind (8.4.5).

From Callirhoe: greetings (χαίρειν) to Dionysius, my benefactor (εὐερ-
γέτῃ) ... Please do not be angry. I am with you in spirit through the son
we share; I entrust him to you to bring up and educate in a way worthy
of us ... Do not let him learn what a stepmother is like ... this letter is
written in my own hand. Fare you well (ἔρρωσο), good Dionysius, and
remember your Callirhoe.

The first line already says it all: Callirhoe no longer addresses
him as husband, but as benefactor, a title appropriate to the man
who had freed her from pirates and slavery. She has dismissed
words of love in favor of those of friendship, respect, and gratitude.[17] But she is still concerned about his reaction: she imagines
how he will feel when he reads her letter, and begs him not to be
angry. She directs his attention to their son as a reminder of their
shared love, but actually her words are a continuation of the lie
she told when she married him to protect Chaereas' child. Her
goal for her son is eventual marriage to Dionysius' daughter from
a previous wife, an obvious substitute for their own failed union.
She goes on to request that Dionysius never remarry, which condemns him to be faithful to her always without actually possessing
her. The last line is meant to ring in his ears forever: "remember
your Callirhoe" (καὶ Καλλιρόης μνημόνευε τῆς σῆς), with the possessive adjective a final irony in this impossible love triangle. Callirhoe writes to Dionysius that he must let her go in body but
remain hers in spirit; Chariton uses her letter to reinscribe the
love affair, to reinforce the eternal triangle.[18] This is the remarkable power of the letter, which can be reread and reexperienced
by the addressee for years thereafter.

Dionysius will keep her last letter, written in her own hand, a
small comfort in the days to come. Her explicit reference to her
own handwriting is understandable in the context of forgery that
has defined the entire episode, and also reflects common practice
of differentiating between letters written by secretaries and those
written by the sender herself. When the queen gives it to Dionysius, as surreptitiously as she herself had received it, he immediately recognizes the handwriting, kisses the tablet, opens it and
clasps it to his breast "as if it were Callirhoe present in the flesh"

---

[17] See D. Konstan, *Friendship in the Classical World* (Cambridge 1997).
[18] See M. Fusillo, *La Naissance du Roman* (Paris 1991) 93.

(8.5.13). His reading is delayed by copious tears and repeated kissing of Callirhoe's name in the opening address.[19] At this point he still assumes that the letter he holds in his hands is a love letter, from his devoted wife who has been stolen from him; the audience, however, knows better.

Once Dionysius opens the letter, he notices the changed address at once, and realizes that he has lost the title "husband" in her eyes. But he is still so much in love that he eagerly misreads her pleas for a spiritual fidelity, and concludes that she left him unwillingly, forced by Chaereas. Callirhoe has carefully constructed her letter to preserve this illusion for him: she calls herself "his" Callirhoe, begs him to remember her always, and avoids all mention of Chaereas. Dionysius would have had no trouble at all interpreting Callirhoe's suggestive blush: she loves him still and blushes for her "spiritual infidelity" to her newly found first husband. But the narrator's cynicism suggests otherwise to the external reader (8.5.14): "love is such an irresponsible thing and can easily persuade a lover that he is loved in return." With this bit of self-delusion, Dionysius finds the strength to return with "his" child to Miletus, where he finds consolation in the many statues of his beloved set up around the city. Letter and statues both offer a physical reminder of the body that is lost to him forever.[20]

Callirhoe's letter attempts to bring closure to a series of events that began with Chaereas' letter announcing that he was still alive. Chaereas' letter immediately went astray, was seen by various unintended readers (Mithridates, Dionysius, Pharnaces), and reached its intended audience only in the courtroom scene in Babylon, when it was read aloud to all present, including the Persian King; the letter's travels mimic Callirhoe's own wanderings, as she falls into the hands of various men who desire to keep her. Callirhoe's letter, however, reaches its addressee directly, and is read and reread by one man alone. Both Chaereas' letter and Callirhoe's are read "incorrectly" by Dionysius; his misreadings frame the narra-

---

[19] While the novel creates pathos in the depiction of Dionysius' actions, and we may find them exaggerated or melodramatic, such behavior is entirely believable in the context of the reception of a letter from a loved one. Koskenniemi (1956) 182–83, offers parallels for this behavior from other novels as well as from actual papyrus letters.

[20] The reader may be reminded of the similar circumstances in Euripides' *Alcestis*, when Alcestis begs Admetus not to remarry after her death, and he promises to devote the rest of his life to the worship of a statue made in her image.

tive, first spurring on and then concluding the action. Dionysius misinterprets Chaereas' message because he refuses to believe that his rival is still alive; he misinterprets Callirhoe's feelings expressed in her final letter because he refuses to believe that she has stopped loving him. Both misreadings, one of self-deception and the other of self-preservation, show the power of a letter to set off a series of unpredicted actions and reactions. In the novel to be discussed next, one letter initially drives the romantic plot forward, but it is curiously an *unread* letter that allows it to continue as long as it does.

LEUCIPPE AND CLITOPHON

In Chariton's novel, letters did not appear until half the story had already been told. By contrast, in Achilles Tatius' *Leucippe and Clitophon*, a letter sets the plot in motion.[21] The novel opens, after an editor's preface, in the first-person voice of the hero, as Clitophon reports a message arriving for his father Hippias in Tyre, announcing that Hippias' half-brother Sostratos in Byzantium was sending his wife and daughter to them for safekeeping during a time of war (1.3.6).

Sostratos to his brother Hippias:
Greetings! This is to announce the arrival of my daughter Leukippe and Pantheia, my wife … Protect my dear family until the fortunes of war are decided.

Hippias rushes down to the newly arrived boat in the harbor to escort the women, providing Clitophon with a first glimpse of his cousin, the divinely beautiful Leucippe.

The letter itself is not critical at this early stage in the narrative; we could have received the same information from an oral message, or from a narrated discussion between Hippias and Clitophon. But the epistolary form serves multiple purposes beyond the basic transmission of data: it breaks up the first-person narrative, thus varying the pace and shape of the story; it allows Clitophon

---

[21] In the introduction to his translation in the Reardon collection, Winkler argues for the third quarter of the second century CE as the date of composition for Achilles Tatius' novel; based on the number of papyri known from the second to the fourth century, his claim is that *Leucippe and Clitophon* was one of the most popular Greek novels in Greco-Roman Egypt. See Reardon (1989) 170–71. The Greek text is that of S. Gaselee, ed., *Achilles Tatius* (Cambridge MA 1947).

to record information that was not meant specifically for his eyes but was either learned by accident or gathered second-hand; and, in reflecting a likely event under the circumstances (i.e. it would be likely that Sostratos would send a letter with his family explaining his actions to their benefactors), it adds a touch of "realism" to the plot. Embedded letters, set off by some conventional editorial feature ("read as follows," quotation marks, or indentation), have a certain documentary value. Direct quotation endows them with a separate identity, a staying power beyond the confines of the rest of Clitophon's narrative.

In this case, the letter does more than announce an arrival: it introduces all the central characters by name and relationship. Surely Hippias does not need to be told that Sostratos is his brother, Leucippe his niece, or Pantheia his sister-in-law. The labels "brother," "daughter," and "wife" are there for the sake of the external reader, who wishes to understand the extended family relationships, and for whom the letter acts as a sort of prologue. The letter provides information already known to its addressee but necessary for the wider reading public. There are other ways to achieve this; in the first paragraph of 1.3, Clitophon goes into elaborate detail about his immediate family background for the benefit of his internal audience, the unnamed "I" of 1.1–2, whom he meets in front of a votive painting in Sidon. But once the action begins, a letter, with the pertinent information thrown in almost as asides, is more dramatic and concise than a sketch of the family tree.

One letter begins the action; the second could have resolved all happily, but that letter, unfortunately for the victims involved, arrives too late. Clitophon and Leucippe fall in love, but thinking that their parents will never agree to the match, they set sail for Alexandria (2.31). After various disasters, including Leucippe's apparent murder at the hands of pirates (5.7), Clitophon's cousin Kleinias catches up with him and reports on a letter that Hippias received the day after their elopement. Hippias returned from a short trip to find a letter waiting for him in which Sostratos offered Leucippe in marriage to Clitophon.[22] Kleinias describes Hippias' reaction to the letter (5.10.3–4):

---

[22] Egger (1988) 58, notes that the epistolary engagement is effected "in absentia," representing an agreement between the two fathers.

He was in a pretty pickle when he read this letter and heard of your flight, vexed to lose this happy match and that Fortune had let it come so close. For none of this would have happened if only the mail had come a little quicker.

Sostratos' letter could have prevented all the misadventures that the lovers have encountered so far, and the three books of wanderings yet to come; in fact, we are informed that the whole novel exists only because the mail between Byzantium and Tyre was slow, and because the addressee happened to be out of town. But of course all letter writing is predicated on absence, and the inopportune absence of the addressee in this case is just a variation on the convention of absence as the requirement for writing in the first place. Both of Sostratos' letters thus effect similar results: one starts the story and the other ensures that it will continue.[23]

Clitophon mistakenly believes he has seen Leucippe decapitated by pirates, and in despair he agrees to marry Melite, a rich Ephesian widow (5.12.2–3). Just as Clitophon arrives on Melite's estate, a slave hands him a letter in secret, and before Clitophon can read even a single sentence, he recognizes the handwriting as Leucippe's. The recognition of handwriting, as we saw also in the case of Callirhoe's letter to Dionysius, creates a moment of intense emotion for the addressee: the simple fact of a letter from the beloved may mean more than the letter's contents. For us as external readers, however, there is an additional appeal: the novel is narrated by its male protagonist Clitophon, and only here, with presumably *verbatim* quotation of Leucippe's letter as we read over Clitophon's shoulder, are we allowed to hear the woman's voice directly.[24]

To return to Clitophon's reaction, the familiar handwriting of the opening address informs him that his beloved is alive, and the actual words provide only further details and explanations. The immediate impact comes from the handwriting, which is all the more easily recognized because ancient epistolary convention

---

[23] I have omitted from the discussion the report of a letter from the governor of Egypt to the general of the army that has rescued the lovers (4.11.1); Clitophon guesses that the letter must have contained directions to proceed with the campaign against local brigands, for the general immediately gives orders for battle.

[24] This is pointed out by Fusillo (1991) 92.

places the writer's name at the beginning rather than the end of the letter (5.18.3–6):[25]

From Leukippe to her master (τῷ δεσπότῃ μου) Kleitophon:
   It is "Master" I must call you, for you are my mistress's husband. You know well all that I have suffered for you, yet now I am obliged to refresh your memory. For your sake I left my mother and undertook a life of wandering. For your sake I went through shipwreck and captivity at the hands of pirates. For your sake ... But while I have struggled through one disaster after another, here are you, unsold, unlashed, now married. If there is any gratitude left in your heart for all the trials I have undergone for you, beg your wife to send me home as she promised. Lend me two thousand gold pieces ... Farewell (ἔρρωσο); be happy in your new marriage. I write this letter still a virgin.

Leucippe addresses Clitophon as "master" because he has married the woman who owns Leucippe as a slave. She uses the epistolary greeting as a way to redefine their relationship, and resigns herself to having lost him to another. But she does not release him that easily from his obligation to her, and reminds him of all she has suffered on his account. In Chariton, whenever the reader seemed on the brink of losing track of the complicated plot developments, the author provided a quick summary of previous events (e.g. 5.1; 8.1).[26] Achilles Tatius does the same in this letter, which reproaches Clitophon for not having protected Leucippe better. We are reminded of their initial flight, of shipwreck, capture by pirates, false deaths, enslavement, work in the fields, and finally lashings. She accuses him of being the source of all her troubles, but promises to disappear from his life forever if he will only set her free with enough money for passage back to Byzantium. The letter closes enigmatically: she wishes Clitophon well in his new

---

25 It may be pertinent to recall in this context the question Ovid's Sappho poses in her letter to Phaon, in which the addressee is expected to recognize Sappho's style and handwriting even before he reads her name (*Her.* 15.1–4): "When you saw these letters from my eager hand/ could your eye recognize the sender/ or did you fail to recognize their author/ until you could read my name, 'Sappho'?" (translation by H. Isbell, *Ovid: Heroides* [London, 1990] 133).

26 T. Hägg, *Narrative Technique in Ancient Greek Romances* (Stockholm, 1971) 332, argues for an oral performance of the novels, and interprets such moments of repetition or plot summary as points of rest for the reciter and listener, or pauses for the sake of clarity: "the frequent use of recapitulation in the romances of Chariton and Xenophon Ephesius reveals something about their 'Sitz im Leben', about the kind of audience these writers addressed themselves to." Bowie (1994) 440, questions the hypothesis of public reading by scribes, but endorses Reardon's suggestion (1982) 15, that there may have been "small reading circles" along with the more common individual acts of reading.

marriage, but informs him that she is still a virgin, effectively announcing her continuing desirability. On the one hand she acknowledges his choice of Melite, and on the other hand she teases
him with information that can only make him think of her as a
prospective bride.

Clitophon is indeed confused. His first reaction is one of conflicting emotions – wonder, doubt, joy, distress – and he asks the
messenger if the letter arrived from Hades, since his Leucippe is
surely dead (5.19.2). But once the situation has been explained,
and he recovers from the initial shock, he rereads more carefully
(5.19.5–7):

> Returning to the text, I scrutinized each word, as if seeing her through
> the letters. I said: "Your charges are all too true, my dearest. You suf-
> fered all for me. I caused you untold troubles." When I got to the part
> about the whips and tortures ... I wept as if I were witnessing them my-
> self. Thinking about it set my mind's eyes working on what the letter said
> and made the visible tangible. I flushed at her criticism of my marriage,
> like an adulterer caught in the act. The letter itself made me feel
> ashamed.

The act of rereading is unique to epistolary form. Having read
the letter through the first time purely for information, Clitophon
now searches for images, "as if seeing her through the letters." His
comments reflect the observations of ancient epistolary theorists
on the power of a letter to bring the writer and reader together, to
make the absent person present, and to reveal a part of the writer's soul.[27] Clitophon addresses the letter directly, as if he were
speaking to Leucippe herself, pleading guilty to all her charges.
He thinks he sees her in the words on the page, and the description of her mistreatment is so vivid that he imagines witnessing the
acts themselves. The letter does not just bring Leucippe to mind at
the moment of Clitophon's reading, but allows him to "see" what
has been happening to her since he left, to break geographical and
temporal constraints in such a way as to cancel out their separation. Her letter makes him present at her sufferings: the moment
of reading rewrites the past, as it will rewrite the future. The letter
transports Clitophon to the scene of Leucippe's torture, but Leucippe, in the guise of the letter, also seems suddenly present in

---

[27] See Koskenniemi (1956) 183–84. Seneca (*Ep.* 40.1) writes "how ... pleasant is a letter,
which brings us real traces, real evidence of an absent friend."

Clitophon's bedroom: although he has yet to consummate his new marriage, he flushes "like an adulterer caught in the act." The letter itself has the power to make him feel ashamed.

Clitophon is so upset by the letter that he despairs of being able to respond properly, but the messenger claims "Eros himself will supply your words" (5.20.4–5):

> Greetings to Leukippe, mistress of my heart!
> I languish in my luxury, noting the absence of your presence, visibly missing in the letters of your letter. If only you will wait for the truth to be told! Don't condemn me without a trial. You will learn that I have imitated your virginity, if that word has any meaning for men as it does for women . . .

His letter opens with a correction of Leucippe's own address. Leucippe must be assured that she, not Melite, is the true "mistress," and that all the wealth offered by his new marriage means nothing to him in her absence. His first reaction to her letter was that it brought with it such a strong image of Leucippe that he believed himself in her presence, and that she could also see him through her letter. But in his response, he emphasizes the negative impact, the physical reminder that she is in fact absent, that the letter replaces her bodily presence and frustrates his desire even more.[28] He focuses on her last words: just as she writes still a virgin, so he has also preserved his virtue. His remark that virtue may not mean the same thing for the two sexes foreshadows his eventual submission to Melite's lust, but at this point he can still write honestly that he and Leucippe are a perfect match. In closing, he begs her to give him a chance to prove his love and explain his actions.

The same messenger who brought Leucippe's letter to Clitophon now returns with his master's answer (5.21), and although we do not see Leucippe receiving or reacting to the letter, we know that she has read it by the next scene (5.22), when Melite, without knowing Leucippe's identity, begs her to help seduce Clitophon with magic herbs. But Leucippe's original letter, rather than Clitophon's answer, brings about the next crisis.

Clitophon has been carrying around Leucippe's letter since he received it, tied inside his cloak on a tassel, hiding it from Melite

---

[28] Thus Cicero (*Ad Att.* 11.4): "if only I might be face-to-face with you once rather than through letters."

(5.24.1). But beyond the obvious need to keep its contents secret from his new wife, the letter has taken on a talismanic property for Clitophon: he finds comfort in bodily contact with an object previously touched by his beloved.[29] In the absence of Leucippe herself, the letter represents her physical presence, and Clitophon thus protects her here just as he was unable to protect her in person during their separation. At an unexpected moment, the letter slips out of his clothing. Clitophon tells us that "Melite picked it up without being observed, for she was afraid that it was one of her letters to me" (5.24.1).[30] Here is a fascinating and somewhat perverse example of epistolary interception. The letter has already reached its proper destination, and has been read (and reread) by its intended addressee. Because Clitophon preserves the letter but then drops it, inadvertantly "sending" it out a second time, Melite has the opportunity to intercept it "without being observed" after it has arrived safely. Here the documentary status of the written message is drawn to the fore: an oral message would in this case have been safer, since more ephemeral.

The same letter is now read for the third time. We already know what information the letter contains, and by whom it is written, but Melite's heart skips a beat at the name of the woman whom she had so often heard spoken of as dead (5.24.2–3). As she reads on, Leucippe's detailed account of her sufferings, intended as a reproach for Clitophon, becomes a clarification of "the whole story" for Melite; the repetition of information familiar to us turns into "news" for this unintended reader. Melite is torn by conflicting emotions, just as Clitophon had felt both pain and joy, but she decides to confront Clitophon one last time with her love. She accosts him letter in hand (5.25.4), and he stands helpless before the incontrovertible physical evidence. In the end he gives in to her desires, having been promised in advance that she will help the lovers escape. Melite realizes that Clitophon still feels loyal to Leucippe, but she finds a way to make everyone happy: Clitophon surrenders his virginity to her, and is then reunited with his long lost love. The novel comes to a conclusion three books later, with no further letters.

---

[29] Thus Cicero (*Ad Fam.* 3.11.2): "I embraced you, absent, in my mind, but I really did kiss the letter."

[30] This is the first we hear of letters between Melite and Clitophon.

The letters embedded in the two novels we have discussed so far reveal a number of shared aspects and functions. Some aspects are familiar from earlier sections of this book: letters bridge the distance between separated individuals, allow the writer to say things which would be difficult to express in person, or use their very physicality for an effect. Many epistolary situations are not limited to the genre of the novel: letters everywhere are liable to be intercepted, delayed, misread. But the letter works especially well as a narrative device in the larger development of prose fiction; the genre's expansiveness offers a friendly environment for embedded letters. For example, the interception of a letter in a novel may appear arbitrary or disastrous at the time, but the letter turns out to be one element in an elaborate plan that gradually leads the hero and heroine back to each other. Letters can begin a chain of events at the start of the novel, or tie up loose ends at its conclusion. The scope of the novel allows multiple letters, and a wide variety of types.

Both Chariton and Achilles Tatius use letters in erotic situations: passionate letters between separated lovers, letters begging for a second chance, and letters ending love affairs. In particular, the letter is frequently at the center of love triangles. The hero writes to the heroine, but his letter is intercepted by a rival, and used fraudulently against him or his beloved. The letter can also be used as a device to expose such a triangle, or to choose between the two rivals: in Chariton's story, the person who receives the letter loses, because no letter is needed to communicate with the favored lover, who is already in his beloved's presence. The novel, with its strong element of romance and adventure, is an ideal host for the love letter.

Many of the texts we have considered thus far may remind us once more of the paradigmatic letter of Bellerophon, and its permutation in Euripides' *Hippolytus*. Letters in erotic contexts always threaten to become repetitions of the Bellerophon story, as Lucian's narrator in *A True Story* suspected above.[31] Before leaving

---

[31] I suspect, but am unable to prove, that a bizarre fragment from Iamblichus' *Babyloniaka* may also reflect the influence of Bellerophon and Phaedra: "he wet his fingers in the blood and wrote further." Was he writing a letter? For text and translation, see S. A. Stephens and J. J. Winkler eds., *Ancient Greek Novels: The Fragments* (Princeton 1995) 216.

the topic of love letters, let us glance briefly at two other novelistic texts that offer more variation on the theme: one by introducing a false accusation in a letter, the other using the letter as a way for a woman to avoid public embarrassment or shame.

In Xenophon's *Ephesian Tale* (*ca.* second century CE), a young woman Manto falls in love with the visiting hero Habrocomes, and writes a passionate letter declaring her love, offering to marry him if he will agree to get rid of his wife, Anthia (2.3–5). She also threatens horrible revenge if he rejects her advances. Habrocomes claims that he would rather die than succumb to her desires, and Manto predictably tells her father that she has been sexually attacked by Habrocomes. Fortunately, Habrocomes had kept her original letter, and shows Manto's father the incriminating evidence: when he recognizes his daughter's handwriting, Habrocomes is absolved of all wrongdoing (2.5–6; 10). Thus Manto's letter, for one man a (failed) tool of seduction, becomes in another man's eyes written proof of her guilt.

The other novel in question expands on the concept of the letter as a "safe" place for a woman in love to express her feelings, feelings that would otherwise be inappropriate if uttered out loud. Phaedra's nurse convinced her that it was no crime to confess her love, but ordinarily, expressing her own erotic desire was forbidden to a woman in antiquity. In the anonymous *Story of Apollonius King of Tyre* (second or third century CE), the shipwrecked hero Apollonius becomes the music tutor to a king's daughter. When suitors arrive to request her hand in marriage, the king asks them to write down their names and the terms of their offers on tablets (20), and then sends the epistolary marriage proposals to the princess, so she can make a final choice. The princess, who has fallen in love with her tutor, writes her response on the tablets (20):

Good king and best of fathers, since you generously and indulgently permit me to express myself, I shall. I desire as my husband the man who was robbed of his inheritance by shipwreck. If, Father, you are surprised that a modest young woman should have written so immodestly, I have entrusted my feelings to wax, which has no sense of shame.

The writer here acknowledges that she is being allowed a voice in circumstances which would normally be out of her control. She thanks her father for permitting her to express herself, in particular for giving her the opportunity of responding in writing: the letter allows her to bypass customary feminine modesty in affairs of the heart, since "wax ... has no sense of shame."[32] Unfortunately, her innate modesty forbids her to mention her beloved's name, even in writing. The king turns to Apollonius for an explanation of the tablets, whose blush upon reading immediately reveals him as the desired bridegroom (21).

There is an intriguing parallel in the fragmentary *The Incredible Things Beyond Thule* by Antonius Diogenes (first or second century CE). We have two papyri (*P Oxy.* 3012 and *PSI* 1177), one which refers to a letter (*P Oxy.* 3012.1–2: "the letter made these things clear"), and another that refers to writing on "a double-leaved tablet of [the sort that] we used to carry to school."[33] In the latter passage, a servant Myrto appears to have difficulty telling her mistress something of greatest importance. The mistress gives Myrto the writing tablet and encourages her to write down what she cannot say, and Myrto "showed] from her face that she would at once [obtain re-]venge and comfort for what she suffered." Although the plot is unclear and the text in large part conjectural, I would argue strongly here for an epistolary context reminiscent of Phaedra's: Myrto is ashamed to describe a sexual scandal, but desperately needs to impart the news to her mistress, who may or may not be implicated in the affair; she turns to writing tablets as a way to express herself, agreeing with Apollonius' princess that "wax ... has no sense of shame."

Thus far, we have discussed only those novels and fragments of novels in which erotic letters play a prominent role, whether in deception or full sincerity. In fact, love letters are so common that a novel which includes letters but excludes love topics must be considered unusual. But this is precisely the case with Heliodorus, whose work we will consider next. Heliodorus' lovers experience most of their adventures together, and therefore have no need to express their love in writing; instead it is the heroine and her biological parents who are separated and exchange letters.

---

[32] By consigning her wishes to the wax tablet, which is personified as a go-between, the princess seeks an intermediary who finds no shame in uttering her lover's name before the union has been sanctioned by her father.

[33] For Greek text and translation of the Antonius Diogenes, see Stephens and Winkler (1995) 148–57.

AN *ETHIOPIAN STORY*

Heliodorus' *Ethiopian Story* is longer and more convoluted in its narrative structure than any of the novels discussed above.[34] Of its ten books, exactly half contain letters embedded in the narrative, and they are scattered in such a way as to create a fairly symmetrical alternation of epistolary and non-epistolary segments: thus books one, three, six, seven, and nine are without letters, while books two, four, five, eight, and ten each contain anywhere from one to five letters. One of the most important objects in the novel is a piece of cloth left with the heroine when she is abandoned by her mother at birth: a belt of silk embroidered in Ethiopian characters with an explanation of the child's parentage and exposure (2.31). In what follows, I define this woven text as a letter, written by mother to child, one which guides the heroine's life from birth to marriage; different readers interpret the script at various points in the narrative, until finally the message returns to its original author in a recognition scene worthy of New Comedy.

The novel begins *in medias res*, with a horrible scene of slaughter on an Egyptian beach, and the introduction of the heroine and hero, Charikleia and Theagenes. They have been captured by pirates along with an Athenian youth, Knemon, who tells them his sad story of treachery by a stepmother and her slave, Thisbe. After a battle in which Theagenes and Knemon escape their captors, they discover a female corpse in the cave where they have hidden Charikleia (2.6). The woman turns out to be Thisbe, and "protruding from her breast was a writing tablet that was tucked under her arm" (2.6). The author alludes throughout to the similar scene in Euripides' *Hippolytus*: earlier his stepmother had called Knemon her "young Hippolytus" (1.10), and his father had flogged him upon hearing the stepmother's accusations of a physical attack (1.11); now Knemon speaks of the corpse telling its tale through the

---

[34] Morgan, in the introduction to his translation in Reardon (1989) 349–52, argues for a date in the fourth century CE, with a dramatic date for the action of the late sixth or early fifth century BCE. Of the novel's complexity, the Byzantine scholar Psellos says "the very beginning of the book resembles the coils of a snake. Snakes hide their heads inside their coils, putting the rest of their body in front; similarly this book, as if assigning the beginning of the plot to the middle into which it slips, brings the middle of the story to the beginning" (quoted in N. G. Wilson, *Scholars of Byzantium* [Baltimore 1983] 175).

letter, and views himself as the "victim of another Attic tragedy, but in an Egyptian setting" (2.11).

The letter begins with a curious address: "To Knemon, my lord and master, from your enemy and benefactress, Thisbe" (2.10). Taking advantage of the chance to define herself in the formal address, Thisbe assumes that Knemon thinks of her as an enemy for her part in the stepmother's plot, but hints that he will soon come to view her as a savior. The letter goes on to say that the wicked stepmother is dead, that Thisbe will be happy to explain the details face-to-face, but that he should take pity and rescue her from the pirates who hold her captive in the cave. She happened to see Knemon walk by her prison, and wrote the letter with the intention of having it delivered to him secretly by an old woman who lived nearby. The details of the events in Athens, of course, will now never be explained, and Knemon feels no pity for Thisbe (2.11):

"Thisbe," said Knemon, "I am glad you are dead, that you were yourself the messenger who brought us word of your misfortunes, for it was your very corpse that delivered your narrative to us!..."

The letter effectively clears up the larger outlines of Knemon's past and allows us to concentrate more on the plight of Charikleia and Theagenes.[35] But it also informs the external reader from the very start that this novel will use letters to advance the narrative. The three protagonists separate temporarily, agreeing to meet again in a nearby town. Knemon arrives first and by chance meets the priest Kalasiris, who miraculously turns out to be the adoptive father of Charikleia and Theagenes (2.23). To complicate matters further, Kalasiris tells Knemon that he received Charikleia from yet another adoptive father, Charikles, who was given Charikleia as a baby. For the next few books, Kalasiris fills in gaps in the story about which both Knemon and the external reader are naturally curious.

During Kalasiris' lengthy exposition, we are given a detailed description of the embroidered belt, the crucial piece of evidence about Charikleia's parentage and origins. Kalasiris had received

---

[35] Winkler (1982) 93–158, comments on Knemon's elaborate life story that "it is almost as if the protagonists of the *Aithiopika* were taking time out from their adventures to read a different novel" (106). For a Greek text, see R. M. Rattenbury, T. W. Lumb, and J. Maillon, eds. and trans., *Héliodore: Les Éthiopiques*, 3 vols. (Paris 1943; 2nd edn. 1960).

Charikleia from Charikles when she was of marriageable age (2.33); since she stubbornly insisted on dedicating herself to Artemis, Kalasiris was asked to convince the girl to take a husband. He reports that he asked to see the mysterious cloth, which he feared might have been inscribed with occult spells that were confusing her soul and causing her to resist marriage (4.5–7). The letter does indeed contain a kind of spell, one that controls Charikleia's life without her knowing it, and offers her a future of which she is totally unaware. The words in the cloth letter define her fate as much as, for example, Meleager's log defines his, but Charikleia fortunately has Kalasiris to act on her behalf. He suspects the truth, that Charikleia has fallen in love with Theagenes, whom she met at a local festival, and resists marriage only because Theagenes is not the intended husband. But what the cloth tells him has nothing to do with Charikleia's present emotions, and everything to do with her past.

Kalasiris tells us that the cloth "was embroidered in the Ethiopian script, not the demotic variety but the royal kind, which closely resembles the so-called hieratic script of Egypt" (4.8).[36] The very writing system used thus reveals an important clue: the creator of the cloth letter is of royal blood, and her royalty is reflected in her choice of alphabet, or rather hieratic pictograms. Fortunately, Kalasiris is a member of the priesthood, and familiar with the Egyptian sacred script that this text closely resembles. He recognizes the writer's name at the opening sentence (4.8):

I, Persinna, Queen of the Ethiopians, inscribe this record of woe (χαράττω τόνδε τὸν ἔγγραφον θρῆνον) as a final gift to my daughter, mine only in the pain of her birth, by whatever name she may be called.

This opening is suggestively epistolary in nature: x writes to y (although the verb χαράττω may be more reminiscent of epigraphy than epistolography), but the Ethiopian queen has not had time yet to name her addressee, the daughter who was born only an hour earlier. Nor will she name her, since she is destined to be exposed on the roadside (4.8):

---

[36] Morgan's note (Reardon [1989] 432, note 111) is helpful here: "According to Herodotus (2.36), the Egyptians had two kinds of writing, sacred and demotic. Diodorus (3.3) adds that in Egypt only members of the priesthood could read the sacred script, whereas everyone in Ethiopia could."

I lied to my husband that you had died at birth, and, in the utmost secrecy, I laid you by the roadside. Beside you I laid as much wealth as I
could afford as a reward to the person who saved your life; but chief
among the treasures with which I bedecked you was this band that I
wrapped around you, the history of your sorrow and mine, written in the
blood and tears shed for you by a mother whose first childbearing was
the occasion of such grief.

The fabric, wrapped around the infant, holds out a vague hope for
the mother that her baby may live. It is addressed to the child but
actually intercepted and read by a host of others first, namely
those who rescue and adopt the child at various stages in her life.
Persinna writes a detailed genealogy, a report of the conception
(Persinna's gaze fell on a painting of Andromeda, magically producing a white baby for her and her husband, an Ethiopian couple), and an explanation of the abandonment. She offers motherly
advice: "if you live, be sure not to forget your royal blood. Honor
chastity ..." Persinna concludes with a reference to the act of
"writing" itself (4.8):[37]

This message (τὸ γράμμα) was the only way I could find to convey all
this to you, since heaven has robbed me of your living presence and the
opportunity to tell you to your face. Perhaps my story will remain unread and useless (κωφὰ καὶ ἀνήνυτα), but perhaps it will one day work
to your advantage. The secrets of fortune cannot be read by men. If you
live, my child whose futile beauty served only to expose me to false allegations, what I have written (τὰ τῆς γραφῆς) will be a token of your recognition; but if that occurs which I pray never to hear of, then it will
take the place of a mother's tears and sorrow at your graveside.

This concluding paragraph is full of epistolary tropes. Persinna
turns to a written text in the absence of the "living presence" (τὰς
ἐμψύχους καὶ ἐν ὀφθαλμοῖς ὁμιλίας) of her addressee. She imagines two possible fates for her letter: it may remain unread (literally, mute) and therefore powerless to help its addressee, or it may
someday find the right reader and expose the truth of the abandoned child's history. She also imagines two fates for her child: if
she lives, the letter will speak to her in her mother's voice, and
allow her to find her way home; but if she dies, the letter will rep-

---

[37] One could also question the amount of time it would take to embroider such a lengthy
narrative, if time was of the essence in spiriting the newborn baby out of the house before its father could see it. Koskenniemi (1956) 189–200, discusses "Der Tempusgebrauch
im Briefstil."

resent the voice and tears of Persinna at the graveside, as the embroidered cloth metamorphoses from swaddling clothes to winding sheet.[38] The challenge for both external and internal readers is to discover the "correct" reading at any given time. At birth, the child herself was a message from her mother that never reached her father; instead, she is wrapped in her own story and sent away, to be delivered and interpreted correctly seventeen years later by the first person clever enough to comprehend the message, namely Kalasiris.[39]

Once Kalasiris reads the letter, he reports its contents to Charikleia, who has never been shown the belt; Charikles kept it under lock and key, supposedly to protect it from the ravages of time. We may imagine the letter's preservation symbolizing that of Charikleia herself, her chastity kept closely guarded by her adoptive father. Kalasiris translates word by word for Charikleia, who has been raised to speak Greek, not her "mother tongue." He also informs her that he has met her mother, and is actually on a mission to find her and return her to her rightful home (4.12). The coincidence is, of course, typical of the ancient novel plot.

The cloth letter, now in Charikleia's possession and preserved throughout her trials, will reappear in the concluding book of the novel. It operates as one of a set of recognition tokens in the story. As such, it admittedly does not wholly depend on its written or verbal-semantic content to work. As with Acontius' apple, the embroidered cloth seems to tease the reader a bit with its marginality: this is a letter, but one which well suits the novel's interest in things non-Greek (pictograms versus alphabet, cloth versus papyrus) and the relativizing of Greek cultural expectations. Particularly at the end of the novel, Greek and barbarian customs confront one another as the piece of cloth is the only thing standing between the hero and heroine and a gruesome death.

But in the meantime, books 5 to 9 lead us through more captures, escapes, separations, and dangers. The letters embedded in

---

[38] The funerary letter also occurs in *The Story of Apollonius King of Tyre* (26), when Apollonius buries his apparently dead wife at sea, and she later washes up on shore where a doctor notices the money and written tablets that had been placed at her head. Apollonius requests a lavish funeral for the corpse, but does not identify the woman or himself as writer. The letter is addressed to "whoever finds this coffin," and ends with a curse if the finder takes the money without burying the body.

[39] This is nicely put by Winkler (1982) 119–20, who discusses the larger question of misinterpretation in the novel.

the narratives of books five and eight are primarily military in nature. An interesting feature of these sections is the delay inserted between the sending and receiving of letters, an effective method of creating narrative suspense.[40] In book five, Charikleia and Theagenes have been recaptured and separated. Theagenes is sent to the governor Oroondates in Memphis, who is then supposed to take him to the king in Babylon, since his beauty is worthy of royal admiration (5.9). After much intervening narrative, book 5 ends with Charikleia's and Kalasiris' resolve to secure the release of Theagenes.[41]

In the interval, Kalasiris dies, and both Charikleia and Theagenes come under the power of Oroondates' wife Arsake in Memphis. Oroondates, away on campaign, hears about the two Greek prisoners; his reaction is one of rage at his wife's infatuation with Theagenes, and of desire at the report of Charikleia's divine beauty. He calls his trusted eunuch Bagoas to act as messenger, and writes two letters with orders that the young people be brought to him as quickly as possible. One letter is addressed to his wife, in which he hints at allegations of her misbehavior; the other is to the head eunuch of his household, Euphrates, in which he threatens to flay the man alive if he does not obey his command (8.3).[42] We are told that the governor sealed the letters with his own seal so that no one would doubt their authority (8.3), and Bagoas departs immediately. But again, the scene of the letters' arrival is postponed for several sections, and we are left hanging while Arsake tries (unsuccessfully) to kill Charikleia and seduce Theagenes.

Bagoas arrives at Memphis dramatically in the dead of night, and wakes Euphrates with his letters, who automatically assumes that he is the bearer of bad news. The unusual time and manner of delivery are enough to frighten Euphrates, just as the delivery

---

[40] Winkler (1982) 97, 103–14, considers "the postponement of wanted information" (97) as a basic feature of Heliodorus' narrative technique, i.e. not limited to epistolary contexts. He views such postponement as a narrative method intended "to provoke the reader to a greater awareness of . . . the conventions of reading fiction" (112).

[41] There are no letters in books 6 and 7, although there is a reference to Mitranes' letter in 7.24, when the person who tried to deliver Theagenes to Oroondates shows the letter to Oroondates' wife, who is in love with Theagenes, to prove to her that the young man is really a captured slave, and therefore required to obey her orders, even to sleep with her.

[42] The tone of the two letters is not dissimilar, even though one is to his supposed equal and the other to a servant. But eunuchs were highly valued in Persian households.

of a government telegram in wartime would automatically alarm any recipient even before opening the envelope. Bagoas replies that he should examine the device on the seal of the letter to satisfy himself that the orders come from Oroondates himself (8.12), and then decide whether or not to forward the second letter to Arsake. Euphrates reads both letters and hands Charikleia and Theagenes over to Bagoas without further discussion. Thus the letter supposedly intended for Arsake never reaches its addressee, as Euphrates' swift action obviates the need for its delivery. Arsake, realizing that her crime has been exposed, hangs herself the next day (8.15).

On their way to Oroondates' camp, the entourage is attacked by an Ethiopian contingent; the fates are slowly conspiring to bring Charikleia back to her homeland. Unfortunately the Ethiopian custom is to sacrifice the first fruits of war (9.1), and the rest of book 9 presents Oroondates and the Ethiopian king, Hydaspes, fighting over the captives. But book 10 opens with a victorious Hydaspes who, as he heads homeward, writes two letters (10.1–22). He chooses two horsemen to carry his messages, telling them to change to fresh horses at every town, so that they can bring the good news of his victory back home as quickly as possible (10.1). The first is to his cabinet, to whom he announces his triumph and extends an invitation to join him at the thanksgiving sacrifices at which Theagenes and Charikleia are to be killed. His letter, in addition to announcing news and extending an invitation, also serves as an acknowledgment of respect for the prophetic powers of his advisors, who had predicted this turn of events. The second letter is addressed to his wife Persinna, and contains the same information about his victory and the upcoming celebration, but worded slightly differently; it also informs us that he has included his letter to the gymnosophists in her own letter; later, a man on horseback hands Persinna yet another letter from the king, stating that he will arrive the next day (10.4). Let us look more closely at the actual messages (10.2):

To the wise men, known as gymnosophists, or naked sages, who form a cabinet that the king consults on matters of policy, he wrote as follows:

King Hydaspes to the most reverend Council.
I write to you with the glad tidings of our victory over the Persians, not in boastfulness at my triumph, for I have no wish to provoke the change-

ability of fortune, but to pay my prompt respects in this letter to your powers of prophecy, which have proved correct now as ever. Wherefore I invite and implore you to come to the accustomed place, where your presence will sanctify for the Ethiopian commonalty the sacrifices to be performed in thanksgiving for my victory.

To his wife, Persinna, he wrote as follows:

I write to inform you that I am victorious and, which is of more concern to you, that I am safe. Make preparations for magnificent pageants and sacrifices to render thanks. Add your own invitation to the sages to that contained in my letter. Then, make haste with them to the glade outside the city walls that is consecrated to our ancestral deities, the Sun, the Moon, and Dionysus.

These two letters are juxtaposed by Heliodorus and joined only by the brief phrase "to his wife, Persinna, he wrote as follows: ..." They are written in deliberately contrasting styles and with deliberately different contents, each according to the status and interest of the recipient.[43] The king opens both letters with an announcement of victory, but the cabinet receives five lines to Persinna's two. He imagines that his political advisors will want to know details (the name of the enemy, the fact that it was a complete triumph), while his wife will want to hear only that he is safe. He reassures the sages that his letter is not to be read as a boast; rather, they should receive it as a letter of respect and praise for their powers of prophecy. Thus Hydaspes includes in the letter advice to his male addressees on how to read it, to which generic framework it belongs. The men are expected to understand the flexibility of the epistolary mode and find the right code of reading. Persinna, in contrast, is expected to read the letter as a personal rather than a political message; her letter reassures her that Hydaspes is alive and well.

The king continues with an invitation in both letters. He "invites and implores" the sages, whose presence at the feast will endow his triumphal sacrifices with their full holiness. The tone throughout this letter is one of respect and admiration; even though he is king, his letter begs rather than commands the wise men to attend

---

[43] "Demetrius" (*On Style* 234): "Since occasionally we write to States or royal personages, such letters must be composed in a slightly heightened tone. It is right to have regard to the person to whom the letter is addressed;" see Malherbe (1988) 19.

him. In contrast, he does command his wife, supposedly his social equal, in one short, crisp phrase, to make all the necessary preparations for the festival and sacrifices. When Hydaspes orders her to "add your own invitation to the sages to that contained in my letter," we realize that Persinna receives both letters at the same time, and is expected first to act as the king's messenger, delivering the letter in person to the sages, and then to accompany them to the spot outside the city where the festival will take place. Persinna, of course, obeys (10.4):

... she handed them the letter from Hydaspes and joined him in begging them to accede to the king's request by gracing the ceremony with their presence, which she would consider a personal honor to herself.

The scene concludes as the sages predict yet another letter informing them of the king's imminent arrival, and indeed, "this was exactly what happened" as Persinna made her way back to the palace (10.4). Heralds immediately proclaim the joyous news to the entire city. Both in Persinna's personal appeal and in the heralds' announcements, we see the novel playing with orality: written messages are normal means of communication, but really important news still takes advantage of an oral complement.

The sacrifice to which the sages have been invited is, lest we forget, the ritual murder of our hero and heroine. Charikleia and Theagenes are prepared for slaughter, and Theagenes implores his beloved to reveal herself to Hydaspes at once, but she understands that the time is not yet right, that her mother, not her father, is the crucial missing piece in the puzzle. To the wrong reader, the embroidered narrative means nothing (9.24):

"The recognition tokens," replied Charikleia, "are tokens only to those who know them or to those who laid them beside me. For those who do not know them or do not recognize every item, they are mere precious trinkets, which might well bring their bearer under suspicion of being a thief or a robber."

The same letter can mean very different things to different readers: to an uninformed or uninvolved reader, it could be interpreted as evidence of criminal activity, a sign of deceit and imposture; to the original author of the text, it can mean only one thing, and will be read as sure proof of the authenticity and true identity of its bearer. The problem that Charikleia faces is finding Persinna before death finds her.

At almost the last possible moment, Charikleia takes off the belt that she wears around her waist, unfolds it, and presents it as "documentary proof" of her identity to Persinna (10.13). Persinna is struck with amazement the instant she sees the object, and she alternates between reading the familiar message and staring in joy at the daughter she never thought to see alive again. When Hydaspes asks her what is wrong, she does not answer, but tells him to "take the band and read it. It will tell you all there is to tell" (10.13). The written text speaks for Persinna at this crucial moment when it proves difficult for her to find words to explain herself. The letter offers at the same time concrete proof of Persinna's story. Hydaspes takes the letter and calls on his advisors to stand beside him and read it with him. He responds with similar amazement but is torn with doubt just as Charikleia had predicted, not about the authenticity of the belt, but about the identity of its bearer: he worries that someone has come across the belt by accident, and is using the girl "as a kind of mask," taking advantage of his desire for a child to carry on his line (10.13). Fortunately, the man who had saved the abandoned baby seventeen years earlier steps forward to corroborate her claim (10.14):

I recognize the band, which, as you can see, is inscribed in the Ethiopian royal script (τοῖς βασιλείοις Αἰθιόπων γράμμασιν), proving beyond any shadow of a doubt that it originated here and nowhere else. That it is embroidered in Persinna's own hand, you yourself are best qualified to confirm.

We return again to the nature of the script, which proves that the letter is Ethiopian in origin even if it guarantees nothing yet about Charikleia's origins. But the suggestion is evident: just as the letter will be acknowledged by Persinna as the product of her own hand, so the child will be acknowledged as the legitimate successor to the throne. Both the letter and its bearer have returned to their source.[44]

Up to this point in the novel, the letter has been the major focus of all attempts at reuniting Charikleia with her native family. But during this scene of recognition, the letter is not enough to convince the hesitant Hydaspes, who questions the paradoxically white skin color of his daughter. The Ethiopian script of the letter

---

[44] The fact that Hydaspes rather than Persinna is asked to confirm that the embroidery is in Persinna's hand has more to do with kingly authority than authorship.

matches its place of origin, but the white skin of the letter-carrier does not. More tokens are produced (10.14): necklaces, a ring, and finally an incontrovertible birthmark on Charikleia's upper arm (10.15–16). The cloth letter is just the first in a series of tokens. The only piece of evidence that is finally and truly believed is the birthmark, the "inscription" of Charikleia's true identity on her body, a symbol that cannot be reproduced independent of her physical identity. Letters can be forged, jewelry stolen; the black birthmark present at her birth is the ideal witness to her parentage and descent.

This dramatic reconciliation would have made a worthy last scene for the novel, but there are a few loose ends left. One more letter arrives, just as Theagenes is about to be sacrificed because Charikleia is too modest to declare her love for him in public (10.34). It is a letter from Oroondates, demanding the return of Charikleia, who belongs to him as a prisoner of war. One of the ambassadors who brought the letter turns out to be her other father, Charikles, who accuses Theagenes of having kidnapped her from Artemis' shrine at Delphi (10.36). All is gradually cleared up, and Charikleia marries her beloved Theagenes.

The novels discussed above share certain narrative elements and techniques, including the embedded letter. At the risk of oversimplifying in the face of such a dizzying array of plots and characters, perhaps we can draw some general conclusions about the role of letters in the novels.

There is great appeal in incorporating letters in a genre that delights in the physical separation and far-flung adventures of its main characters, the young men and women in love.[45] Letters function as intermediaries at every stage of love affairs: Manto's attempted seduction, Clitophon's and Chaereas' letters begging their beloveds to give them another chance, Callirhoe's farewell love letter to her second husband. In most cases the separation is physical, but occasionally the writer turns to letters in the game of love because of modesty, as happens in the case of the princess who receives and answers marriage proposals on wax tablets.

The romantic adventures of the lovers also often involve near-death experiences, and letters are convenient methods of contacting a person who has given up all hope of the beloved's survival. A

---

[45] On this see Koskenniemi (1956) 180.

sudden appearance might be too much of a shock; the letter both informs the addressee of the change in circumstances and predicts the imminent arrival of the writer. A return from the dead, however, is not easily believable, and letters are obsessed with issues of authenticity; the writer accordingly includes information that will convince the reader of the letter's genuineness: the familiar handwriting is explicitly referred to, or experiences shared in the couple's past are listed. The issue of forgery haunts these novels, but curiously enough we read only of true letters that are misinterpreted as forgeries (Chaereas' letter, Charikleia's cloth narrative) rather than of actual forgeries themselves.

Another way in which the novels reveal an anxiety about epistolary authenticity is their great concern with details of sending and receiving letters. We are given precise details in order to be convinced of the verisimilitude of the epistolary device: messengers are named and their presence explained (e.g. Thisbe uses an old woman who lives nearby although she never reappears in the story), the time and circumstances of writing and delivery are documented, and letters may be preserved for a future cameo appearance in the plot (Manto's letter, Persinna's letter). The novels often keep the readers, both internal and external, in suspense about the contents of the letters: thus a letter written in one scene may not be read until after a digression or scene change to another plot line. This suspense may be meant to mimic the actual time it takes for the letter to arrive at its destination.

In the ancient novel, as in other genres we have considered in earlier chapters, the embedded letter offers a way to vary a third- or first-person narrative. It piques the reader's interest, who reads over the shoulder of the addressee, and adds a certain weight to the narrative by simulating a "real" epistolary exchange, a document that gives the illusion of being separable from the rest of the novel. The novel's enjoyment of the textuality of the letter is connected with its overall fascination with intertextuality and allusiveness, and its dialogue with other genres and time periods, so characteristic of literary products of the Second Sophistic.

CHAPTER 7

The Alexander Romance

The storie of Alisaundre is so commune
That every wight that hath discrecioun
Hath herd somwhat or al of his fortune.

Chaucer, The Monk's Tale 7.2631–33

The previous chapter explored a number of ancient novels that included letters embedded within a third-person narrative. The following three chapters will investigate further variations on epistolary prose form: the novel or romance that alternates between the epistolary first- and third-person narration; epistolary collections that sustain the first-person epistolary voice but are not necessarily "novels;" and a novel written entirely in epistolary form. The *Alexander Romance* belongs to the first category. It could logically have been discussed in the context of Hellenistic epistolary experiments, since, as we shall see, its core may be dated to that period. But instead I have organized this section of the book, where dating and provenance become extremely difficult to prove, according to the development of epistolary narrative technique, moving from a work with some embedded epistolary sections in it, to a work written entirely in epistolary form; the existing *Alexander Romance* falls relatively early on that continuum.

The *Alexander Romance*, the story of the life and times of Alexander the Great (356–323 BCE), King of Macedon, son of Philip II and Olympias of Epirus, was one of the most popular works in antiquity. Its success can be measured by the approximately eighty versions in twenty-four languages which appeared in places as distant as fifth-century Armenia and medieval France.[1]

---

[1] I use the translation and introduction by Dowden in Reardon (1989) 650–735. Much valuable information is also to be found in the translation and introductory remarks of R. Stoneman, *The Greek Alexander Romance* (London 1991), and in L. L. Gunderson, *Alexander's Letter to Aristotle about India* (Meisenheim am Glan 1980). For the Greek text, see R. Merkelbach, *Die Quellen des griechischen Alexanderromans*, 2nd edn. (Munich 1977).

But, as is often the case with works that fall outside the established canon, its authorship and date are obscure. The first manuscript dates from the third century CE, which narrows the time of composition to a six-hundred-year span after Alexander's death in 323 BCE. Some fifteenth-century manuscripts of the *Romance* attribute it to Alexander's court historian, Kallisthenes, but his murder during Alexander's Asian campaign eliminates that theory.[2] The issue is complicated by the likelihood that the "author" was really more of a compiler or editor of various versions of Alexander's life which began to circulate in the century following his death.

Scholars draw different conclusions about the chronology of the work, based in part on their interpretation of its generic affiliation. Some view it as a piece of fiction written long after the death of its main character: thus K. Dowden, translating the work for inclusion in B. P. Reardon's edition of ancient Greek novels, declares it a novel written by a "Greek-speaker living in Alexandria at some time between A.D. 140 and 340."[3] In contrast, R. Stoneman views it as a biographical "romance," a kind of adventure narrative with a historical hero, and argues that most of the component elements were already circulating within fifty to one hundred years after its hero's death: "the *Alexander Romance* would by no means be out of place in the literary context of third-century-BC Alexandria."[4] J. Romm also categorizes the work as part of the tradition of romance, and connects it with other literary journeys to view the "wonders of the east" (such as Philostratus' *Life of Apollonius of Tyana*), suggesting that in this case, as in others, the geographical exploration parallels the hero's quest for immortality or spiritual enlightenment.[5]

The conventional title seems to set this work apart from other

[2] Stoneman (1991) 8.
[3] Dowden (1989) 650; see also Hägg (1983) 125–43, and Merkelbach (1977).
[4] Stoneman (1991) 8–17. S. Burstein, "*SEG* 33.802 and the Alexander Romance," *ZPE* 77 (1989) 275–76 argues that a papyrus from the reign of Tiberius (first century CE) contains fragments of a letter from Darius to Alexander also found in the *Alexander Romance* (2.17), which implies that the historical sources may have been aware of the epistolary novel based on Alexander's exploits, thus challenging their independent status. Merkelbach responds in "Der Brief des Dareios im Getty-Museum und Alexanders Wortwechsel mit Parmenion," *ZPE* 77 (1989) 277–80, arguing for the presence of letters in the historical sources as well as in the separate epistolary tradition.
[5] J. S. Romm, *The Edges of the Earth in Ancient Thought* (Princeton 1992) 108–16.

novels, and to put it squarely in the camp of "romance."[6] Is this
a "romance" because its adventure tales (Egyptian magic, the
"fountain of youth," the Amazons) are remote from everyday life,
more reminiscent of Lucian's fantastic *True Story* than sober biography or historiography? If its main character were not a famous
historical figure, and if we therefore did not expect the narrative
to offer a credible representation of real life, would we still call it
a "romance?" Do the lack of a continuous plot and the shifts in
narrative technique keep us from granting it the literary status
implied in the term "novel?" The search for the appropriate
terminology for ancient prose fiction has been going on for three
centuries, and will no doubt continue for many more.[7]

Whatever generic label we attach to the work, its literary ante-
cedent is clearly the fabulous adventure narrative of Homer's
Odyssey.[8] Both highlight the prolonged wandering of the hero, fights
with monsters or fierce enemies, some love interest (although sub-
stantially less in Alexander's story), and a fascination with unknown lands and peoples. The hero of the later work, however, is
a well-documented historical figure, and its fictional narrative is
woven around a core of historical fact, namely Alexander's biography. I agree with Richard Stoneman's assessment that "the
Alexander Romance is a text which uses the freedom of fiction to explore more fully, through philosophical and psychological means,
the quality of a particular historical epoch."[9]

Although we may not be able to specify exactly when or by
whom this work was composed, or even to what genre it belongs,
we do know that its compiler drew on several distinct sources. The

---

[6] For a general discussion of the assumptions implicit in the division "romance" vs.
"novel," see Hägg (1983) 4, and M. McKeon, *The Origins of the English Novel, 1600–1740*
(Baltimore 1987) 1–22. On the term "novel," see J. Tatum, ed. *The Search for the Ancient
Novel* (Baltimore 1994) 1–19. Stoneman (1991) 17–23 discusses the genre of the *Alexander
Romance*; see also Stoneman, "The Alexander Romance," in J. R. Morgan and R. Stoneman, eds., *Greek Fiction: The Greek Novel in Context* (London 1994) 117–29, esp. 117: "The
Greek romances have been so called mainly because of a reluctance by critics to refer to
them as novels, implying a nineteenth-century model of character development and psychological analysis." On the whole issue of whether or not there is a literary kind that can
be called "the ancient novel," see D. L. Selden, "Genre of Genre," in Tatum (1994) 39–
64.

[7] The influential *Traité de l'origine des romans* of Pierre-Daniel Huet was published in Paris in
1670; the collections of Morgan and Stoneman (1994) and Tatum (1994) continue to debate questions of naming and typification.

[8] Stoneman (1991) 17–19.

[9] Stoneman (1994) 118.

main historical source was a biography of Alexander written by Kleitarchos (*ca.* 300 BCE), who was said by some to have emphasized the dramatic in his writing, and to have been more interested in sensationalism than in factual reporting; this reminds us to what degree Alexander's extraordinary character and deeds invited literary elaboration even during his own lifetime.[10]

But the fictional sources most interesting for our purposes are two kinds of letter collections: (1) an epistolary "novel" dated to *ca.* 100 BCE, no longer extant in its entirety, which presumably originated in the historical report of an actual exchange of letters between Alexander and his adversary, the Persian king Darius;[11] (2) a separate series of longer letters describing marvels and monsters at the ends of the earth, supposedly sent by Alexander to his mother Olympias and his tutor Aristotle.[12] Other sections which include epistolary passages are Alexander's meetings with the famous naked wise men in India (the "gymnosophists"), the Amazons, and Queen Kandake of Ethiopia, and, at the very end of the work, Alexander's deathbed scene.

The compiler of the *Romance* used letters in a variety of ways throughout the work, which consists of three books of forty to fifty chapters each.[13] The first letter quoted in full (1.35, to the Tyrians) appears only after a lengthy third-person narration of Alexander's birth and upbringing. We will see that Alexander's coming of age coincides with his awareness of the power of letters to define status and power. Thereafter, letters are an integral part of his life story. The letters between Alexander and his enemies, Darius and Porus, occur in 1.36 through 2.22, and again briefly at 3.2. Their military campaign is described through a lively epistolary exchange within the larger framework of the action; the letters are kinetic, both causing and reacting to events. Throughout this section we read letters written back-to-back, with little narrative

---

[10] Merkelbach (1954) 9; Dowden (1989) 650–51; Hägg (1983) 115–16, 126.

[11] Merkelbach (1954) 38; Dowden (1989) 650; Hägg (1983) 126; Stoneman (1991) 9 and note 18 discusses the papyrus published in the late 1940s of a cycle of letters between Darius and Alexander which closely resembles the correspondence in the *Romance*.

[12] Merkelbach (1954) 40, discusses the differences between the first and second types of letters: the second set reveals a primarily descriptive function, and no longer reflects as strongly the rhetorical influence of *prosopopoeia*.

[13] Dowden's translation (1989) is based on his choice of a particular recension of the text. Some of my comments would not apply to a different transmission.

interspersed other than the occasional "and then he wrote back as follows."

As the phase of expansion and conquest draws to a close, Alexander shifts his epistolary energy to letters home to his mother Olympias and his tutor Aristotle. The long letter home at 2.23–41 summarizes the conclusive battle with Darius and then chronicles Alexander's travels east, where he encounters killer crabs (2.38) and the water of immortality (2.39), and explores the ocean floor (2.38) and the upper atmosphere (2.41). Alexander takes advantage of the fact that the letter itself is an extremely flexible form which allows different narrative modes within its borders: in addition to the narratives of adventure described above, he also includes direct quotations in the first person, the texts of oracles (2.38), and the wording of an inscription from an arch built at his command at the end of the earth (2.41). His letter provides his mother (and the external reader) with a full and well-documented picture of his time abroad. But these letters, in contrast to those of the previous section, are for the most part static and descriptive: the stories are recounted *in* rather than *through* the epistolary medium.

Book 3 reveals yet another use for letters, reminiscent of the military communications of the first book. Alexander visits the gymnosophists, the Amazons, Queen Kandake, and other foreign hosts. These letters are embedded in third-person narrative, and do not dominate the text as they did in the earlier segments.[14] So, for example, after the gymnosophists write one letter to Alexander (3.5), requesting that he come in peace, the narrative resumes not with a return letter from Alexander, but with the two sides meeting for a philosophical debate. Similarly, after Alexander introduces himself by letter to Queen Kandake and she responds by return mail (3.18), Alexander visits the Queen in person, thus losing the opportunity for further writing. The epistolary exchange with the Amazons is slightly more extended, but ends again with Alexander visiting their country (3.25–26); he then writes his mother an account of his doings in Amazon territory (3.27–29), so we can compare the information given and the manner of its presentation in the two kinds of letters: one kinetic, the other static.

---

[14] All of book 3, with the exception of a first-person letter home to Olympias (3.27–30), is in the third-person voice.

The overview above should give the reader a sense of the frequency and variety of letters in the *Alexander Romance*. At times they alone constitute the narrative; at other times they emerge as threads in the fabric of the surrounding text. In what follows, I explore the letters of the *Alexander Romance*, considering first the letters written on campaign to Darius; then two separate epistolary adventures with remarkable women, Queen Kandake and the Amazons; and finally the individual letters written to Olympias and Aristotle, including the last letter of the book, written by Alexander on his deathbed.

With the *Alexander Romance*, we begin to see a new development in epistolary usage: a movement from individual letters scattered about or embedded in an ancient novel, discussed in the last chapter, to the more formally sustained epistolary voices of the pseudonymous letter writers and *Chion of Heraclea*, to be treated in the next chapters. A unique feature of this romance, as I have suggested above, is that Alexander uses the letter form in so many different ways. Yet while they are formally and rhetorically distinct (letters of persuasion, of hostility, of filial affection, etc.), all the letters written by Alexander are united by his authorial voice and personal style. We will see in the following pages how Alexander reveals himself as "master writer" of letters, particularly when he turns to letters as documents of self-exaltation and imperial aggrandizement. His letters reveal a tension between the conventional Hellenistic letter form of civility and conversation, and the epistolary rhetoric of a conquerer. On campaign, often the first letter in a series will politely test his audience, or firmly demand allegiance, while the second begins to menace or threaten. In true epistolary fashion, this "master writer" is also a "master reader" of his correspondents' replies, and Alexander learns quickly how to twist epistolary conventions to serve his specific needs at any given time.

LETTERS TO THE ENEMY

Through epistolary means, Alexander defines his relationship with Darius and his own royal nature well before he sets out on a campaign. During his father's reign, envoys from Darius come to demand the usual tribute from Philip. Alexander rudely rebuffs the envoys, threatening to come in person and reclaim the total trib-

ute paid in previous years, and "with these words he sent away the
emissaries, not even deigning to write to the king who had sent
them" (1.23).[15] Here Alexander asserts his power by *not* writing a
letter, by refusing to enter into communication with "barbarians,"
as he calls the Persians. While paying tribute is an explicit acknowledgment of one's allegiance to a higher authority, Alexander
implies that letter writing in this case is also an act of submission
to the Persians. He declares his independence by withholding both
money and writing. Philip is delighted at his son's daring, but the
emissaries respond in an unexpected manner: they commission a
painting of Alexander which they then take back to Darius, to
whom they report everything that was said at the meeting. If a
letter reflects the character of its writer, so, too, does a painting
reflect and represent its subject; the two media (writing and painting) are understood as *eikones* of the soul. In spite of Alexander's
refusal to give them anything at all, they take back with them
Alexander's portrait, accompanied by an oral report based on
their interview, and present these as "tribute" to Darius.

After Philip's death, Alexander assumes the throne and sets out
to conquer foreign territory. Before confronting Darius, he hones
his diplomatic skills on the inhabitants of Tyre. Intending to sack
the city, he is told in a dream that he should under no circumstances go personally into Tyre; he interprets this to mean that he
should send a letter instead, and writes as follows (1.35):

> King Alexander, son of Ammon and King Philip, I who am greatest
> King of Europe and the whole of Asia, of Egypt and Libya, to the
> Tyrians, who no longer exist:
> Journeying to the regions of Syria in peace and lawfulness, I wished
> to enter your land. But if you Tyrians are the first to oppose our en-
> trance as we journey, then it is only by your example that others will
> learn the strength of the Macedonians in the face of your mindless
> action and shall cower in obedience to us. And you may rely on the
> oracle you have been given: I shall come through your city.
> Farewell, men of sense – or otherwise, farewell men of misfortune!

The opening address is elaborate: Alexander resolves doubts
about his paternity by identifying two fathers, one immortal
(stated first), and one mortal. He claims Europe, Asia, Egypt, and

---

[15] This scene is based on a tale of Alexander's questioning the Persian envoys in his father's
absence (Plutarch *Life of Alexander* 5), but the demands for tribute and the rude rebuff are
probably fictional embellishments. See Dowden (1989) 669, note 18.

Libya as parts of his own realm, quite boastfully, since he has just begun his Asian campaign. So far, all fits with epistolary convention in a military dispatch, as the writer tries to intimidate his opponents verbally in order to encourage surrender and avoid bloodshed. But while working within the form of a conventional epistolary opening, Alexander breaks with all form and civility by addressing them as the Tyrians "who no longer exist." His wording and tone elevate him while demoralizing the enemy. Three days later, Alexander will raze the city, as their oracles and his destiny have predicted; but his address forces them to acknowledge that they have already ceased to exist at the very moment of reading the letter.

If the opening address is an act of aggression in itself, the closing formula gives the Tyrians one last chance to submit without violence. They would prove themselves to be "men of sense" if they were to allow Alexander to enter their land peacefully; otherwise, he will call them "men of misfortune" for stubbornly calling down disaster on their own heads. It is entirely up to them which line they wish to "read." The double "farewell" serves a double purpose: first, it is an epistolary convention to acknowledge that the letter has ended; but second, if the Tyrians insist on being "men of misfortune," the "farewell" will ring as their death knell, a farewell to life as Alexander kills the citizens who dare to oppose him. The Tyrians refuse to surrender, and the second reading is fulfilled.

This letter to the Tyrians shows how, within the framework of formal letter writing, it is not just what is said, but how it is said that creates meaning. The simplest convention of address and closure may be used not just to get the attention of the reader (Jakobson's "phatic" function[16]), or to mark the end of the letter, but also to stake out one's position, establish a hierarchy, to force the reader to submit to authority. Because a conversational letter is conventionally so formulaic and civil, the distinctiveness of Alexander's letter is all the more effective. Alexander takes full advantage of the potential tension between form and content, giving added punch to customary greetings and farewells.[17]

[16] R. Jakobson, "Closing Statement: Linguistics and Poetics," in T. A. Sebeok, ed., *Style in Language* (Cambridge MA 1960) 350–77.

[17] A modern parallel is the "Dear John" letter, in which the "dear" is demanded by epistolary convention even if the label is no longer appropriate under the circumstances.

Let us now look closely at the correspondence between Alexander and his main foe, Darius (1.36–2.22). Some twenty-three letters tell the story of their hostilities, including not only the letters exchanged between the two of them, but also letters to allies and family members. At times the narrative at this point in the *Romance* is almost entirely epistolary, with only brief transitional passages; at other times the letters seem embedded in a larger sequence of impersonal third-person historical biography.

Consistent with his earlier behavior (1.23), where a younger Alexander refused to acknowledge Darius by return letter, Alexander does not initiate the correspondence. But in reaction to the Tyrian campaign, Darius sends emissaries to Alexander with a letter and some odd gifts: a strap, a ball, and a box of gold (1.36). We are told that "Alexander accepted the letter of Darius, King of Persia."[18] Darius intends the letter to function as a warning, to scare the young man and send him back home. Darius introduces himself as "kinsman of the gods, I who rise to heaven with the Sun, a god myself," and writes to "my servant Alexander" (Δαρεῖος Ἀλεξάνδρῳ ἐμῷ θεράποντι τάδε προστάσσω), not bothering to greet him conventionally, but giving him orders to "return to your parents, to be my slave, and to sleep in the lap of your mother." The gifts, as Darius spells out for us, are meant to humiliate and infantilize Alexander: the strap is for the whipping he deserves, the ball so he can play with children his own age, the money to feed the army on its way home. Darius closes with threats and yet another manipulation of Alexander's identity: "you will not be educated as the son of Philip but crucified as a rebel." The epistolary tactics of intimidation resemble those employed by Alexander himself against the Tyrians.

Alexander receives the letter and reads it out loud to his troops. He will continue to include his men in his writing and reading activities, in contrast to the atmosphere of tyrannical secrecy that marks the letter writing of the barbarian kings.[19] When the troops become frightened at the threats in the letter, Alexander scoffs at the empty words (1.37):

---

[18] For a similar delivery of symbolic gifts in Herodotus, see 4.131, where the Scythians send Darius a bird, a mouse, a frog, and five arrows. Darius interprets the objects metaphorically, but his advisor offers a more accurate literal reading of the tokens. The Herodotean passage is discussed by Steiner (1994) 175.

[19] On this topic, see Steiner (1994) *passim*.

... why are you upset at what Darius has written, as though his boastful letter had real power? There are some dogs too who make up for being small by barking loud, as though they could give the illusion of being powerful by their barking. That is what Darius is like ...

Not all letters are powerless, of course. Alexander himself used the power of a letter against the Tyrians, and in turn will send threatening letters back to the Persian king, entering into an extended diplomatic exchange. But he refuses to take Darius' letter seriously because Darius refuses to take him seriously; Darius' words are characterized as boastful, excessive, not representative of what Alexander perceives as their equal footing. Darius tried to intimidate Alexander by treating him as a harmless child. Alexander responds in kind by manipulating Darius' identity with a vivid and insulting simile: Darius is a dog whose bark is worse than his bite. Alexander's public reception and reading of the letter, done in front of the troops, is staged for the sake of army morale. He makes the letter public in order to undercut its claim, and convinces his men of Darius' impotence by redefining the king's words as loud but ineffectual. In this way Alexander sustains his role as both master writer and master reader; his manipulation of the epistolary situation parallels and foreshadows his mastery of military strategy.

His rejection of the power of Darius' words is curiously contradicted, however, in his subsequent dealings with the messengers. He orders them to be crucified, and when the men object that they have done nothing to deserve their fate, he answers cleverly (1.37):

Blame King Darius, not me: Darius sent you with a letter like that, as though it were to a brigand chief, not to a king. So I am killing you as though you had come to a ruthless man, not a king.

When it is convenient for him to take the letter "seriously" he does so, allowing Darius to invent a role for him as a ruthless brigand. But to his own troops he denies that the king's words have any power to affect him. In the end, in order to show the envoys the difference between a Greek king and a barbarian despot, he relents and lets them return safely to Darius' camp, carrying a letter in answer, a letter which he reads first in full to his own troops, before sealing it (1.38).

We are accustomed to reading letters over the shoulder of the receiver, not the sender. Variation in the divulging of a letter's contents lets us see the situation from the Greek perspective, through the eyes of the Greek army rather than those of Darius himself, and confirms Alexander's democratic and civilized approach to campaigning. It also removes the feeling of "eavesdropping;" we are invited to participate fully, not as marginalized secondary audiences. By including the external reader in the story in this way, by making all public and open, Alexander as "master writer" gives us the impression that we are part of his group, and guarantees our allegiance.[20]

Alexander's letter responds point by point to Darius' insults. It is tactically useful for him to emphasize his own mortal beginnings ("King Alexander, son of King Philip and his mother, Olympias") in contrast to Darius' lofty claims to divinity. If we read just the opening address, we may think that Alexander is acknowledging the superior power of his enemy: "to the King of Kings, enthroned with the gods, who rises to heaven with the Sun, a Great God, King of the Persians, greetings" (χαίρειν). But this is immediately sabotaged by what follows, as Alexander writes (1.38):

It is a disgrace if someone priding himself on such great power and "rising with the Sun" eventually falls into base slavery to a man, Alexander ... you have no power over us, but usurp the title of the gods and attribute their powers on earth to yourself. I am going to wage war on you in the view that you are mortal ...

Alexander accepts Darius' claim to divinity only to threaten the "god" with enslavement to a mere mortal; but by the end of the paragraph he has exposed Darius as a mortal pretending to be divine, and promises to meet him on equal ground: they are both mortal, and fate alone will decide who is destined to conquer. Darius' letter continues to be his own undoing, as Alexander imagines a scenario in which Darius will never "win." If Darius is defeated, Alexander will have all the glory of having killed a mighty king; but if Alexander is defeated, Darius will be famous only for killing a brigand, "according to your letter to me." Alexander finishes his letter by reinterpreting the items sent by Darius: the strap will be used to whip the barbarians, the ball represents Alexander's power over the whole world (which he per-

---

[20] We are told explicitly that Alexander reads out the letter in the absence of Darius' letter carriers (1.38). He may assume that if they knew the insulting contents of the letter, they would refuse to carry it to their master.

ceives as spherical), and the gold is the first installment of much
tribute to come. Thus Alexander takes complete control of the
production of meaning in both his and Darius' letters; he is the
omnipotent reader who can determine "meaning" according to his
own will or judgment, can use the same words to mean totally different things, and can convince others to agree with his interpretations. His control of language in the letters foreshadows his
conquest of empire.

Preliminaries over, the two settle down to an extended battle of
words, which will last until they meet face-to-face. The correspondence fuels their mutual dislike and builds tension while deferring
a physical confrontation. They use letters to threaten, insult, bluff,
and eventually arrange terms of surrender. Darius is disturbed
by the "forcefulness" of Alexander's first letter, and writes to his
allies, hoping that they will arrest the man for him;[21] when this
plan fails, Darius camps near Alexander, and writes another letter.
He still advertises himself as "King of Kings, Great God Darius
and Lord of Nations," but his addressee is now grudgingly
"Alexander, who has plundered the cities." Darius can admit this
much, but he prophesies that Alexander cannot continue to succeed in his campaign. He claims that his adversary is wasting his
time conquering poor and isolated cities which Darius himself has
ignored, and he concludes thus (1.40):

I have written to you to come and do obeisance to King Darius – and I
swear to you by Zeus, the greatest god and my father, that I will not hold
against you what you have done. But you persist in another, foolish,
course; so I shall punish you with an indescribable death; and those with
you who have failed to instill good sense in you shall suffer worse than
you.

We are told that "when Alexander received the letter of Darius
and read it, he was not incensed at Darius' haughty words" (1.41);
realizing that letters were no longer useful, that Darius was simply
repeating empty threats and would not be convinced to surrender,
he attacked at Issos, routed his enemy, and took Darius' family
hostage.

As Darius tries to regroup his forces, we are told of other letters

---

[21] Some letters may have fallen out at this point (1.39). Darius makes obscure allusions to
the ability of the satraps and generals to quench lightning bolts, a boast they may have
made in an earlier letter; see Dowden (1989) 683, note 43.

but are not given the actual texts: Darius writes to allies asking for
help, and these activities are reported in letters from spies to
Alexander. The next letter quoted verbatim is from Alexander to
a general (1.42), two brief lines of military orders. Before the enemies meet again, Alexander falls ill and, about to drink medicine
prescribed by his doctor Philip, is warned by letter that the doctor
plans to poison him (2.8):

Darius told the doctor Philip to poison you when he had the opportunity, promising to give him his sister in marriage and to make him a
partner in his kingdom; and Philip agreed to do this. So be on your
guard, King, against Philip.

Alexander swallows the medicine and only afterwards shows the
doctor the letter, proving his great trust in the man. It turns out
that the writer of the letter, the general Parmenion, had himself
tried to convince Philip to poison Alexander, even offering him
Darius' sister in marriage, but after being refused, wrote the letter
to implicate the doctor in his crime.

Thus in the middle of a narrative of war and a historical novel,
we find an epistolary situation familiar from Attic tragedy. The
poisoning scene could be straight out of Euripides' *Ion*: a murder
plot, the dramatic drinking of the poison, revelation of the guilty
party, and revenge. The vignette adds interest to the narrative and
foreshadows Alexander's eventual death at the hands of another,
more successful poisoner (3.32). But faced with a letter purporting to warn him of Philip's treachery, how can Alexander be so
sure of his doctor's character that he stakes his own life on it?
Alexander rejects the letter as not being "an accurate picture" of
Philip, and trusts his own instincts over the written word. Yet part
of the picture is shown to be a likely one; in fact, Philip admits
that the terms of the letter are correct, except for the small detail
that he rejected Parmenion's plan. What makes Alexander suspicious is perhaps not the precise circumstances of this particular
letter, but rather the age-old association of letters and deception.
He reads this letter in the framework of Homer's Bellerophon and
Euripides' Phaedra. We read the whole scene as a testimony to
Alexander's skill at "reading" correctly, and to his courage in
drinking the medicine before confirming his conclusions of epistolary deceit.

Eight letters then appear in rapid succession, with no linking narrative material other than "x received y's letter and replied as follows" (2.11–12). Darius' allies write first to warn him of Alexander's imminent arrival in his territory, and then again to inform him of the numbers of deserters and dead soldiers; Darius writes to gather his allies, and requests assistance from Porus, king of India.[22] Even Darius' mother gets involved, writing secretly from her captivity, begging her son not to fight Alexander again, but rather to find some honorable peace. "Darius read and wept, remembering his family bonds, but at the same time he was in confusion and came down on the side of war" (2.12).

Also in this sequence are two letters between Darius and Alexander. Darius writes first, a letter in which he rejects the civilized convention of opening and closing address, and claims he no longer cares how Alexander treats the prisoners: his captured family is dead to him, and he will never cease seeking revenge. Alexander answers with the briefest of greetings, "King Alexander to Darius," scolds him for his "gabbling and ineffectual talk," assures his enemy that he will treat the prisoners with courtesy but not out of fear of Darius, and announces in closing that this is the last letter he will ever write to Darius.

This is an awkward vow, since Alexander will wish to communicate with Darius once again before they meet in combat, and we as readers have grown accustomed to the epistolary medium for their exchanges; it seems odd now to revert to the system of an oral message. Why does he suddenly decide to cease writing altogether at this point? And why did he decide to attack at Issos rather than continue his epistolary demands for surrender? Alexander may feel that Darius is no longer capable of rational thought, that all that could be said has already been said, and now it is time for action. For this reason he is no longer "incensed at Darius' haughty words" (1.41), but simply tired of the debate. We

---

[22] The text of the letter to Porus is not given, but a letter corresponding to the stated contents appears at 2.19; it seems that the chronological order of some of these letters is not wholly followed. See Dowden (1989) 695, note 64. What I find most curious about this letter to Porus is that Alexander is said to learn about it from a deserter from Darius' camp, and "as soon as he had read it," he took his whole force toward Ekbatana. If Alexander intercepts the letter, did it ever reach Porus? Something must have reached Porus at 2.12 for him to have answered as he did, so presumably these are two separate letter writing incidents which just happen to ask for the same thing, namely reinforcements in battle.

should keep in mind that refusing to write is also an act of power and domination, a way to cut off all ties before the inevitable end: it may be harder to kill a man with whom you have had a correspondence, as the act of writing marks him as somehow less barbarian. But the decision also offers a pleasing moment of literary symmetry. In portraying Alexander's refusal to write, the author asks us to remember the initial rejection of writing that defined Alexander's relationship with Darius. Things have come full circle, and Alexander's vow as a child to reclaim Macedonian tribute from Persia is about to be fulfilled.

Ironically, of course, as the letters end, so should our story; yet Alexander manages to find a way to continue writing. Letter writing has become for him the critical tool in his government, his system of challenge and conquest. Darius, too, seems caught up in the system. In the long-awaited final battle, narrated briefly but powerfully in one paragraph (2.16), Darius is badly beaten; crawling back as a fugitive to his own palace, he sits down to write yet another letter, which will turn out to be his last to Alexander. He admits complete defeat in the greeting: "Darius to my master Alexander, greetings" (Δαρεῖος Ἀλεξάνδρῳ τῷ ἐμῷ μεγάλῳ δεσπότῃ χαίρειν). Darius offers his enemy all his lands and countless treasure as ransom for his wife, mother, and children. Alexander, in his usual fashion, reads the letter aloud to his whole army, refuses its terms, and sends a messenger – but without a letter – to inform Darius of his answer.

We read next of Darius' death by assassination and Alexander's civilized behavior as conquering hero. Alexander wraps up the Persian campaign with a lengthy public letter to the city, letters to Darius' family, and a letter to his own mother (2.21–22). Alexander's letter to Darius' mother, wife, and daughter contains an explanation of how Darius died, and we can compare his epistolary version with the third-person narration of Darius' final moments at 2.20. Alexander offers an abbreviated version of Darius' deathbed speech, which had included moralizing about fate as well as contemplation of the children that would spring someday from their united families. Alexander focuses on the part most relevant for the abandoned women, and writes to them (somewhat inventively), "he said nothing to me except this: 'I entrust to you my mother and my wife, and particularly Roxana, my daughter and your wife.'" Roxana, however, has presumably already guessed at her fate from the letter's address: "King Alexander to Stateira and Rodogoune and my wife, Roxana, greetings."

Rodogoune and Stateira answer promptly, their letter full of flattery and oaths of obedience, almost embarrassing to the modern reader in their abasement before their new ruler. They inform Alexander that they have taken it upon themselves to send letters throughout the kingdom declaring their new allegiance and encouraging others to follow suit. Alexander writes a quick reply thanking them for their sentiments. We are told that "in another letter he wrote to Roxana of his decisions," and then sent a letter to his mother asking for jewelry and clothing for his bride and her family. So women do participate in this story as both writers and readers, and others will play important parts later on. But Roxana herself is mute, a person who is written about but never writes herself, an object of exchange between kings, much like the letters themselves.

Thus far, letters have been used primarily in military contexts: to threaten the enemy, ask for reinforcements, and arrange details concerning prisoners-of-war.[23] But as the *Romance* continues, travel and tourism take their place beside conquest, as Alexander explores the far reaches of the world. The next set of letters begins by voicing the familiar demand for tribute from foreign peoples, but develops into something more unusual, perhaps because Alexander's addressees in this case are not just ordinary foes, but a queen who beats the king at his own game, and the exotic tribe of Amazons.

EPISTOLARY HEROINES AND LETTERS HOME

After his conquests in Persia and India, Alexander decides to visit the famous palace of Semiramis, which our author connects with the palace of Queen Kandake at Meroe, on the Nile in central Sudan.[24] He writes politely to Kandake, saying that he has heard

---

[23] I have omitted the section on Alexander and King Porus of India, which parallels the downfall of Darius. Letters seem to follow Alexander wherever he goes. When the Indian sages learn that the king is on his way to see them, they send their best philosophers to meet him with a letter, addressed pointedly to "the man Alexander," asking him to come in peace (3.5).

[24] It has been suggested that the Kandake episode existed originally as a separate short novel, not necessarily epistolary. See Dowden (1989) 720, note 86.

wonderful things about her country, and then requests tribute at her discretion: "take advice and send what seems appropriate to you" (3.18). The queen responds with generous, if somewhat impractical, tribute, oddly matched with an imperious tone:

Queen Kandake of Meroe and all the princes, to King Alexander, greetings:
Do not think the worse of us for the color of our skin. We are purer in soul than the whitest of your people. We are in number 80 squadrons ready to do harm to aggressors. The emissaries sent by us bring you 100 solid gold ingots, 500 Ethiopians not yet mature, 200 chimpanzees, an emerald crown [and so forth] ... So send us immediately the men you want to receive the presents. And write to us about yourself when you have become king of the whole world. Farewell.

Kandake begins her letter with an assumption of how Alexander must view her people. She assumes they are being judged as "worse" than the Greek army because of the color of their skin, which may be seen to hide their pure and noble souls.[25] Kandake's words imply that she thinks Alexander has misjudged the power of her army, and she quickly corrects him on this point, not directly threatening him, but declaring their willingness to fight against "aggressors," if he chooses to identify himself as such. Her letter reveals her concern with what he must be thinking as he approaches her city: it offers in response a diplomatic mixture of veiled threat and immediate obedience to Alexander's request for tribute.

But what are we to make of the tone of her closing sentence? "And write to us about yourself when you have become king of the whole world." We could read it as sincere, assuming that Kandake is curious to find out more about such an enterprising and successful leader. This interpretation fits with Kandake's commission of a painting of Alexander, made without his knowledge, which she hangs in her palace (3.19), reminding us of the Persian emissaries in book 1 who had done precisely the same thing for Darius. On the other hand, if we read it as hostile or ironic, it suggests that no one could possibly become king of the whole world, so she will not have to worry about hearing ever again from Alexander; in this case, it is an indirect way of saying "don't write back."

[25] On the issue of race, see K. Snowdon, *Blacks in Antiquity* (Cambridge MA 1970).

The story does not end here, especially since Alexander has not yet seen the palace he is so eager to view. After serendipitously rescuing the family of Kandake's son from a rival prince, Alexander has the opportunity, disguised as a letter-bearer accompanying a convoy of gifts, to visit the queen herself (3.20–22).[26] This particular disguise is wonderfully appropriate for the ruler who defines himself by letters. But after the narrative satisfies Alexander's (and our) curiosity about the marvels of Kandake's palace, we hear no more about the letter supposedly containing greetings from Alexander to Kandake; perhaps Alexander, once he had used it as an excuse to get into the city, remembered that no letter was to pass between them until he had conquered the world. Kandake sees through Alexander's disguise, thanks to her portrait of him, and gloats that she has managed to outwit the destroyer of Persia, India, and the whole East. She says to his face "you must now realize, Alexander, that whenever a man thinks that he is brilliant, there will be another man still more brilliant than him. Kandake's mind has been more than a match for your ingenious plan, Alexander" (3.22). Ironically, Kandake does not attribute her brilliance explicitly to her gender: the gnomic statement retains its generic "man" rather than, specific to this case, "woman." But we may recall previously discussed examples of women depicted as prime "discoverers," whether Atossa as the mythical inventor of letters, or Herodotus' story of the Spartan Gorgo, wife of Leonidas, who discovered a message hidden underneath the smooth wax of the tablet.

By pretending to be the messenger for his own letter, Alexander creates a doubled identity: disguised man and letter both are meant to represent Alexander, sent in his place to protect the real Alexander from any physical confrontation with the enemy. We see yet again the familiar connection between letters and deception originating in Homer, even when the deception is wholly invented by Alexander for the thrill of the chase. But Kandake shrewdly matches the written and oral messages, and she exposes him as the true author (and single referent) of confusing signs, matching flesh and blood with yet another representation, the portrait hanging on her wall. The letter as a "portrait of the soul"

---

[26] We are reminded that Alexander tricked Darius in a similar manner, although no letter was involved in the prior situation (2.13–15).

ought to offer deeper insight, but in this case it loses out to a "portrait of the body," because the letter lies by implication, suggesting that the sender is absent when in fact he is present. Fortunately, Kandake is more merciful than Alexander himself, and all ends happily, although curiously without even a hint of a love affair.

The next stop on Alexander's epistolary tour is the land of the Amazons (3.25–26). Alexander sends the expected letter introducing himself to the group as a whole (3.25): "King Alexander to the Amazons, greetings" (Βασιλεὺς Ἀλέξανδρος Ἀμαζόσι χαίρειν). He opens with a catalogue of all his recent conquests: Darius, the Indians, the gymnosophists who offered up tribute. He concludes with their present plans:

After that we are marching to you. Meet us with joy; we do not come to do you ill, but to see your country and at the same time to do you good. Farewell.

The catalogue of war victims for whom Alexander claims personal responsibility impresses the Amazons more than his conciliatory last words, and they respond in the voice of "the leading Amazons and the mightiest, to Alexander, greetings" (3.25):

We have written to you so that you may be informed before you set foot in our land and not have to withdraw ignominiously. By our letter we shall make clear the nature of our country and of ourselves, who have a way of life to be reckoned with.

What follows is a combined autobiography and ethnography, an epistolary guide to the wonders of Amazonian culture. The tone is proud, and the women are unafraid of hostile male forces. We read of an island surrounded by a circular river, 270,000 women living in armed readiness, daughters conceived with men on the other side of the river and sent to live with the Amazons at age seven; the Amazons have their own culture of war, honoring brave fighters and paying good money for enemy corpses. They know that defeat at their hands brings with it great shame for men, while conquest of mere women would bring no glory.[27] They threaten Alexander with this double jeopardy, and ask him to write a reply when he has reached his decision.

---

[27] Cf. Alexander's interpretation of the "no-win" situation for Darius (1.38).

This letter of the Amazons goes far beyond a simple answer to Alexander's greetings. Alexander presumably has already heard of their exploits and customs; he would not be writing to them in the first place if he was not familiar with their situation. The women claim that their letter will make clear to the intruder that they are a force to be reckoned with, but the letter offers its narrative more for our benefit than for Alexander's. For the external reader, this truly is the first introduction to the Amazon nation. We take in the details and suspend disbelief while the "leading Amazons and the mightiest" sketch for us a portrait of their way of life. The epistolary form here is a convenient envelope, made realistic by Alexander's previous epistolary exchanges with the enemy on the verge of battle. The body of the letter has more in common with Alexander's descriptive letters home to his mother than the kinetic, action-producing correspondence of Darius and Alexander. The difference remains, however, that the Amazons are describing themselves, while Alexander's letters home describe others.

The letter produces an unexpected response from Alexander, who smiles as he reads it (3.26). How do we read his smile? Does he find it incongruous that women should threaten him? Does he laugh at their assumption that he will "have to withdraw ignominiously?" His return letter implies that he feels obliged to fight the Amazons: "a legacy of shame will be left to us if we fail to campaign against you." The Amazons had asserted that to fight women would bring the army only shame, whether they succeeded or failed in their attempt. Alexander turns that argument around in his response and claims that *not* to fight will surely bring shame upon his men. But he offers both sides a way to resolve the crisis in which no one will be hurt: the women are to advance to the border, let themselves be seen by Alexander's army, offer whatever tribute they wish to give, and Alexander will promise not to enter their land. He demands in addition a tribute of live Amazons; whether they are to work as mercenaries or concubines is unclear: "we shall give each person you send an allowance of a stater of gold per month and maintenance. After a year these will return, and you must send replacements" (2.26). The women are asked to present themselves as tourist attractions, a curiosity for the advancing army, and to serve foreigners in an annual reenactment of their submission to his will. Alexander closes his letter by adopting the Amazon's closing formula: "When you have reached a deci-

sion, write us a reply" (βουλευσάμεναι οὖν περὶ τούτων ἀντι-
γράψατε ἡμῖν).

When Darius and Alexander played their game of epistolary
"chicken," the exchange lasted a good long while; the Amazons,
by contrast, capitulate after the second letter. They permit
Alexander to travel through their country, offer him gold, horses,
and their own people. They emphasize their allegiance to him, his
mastery over them achieved not by the sword but by the word:
"We have decided to write to you, to live in our own land, and to
be subject to you as master." The very act of writing back to
Alexander is the first step in submission: they are bullied by his
letter, tempted by his terms. Writing to declare their allegiance
enacts the deed itself, and as the letter is handed to the king, so
their nation transfers itself from independence to subject status,
puts itself in the hands of the king. When they say "we have
decided to write to you," they admit fully the import of writing
back, just as Alexander in his youth had understood the power of
withholding letters. To write back is to submit, to give in to the
terms of the enemy. But they vainly attempt to retain some shred
of self-respect as they phrase their surrender with the words "we
have decided," as if it were a totally voluntary act, not a forced
capitulation.

We are fortunate to have two versions of the conquest of the
Amazons, one in the passages just discussed, and the other in the
section immediately following (3.27), in the form of a letter from
Alexander to his mother, Olympias. What strikes the reader first
in Alexander's letter to his mother is how little material about the
Amazons is repeated from the earlier passages. The lack of overlap is surely for the sake of external readers, who would be bored
by an immediate repetition of the same story. The Amazons' letter
of capitulation is divided from the letter to Olympias by only one
sentence ("After this exchange of letters, Alexander wrote to his
mother, Olympias, this account of his deeds" 3.27), but the information he thinks worth passing on is completely different from the
Amazons' own account in their ethno-autobiography. Alexander
writes to his mother of their physical appearance, clothes, weapons, and intelligence, perhaps because he thinks she will be interested in precisely these, more "feminine," details (3.27).

It is for both his own and his mother's sake that Alexander depicts worthy opponents, exceptional in their physical and mental

abilities; but in his letter to the Amazons he had emphasized just the opposite, that he would be ashamed if mere women were to intimidate his army (3.26). The letter writer composes with the reader in mind, and a single event is presented quite differently in two letters. Alexander is well aware of the power of the written word: he remarks in this letter on the effectiveness of his earlier letter in convincing the Amazons to surrender without a fight (3.27): "we persuaded them by our letters to become subject to us."

Alexander's letter to Olympias about his adventures continues for two short chapters (3.27–28), and is filled with reports of amazing sights encountered abroad, including magical mountains, talking birds, and gigantic golden wine bowls. He ends this letter by throwing up his hands at the impossibility of describing in words the quality and quantity of the marvels he has seen, quite a tease for his mother and for us, who would love to hear more stories about the wonders at the edges of the earth. In other works, epistolary aposiopesis is often predicated on physical challenges: tears blur the eyes, the hand is weary, the paper supply running short. But Alexander stops in full flow out of aesthetic or artistic failure: language simply cannot do justice to the wonders he has seen.

Such letters home do not function as agents themselves, but describe events in a narrative not unlike that of the third person; the epistolary form here stands in for third-person narrative. The author of the *Romance* uses Olympias, and an absent son's natural filial piety, as an excuse to include lengthy epistolary narratives on all sorts of subjects, narratives that are livened up by the pretense of reading over someone else's shoulder. Earlier in the book Alexander had written an epistolary travelogue to his mother and his tutor Aristotle that went on for a full eighteen chapters (2.23–41). By the time the reader reaches the "farewell," only the first-person formulation keeps her from forgetting that this is a letter. Later, we are told that Alexander writes another letter to his mother, when he is in Babylon, unaware that the day of his death is approaching (3.30). But the final letter to his mother, which also happens to be the final letter of the *Romance*, is transmitted in its entirety, written by a scribe who attends Alexander on his death-bed (3.33):[28]

---

[28] Although the material could be analyzed from an epistolary angle, I will not discuss Alexander's last will and testament here. For the text, see Stoneman (1991) 152–55.

King Alexander to my dearest mother, greetings:
When you receive this, my last letter, prepare an expensive meal to
thank Providence above for having given you such a son. But if you wish
to do me honor, go on your own and collect together all men, great and
humble, rich and poor, for the meal, saying to them: "See, the meal is
prepared! Come and feast!" But no one who now or in the past has experienced suffering should come, as I have prepared a meal not of suffering but of joy.
Farewell, Mother.

The convention of a farewell letter is that it be serious: last
words are given a mysterious weight and value, as if the speaker
were already sharing some divine intelligence from beyond the
grave. But Alexander, in the process of dying as he dictates the
letter, writes humorously to his mother about his own death.
Olympias is caught unawares by this epistolary anomaly. Alexander dictates the precise words that his mother is to say in
public after he dies, and she follows his script exactly. Only after
she utters the words does she comprehend the full meaning of his
letter, that no one on this earth lives without suffering, and that
her own grief is to be understood in the light of all human grief.
She realizes that this strange letter is not just a death announcement, or the model for a bizarre dinner invitation, but a letter of
consolation, precisely the right kind of letter to write under the
circumstances. Alexander writes to console his mother for his impending death; we shall see a comparable letter (17) at the end of
Chion of Heraclea, in which the hero, facing certain death, writes
not to his parents, but to his teacher Plato, reassuring him that he
remains true to his philosophical faith to the very end.

The *Alexander Romance* begins with a refusal to write (to Darius)
and ends with a letter whose "farewell," lacking an explicit reference to death, is all the more poignant for Alexander's actual
death. Along the way, we come to know the hero through his
letters, as he uses the epistolary form to transmit a wide variety
of messages: military commands, challenges to enemies, diary-like
descriptions of his travels, his engagement to Roxana, and demands for tribute or submission. He likens his letter to the Amazons to an endeavor at persuasion: when he writes, his letters are
sincere and powerful, his word is law; but when enemies write, he
scorns their letters as empty and impotent, unable to frighten him
into surrender. Alexander uses letters as an excuse to travel deep
into enemy territory, disguised as a letter-carrier, in order to view

his victims in their own homes and gain an advantage over them in time of attack. He is depicted as a master letter writer and manipulator of words, pushing epistolary convention to its limits as he infuses even opening and closing formulas with added meaning.

At the beginning of this chapter, I mentioned briefly that most scholars argue for an epistolary core to this work, a core that gradually attracted layers of narrative accretion over the years. The strength of its epistolary nucleus is revealed in the curious irony that a man such as Alexander, famed for his military exploits and active life, is represented in the *Romance* as a constant scribbler, an obsessive letter writer who accomplished many of his most famous deeds not by brute strength, but by persuasive or intimidating words, and whose final act in life, writing home to his mother, is worthy of the plot of the most sentimental eighteenth-century epistolary novel.

CHAPTER 8

Pseudonymous letter collections

In a man's letters, you know, Madam, his soul lies naked, his letters are only the mirrour of his breast; whatever passes within him is shown undisguised in its natural process; nothing is inverted, nothing distorted; you see systems in their elements; you discover actions in their motives.

Dr. Johnson, "Letter to Mrs. Thrale"[1]

There is, indeed, no transaction which offers stronger temptations to fallacy and sophistication than epistolary intercourse.

Dr. Johnson, "The Life of Pope"[2]

This chapter will address the controversial subject of pseudonymous letters, that is, letters written by an anonymous writer or writers in the name of a famous person, sometimes mythical, sometimes historical.[3] The category occupies a middle ground between embedded letters, such as those discussed in the ancient novels and in the *Alexander Romance*, and the epistolary novel: pseudonymous letters are influenced by the former, and suggestive of the latter. Thucydides' use of embedded historical letters may have inspired later pseudonymous letter writers, particularly in the case of Themistocles, whose letter to Artaxerxes is quoted extensively in Thucydides (Thuc. 1.137.4), and who is the alleged author of a famous collection of letters.[4] The pseudonymous letters in turn may also play a part in the development of the epistolary novel; several of them tell a carefully shaped story through letters,

---

[1] B. H. Bronson, ed., *Samuel Johnson*, 3rd edn. (New York 1971) 25.

[2] Bronson (1971) 470.

[3] Sykutris (1931) 185–220. See esp. 208: "Der fingierte Brief ... Mit diesem Namen bezeichnen wir diejenigen Briefe, deren angeblicher Schreiber bezw. Adressat entweder nicht existiert oder aber die ihnen beigelegten Briefe, mindestens in dieser Form, nicht geschrieben bezw. erhalten haben."

[4] A. J. Podlecki, *The Life of Themistocles* (Montreal 1975) 129, who cites C. Huit, "Les Epistolographes grecs," *REG* 2.6 (1889) 149–63, esp. 157.

with a clearly defined narrative structure. The question of categorization will occupy both this and the following chapter, when we turn to the epistolary novel *Chion of Heraclea*.

Many of the pseudonymous letter collections, while admittedly hard to date, may originate in the first or second century CE, the same general period in which the epistolographers of the Second Sophistic and the author of *Chion of Heraclea* flourished.[5] We can read them for clues to the general interest in fictional letter forms among the writing and reading public of that era. Also, they are our first example of free-standing epistolary collections, a group of letters organized and edited to sustain characterization of the writer(s), to advance a plot, or to replicate the patterns (orderly or disorderly) of a correspondence over time. This chapter will consider how some of the pseudonymous collections function as specifically epistolary fictions, namely how they tell their narratives through an exchange of letters, and whether they reveal a self-consciousness about their epistolary medium through references to the acts of reading, writing, and sending.

BENTLEY'S LEGACY

The only modern reference work which contains all the pseudonymous letter collections is still R. Hercher's anthology of Greek epistolary texts, *Epistolographi Graeci* (Paris 1873), although new editions of individual authors have since appeared.[6] Hercher's edition contains the Greek texts (with facing Latin translation) of letters attributed to Aeschines, Anacharsis, Aristotle, Artaxerxes, Brutus, Chion, Crates, Demosthenes, Diogenes, Dion, Euripides, Heraclitus, Hippocrates, Isocrates, Lucian, Periander, Phalaris, Plato, the Pythagoreans, Socrates and the Socratics, Solon, Thales, Themistocles, Xenophon, and Zeno; in addition to the pseudonymous writers, Hercher includes the letter collections of Aelian, Alciphron, Philostratus, Aristaenetus, Theophylactus, and many Christian writers. His work is massive in its scope and scholar-

---

[5] Sykutris (1931) 210, notes that pseudonymous letters are rare in Latin literature, a fact which he is at a loss to explain. Perhaps the existence early on of Cicero's "real" letters dissuaded prospective pseudonymous authors.

[6] For a general overview of pseudonymous letter writers, see F. Susemihl, *Geschichte der griechischen Litteratur in der Alexandrinerzeit*, 2 vols. (Leipzig, 1891–92), vol. II, 579–601, and Speyer (1971).

ship, totalling 843 pages with indexes and critical notes, including approximately 1,600 letters by sixty different authors.

The reason for the paucity of editions other than Hercher's is clear: the letters attributed to famous men of antiquity have never recovered from the scorching denunciation of Richard Bentley, in his *Dissertation upon the Epistles of Phalaris, Themistocles, Socrates, Euripides, and Others* (London 1697), who boasted that it would be "no unpleasant labour ... to pull off the disguise from those little pedants, that have stalked about so long in the apparel of heroes."[7] Scholars now generally agree that most of the pseudonymous letter collections are literary inventions composed after the lives of the "heroes" in question, even if they may include some original material or be based on genuine collections no longer extant. But, while much ink has been spilled on arguments for and against authenticity, few have questioned Bentley's original assumption that their authors intended to deceive the reading public, and consciously adopted a "disguise." While I do not believe that we can uncover the primary "intent" of these pseudonymous writers any more than we can uncover their identities, we have insufficient information about their impact upon their contemporaries – indeed, one of the common traits of these works is that they were rarely commented on in antiquity, a fact which is often used against them – to conclude that the authors wished to pass themselves off as the genuine article.

Modern scholarship in its eagerness for classical material has often incorporated into the classical canon pages that have, upon closer inspection, turned out to be products of a post-classical age. The rejection of such "forgeries," once discovered, as worthy of study stems mainly from embarrassment at our own naiveté.[8] R. Syme questions whether "forgery" is the proper term for all such items: "the word exudes an odour of personal guilt and criminal handiwork."[9] He prefers the word "impostures," and reminds us that a large number of literary impostures were doubtless created without any serious intent to deceive:

---

[7] The German scholar Leibniz was working on the same problem as early as 1675; see B. Kytzler, *Erotische Briefe der griechischen Antike* (Munich 1967) 287.

[8] I have written on this subject with reference to the anacreontic poems in *The Poetics of Imitation* (Cambridge 1992).

[9] R. Syme, "Fraud and Imposture," in Entretiens Hardt 18 *Pseudepigrapha* I (Geneva 1972) 3–17, esp. 13. See also A. Gudeman, "Literary Frauds Among the Greeks," in *Classical Studies in Honour of Henry Drisler* (New York 1894) 53–74.

When for one reason or another an author has chosen to write under an invented name, the deceit may be mild, venial, or temporary; he may not be loath to allow the truth to percolate. Most important, a deed of deception may actually be intended to be seen through sooner or later.[10]

Many questions remain about the social context of imposture and literary impersonation. Can we determine if exercises of stylistic emulation in the schools led directly to impersonation in letter collections? Did the canonization of authors and the payment for original manuscripts encourage attempts by imposters to "discover" lost works? Who was the audience for pseudonymous epistolary fictions? These issues seem to me more interesting, and certainly more susceptible to scholarly inquiry, than the categorization of an epistolary collection as authentic or fake.[11] In what follows, I will follow Syme in avoiding the word forgery, but will retain the term "pseudonymous," by which I mean an anonymous author who writes under an assumed name which, in the case of epistolary fiction, usually belongs to a well-known historical figure. This term remains neutral about the intention of the author to deceive or not to deceive his audience.[12]

THE GENRE OF PSEUDONYMOUS LETTERS

In *Der griechische Briefroman*, N. Holzberg argues for certain genre requirements of the Greek "novel in letters": the story will represent scenes from the life of a famous person from Greek history in the fifth or fourth century BCE through that person's letters; the letters will give the impression of having been really written by that person by imitating dialect and reflecting historical setting, but this same attention to detail will create opportunities for inad-

---

[10] Syme (1972) 14, and the discussion of terminology for literary forgeries in Speyer (1971) 13–21.

[11] These questions are discussed by Huit (1889) 152. See also Gudeman (1894) 55: "literary frauds cannot thrive in an age of intellectual productivity. It was not till a *reading* public had arisen in Greece ... that such practices found more favourable conditions of growth." Speyer (1971) 133 discusses the effect on forgery of Hellenistic rulers "buying" manuscripts of famous authors' works.

[12] Speyer also differentiates between a pseudonymous work and a forgery: Speyer (1971) 13: "Ein Pseudepigraphon ist ein literarisches Werk, das nicht von dem Verfasser stammt, dem es der Titel (Die Subscriptio), der Inhalt, oder die Überlieferung zuweisen ... Eine Fälschung liegt dann vor, wenn der wirkliche Verfasser mit dem angegebenen nicht übereinstimmt und die Maske als Mittel gewählt wurde, um Absichten durchzusetzen, die ausserhalb der Literatur, das heisst der Kunst, lagen. Nur wo Täuschungsabsicht, also dolus malus, vorliegt, wird der Tatbestand der Fälschung erfüllt." For terms for "Fälschungen" in ancient Greek and Latin, see Speyer (1971) 16, where a common metaphor for forgery is that of a family relationship: the forgery is an illegitimate child, *nothos* as opposed to *gnesios*.

vertent anachronisms; as information is gradually revealed during the collection, the protagonist will explore his feelings, thoughts, and experiences, usually with clear inner development (e.g. Chion, Hippocrates), but at other times reflecting confusion according to the circumstances (e.g. Themistocles).[13] While I would hesitate to categorize all the *pseudonymoi* as "novelistic," Holzberg's list of elements applies equally to the collections discussed here. The most obvious shared trait of all the pseudonymous collections is their supposed historicity.

The principal impulse behind the role playing of a pseudonymous letter writer may have been precisely a glimpse into the glorious Greek past from a more personal angle, and the illumination of a particular historical figure. This interest in classicizing and a fascination with the documents of the past are symptomatic of both Hellenistic and later imperial times.[14] In this case, the author focuses on one individual and illuminates his life through imaginary letters. The letter writer presents an "apology" for the hero's life, or challenges a later generation to admire his accomplishments, viewing and interpreting historical events through the lens of one man's personal correspondence.[15] The epistolary genre implies a focus on the inner life of the "hero," and the reader is then invited to identify with the *ego* of the letter.[16] This type of writing has its roots in the rhetorical character sketches (*ethopoieia*) mentioned previously. By the Roman imperial period, the imaginative composition of letters to and from famous men had become a standard component of the rhetoric syllabus, and is clearly related to the fictitious speech put into a character's mouth and delivered on a specified mythical or historical occasion.[17] These literary

---

[13] N. Holzberg, *Der griechische Briefroman: Gattungstypologie und Textanalyse* (Tübingen 1994) 47–52 offers a convenient synopsis of the whole genre typology.

[14] A useful discussion of classicizing is that of A. Dihle, *Greek and Latin Literature of the Roman Empire*, trans. M. Malzahn (London 1994) 49–61.

[15] Syme (1972) 7–9, offers the following motives for literary fraud: a political purpose, national pride, defense of religious or philosophical doctrines, or the satisfying of curiosity about the lives and writings of authors who subsequently achieved the rank of "classics." Speyer (1971) 106 and 131–50 distinguishes between personal motives and motives involving another person or a wider social group.

[16] Holzberg (1994) 2–3.

[17] See D. A. Russell, *Greek Declamation* (Cambridge 1983) 1–20; Podlecki (1975) 129–30; Syme (1972) 6; Speyer (1971) 32–33: "Die Arbeiten der Rhetoren, ihrer Schüler und der von ihnen beeinflussten Schriftsteller haben bewirkt, dass die Grenze zwischen echter und frei erfundener Urkunde weithin unsicher wurde. Bei einem antiken Brief, der unter dem Namen einer bekannten Persönlichkeit umläuft, ist der Verdacht gross, dass ein Rhetor ihn erfunden hat."

exercises in turn grew beyond the schoolroom into the forum of
declamations on fictional topics, both judicial and historical: public performances for the entertainment and edification of adult
audiences.[18] While not engaged in public performance in the same
way, since their medium was written rather than oral, the pseudonymous writers developed an even more sophisticated pattern of
impersonation: some record the writings of a single correspondent
(e.g. Chion's univocal letters), while others include a number of
writers within a related group (e.g. the Socratic letters). Almost all
the collections, on stylistic or other grounds, have been shown to
be the product of more than one author; this may reflect an act of
collaboration, or, perhaps more likely, an accretion of invented
letters around an original core.

The urge to read the private words of famous historical figures,
such as tyrants or philosophers, reveals a kind of antiquarian interest in great men, similar to a contemporary fascination with the
diaries and letters of Virginia Woolf, for example, or the private
letters of former presidents. The curious reader hopes to find in
the author's writings a "mirror of the soul," to use an image popular in the writings of ancient epistolary theorists (e.g. "Demetrius" *On Style* 227).[19] One could call our readings of such letters
"voyeuristic," as we seek glimpses into the private thoughts of a
public figure. But the shift from reading available material to producing a "version" of one's own is a momentous one. The individual reasons for such a decision will never be clear, but critics
point to an interest in the historical past, or in the personal lives
of famous long-dead authors, an eagerness to supplement existing
information or to replace information that had been lost over the
years, and the invention of an older authority for a particular belief or movement, as in the case of the Cynics' adoption of Anacharsis as their "culture hero."[20] The goal of the pseudonymous
epistolographer was thus to work the bare bones of a biography
into a compelling life story. He was both scholar and creative artist, researching historical materials in order to define the bounds

---

[18] E. L. Bowie, "Greeks and their Past in the Second Sophistic," *Past and Present* (1970) 5.
[19] The texts of the ancient epistolary theorists are conveniently collected in Malherbe
(1988). Malherbe dates "Demetrius" to the period between the first century BCE and the
first century CE.
[20] See Speyer (1971) 106 and 131–50.

of the tradition, and using his imagination to elaborate creatively and dramatically on that tradition.

Did letters in particular, more than other genres, offer fertile ground for pseudonymous composition? In the opinion of A. Gudeman, writing in the late 1800s,[21]

in a letter, artistic unity, cogency of reasoning and rhetorical finish are not prerequisite qualities; an easy abandon, on the contrary, variety and multiplicity of topics, and a greater stylistic freedom in their treatment, constitute some of the characteristics of all confidential communications. The author in this field had therefore a comparatively easy task to accomplish, and his production, whether composed with a view to deception or written as a rhetorical school-exercise, would easily pass critical scrutiny as to its genuineness, if a reasonable amount of care was taken in preserving consistency in the characterization and if his treatment kept within the bounds of biographical accuracy or historical probability.

Gudeman's appeal to a standard of consistency in characterization reminds us that the writing of pseudonymous letters depends first of all on the established reputation of the person in whose voice the letters are written. Epistolary fiction often depends on the paradigm of a previously defined personality, whether a historical type, as in the case of Socrates or Chion, or a socio-literary stereotype, as in the parasites of Alciphron (all to be considered below and in later chapters). In our modern epistolary fictions, we are accustomed to learning about the correspondents as they write: Richardson's Lovelace and Clarissa do not exist before we come to know them through their letters. In antiquity, however, it is rare to find a fictional letter collection that does not assume prior knowledge of the subject: thus the letters of Plato are read against his wider corpus, the letters of Chion are compared with historical data from other sources, and Alciphron's colorful characters step straight out of Menander's Athens. This dependence on "history" or literary tradition may spring from the original impulse of the rhetorical exercise. No self-respecting teacher in the ancient world would assign a student to write a letter based on what the baker's assistant in the house next door said when he found mice in the flour bins. The use of well-known names, specific places, even precise dates was required if the author wished

---

[21] Gudeman (1894) 65.

the details of his letter to ring true, and if the teacher was to evaluate the work according to conventional standards of verisimilitude and probability.[22] When mismanaged, however, these attempts at historical accuracy allow scholars to challenge the work's authenticity.[23]

A further consequence of the historical nature of most pseudonymous writings is that we may wonder how the editor of any given collection came across the letters, and whether he presents them as he found them, or if they have been reorganized or edited in some way. If the editor or collector himself is one of the participants in the exchange, the explanation is somewhat easier: he may have kept copies of his own letters, or asked his addressee to return both sides of the correspondence at a later date. If he is merely an interested observer, he needs a more elaborate excuse for possessing them: a friend gave him the letters, they were found in an abandoned castle, or a whole bag of letters came from a "postboy robbed of his mail."[24] This kind of explanation occurs also in the context of novels: Antonius Diogenes has a two-fold explanation of his sources for *The Incredible Things Beyond Thule.* Two letters preface his work, with what appear to be mutually exclusive sources: one describes the author's library of historians' and travelers' reports that he used in composing his (true) story; the other relates how the cypress tablets on which the novel was written were originally found in a crypt along with six coffins, and then passed to different owners as war plunder.[25] Similarly, two fictitious eye-witness accounts of the Trojan War by authors writing in imperial times are both prefaced by a dedicatory letter in-

---

[22] J. Sykutris, *Die Briefe des Sokrates und der Sokratiker* (Paderborn 1933) 116: "Die Fiktion eines Briefwechsels fordert, dass man entweder eine konkrete Einzelheit auf eine bestimmte Person bezieht oder aus anderen Quellen mehr oder weniger entlegene Namen heranzieht."

[23] R. J. Lenardon, "Charon, Thucydides, and 'Themistokles'," *Phoenix* 15 (1961) 36. Speyer (1971) 82 claims that the more specific the details are, the more likely it is that the letters are false, as the author's anxiety reveals itself in an overzealous attempt at particulars.

[24] The title of Charles Gildon's epistolary novel from 1692–93: *Post-Boy Rob'd of His Mail.* The work is mentioned in R. A. Day *Told in Letters: Epistolary Fiction Before Richardson* (Ann Arbor 1966) 40ff., who discusses in that context the fashion of epistolary "secret histories" in English writing of the seventeenth and eighteenth centuries. Jost (1968) 122 considers various ways that an editor may justify the existence of an epistolary collection.

[25] See Stephens and Winkler (1995) 102–03.

forming the reader how each respective text was discovered and then translated from Greek to the more accessible Latin.[26]

Looking more closely at the list of names associated with pseudonymous compositions, it becomes clear that certain types were favored; many of the names represent either philosophers and wise men, or politicians and tyrants. To turn to the former, if letters were indeed considered images of the soul, they could offer insights into a philosopher's mind, which would in turn presumably deepen his disciples' understanding of his public teachings. We can see this principle at work in the letters of several philosophers (Plato, Heraclitus, the Cynics), but particularly in the case of Socrates and his disciples.[27] Here we have a man famous for his genius, surrounded by a group of supporters who desire nothing more than to follow his teachings. The writings of his followers, whether in his name or in their own voices after his death, praise the actions and words of their hero, confirm the importance of his beliefs, and transfer the oral tradition that developed around him into a more permanent written form. The resulting letters, while containing little philosophical material, offer a lively and flattering picture of the great man. The impulse is similar to that of Xenophon's narratives of Socrates, namely intellectual association with great men, but the epistolary form brings a great deal more vividness and emotion to the texts, particularly when several voices are allowed to speak consecutively. The plurality of voices also works as confirmation of the facts: individual writers presenting roughly the same version of the events are more likely to be accepted as trustworthy sources.

In the collection of Socratic epistles, we also find two rival schools, each offering justification and glorification of its own beliefs: Antisthenes furnishes the rigorous and Aristippus the hedonistic interpretation. In this case, the epistolary exchange offers

---

[26] The authors are the pseudonymous "Dictys Cretensis" and "Dares Phrygius"; see S. Merkle, "The Truth and Nothing But the Truth: Dictys and Dares," in G. Schmeling, ed., *The Novel in the Ancient World* (Leiden 1996) 564–80. Similar assurances of authenticity appear in the story of the discovery of Pythagorean texts in the grave of Numa (Pliny *NH* 13.84–87; Livy 40.29.3–14; Plutarch *Numa* 22); and in the role of Damis in Philostratus' *Life of Apollonius of Tyana*. Merkle calls this technique a "Beglaubigungsapparat," an authentication strategy.

[27] For bibliography on the Socratic epistles, see Sykutris (1933), and the references in Holzberg (1994) 188–89.

opportunities for invective against the rival group as well as propaganda for their own "correct" lifestyle. A treatise on the subject could be rejected as just another (mis)interpretation of the philosopher; but a letter in the voice of the great man himself, or in that of his most highly regarded disciple, would be hard to refute. Additionally, the exchange of letters could reveal debates in progress in a way that only a dialogue otherwise could; when the debaters are geographically separated, letters seem the obvious choice. Letters may even permit a more polemical tone than a dialogue is likely to encourage, making for fascinating reading.

The plurality of voices in the Socratic collection contrasts with the single voice of Plato's *Epistles*, among the most disputed texts of antiquity. Scholars debate whether to read the letters as forgeries, because they are so alien to the thought and character of the philosopher Plato familiar to us from the dialogues, or, for the same reason, to accept them as genuine revelations of the life of the man Plato.[28] This Plato, unlike Socrates' great teacher, is willing to put his beliefs in writing, and his letters are addressed to tyrants, as gradually in his correspondence he develops the idea of a mutually beneficial relationship between philosopher and tyrant. He offers advice and criticism in an attempt to turn the tyrant into a wise ruler, describing the ideal situation in letter 7, where philosophers rule the cities and the former rulers have in turn become philosophers. The observations on contemporary politics, and the concern about proper government and the philosopher's duty as a citizen in Plato's *Epistles* may have influenced the author of *Chion of Heraclea*, who approached these same concerns through the figure of a young student of philosophy confronted with a tyrant ruling his city.

Turning to our second category, the connection specifically between tyrants and writing has been treated by D. Steiner, as we have remarked already, who explores fifth-century representations of tyranny and "how frequently documents, scribes, and writing equipment feature in the retinue of despotic Oriental kings."[29] As we have seen in Herodotus, Eastern monarchs are repeatedly shown in the pose of writing decrees, dictating dispatches, and

---

[28] See, most recently, V. Wohl, "Plato avant la lettre: Authenticity in Plato's Epistles," *Ramus* 27 (1998) 60–93, who also refers to earlier literature.

[29] Steiner (1994), 6–7, and esp. chapter 4: "The Tyranny of Writing," 127–85.

using letters not just to supplement but to replace face-to-face interactions with their own people as well as with other nations. Steiner argues that, while writing must have played a major role in the complex administration of large kingdoms, Herodotus surrounds such writing with sinister associations. She points out that the elaborate Persian postal system, for example, had its darker side: the royal monarchy carefully controlled the flow of letters in its territories, and effectively blocked all other attempts to communicate in writing – hence the fanciful ruses of secret dispatches, such as the slaves' shaved heads and eviscerated rabbits which we have discussed previously.[30] I suspect that the links drawn in fifth-century literature between tyrants and writing systems contributed to the popularity of tyrants (such as Artaxerxes, Periander, and Phalaris) as letter writers in the pseudonymous epistolographers. In addition, this popularity is strengthened by an eternal human fascination with the monstrous exercise of power. Fictional or forged letters offer an opportunity to explore aspects of history that could never have been part of the standard historical record. There is no real "news" content to such letters, just events in the daily lives of the rich, famous, or horribly evil. The appeal to read such mundane details is universal and timeless.

If the writing figures in the pseudonymous collections are limited to men already famous from other texts and contexts, the actual types of letters written in their voices are many and varied. Some are familiar from taxonomies of letter writing: letters of consolation, invective, invitation, recommendation, request for payment of debt; there are diatribes in letter form, and didactic treatises.[31] In addition we find personal letters about family affairs, propagandistic messages glorifying a particular political or philosophical cause, letters that attempt to convert their readers to a certain belief, and letters filled with narrative description. The collections themselves may be grouped by the occupations of their supposed writers: philosophers (Socrates, Heraclitus, Plato, the Cynics), wise men (Anacharsis, Apollonius of Tyana, Democritus, Hippocrates), literary figures (Euripides, Xenophon), orators (Demosthenes, Isocrates), and politicians or tyrants (Themistocles,

---

[30] Steiner (1994) 127, 150.
[31] These taxonomies are found in two handbooks: the *Epistolary Types* of Pseudo-Demetrius and the *Epistolary Styles* of Pseudo-Libanius; see Malherbe (1988) for texts.

Phalaris, Artaxerxes, Periander). It is impossible within the scope of this chapter to discuss all the pseudonymous collections, or even fully to address questions of authenticity, provenance, or compilation. I will therefore first summarize some general traits all the collections share, and then select four specific correspondences, not because they are necessarily typical of the rest, but because they allow me to ask certain questions of the whole genre. I have chosen the letters of Anacharsis mainly because the anthology is fairly short (ten letters), and therefore easier to summarize. I will also consider the correspondence between Crates and Diogenes, between Democritus and Hippocrates, and the 148 letters of Phalaris. This chapter will close with a discussion of the letters of Themistocles, asking yet again whether we can apply the term "novel" to any of the pseudonymous collections.

THE ANXIETY OF FICTION

I first turn to a general trait of the pseudonymous letters (and of fictional letters in general) that may be interpreted as reflecting an anxiety about their own fictitiousness. By frequently referring to the act of writing, reading, or sending a letter, the collections respond to a set of assumptions or expectations on the part of their readers, who know that the letters they are reading are not "real," but still enjoy the pretense of reality. This self-referentiality is not limited to pseudonymous or even fictional works; it is, rather, characteristic of all letters, and another indication of the hospitality of the letter form to reflections on its own production and reception. In the case of fictional letters, however, it is an ongoing attempt to give the fiction at least the veneer of genuineness. By this I do not mean to imply that the writers wanted their products to be taken for actual letters of great men. But playing the literary game, whether as a student of rhetoric or as a seasoned author, involved following rules of verisimilitude, and writing a letter was no exception: hence the references in pseudonymous letters to the physical nature of epistolarity: acts of writing or reading, methods of sending, enclosed letters, and epistolary formulas.

In the collection attributed to Themistocles, the letter writer praises swift messengers (*Letter* 3), informs his correspondents where he is at the very moment of writing (on shipboard; in a certain city; in a carriage on the way to Persia), and relates the tale of

Pausanias' elaborate postal system, in which the messenger is killed upon delivery of the letter (16).[32] In a letter which should not have made it into the collection in its entirety (8), the cautious Themistocles orders his reader to

show your friends the first part of this letter up until this point if you wish and read it aloud, but either erase and destroy the section that follows or cut it off and keep it and let it be known to no one except you alone.

What Themistocles wishes to be kept from posterity is the information that he is on his way to Persia, has sent a letter announcing his arrival, and has already received a welcoming reply. We read the rest even more eagerly for the warning.

Whereas Themistocles writes "to the moment," Phalaris is well aware of the time lag that dogs any epistolary delivery. In *Letter* 55, a military dispatch reporting the capture of a castle, he notes that the surrender occurred so quickly that "I believe it was taken even in less time than this letter can possibly take in reaching you." Diogenes expresses a similar sentiment somewhat more dramatically (22): "To me life is so uncertain that I am not sure of lasting till I finish writing you this letter."

Several correspondents write about enclosed documents, asking the reader to imagine an additional letter whose contents may or may not be revealed. Thus Phalaris (117) tells the Milesians that he is sending back their ambassador with his letters unopened, not out of contempt, but because he feels he is not a fit subject for their praise. How he knew that the ambassador carried letters praising him is left unexplained, since the letters themselves remain sealed. Apollonius of Tyana (62) receives a letter from the Spartans informing him of a decree voting him state honors; an official copy of the decree is included for both his and our perusal. Layers of embeddedness can become convoluted, as in the case of Hippocrates' *Letter* 7: Hystanes, commander of the Hellespont, writes to King Artaxerxes that he forwarded the king's letter of invitation to Hippocrates and received a response, which he has enclosed in this dispatch. We, of course, see only the cover letter, but the larger collection offers us both the king's request (3) and Hippocrates' refusal (5).

---

[32] The letter-cum-death warrant is a familiar motif from other sources. Steiner (1994) 150–54, discusses similar cases.

Some letters play with the rules of epistolary formulas; others take the opportunity to comment on possibly contemporary theories of epistolary discourse. When the Socratic disciple Dionysius writes in jest to Speusippus about the conventions of epistolary opening formulas, we may be hearing, in his "literary" letter, an echo of a more formal epistolary handbook (34):[33]

I want to speak to you boldly in sport, since you have already made remarks about me in this manner. I use "Do well" [εὖ πράττειν] in greeting you, if indeed it is better than "Joy to you" [χαίρειν] (which it is not). But it is better than "Enjoy yourself" [ἥδεσθαι], which Lasthenia and Speusippus use.[34]

Closing formulas are more often the topic of conversation than opening. Diogenes (40) takes the closing formulas quite literally when he writes in conclusion to Alexander "it is not right for me to write salutations [ἐρρῶσθαι] and farewell [χαίρειν]" until, he says, Alexander learns to live a good life; similarly, he tries to convert a certain Aroueca to his Cynic ways, and ends the letter (49) "my greetings and salutation have been sent on the condition that you not disregard what is written." Heraclitus plays a similar game when he ends his letter (6) by saying farewell (χαίρειν) to those doctors who are frauds and cannot heal him; this dismissive gesture contrasts with the sincere farewell to Hermodorus at the end of *Letter* 9, which also ends the collection as a whole: "be of good cheer, for you are good" [σὺ δὲ χαῖρε ἀγαθὸς ὤν].

Apollonius of Tyana goes beyond a commentary on the formulaic aspects of letters to connect the letter's style with its writer. Addressing the citizens of Caesarea, he praises the "Greekness" of this city in Palestine, which is evident in the letter itself (11):[35]

I was pleased by your city's Greek culture, which manifests its distinct excellence even in your official correspondence.

---

[33] Examples of later handbooks may be found in Malherbe (1988): Pseudo-Demetrius' *Epistolary Types*, and Pseudo-Libanius' *Epistolary Styles*.

[34] Greek text and translations are from A. J. Malherbe, *The Cynic Epistles* (Missoula MT 1977), who says of the author of the Socratic letters, "that he had thoroughly studied rhetorical letter theory is evident from the fact that he had worked into *Ep.* 33:1 a rule that we know from Cicero, *Ad Fam.* 2.4.1" (28); he refers the reader to Sykutris (1933) 118ff., and L. Köhler, "Briefe des Sokrates und die Sokratiker," *Philologus*, Suppl. 20.2 (Leipzig 1928).

[35] Translation from R. J. Penella, *The Letters of Apollonius of Tyana: A Critical Text with Prolegomena, Translation, and Commentary* (Leiden 1979).

Apollonius claims to recognize a high level of culture in an entire city from the language and style used by its officials in letters. In *Letter* 19, he explains his assumption further, arguing that "first in rank is the style that is proper to a person because it is in accordance with his innate capacity or nature." On a more mundane level, Apollonius answers a friend's letter by interpreting an "amiable" tone as an invitation to visit: the friend who reveals true friendship in his letter is rewarded with a friendly visit (49):

I thoroughly enjoyed the letter that you sent me; it had a very amiable tone, and showed how much you remember about my family ... Therefore, I shall come to visit you as soon as possible.

The focus on writing discussed above, whether a reference to the physicality of the letter itself or a more complex analysis of epistolary style, testifies to a self-consciousness on the part of the writer, an anxiety that his letter fit the expectations of the genre (of "real" letters, that is). The more realistic the epistolary moment appears, both in terms of the occasion and the specific letter, the more convincing it will be to its readers, who seek the literary thrill of reading someone else's private messages. The late second-century CE sophist Philostratus compares Apollonius of Tyana's letters to an archaic type of secret military dispatch, praising their effect: (*Vita Apoll.* 7.35: "they are as laconically brief as if they had just been unwound from a Spartan herald's message stick"; cf. also *Vita Apoll.* 4.27). But occasionally the mimetic conventions of letter writing come into direct conflict with the conventions of epistolary fiction. The complication stems from the tension between the worlds of the internal and external readers, and the need to balance the intimacy of a private exchange with the needs of a general reading public. The issues at stake are the explicit identification of the writer in the body of the letter, rather than in the heading, and the dissemination of information clearly already familiar to his correspondent(s).

For the most part, all readers are guided by headings and addresses, so that the correspondents' identities are made clear at the start. External readers expect to sit down to read a collection, not an individual letter, the assumption being that the same voice, or at least a limited group of voices, will recur throughout. But in fictional letters, the narrator is made to refer to himself remarkably often in the third person, and I suspect that this stylistic idiosyncracy may have come about because the information it conveys is often critical for an understanding of the narrative. As an example, here are the opening lines of the Socratic collection (1):

You seem to have misunderstood my intention, for otherwise you would not have written a second letter and even promised to increase your contribution. But you seem to suspect that Socrates, too, is a retailer of education like the Sophists, and that he wrote what he did earlier, not simply to refuse your offer, but to get even more than you had given earlier.[36]

The letter opens with a pointed reference to a previous correspondence, reminding the reader that most letters presuppose an earlier communication of some sort. It seems that King Archelaus of Macedonia had invited Socrates to his court and offered to pay for his teachings; although Socrates rejected his overtures, we are told that the king then sent a second letter, with promises of even greater rewards.[37] We now read Socrates' second letter of refusal to the king. Although the addressee remains unnamed, the writer, by shifting initially between first- and third-person narrative when referring to himself, orients the reader at this crucial moment. The first sentence uses *moi*, the second names Socrates in the third person, and the third and remaining sections will revert to forms of *ego*. The shifting may seem awkward stylistically, but identification of the writer in the body of the letter, while presumably unnecessary for the king's purposes, is potentially helpful for later readers, especially if the heading were to fall out at some point in transmission.

The communication of information unnecessary for the comprehension of the purported addressee, but crucial for the appreciation of the external reader, is a frequent reminder of the fictionality of pseudonymous letters.[38] In Themistocles' collection, the writer uses *Letters* 6 and 7 to repeat to his banker in detail much of what his banker had apparently written him in a previous (unincluded) letter, solely for our benefit as readers; in *Letter* 14, he tells Pausanias many things about himself that he would already know; and in *Letter* 20 he defines personal names ("Gelon the tyrant

---

[36] The translation is by Stowers in Malherbe (1977) 219.
[37] The identification of the addressee as King Archelaus is discussed in Sykutris (1933) 13.
[38] The opposite reaction is to leave obscure items unexplained, as in the last three Socratic letters (33–35).

of Syracuse"; "Admetus the king of the Molossians"; "Alexander ruler of Macedon") in such a way as to inform fully not just a general reader, but a reader not necessarily contemporary with the work.[39] Such clarification simultaneously informs us by filling in much needed detail, and alerts us to the public nature of the literary letter, written with posterity in mind.

The previous paragraphs delineated traits shared by all epistolary fictions, namely references to the physical nature of epistolarity: acts of writing or reading, the method of sending, enclosed or embedded letters, and epistolary formulas. We encountered these issues previously in chapters on embedded letters in historical narrative and on the tragic stage. But unique to the pseudonymous letter collections is the lack of connective material: these letters tell their stories both in and through letters, without a separate narrating voice. The collections replicate the patterns of a "real" correspondence over time, but also attempt to advance a plot and sustain characterizations. They simultaneously reflect an epistolary exchange and tell a story, and at times these two roles clash and contradict one another, as will become apparent. Earlier we had formulated this clash in terms of external and internal audience: the fictional letter writer feels a tension between what the internal audience supposedly already knows and what the external audience must be told. Here the added temporal element, the fact that the letters tell a story over time, further complicates the picture. We can begin to explore these issues through the letters of Anacharsis.

THE LETTERS OF ANACHARSIS

The ten letters written in the voice of the Scythian sage Anacharsis probably date from the early Hellenistic period.[40] There is no question of authenticity here, since the historical sixth-century Scythian prince could not have been writing three centuries after

---

[39] See discussion in N. A. Doenges, *The Letters of Themistocles* (New York 1981) 25. This stylistic specificity is not particular to letters: in the case of lyric poetry, see my comments in Rosenmeyer (1992) 159–61.

[40] The most recent work on Anacharsis is J. F. Kindstrand, *Anacharsis* (Uppsala 1981). There is a good introduction to the epistles in Malherbe (1977) 6–8. See also F. H. Reuters, *Die Briefe des Anacharsis* (Berlin 1963). Reuters dates *Letter* 10 in the fifth or fourth century BCE, *Letters* 1–9 to the period 300–250 BCE, mainly on linguistic grounds.

he is said to have visited Athens.[41] If our dating is correct, the letters are the earliest representatives of the genre of pseudonymous epistolary fiction. The first nine of the letters appear to be by the same author, while the tenth was most likely written and circulated independently. All ten letters are preserved under his name as early as Cicero (*Tusc. Disp.* 5.32.90).[42] Anacharsis himself appeared in literature first in Herodotus' descriptions of Scythia (4.76), and he became very popular as the exemplary barbarian wise man later in the second and third centuries CE: Lucian, for example, devotes a whole dialogue (*Anacharsis*) to an imagined conversation between Solon and Anacharsis on the subject of Greek athletics.

In the pseudonymous letters, Anacharsis challenges the ethnocentric view that Athens and her culture are superior to all other cultures, and his letters, addressed to a variety of leaders, resemble short lectures on nobility and mutual respect. As J. F. Kindstrand points out, the idea of making a non-Greek offer fictional criticism of Greek customs appealed to writers with ethnographical interests and a sharp eye for social and cultural differences.[43] A barbarian can view the issues with a sense of detachment that a native Greek could not sustain. In the case of Anacharsis, the repetitiveness of approach – the same cultural criticisms are delivered to a variety of addressees – impedes any effort to trace the development of character over time. But Anacharsis' static personality contrasts both with the ever changing backdrop of setting, as he wanders throughout Greece, and with each individual internal audience, as he writes to nine different addressees.

Before considering the content of the collection, we can make two important points about its form and context. First, although the letters are unified in the moralizing voice of Anacharsis, the collection is not particularly dependent on individual epistolary forms. As will be the case with most of the Cynic epistles, only the opening formulas are preserved (e.g. *Letter* 1: "Anacharsis to the Athenians"), since they are necessary for the identification of the addressee, which in turn allows a better appreciation of the indi-

---

[41] Kindstrand (1981) 7.
[42] Kindstrand (1981) 9: see also Diog. Laert. 1.105; Clem. Alex. *Strom.* 1.16.77.3–4.
[43] Kindstrand (1981) 60.

vidual piece; closing formulas, on the other hand are uniformly ignored. But not all opening formulas sustain the illusion of a "genuine" personal correspondence. *Letter* 7, for example, has the heading "Anacharsis to Tereus, the cruel despot of Thrace." Would Anacharsis really expect Tereus to read beyond such an insulting opening line? The pejorative address and the biographical information implied were obviously designed not for the fictional internal addressee, but for external readers, who would relish the incongruity of formal address and insult, and for posterity, who may have forgotten who Tereus was.[44]

Second, while the writer does not mention details which typically enhance epistolary verisimilitude (messengers, the difficulties of postal delivery, or other mundane aspects of writing and sending), he does choose a situation for his letter writing which is intrinsically plausible. Anacharsis is depicted as wandering throughout the Greek world, visiting tyrants, kings, and wise men, and writing to his new acquaintances en route. We find a similar situation repeated in almost all the epistolary collections: the writers travel, live in exile, are temporarily separated from their families, or have been caught up in military actions far from home. When Anacharsis writes to Solon (2), he had already attempted to visit him, but was turned away at the door:

because it was Anacharsis who came knocking on your doors with the desire to become your house guest, you refused and replied that I should seek hospitality in my own land ... To me, Solon, you wise Athenian, this does not appear to be right. And my spirit bids me to come again to your doors, not to ask what I did earlier, but to learn what the case is with respect to what you declared about hospitality.[45]

This passage offers the reader both a narrative of a previous event – Anacharsis' failed attempt at a meeting with Solon – and an announcement of his impending return. Since Solon had refused to meet him face-to-face, the sending of a letter seems plausible. Thus, albeit indirectly, the letter provides its own reason for being, and the reader accepts the fiction as a likely occurrence under the circumstances. The reader, ancient or modern, while not necessarily convinced of the authenticity of a letter, still expects

---

[44] There is always the suspicion, of course, that the heading is a later editorial addition, since titles and title-like formulas are particularly vulnerable to such treatment.

[45] The translations of Anacharsis' letters are by A. M. McGuire, in Malherbe (1977) 37–51.

some attempt at epistolary verisimilitude, and resents any obvious incongruities.

The collection begins with an open letter to the Athenians, warning them not to reject automatically all that is non-Greek (*Letter* 1):

You laugh at my speech, because I do not pronounce the Greek sound clearly. In the opinion of the Athenians, Anacharsis speaks incorrectly, but in the opinion of the Scythians, the Greeks do. It is not in their speech that men differ among themselves in their importance, but rather in their judgments, in which, indeed, even Greeks differ from Greeks.

Every opening letter stands as both a guide to the collection that follows, and a general "letter of introduction" to later readers. Thus, when the Athenians are scolded for their mockery of Anacharsis' accent and their refusal to take his words seriously, we as external readers may read these words as a warning not to dismiss the letters that follow as unworthy of notice. The letter goes on to point out how unimportant speech itself is in relation to argument:

A speech is not poor if good intentions stand behind it and good actions follow upon the words. But the Scythians judge a speech poor only when its arguments are poor ... Look, rather, when people speak, at the things that are actually said.

The author of the letters, in addition to arguing to the moment, may also be asking our patience with his epistolary inventions, hoping that later readers will see the value of his literary work rather than condemning it as a forgery. Just as the barbarian Anacharsis attempts to speak Greek to communicate with his audience, so the anonymous writer has taken on the voice and language of another man (Anacharsis) in order to transmit his message to us as readers. This kind of double vision is always present in epistolary fictions, whether pseudonymous or not, by virtue of the double readership: internal and external, contemporary and later.

The rest of the collection is addressed to a variety of rulers (2: Solon; 3: the tyrant Hipparchus; 4: Medocus; 5: Hanno the Carthaginian; 6: the son of a king [unidentified]; 7: Tereus; 8: Thrasylochus; 9 and 10: Croesus). The writer moralizes about proper behavior among civilized men, and the dangers of a life of luxury and excessive emotion. In *Letter* 7, in connection with Tereus' villainy toward his family and his people, a cruel despot is compared to a bad shepherd:[46]

> No good ruler ruins his subjects, nor does a good shepherd harm his sheep. But your whole land is empty of subjects, and poorly managed by your officials.

Letter 8, to a man who is unkind and angry at his friends, sets up a positive image of loyalty at its start, but shifts quickly to a condemnatory tone:

> The dog is a good animal at heart, in that he remembers kindnesses. He guards the house of his benefactors, maintaining its order until he dies. But you fall short of the kindnesses of a dog ...

Other letters sustain the diatribe but the discussion shifts from public behavior to private: thus the tyrant Hipparchus is chided for his excessive wine drinking (3: "Much undiluted wine is an enemy of properly performing one's duties"); later Medocus is blamed for lack of self-control: (4: "Envy and passion are clear signs of an inferior soul").

The opening lines of *Letters* 3 and 4 above show how some letters resemble series of apothegms more than epistles. While *Letters* 3 and 4 proceed to dwell for several lines on the iniquities in question, in certain letters attributed to Apollonius of Tyana, for instance, the pithy phrase itself without further discussion constitutes the whole letter: *Letter* 83: "to speak falsely is the mark of a slave, but the truth is noble"; *Letter* 86: "a quick temper blossoms into madness"; *Letter* 100: "assuage your grief by considering the troubles of others."[47] Many of these *topoi* are not specifically epistolary in nature; here the letter form is used as a forum for opinions which are familiar to us from archaic Greek lyric poetry. But while lyric poets can choose to speak in general or specific terms, letters always direct their moral instruction or criticism toward a named individual.

---

[46] Cf. Socrates and Thrasymachus in *Resp.* 1 and Socrates in Xen. *Mem.* 1.2.32ff. Also, see O. Murray, "The Idea of the Shepherd King from Cyrus to Charlemagne," in P. Godman and O. Murray, eds., *Latin Poetry and the Classical Tradition* (Oxford 1990) 1–14.

[47] These brief lines come from Stobaeus' collection, and there is some question whether the letters have been transmitted in their entirety. I am using the translations of Penella (1979). On Apollonius of Tyana, see also W. Speyer, "Zum Bild des Apollonios von Tyana bei Heiden und Christen," *Jahrbuch für Antike und Christentum* 17 (1974): 47–63, esp. 48–53.

Several of Anacharsis' letters praise the austere life of the typical Scythian himself, content with his personal freedom, the clothes on his back, and a bit of food. These letters show a great deal of similarity in theme to Cynic ideas, which we will explore below in the letters of Diogenes and Crates; but rather than posit a direct connection between the two, scholars explain the similarity by the subject matter: praise of the simple life was not confined to the Cynics in antiquity.[48] Here is *Letter* 5 in its entirety, in which Anacharsis embraces personal freedom and independence from material goods:

For me, a Scythian cloak serves as my garment, the skin of my feet as my shoes, the whole earth as my resting place, milk, cheese, and meat as my favorite meal, hunger as my main course. Therefore, since I am free from those things for which most people sacrifice their leisure, come to me, if you need anything of mine. For the gifts in which you delight, I will give you others in return. But you, give them to the Carthaginians, or dedicate your thankfulness to the gods.

Letter 6 continues in this vein, asking the king's son to throw away his money and possessions, and come to live a free life with the Scythians.[49]

Letter 9 is addressed to Croesus, and is somewhat longer and chattier than the rest of the letters. It covers a wide range of subjects: the first part resembles a one-page summary of the Hesiodic cosmogony and rise of mankind, which, combined with a local story about robbers and loot, and contrasted with the noble and free life of the Scythian people, is then used to urge Croesus to abandon his life of excessive wealth and misguided happiness. The collection ends with a flattering address to Croesus (*Letter* 10, *in toto*):

I, King of the Lydians, have come to the land of the Greeks to be taught their customs and way of life. I have no need of gold, but am content to return to the Scythians a better man. Therefore, I have come to Sardis, considering it an honor to make your acquaintance.

This concluding letter cannot close the collection as it stands. It purports to introduce Anacharsis to his new host, Croesus, yet in *Letter* 9, perhaps the original closing piece of the group, Anachar-

---

[48] Kindstrand (1981) 82.
[49] Kindstrand (1981) 12 points out that this letter reflects a common ancient idea that Scythian food consisted almost exclusively of horses' milk; see also Homer *Il.* 13.5–6.

sis appears to know his host well enough to speak quite openly and critically to him. Even the phrase "King of the Lydians" seems odd in light of the previous letter's casual tone and address. Such internal self-contradiction appears in many of the pseudonymous letter collections, and we are forced either to challenge the authenticity of the offending piece, to rearrange the manuscript order, or to question our own expectations of "order" and "unity" in a collection.

What exactly are our assumptions of organization and order in an epistolary collection? No one, I suspect, would agree with the seventeenth-century editor of Themistocles' letters, who placed all the letters alphabetically in accordance with the names of the addressees – using the Latin alphabet.[50] But the collecting of individual letters into an anthology seems to us to presume some sort of organizing principle, whether by chronology, by addressee, or by subject matter. We also assume that a sequence of narratives will reveal a development of plot or of character. Again, N. Holzberg offers some useful observations on narrative structure in a "Briefroman."[51] He notes a mostly chronological organization, with some "novels" falling into clear patterns of grouping in blocks (Euripides, Aeschylus) or symmetries (Plato, Chion, Themistocles); occasionally some have letter groups at the end of the work that are linked together only thematically (Plato 9–13; Hippocrates 18–24); elsewhere there should be chains of motifs connecting letters to one another; frequently the structure is that of gradual revelation of information that is explained fully by a longer explanatory letter at the end. The perspective of the narrator may also affect the ordering of the letters: when the perspective is based on that of one narrator, the order is mostly linear, but in a polyphonic collection, the order is more of a mosaic, reflecting the relationships of multiple narrators.[52]

Holzberg's assumption of chronology and gradual revelation works in some but not all cases that we are discussing. In an epistolary collection, if we read sequentially, the meaning of each text is determined by that of the one that precedes it, but an interrup-

---

[50] E. Ehringer, *Themistoclis Epistolae Graeco-Latinae a Biblioteca Ehringeriana* (Frankfurt 1629), quoted in Doenges (1981) 24.

[51] Holzberg (1994) 50–52.

[52] C. Arndt, "Antiker und neuzeitlicher Briefroman," in Holzberg (1994) 53–84, esp. 79.

tion can threaten the understanding of the whole sequence: insufficient information may plague the reader because of a lost, stolen, suppressed, or intercepted letter. At some point, in some way, the information must be transmitted for the story to continue: "the letter in the epistolary network does not always arrive within the récit, but it must always arrive in the histoire."[53] But the information is not always transmitted chronologically.

The openings *in medias res* further complicate the reader's reconstruction of the plot, and the beginning of a series of letters may appear arbitrary, as the first letter frequently alludes to prior correspondence that is not included. But endings are much more complex. Epistolary endings, that is the end of an individual letter as well as the end of a series, waver between two contradictory impulses; the potential finality of any single letter with its conventional closing formula exists in tension with the intrinsic open-endedness of the sequence, which could easily continue as long as a return letter arrives, demanding in turn yet another response.[54] If writing implies love, friendship, or some other emotional connection, there is a limited number of ways to end the exchange naturally: death, reunion, renunciation of the relationship. In literary contexts, boredom or neglect rarely serve as an excuse for closure, and the correspondents usually require a more violent reason to stop writing. Some letters focus self-consciously on the fragility of correspondence, threatening to stop writing back. If the collection does end abruptly, the editor is sorely tempted to write one last commentary, beyond the frame of the collection, by way of explanation. The author of *Chion of Heraclea*, as we will see in the next chapter, resists this temptation, leaving the reader in suspense as to the fate of the young writer, who writes his last letter as he is about to attempt to assassinate a tyrant. The lack of closure gives added power and poignancy to the collection, leaving the details of the narrator's death to the imagination of the reader. But in that case, since Chion is a historical figure, history completes the story.

The collection of Anacharsis has already begun to challenge some of our assumptions about organization and narrative struc-

---

[53] Meltzer (1982) 518.
[54] This is the curious power behind the "chain letter," which imposes a sense of obligation to continue the sequence even upon complete strangers.

ture. In terms of Holzberg's final point alone, that the "novel" should end with some sort of explanatory or concluding letter, we see that the Anacharsis collection fails to conform to his typology. These assumptions will be challenged further by other extant pseudonymous letter collections.

THE LETTERS OF HIPPOCRATES AND DEMOCRITUS

We noted above that the letters of Anacharsis do not reveal any development of character; this may be connected to the fact that the writer shifts addressee in every letter except the last, thus preventing a continuous dialogue with the same person. But when letters are exchanged over a period of time between two persons, we instinctively expect some sort of growth, as the writers learn from one another, influence one another's views, and explore new ideas together. This is evident in the fictional correspondence between Hippocrates and Democritus, an epistolary meeting of great minds, which tells of Hippocrates' visit to Abdera to cure the philosopher Democritus of his "laughing sickness."[55] Their twenty-seven letters are arranged roughly chronologically, but with great diversity of form, such as transcriptions of decrees or speeches, and scientific treatises; while the latter texts clearly stretch the epistolary definition, it is difficult to know what else to call them, and we will return to this question below.[56] Scholars agree that the collection grew by accretion: ancient papyri contain

---

[55] For general background Doenges (1981) 43–48; W. D. Smith, *Hippocrates' Pseudepigraphic Writings* (Leiden 1990); T. Rütten, *Demokrit: lachender Philosoph und sanguinischer Melancholiker* (Leiden 1992); for a critical edition of the Greek text, see D. T. Sakalis, *Hippokratous Epistolai* (Joannina 1989). Speyer (1971) 120 offers ancient views on the authenticity of the Corpus Hippocraticum. For a comparable fictional correspondence between great men in Christian times, see the *Epistolae Senecae et Pauli*, fourteen letters composed in the third or fourth century CE, which purport to be an exchange between Paul and his philosophic contemporary; the letters are discussed by A. J. Malherbe, "Seneca on Paul as Letter Writer," in B. A. Pearson, ed., *The Future of Early Christianity: Essays in Honor of Helmut Koester* (Minneapolis 1991) 414–21.

[56] *Letters* 1–9 are set in Persia, as King Artaxerxes attempts to bring Hippocrates to court; the group ends with a decree of the Koan people to protect Hippocrates. *Letters* 10–16 describe to a variety of addressees the preparations for Hippocrates' trip to Abdera. *Letter* 17 narrates the trip to the ship owner. *Letters* 18–24, written after Hippocrates returns home, are an exchange of scientific ideas, and *Letters* 25–27 are three decrees. Smith (1990) 2 argues that the speeches and decrees seem to be the earliest pieces, while the letters grew by accretion, later additions expanding and interpreting themes from previous periods.

only *Letters* 3–6 and 11. We know of one edition at least that was current during Cicero's lifetime, and then presumably revised and expanded shortly after 44 BCE.[57]

The collection opens with a brief exchange between King Artaxerxes and his subjects, who are trying to bring Hippocrates to Persia to cure the plague that is ravaging their country. Hippocrates' staunch refusal to help the enemy, in spite of the offer of a reward, creates a dramatic contrast with his immediate willingness to answer the call of the Abderites, when they beg him to cure their most distinguished citizen, Democritus, who appears to have gone mad (10). He answers the Abderites in *Letters* 11 and 12, saying "I am coming, prepare to receive me" (12).

Then comes a series of letters from Hippocrates to his friends in preparation for the trip (13: settling affairs at home; 14: renting a ship; 16: collecting medicinal herbs). In writing to Damagetes of Rhodes, the shipowner who will rent him a vessel in which to sail to Abdera, Hippocrates expresses impatience: "your ship is wasting time even while I am writing to you." The correspondence naturally ceases while Hippocrates and Democritus converse together. We later learn about Hippocrates' experiences in Abdera from a single letter rather than an exchange. This is *Letter* 17, a lengthy piece (in comparison with the rest of the corpus), nominally a letter of thanks to Damagetes, but really a narrative of his encounter with the laughing philosopher. Hippocrates writes that Democritus, far from being mad, actually taught him something, namely the utter pettiness of most human concerns. He found Democritus sitting in his garden, studying dissected animals, and writing a treatise on madness.[58] When Hippocrates wished for more time for his own writings, Democritus laughed, and explained his laughter as the only logical reaction to vain human striving and inconsistency: if he wants to write, he should simply give himself enough time to write rather than wasting his time on activities of no value. After listening to a long diatribe on the evils of mankind, Hippocrates is converted to Democritus' point of

---

[57] On the history of the ancient editions, see Doenges (1981) 47 and Smith (1990) 2–18.

[58] "Democritus investigates madness by investigating its seat, an activity that seems simple and straightforward to us, and did to later antiquity, but is too sophisticated for the period that provides the dramatic date of the letter, and probably before the first century B.C." (Smith [1990] 26).

view, acknowledging that the sage is far from mad; in fact, he is the wisest of men.

It is an interesting choice on the part of the pseudonymous writer to describe Hippocrates' "conversion" in the narrative of *Letter* 17, rather than in an exchange of letters between the two men. It is also the only choice he could have made to keep the illusion of verisimilitude: once the two men met, they could interact in speech rather than by letter. Thus the story of their meeting and Hippocrates' enlightenment must be told *in* a letter rather than *through* letters. Hippocrates' perspective on medicine and life is exposed as flawed in his encounter with Democritus; he admits his failings and writes about them to his friend the shipowner.

We watch Hippocrates' character gradually come into focus through the first sixteen letters: he is not interested in money, but is a skilled physician loyal to his homeland. His letters reveal impressive scientific knowledge (medicinal herbs, physiology of melancholy) combined with ethical and moral integrity; they also show that he is a very careful planner as he prepares for his trip. But in *Letter* 17, when Hippocrates reports that he was scolded by Democritus for allowing mundane affairs to intrude upon his time to think and write, the details of the earlier letters undergo a witty reevaluation: these details, now illuminated as vain distractions, are precisely what stand in the way of higher pursuits.[59]

Letter 17 has been called the "climax and intellectual center of the novella,"[60] but the collection continues with five more communications exchanged between the two men after Hippocrates returns home. Democritus' *Letter* 18 announces the treatise that follows as *Letter* 19 (*A discourse on madness*), while Hippocrates' *Letter* 20 serves as a cover letter for a discourse on hellebore (*Letter* 21: *On treatment with hellebore*). Other scientific tracts are sent back and forth before the collection concludes with three formal speeches: *Letter* 25: the "decree of the Athenians" granting Hippocrates citizenship; *Letter* 26, Hippocrates' "speech at the altar" to the Thessalians; and *Letter* 27, Hippocrates' son's "ambassadorial speech" to the Athenians on behalf of Kos. None of the last group of texts qualifies formally as a letter, as I mentioned above, but they are nevertheless incorporated into the larger epistolary collection; nowadays one might call them "enclosures" and identify them as

---

[59] Smith (1990) 23.   [60] Smith (1990) 21.

such on the bottom of the cover letter. They are what the epistolary theorist "Demetrius" had in mind when he objected to letters
so lengthy that they deserve the name of "treatise" (*On Style* 228).

These letters on philosophical and medical subjects problem-
atize our (and the ancients') definition of "letter." They are obviously treatises, but they are just as clearly connected by some
earlier editorial hand to the epistolary collection of Hippocrates.
N. Holzberg refuses to include 18–24 in the "novel," arguing that
they do not reflect narration and therefore must have been tacked
on later; they do not fit his typology of the genre.[61] But I would
argue that the incredible flexibility of the letter form allows these
treatises to remain an integral part of the work, and that the
editor took care to connect the treatises with the earlier epistolary
material. Thus the exchange of treatises is integrated into the collection through cross-references to prior events: *Letter* 18 summarizes the visit in Abdera from Democritus' perspective, and *Letter*
20 repeats the diagnosis of *Letter* 17, as Hippocrates restates that,
although he had been told that the philosopher was insane, he
realized immediately that the diagnosis was incorrect. But it is
true that the direct correspondence between Hippocrates and Democritus tells us less about the men than about their studies; whoever wrote *Letters* 18–21 was not as interested in the "Cynic drama
of conversion" as in the literary possibility of an intellectual exchange between two famous men with whose work he was familiar.[62] So our assumption about character development in an
exchange of letters is once again challenged by the nature of the
particular letters: *Letters* 18–21 function primarily as cover letters
for scientific treatises, while *Letter* 17 provides a summary of spiritual or intellectual growth during the encounter in Abdera.

I mentioned above that the collection unites two disparate segments through an internal reference system: events or characters
that are touched upon more than once, sometimes by more than
one voice.[63] An extension of such cross-referencing is the creation
of a short sequence of letters within a larger collection that narrates a self-contained story, an epistolary subplot as it were. The

---

[61] Holzberg (1994) 22–28.

[62] So Smith (1990) 31, who claims that the two groups of *Letters* (1–17, 18–21) are by different authors, perhaps even independent of one another.

[63] This technique is also used in the Socratic letters, with great success. See Sykutris (1933)
45ff.

internal unit may consist of sequential letters, or the story may be
spread throughout the collection, united by subject or addressee
rather than textual order. When the sequence appears to be in-
adequately synchronized, it challenges our assumptions of chronological consistency. Let us explore this phenomenon in two
other collections: the fictional letters of Crates and Diogenes, and
those of Phalaris.

THE "HIPPARCHIA" LETTERS

The letters of Crates and Diogenes provide us with a model, an
epistolary subplot that lives up to our expectations of consistency
and order, centered around the figure of Hipparchia, Crates' wife
and philosophical companion.[64] We have some information on the
historical background. The fourth-century BCE Cynic philosophers
Crates of Thebes and Diogenes of Sinope may have originally
written their own letter collections which inspired later imitators.
Diogenes Laertius (6.98) reports that a collection of Crates' letters
was in circulation some six centuries after the author's *floruit*, while
the letters of Diogenes of Sinope are referred to by Epictetus
(4.1.29–31, 156), Julian (7.212D), and again Diogenes Laertius
(6.80), who provides a catalogue of letters which were regarded as
genuine by Sotion (*ca.* 200 BCE). Neither one of these early collections has been preserved, and it is impossible to judge whether
they represented authentic letters or rather were products of the
extensive pseudepigraphic tradition which quickly developed
around the philosophers' names. It is clear, however, that our collections of 36 (Crates) and 51 (Diogenes) letters come from a much
later period. The letters attributed to Crates, a pupil of Diogenes
and an influential Cynic in his own right, have been dated according to their similarity to the letters attributed to his teacher, and
scholars have concluded that Crates' collection is in part influenced by and thus later in composition than Diogenes'. Both collections appear to be the work of multiple authors, which may

---

[64] On the letters of Crates and Diogenes, see the discussion in Malherbe (1977) 10–21, and
his bibliography. I use the text and translation in Malherbe (1977): the letters of Diogenes
are translated by R. F. Hock in Malherbe (1977) 54–89, and those of Crates by B. Fiore
in Malherbe (1977) 92–183. On Crates, see O. Gigon, "Kynikerbriefe," *Lexikon der Alten
Welt* (Zurich 1965) 1658ff.; H. Dörrie, "Krates," *Der Kleine Pauly*, vol. III (1969) 327ff.; U.
Criscuolo, "Cratete di Tebe e la tradizione cinica," *Maia* 22 (1970) 360–67.

explain the inconsistencies and occasional repetitiveness (e.g. Crates 26–27, 30–32) within each group.

Crates' collection opens with his dramatic command to Hipparchia that she return at once if she wishes to see Diogenes once more before he dies (*Letter* 1):

Return quickly. You can still find Diogenes alive (for he is already near the end of life; yesterday, at any rate, he all but expired) in order to greet him for the last time and to learn how much philosophy can do even in the most terrifying circumstances.

As external readers, we may or may not know from other sources that Hipparchia is Crates' wife, but we have no idea where Hipparchia must travel from or what her destination should be, nor any details of Diogenes' illness; the writer does not break the epistolary illusion by giving us that information. This opening letter, forecasting the imminent death of the master and, presumably, the consequent passing on of the torch of philosophy to Crates himself, is contradicted by *Letter* 8, in which Crates declares himself ready to sail to Athens to join his beloved Diogenes, apparently alive and well. We are left to conjecture either a missing narrative of miraculous return to health, or perhaps a flashback to an earlier stage in Crates' training. If we were certain about the transmission of the texts in the given order, we could argue more strongly for an editorial attempt at suspense; as it is, we may equally suspect an error in placement.

Fortunately we learn more in later letters, at least about Hipparchia herself. *Letters* 28–33 form an internal unit addressed to Hipparchia in which Crates explicitly identifies himself as her husband (28). Diogenes also writes to Hipparchia, in his third letter, as he attempts to explain the Cynic lifestyle.[65] He challenges her to compete with Crates in her dedication to the cause, and encourages her to write to him frequently (*Letter* 3):

I admire you for your eagerness in that, although you are a woman, you yearned for philosophy and have become one of our school, which has struck even men with awe for its austerity. But be earnest to bring to a finish what you have begun. And you will cap it off, I am sure, if you should not be outstripped by Crates, your husband, and if you frequently write to me, your benefactor in philosophy. For letters are worth a great deal and are not inferior to conversation with people actually present.

---

[65] On Diogenes, see Malherbe (1977) 14–18, and V. E. Emeljanow, "The Letters of Diogenes" (Diss. Stanford Univ. 1967).

The final sentence reveals the standard epistolary trope of presence and absence, which Diogenes uses elswhere in his collection (e.g. *Letter* 17). This letter tells us that Hipparchia has become a good Cynic, but Diogenes' admonition to "finish what you have begun" presents us with the possibility that she may yet fail. He ends optimistically, expecting her to excel in her endeavor, and in general seems to have a more idealistic image of her as a disciple than Crates himself does. However, we see only this one letter from Diogenes, whereas Crates' letters gradually reveal more sides to his wife's personality.

Diogenes' *Letter* 3 is written when Hipparchia still lives as a good Cynic, wandering the country with her husband. We discover from Crates' *Letter* 28 that she has returned home, and her husband writes to her during their separation. He begins with the enlightened statement that "women are not by nature inferior to men" (28), and urges her to return to him: "for you would not convince us that you are enfeebled at home" (28); "stand fast, therefore, and live the Cynic life with us" (29).[66] Time passes, during which Hipparchia weaves a cloak and sends it to him; he returns the gift and scolds her for acting as a conventional wife, when he married her "for the sake of philosophy" (30). He writes three letters in which he chastises her unmercifully for returning to mindless activities in the house and neglecting their common philosophical cause (30–32).

Since the author chose not to include any of Hipparchia's replies, we are in the dark for some time about her motivations for the abandonment of her previous lifestyle. The absence of her voice adds suspense to our reading, and a cloak of mystery surrounds this unusual woman-philosopher. But Crates seems equally uninformed, for his *Letter* 33 expresses great surprise at the sudden new development in their lives:

I hear that you have given birth – and that quite easily, for you have said nothing to me. Thanks be to God and to you.

Her return to the home and to traditional female tasks now makes sense to him, as pregnancy could only have been a disadvantage on the road. His letter shows an abrupt *volte-face* comparable to her sudden disappearance, as he enters into the mundane details

---

[66] His feminism extends only to those women who agree with his philosophical program, as he says in *Letter* 32: "leave the spinning of wool, which is of little benefit, to those other women, who have aspired to none of the things you have."

of child-rearing. No longer eager for his wife to be his equal as a philosopher, he has not lost all his lofty philosophical ideals: now his attention is focused solely on the child as a potential companion in his wanderings (*Letter* 33):

Therefore let his bath water be cold, his clothes be a cloak, his food be milk, yet not to excess. Rock him in a cradle made from a tortoise shell, for this, they say, protects against childhood diseases. When he is able to speak and walk, dress him ... with a staff and cloak and wallet ... and send him to Athens.

The letter closes with a joke on the realities of one's dependence on children in later years, and the impracticality of a Cynic life: "I will be careful to raise up a stork for our old age, not a dog (ἀντὶ κυνός)." Thus far has Hipparchia come, from the travels of a Cynic philosopher to home duties, the husbandless mother of a "little puppy" (τοῦ σκυλακίου).

If we finally turn back to Crates' *Letter* 1, we are left with two possibilities. Either the letter is sent before the events reported by *Letters* 28–33, in which case Hipparchia has not always been at his side, or Diogenes has fallen ill after the birth of their son, and Crates calls on her to remember her former involvement with the great man, leave home, and attend to him in this crisis. The rest of the collection does not afford us any clues as to which interpretation is the likelier one. But the separate letter, partially by virtue of its placement in the collection, does not disrupt the unity and order of Hipparchia's "story" as told through Crates' *Letters* 28–33.

THE LETTERS OF PHALARIS

The final example of an epistolary subplot I will discuss is found in the letters attributed to Phalaris, and it presents multiple problems of interpretation. Scholars do not agree on a date for the work, which is composed of 148 letters written in the voice of Phalaris, although most would agree that the collection as a whole is not earlier than the fourth century, with some parts added as late as the Byzantine period.[67] Part of the problem with "organizing" the

---

[67] D. A. Russell, "The Ass in the Lion's Skin: Thoughts on the Letters of Phalaris," *JHS* 108 (1988) 94–106, esp. 97.

letters of Phalaris in the first place is that, thanks to Bentley's opprobrium, there is still no modern critical text. The corpus is preserved by ancient and medieval compilers in various selections and orders, but none of the transmitted orders appears to be based on any recognizable thematic or chronological principle.[68] The standard edition remains Hercher's *Epistolographi Graeci* (Paris 1873), whose numbering system I will use below.

If, for the sake of argument, we assume that the manuscript tradition adopted by Hercher is indeed correct, then the letters seem deliberately arranged in chronological *dis*order. The arrangement may reflect an attempt at historical verisimilitude: the disorder is meant to suggest the absence of editorial intervention, and the reader is encouraged to accept the collection as a random assortment from the hand of the author himself. We are asked to believe not that the author wrote out of chronological sequence, but that the letters, retrieved from their respective addressees, were bound together as they came in, without regard for date or subject matter. In other words, this is like a jumble of "real" letters in Phalaris' attic, not a sophisticated literary anthology.

Phalaris was a tyrant in Agrigentum in the sixth century BCE with a vivid reputation for cruelty to his fellow man. Pindar refers to him in *Pythian* 1.95–96, and he is best known in literature for his horrible habit of burning enemies alive in a huge bronze bull invented just for that purpose.[69] But the overlap between earlier tradition and the letters attributed to Phalaris is quite small, and the tyrant is presented in this collection in a kinder light. This should not surprise us, since Phalaris would be unlikely to present himself in his own letters as wholly evil. The impulse behind the true authors of the letters may have been an interest in revealing or inventing sides of the tyrant that were precisely untreated in previous sources. Beyond this anecdotal aspect, D. A. Russell speculates that the authors may have attempted to portray the

---

[68] Russell (1988) 94, where he also discusses the early modern editors of the letters. On the letters in general, see also S. Bianchetti, *Falaride e Pseudofalaride: Storia e Leggenda* (Florence 1987); O. Bruno, "L'epistola 92 dello Pseudo-Falaride e I Nostoi di Stesicoro," *Helikon* 7 (1967) 323–56; and the somewhat dated English translations of T. Francklin, *The Epistles of Phalaris* (London 1749).

[69] See Callimachus *Aet.* fr. 46–47 Pfeiffer, Ovid *Trist.* 3.11.39–48; Prop. 2.25.11, and Lucian's two declamations, *Phalaris* 1 and 2; also mentioned by name alone in Lucian *Ver. Hist.* 2.23.

ethos of the tyrant through letters for educational or moral purposes, and he quotes "Demetrius" (*On Style* 292):

Dynasts ... do not like to hear of their own faults. In advising them against these, we shall therefore not speak in direct terms, but either criticize others who have done the like – e.g. in addressing the tyrant Dionysius we shall speak against the tyrant Phalaris and his brutality – or else praise those whose behaviour has been the opposite.

Russell also points out the large number of Phalaris' letters that may be classified under the headings of epistolary taxonomy, suggesting another raison d'etre for the collection, namely to provide its readers with practical examples of letter writing: there are letters of reproach (2), reproof (3), irony (8), menace (13, 14, 24, 30, 89, 128), invitation (23), gift giving (119), and consolation (103), to name a few.[70] With the letters of Phalaris, as with other pseudonymous collections, we can assume a number of reasons for composition, including but not limited to those mentioned above.

The lengthy collection consists of letters from Phalaris to many different addressees, but interspersed among the unconnected letters are series of related letters to the same person. Phalaris writes one set of related letters to his wife and son (18–20, 40, 67–69), and another set to the poet Stesichorus and a friend Nicocles, whose wife had just died, requesting a poem in her honor (78–79, 144–46).[71] As is evident from the numeration, these series include letters placed together by Hercher but also others scattered through the collection. The third series, which we will investigate more closely, includes six letters and revolves around Phalaris' involvement in the marriage of Theano, daughter of Philodemus (59, 80, 131, 135, 142, 143). I have chosen this series because the topic of Theano's marriage is easily marked off from other epistolary subplots in the collection, and it tells a connected story from start (recommendations for arranging a marriage) to finish (celebration of the marriage). We do not know Theano, the girl to whom Phalaris sends a dowry, from any other literary or historical source, but the situation is closely paralleled in two other epistolary contexts: first, when Chion sends a dowry to a relative of Plato (*Chion of Heraclea* 10), and second, in the Platonic letter col-

---

[70] Russell (1988) 103.
[71] The letters also tell the story of Stesichorus' pursuit and capture by Phalaris in *Letters* 88, 92, 93, 108, 109, 121, 147; see Russell (1988) 98–99.

lection, when Plato himself tries to provide a dowry for his nieces from money supplied by the tyrant Dionysius (Plato *Letter* 13).[72] But the issue under investigation here is the ordering of the letters in the larger collection, which challenges our notion of linear narration. If we follow the order of letters as they stand, we will find ourselves quite confused.[73]

The first reference to the marriage comes in *Letter* 59, addressed to one Nausicles, in which Phalaris announces that he has sent gifts, as he had promised, to the newly married daughter of Philodemus, in spite of opposition from others:

> although I am a tyrant, and in no way related to her, yet if I have acted as a parent, I think I am at least entitled to an equal, if not a larger share, of praise and gratitude.

This letter leaves us with a number of questions: why does Phalaris get involved with this particular family, and why does he write defensively about his motives? Further information is provided by *Letter* 80, to Theano and her mother Kleainete. Phalaris thanks them for their kind words, but warns them that, in view of his reputation, it would perhaps be better if they said nothing at all; he presents himself as a misunderstood but essentially noble man forced by circumstance to perform ignoble deeds. It is unclear whether this letter comes, in the fictional framework, before or after *Letter* 59: in the former case, it may be the motivation behind his kind gesture to the bride, but in the latter case, it may be interpreted as a response to their thank-you note for his wedding gifts. At this point, we are still left uninformed.

Later comes a letter from Phalaris to Philodemus himself. In *Letter* 131, the tyrant writes that he has sent him money for his daughter's wedding, but that if Philodemus so wishes, he should pretend that the money is really his own, and bestow it as a formal dowry. The letter ends with an apparent reference back to *Letter* 80:

> That Theano has expressed her gratitude to me in such a manner, gives me the greatest satisfaction; and I am pleased to see that the favors she received before marriage are so thankfully acknowledged after it.

---

[72] Russell (1988) 99.

[73] But note that the Dutch scholar van Lennep (1777) rearranged the letters towards the end of his edition to follow the chronology of the affair (using Hercher's numeration): 142, 143, 138, 135, 131, 59, 25, 80; see Russell (1988) 94 note 6, and L. O. T. Tudeer, *The Epistles of Phalaris: Preliminary Investigation of the Manuscripts* (Helsinki 1931). Similarly Russell (1988) in his article automatically re-organizes the sequence and reads it in the order of the events.

This allows us to understand that some sort of gift has arrived, the marriage has taken place, and the previous letter was indeed a thank-you note.

Things become more complicated in *Letters* 135 and 142, each addressed to a mutual friend of Phalaris and Philodemus, a certain Teucer, who will turn out on closer scrutiny to be Phalaris' financial advisor. Phalaris writes "I heard of the marriage of Philodemus' daughter before your letters came to inform me of it." Letters sent *to* the tyrant are, not surprisingly, not included in the collection. *Letter* 135 continues with the command to Teucer that the married couple, Theano and Leo, be allowed to remain in the house in which they were wed. But *Letter* 142 reflects a time prior to the wedding or even the engagement. Phalaris states that he had intended to talk to Kleainete about the marriage of her daughter, but other business intervened, and he now asks Teucer to go to Kleainete in his place and promise her daughter five talents as a gift as soon as she marries; Teucer should offer the money as if it were a debt owed to Philodemus. We are also told that Leo has gone to Phalaris to solicit assistance in presenting his case to his future mother-in-law. Phalaris quickly adds that the money should be given regardless of the identity of the man chosen. Looking ahead to the happy event, Teucer is told,

on the day of the marriage, send four servants her age, together with the clothing I sent you, and sixty pieces of gold. If the marriage is delayed, hasten it as much as possible, and do not fail to do everything with the utmost willingness, so that you may share in part of the praise that Phalaris will receive [for these deeds].

These are the details missing from *Letters* 59 and 80, when Phalaris alludes merely to "gifts" in general.[74]

This trip backwards in time is confirmed by the last letter on this subject, *Letter* 143 to Kleainete, which opens as follows:

Your husband (and my invaluable friend) Philodemus is abroad ... yet it is the greatest misfortune that your daughter, now twenty years of age, is left behind unmarried.

This reminds us that Phalaris had wanted to talk directly to Kleainete on this matter, but was distracted by other business; perhaps

---

[74] Because of Phalaris' elaborate ploy to funnel the five talents through Philodemus, Theano and Kleainete cannot possibly be thanking him for money in *Letter* 80.

this letter is written while he is still on that journey. Phalaris goes on at some length about how unfair it would be to Theano to insist on waiting for Philodemus' return to arrange a marriage, simply in order to keep the girl by her side for company while her husband is away. He informs Kleainete that her husband actually left five talents with him for his daughter's dowry:

Teucer will give you the portion whenever you wish, and supply you also with anything else that you may require for the occasion.

We are not given the name of the prospective bridegroom in this letter, but we can conclude that it was written just before or at approximately the same time as the letter to Teucer (142) which asks him to help persuade Kleainete with friendly advice and the five talents.

As I hope has become clear from this exposition, the letters of Phalaris on the marriage of Theano do not function according to our expectations of sequential action. As we read further in the collection, we find ourselves going back in time, from the first letter of thanks for wedding gifts received to the final letter of advice to a mother who resists even thinking of marrying off her only daughter, her companion in solitude. In addition, the series is complicated by the letter to Philodemus, announcing the gift of five talents, which contradicts the later letters to Teucer, identifying him as the intermediary for the dowry.[75]

The latter issue could be explained away by a missing letter, a constant threat in any letter collection; we can always postulate a piece of information that has gone astray that will explain all the inconsistencies and apparent contradictions. But it is precisely this instinct to "explain away," to fit all the parts into a consistent and chronologically smooth whole, that may be counterproductive in reading epistolary fictions. Series of letters have a marvelous ability to explore alternative modes of narration. The genre delights in playing with all possibilities: twisting time, showing a Jekyll and Hyde in two letters written to different addressees, leaving

---

[75] Russell (1988) 99–101 traces even more evidence of internal inconsistency in the subplot of Theano's marriage, and concludes that the story has been worked up by two or three writers, and facts and details have been omitted in all versions. His solution is to read the correspondence as the tyrant's own hypocritical version of some discreditable events: he makes Phalaris the father of Theano's child, and imagines him bribing Leo to marry the girl, a reading that he readily admits reflects how we would expect Phalaris to behave from tradition, but not from this letter collection. See Russell (1988) 101.

the reader with gaps she can fill in only with her own imagination. I therefore resist reordering the letters of Phalaris to form a "proper" narrative. Part of the epistolary game is to create a situation which demands the active participation of the reader. Each letter gives the reader a little more information to work with, until we finally convince ourselves that we have reconstructed a reasonable facsimile of "what really happened." The procedure, however, is neither wholly linear (past to present) nor a flashback (present to past), nor entirely consistent in its details.

When N. Holzberg brings his classificatory scheme of "Briefroman" to bear on the issue of Phalaris' letters, he concludes that it fails on two counts: first, as we have observed, while the letters are related thematically, they follow no chronology or order; second, any remaining unity is broken up by letters on the subject of popular philosophy, inserted into the larger "plot."[76] He suggests instead that the current text may have been built around the framework of a chronologically ordered "Briefroman," but concedes that the current text cannot be so called. As I have argued above, the letters of Phalaris are a prime example of epistolary fiction, as are the rest of the pseudonymous collections, but that the addition of the label "novelistic," with its accompanying typology, will only cloud our appreciation of the material, and lead us to fault the genre for missing certain traits (chronological organization, a modern sense of unity) it never was meant to possess.

We have now touched on most of the issues raised at the start of this chapter: consistency of characterization, chronological arrangement within a collection, the multiplicity of topics and styles found in pseudonymous letter fictions. We have also considered certain traits within letters which imply an anxiety about their pseudonymous status: references to the epistolary process itself (writing, sending, reading), and lapses in the epistolary illusion because of the constant tension between the needs of internal and external audiences. We have avoided, however, a crucial question of labeling: is there a difference between an epistolary collection that tells a carefully shaped story through letters in such a way as to form an artistic whole, and an epistolary novel? I do not consider these pseudonymous letter collections to be novelistic, but is there any such thing as an epistolary novel in antiquity? Let us

---

[76] Holzberg (1994) 5.

conclude this chapter with a very brief glance at one letter collection that does come close to fitting the typology of "Briefroman": the letters of Themistocles.[77] By analyzing how this ultimately fails to live up to "novel" status, we will be able to argue better on behalf of *Chion of Heraclea*.

THE LETTERS OF THEMISTOCLES

The twenty-one letters of Themistocles are the product of multiple hands, probably from the late first or second century CE, although, as we have suggested before, the actual literary antecedents may be considerably more ancient, as we suspect when reading Thucydides' incorporation in his *History* (1.137.4) of a letter from Themistocles to Artaxerxes.[78] As with most of the material we have been dealing with, there is some doubt as to the correct order of the collected letters, and whether the series is complete as it stands. The letters all purport to be from Themistocles, and are addressed to different people, some historical figures and some apparently fictional characters, who would have been likely candidates for such a correspondence at that time in his career, namely during his exile from Athens and his subsequent escape to Persia.[79] The collection reveals a mixture of solid historical evidence with imaginative invention, one which dramatizes Themistocles' political and philosophical outlook.

It has been said that "above all, these letters should be enjoyed as a kind of historical novelette in epistolary form."[80] But objections have been made that the letters do not follow chronological order, and that certain inconsistencies within the collection, both of fact and of characterization, keep the work from being a "novel." There are irreconcilable accounts given of Themistocles'

---

[77] One could also argue for the "novel" status of the letters of Socrates and his disciples; see Holzberg (1994) 38–47.

[78] For discussion of the dating, see among others: W. Niessing, *De Themistoclis epistulis* (Freiburg 1929); C. Nylander, "Assuria Grammata: Remarks on the 21st 'Letter of Themistokles'," *Opuscula Atheniensia* 8 (1968) 119–36; Podlecki (1975) 129–33; R. J. Lenardon, *The Saga of Themistocles* (London 1978) 154–55; Penwill (1978) 83–103; Doenges (1981). Suggested lost ancient sources include Hellanicus and Charon of Lampsacus.

[79] For example, his family and friends in Athens, prominent cultural figures (e.g. Aeschylus and Polygnotus), military leaders (e.g. Xerxes, Artaxerxes, and Pausanias). Lenardon (1978) 155 calls the situation "an ideal scenario for epistolary fiction," although the collection presumably is not a strict reflection of Themistocles' real letters.

[80] Lenardon (1961) 28–40, esp. 35, and Lenardon (1978) 155.

experiences at the court of Admetus in *Letters* 5 and 20, for example, and the personal characteristics of Themistocles in the latter part of the collection seem very different from those of the earlier part. So C. Nylander argues for a very loose arrangement: "what we have here is clearly not a structural whole and it seems useless to look at these letters as a unit in a more than formal and superficial sense."[81] But J. L. Penwill suggests a reconsideration of the sequences so as to read *Letters* 1–12 and 13–21 as distinctly ordered segments, a diptych as it were.[82] This approach solves the chronological problem by showing two parallel time frames at work, and reduces the issue of inconsistency to one between the distinct segments, never within them. The collection is then read as a two-part exploration of Themistocles' distinct personas, that of the unscrupulous politician on the one hand, and that of the noble patriot on the other.[83] We then are left with "a double correspondence [that] develops two coherent, yet incompatible, personae for the statesman, each of which implicitly critiques the other."[84] The balance of compatible and incompatible information encourages us as readers to choose for ourselves which "side" we are on, while simultaneously undermining our sense of confidence in that reductionist act.

The debate over the "unity" of this collection continues, but it reminds us once again of the danger of typologizing in dealing with the ancient epistolary novel. The answer one comes up with will depend entirely on the typology invented for the purpose. I have been arguing throughout this chapter that the great power of the epistolary form lies in its flexibility, its ability to contain multiple other forms: it constantly criticizes or contradicts itself, invites the reader to create yet another scenario or explanation, and always keeps us waiting for the next letter which will fill in all the gaps, as it were. N. Holzberg points out the rather modern psy-

---

[81] Nylander (1968) 131.
[82] Penwill (1978).
[83] Penwill's arguments for a novel of psychological development, whereby the author chose the epistolary form not to tell "history" but to explore the character of Themistocles, and to show how he reacted to different situations that confronted him (1978) 92–93, contradict Sykutris' insistence that ancient novels are specifically not psychological novels in our modern sense of the word (1931) 213–14. While Sykutris is right to warn against the danger of adopting modern critical assumptions without question, I find it hard to believe that the ancient novel, epistolary or not, was not in some sense an exploration of human motivations.
[84] Selden (1994) 39–64, esp. 49.

chological complexity involved in Themistocles' letters: the reader may be irritated that the temporal and logical lines of narration are unclear, but this both calls for sophistication on the part of the reader, and actually reflects Themistocles' own inner confusion; thus, instead of the sustained inner development of a heroic Chion, which we will explore in the next chapter, we witness the inner turmoil and vacillation of an unwilling and unhappy exile.[85] If we continue to argue for a Richardsonian definition of the epistolary novel that demands consistency in characterization and logical chronology, then *Chion of Heraclea* will be the only letter collection to fit the requirements of the genre.

[85] Holzberg (1994) 36–37.

CHAPTER 9

Chion of Heraclea: *an epistolary novel*

It is always in a man's letters, more than in his other works, that one must seek the imprint of his heart and the trace of his life.

Victor Hugo *Choix moral de lettres de Voltaire*[1]

This last chapter in the section on epistolarity and the ancient novel will finally combine the two elements into one. Previously we considered letters embedded in various novels; a novel or romance probably based on an original epistolary core but including additional non-epistolary narrative; and purely epistolary collections which presented a series of letters purportedly by a single, pseudonymous author. None of these examples, although epistolary on one level and novelistic on another, could be classified unquestionably as an "epistolary novel." If we accept a basic definition of the genre which allows only prose fictions composed of chronologically organized sequences of letters, without supplementary narrative, that cohere to create a single unified story, then *Chion of Heraclea* is our only surviving example of the ancient epistolary novel.

The work contains seventeen letters from the young, aristocratic Chion, addressed variously to his parents, a friend, the tyrant Clearchus, and Plato. The bulk of the correspondence, however, is from Chion, studying in Athens, to his father Matris, at home in Heraclea in Pontus. The letters depict the hero setting off somewhat unwillingly at his father's request to study philosophy with Plato, learning the value of personal commitment to an ideal such as political freedom; he returns home to sacrifice his life attempt-

---

[1] This phrase is quoted in S. Gaudon, "On Editing Victor Hugo's Correspondence," *YFS* 71 (1986) 177–98, esp. 177. It prefaces a selection by Hugo of letters by Voltaire; see V. Hugo, *Choix moral de lettres de Voltaire*, 4 vols. (Paris 1824) x.

ing to oust the tyrant Clearchus from his city. The collection opens *in medias res*, and Chion's death, never explicitly stated, cuts off any possibility of a sequel.

The basic story reflects historical events recorded by numerous ancient sources.[2] In the mid-fourth century BCE, the city of Heraclea in Pontus was taken over by the tyrant Clearchus, who was killed twelve years later (353/52) by conspirators under the leadership of a man named Chion. We can thus accept a historical Chion, but we cannot defend the authenticity of the letters as productions of the same man. Chronological inconsistencies argue against the attribution: for example, *Letter* 3 shows Chion meeting Xenophon in Byzantium, which must have happened *ca.* 400/399 BCE, but we are also told that Chion returned home five years later to kill Clearchus; this leaves an unexplained gap of over forty years. The language and style of the letters, and the absence of detail about Chion's experiences in Athens, appear to rule out authorship contemporary with the events. The evidence points to an anonymous author writing in the first century CE, combining a core of truth with layers of literary creativity. We cannot determine if the author found inspiration in an existing epistolary genre, although we have discussed above the prevalence of epistolary experimentation in this period; possible contemporaneous non-epistolary influences include the novels of Chariton of Aphrodisias and Xenophon of Ephesus, written perhaps for a similar readership, namely Greek-speaking subjects of the Roman empire.[3]

Knowing so little about the creation and reception of this collection, it is difficult to define its literary character or intent. Was it a variation on a rhetorical school exercise written in epistolary style from the perspective of a famous person in a specific situation (*ethopoieia*)? Was the novel meant primarily to entertain as the adventure story of a young and sympathetic hero? Although it contained no romantic plot, it included other important elements of the ancient novel, in particular travel and mortal danger for the protagonist. Or was its main goal to instruct readers in the value of a philosophical education for the practice of civic virtue? In

---

[2] The references are collected in I. Düring, *Chion of Heraclea: A Novel in Letters* (Göteborg 1951) 9–13.

[3] On probable readers, see D. Konstan and P. Mitsis, "Chion of Heraclea: A Philosophical Novel in Letters," *Apeiron* 23 (1990) 258.

this way, it followed in the footsteps of the fourth letter attributed
to Plato, most probably composed by a member of the Academy
shortly after his death, which celebrates Academic political activity and argues for the practical role of philosophy.[4] Other letter
collections attributed to philosophers (e.g., Heraclitus, Aristotle)
were written in Hellenistic and imperial times, and could equally
have influenced the author of *Chion*.

As a third option, perhaps the work was meant to encourage
others to consider rebellion against cruel tyrants. Since there are
no allusions in *Chion* to any contemporary events, it is unlikely that
the work is a veiled exhortation to a specific act of tyrannicide,
although any given political climate might have inspired such a
literary response.[5] But *Chion* fits a larger literary pattern of tyrannicide narratives. To give just one example from the century before
the probable composition of the work, in 49 BCE, Cicero, trying to
decide whether to join Pompey in the East, asked himself questions very similar to those asked by Chion: "should a man remain
in his country when it is ruled by a tyrant?"; "should a man use
any means to upset tyranny, even if the safety of the state is
thereby endangered?" (Cic. *Att.* 9.4).[6] A tyrannicide narrative can
appeal to an audience with classicizing tastes even if the question
of contemporary tyrannicide does not arise. The tyrant-slayer
was a *topos* in Greek and Latin literature as early as the melic
poet Alcaeus of Lesbos (fr. 332 celebrating the death of the tyrant
Myrsilus in sixth-century Miletus), and even more famously in
Thucydides' and Herodotus' narrations of the glorious deeds of
Harmodius and Aristogeiton (e.g. Hdt. 5.55, 57–61; 6.109, 123;
Thuc. 1.20; 6.53–59).

Thus the author of *Chion* may have wanted to give added fame
to his protagonist by presenting his story as a tyrannicide narrative. The enduring power of such a story is made clear by the following anecdote from the Italian Renaissance: a young scholar of
Latin living in Milan under the tyranny of Duke Galeazzo Maria
Sforza plotted with two friends to kill the duke. In 1476 they slew
him while he was at church; two conspirators died immediately,

[4] Konstan and Mitsis (1990) 275.
[5] This is suggested by Konstan and Mitsis (1990) 258 note 4.
[6] Konstan and Mitsis (1990) 278, referring to M. Griffin, "Philosophy, Politics, and Politicians at Rome," in M. Griffin and J. Barnes, eds., *Philosophia Togata: Essays on Philosophy
and Roman Society* (Oxford 1989) 34.

but the third was sentenced to be tortured and quartered alive. Facing his executioners, he declaimed in Latin and boasted of having achieved his goal of slaying a tyrant: "his death would be bitter, but his fame would be perpetual, because he would join the ranks of all of the other tyrant-slayers of Greek and Roman literature."[7]

Whether adventure story, philosophical teaching text, or political manifesto (or some combination of all three), *Chion of Heraclea* defines itself first and foremost through its epistolarity. The following discussion considers both the contents of the letters and the epistolary conventions shaping the work.

CHION'S LETTERS HOME

Since *Chion of Heraclea* is less familiar to most readers than other works of this period, it may help to begin with an overview of its contents.[8] The first letter introduces Chion "consoling" his parents for his absence (*Letter* 1: to Matris):

On the third day of my sojourn here near Byzantium, Lysis arrived with your letter, telling me how worried you and the whole family are. Another than I would have summoned all possible arguments to console you, enumerating the prospects that my journey raises, and by such remarks he would have roused cheerful thoughts as a counterpoise to sorrow. The prize that I ask you to establish for the virtue that you hope I shall acquire is that I make you happy parents, but not that you expect solace from my studies or rather happiness, since you must be grieving for me . . .

Chion plays with both content and form here. His parents expect to read a standard consolation letter, but he informs them that he will not summon arguments to rouse cheerful thoughts in their minds, but rather redefine the whole situation as one in which they should endure the immediate pain for the sake of a higher goal, namely the happiness they will find when he completes his education. On the level of form, Chion's letters ignore formal epistolary greeting and farewell; while this seems to veer away from verisimilitude, it is also an argument for the novelistic quality of the work. The shape of the collection allows the reader

---

[7] See S. Jed, *The Violence of Representation* (London 1989) 33.
[8] I use the serviceable translations of Düring (1951) throughout this chapter.

to take epistolary conventions for granted; all we need to know in each case is the identity of the addressee, which the manuscript tradition gives us in the form of a name (*Letter* 1: "Chion to Matris"), or in the highly artificial editorial prescript of "to the same person" (e.g. *Letter* 2). We are told very little at this stage, as the author, at this level at least imitating a "real" letter home, presumes the family knows why Chion visits Byzantium, what his final destination is, and what studies he will pursue. We gather from reading between the lines that Chion's family is wealthy, having a servant to spare as a messenger ("Lysis arrived with a letter").

The next two letters find Chion still in Byzantium. *Letter* 2 is written on behalf of the merchant Thraso, whom Chion commends to his father's hospitable care in Heraclea. What appears to be a conventional recommendation manages also to inform us of Chion's own activities: Thraso hosted him in Byzantium, and Chion wishes to repay his kindness. The second letter's ending is linked closely with the beginning of *Letter* 3: both comment on the winds that delay Chion's plans to sail. Repeated references to the forced deferral of the journey add tension and a sense of the unexpected to the narrative.

Letter 3 is a lengthy description of a chance encounter with Xenophon, who was leading troops through Byzantium. The narrative includes a historico-biographical digression introducing Xenophon, praise of his beauty and wisdom, and description of a narrowly averted battle which Chion both participates in and chronicles. Chion concludes by eagerly embracing his future as a student of philosophy, having seen the effects of such an education on Xenophon. Chion is enthralled by Xenophon's eloquence as he keeps his mutinous troops from sacking the city; here is proof that philosophy makes men useful citizens without enfeebling their potential for action. Chion's letter gives an impression of youthful naiveté as he praises Xenophon and gets caught up in the atmosphere of military excitement. The letter closes with a flashback to Chion's initial resistance to his father's plans for his education, and a statement of his present goals: he hopes to become a better man, not less brave (ἀνδρεῖος) but certainly less rash (θρασύς).

Letter 4 finds him finally on his way again to Athens, although not without additional adventure. Chion tells how his crew refused to listen to his warnings of storms at sea, with the result that they barely escape alive, only to face further danger from hostile Thracians on shore. All ends well, obviously, or Chion would not have survived to write this letter home. The letter functions here as a witness to a living voice, but simultaneously points forward to the final letter of the collection (*Letter* 17), where the letter survives but Chion does not, and the unavoidable temporal gap between writing and receiving results in the addressee's reading the words of a dead man.

The next letter (*Letter* 5) marks Chion's arrival and initial meeting with Plato, quite understated after the fulsome hero-worship of Xenophon:

We have arrived in Athens and talked with Plato, the disciple of Socrates. He is a wise man in all respects and endeavours to make philosophy appear to his disciples as not incompatible with an active life, in fact as something with its face turned towards practical life as well as towards quiet contemplation ... I am anxious not to fall short of Plato's friendship but be reckoned among those from whom he professes to draw benefit because he can do them good. For he says that there is no less happiness in making men good than in becoming good oneself ...

We now realize that Chion plans to study at the Academy. There is no physical description of the great man, nor information about Chion's immediate reactions; instead we (and Chion's father) are introduced to Plato the Socratic disciple, a wise man proclaiming a philosophy compatible with an active life. Chion quotes Plato's words in his letter home, a sign that he is already under the philosopher's pedagogical spell, and says he is eager to become part of Plato's circle.

From *Letter* 6 to *Letter* 13, Chion studies in Athens, and we are told in passing that five years elapse. The author hints that many letters have disappeared: some omissions are explicit (e.g. *Letter* 13 alludes to information in a letter not in our collection), while other missing pieces may be suggested by the relatively small number of letters written (eight in five years). By not "inventing" letters to fill in the gaps, the author appears to gain his readers' confidence. In the extant letters, Chion neither discusses daily routines nor debates deeper philosophical issues; this seems odd since his father, a former student of Socrates, would have an interest in the workings of the Academy. But what Chion does write both reveals an "image of his soul" and his developing views on friendship and duty.

Letter 6 acknowledges the receipt of gifts from home, as Chion lists each item to check if all that was sent has indeed arrived:

Phaedimus arrived with pickled fish, five jars of honey and twenty jars of wine flavoured with myrtle and in addition three silver talents. I praise his faithfulness and I recognize your kind consideration ... I do not want money at all, particularly since I have now arrived in Athens and attend Plato's school. For it would be quite out of place if now, when I have sailed to Greece in order to become less fond of money, love of money should none the less sail to me from Pontus. Please do send me such things as remind me of my country, not wealth.

Chion asks his father not to send money, but rather local goods such as food and wine that remind him of home and allow him to entertain friends. For although Plato on principle refuses gifts, he can be "tricked" into accepting culinary contributions. The details in the opening of the letter of specific numbers of jars and the type of wine may be a safeguard against theft along the way; Chion's father is reassured by this catalogue that the items he sent have indeed arrived safely without loss or substitution, and the slave Phaedimus is praised accordingly for his faithfulness as a courier. The letter is a wonderful example of the mundane uses to which a letter may be put: an inventory of gifts, or thanks for the objects listed, reminding us of the Hellenistic letter-poems that were composed to accompany gifts, and also of the many papyrus letters of this sort. There is a focus in this letter on entertainment rather than on serious education (although intellectual discussion surely played a major part in the symposium), and a hint of homesickness, yet Chion never explicitly requests news of his family or city.

Letter 7, a confidential cover letter, and *Letter* 8, a formal recommendation, contrast sharply with the heartfelt praise of *Letter* 2. *Letter* 7 is both a devastating character sketch and a private warning: a certain Archepolis, who recently abandoned philosophy for business, is said to be untrustworthy and reckless. After frequently insulting Chion, he has now demanded a letter of introduction for business ventures in Pontus, and Chion sends him to stay with his parents. Chion refuses to write a duplicitous letter, the literary model for which he finds in Homer: "although he is unworthy, I will avoid the model of Bellerophon; I have given him another letter, in which I wrote nothing false." While Chion makes explicit reference to Bellerophon, the literary paradigm so strongly evident in Euripides and the ancient novels is now reduced to passing literary allusion. But the allusion is still strong enough that Chion needs merely to mention the name "Bellerophon" to denote a particular type of letter writing, namely a false one.

The "honest" letter is reproduced as *Letter* 8, a brief note resembling Pseudo-Demetrius' commendatory type,[9] and the irony in reading it directly after the previous document is intense. Clearly the trusted servant carrying the first letter was meant to arrive before Archepolis with his official version. Chion asks his father to accommodate the guest, but to reveal at his departure how Chion knowingly returned good for evil, even if Archepolis is too stupid to learn from the experience. Both letters affirm Chion's views on friendship: a good man (ἀγαθός) helps both friends and enemies, and it is an advantage (κέρδος – material or spiritual profit) to make every man your friend. Understanding these views to be the result of Chion's philosophical education, we perceive a certain maturation which will peak later in his sense of duty towards city and family.

Letter 9 continues the theme of friendship, as Chion writes for the first time to someone other than his father, in this case to his friend Bion:

I would not have expected you to care so little about me and I am not willing to interpret it that way. I wonder what has happened and why I still have received no letter from you, although letters often arrive from my other friends. Well, for what has so far happened I myself shall find excuses for you, but for the future, if those who were sent with letters to me are guilty, try to avoid such mishaps by writing often, for at least some letters will arrive safely. If you yourself are guilty through not writing, avoid going on with that, for it is easy to avoid. Surely we were such close friends that these difficulties can be surmounted.

Chion complains to his friend that he receives no letters from him, and suggests two possible reasons (and solutions): either the messengers are at fault, in which case Bion should write more often in order to increase the chance that some letters might arrive safely, or Bion himself is remiss, which is easily remedied by putting pen to papyrus. Bion should "write often as one who remembers our friendship to one who likewise remembers it." The letter is perceived, as in many other sources on the epistolary mode, as a sign

---

[9] *Typoi Epist.*, type 2 in Malherbe (1988) 30–32. See also Pseudo-Libanius *Epist. Char.* in Malherbe (1988) 66, 68, 74, and Julius Victor *Ars Rhet.* 27: "Commendaticias fideliter dato aut ne dato" in Malherbe (1988) 64.

of friendship.[10] The bond forged while together must be sustained while apart, and ignoring a friend by not writing implies a low opinion of their friendship.

Thus in four of the first nine letters, Chion writes about connections with his fellow man. *Letter* 9 shows an established long-term friendship, *Letters* 7 and 8 the undeserved decent treatment of an opportunist, and *Letter* 2 favors exchanged with an honest man. Chion's philosophy is to do good to others. *Letter* 10 picks up themes raised earlier in *Letter* 6, namely Chion's relationship to Plato and his friends.[11] But now philanthropy takes the form of convincing Plato that, in spite of reservations expressed earlier, money can be a good thing when used appropriately. Applying "sincere and just argumentation" to turn cash into an honorable gift, Chion presses a sum of money on Plato for his grand-niece's dowry. Chion proudly informs his father of his generosity, calling it a great profit (κέρδος). But we note an undertone of boasting as he quotes the very words used successfully in debate with his teacher.

Chion has been in Athens for five years when his father calls him back, claiming longer absence will turn him into a stranger. We learn this from Chion's own reply (*Letter* 11: "with Bianor came a letter from you in which you asked me to return home"); he repeats his father's words, responding in turn to each question and request. Chion admits feeling homesick, but insists that another five years with Plato will make him even more virtuous and useful to his country. Explaining the decision to stay, he recalls his first letter, in which Chion asked his father to rejoice at his absence. He closes the letter with a bit of humor: it is not the journey to Athens that makes one a good man, but the time spent studying there. Perhaps if Chion had written more about philosophy and less about generous gifts, his father might have had more confidence in the educational investment. All this changes in *Letter* 12, quoted in full:

As I wrote to you some time ago I intended to stay in Athens ten years before returning home. But since I learnt about the tyranny in Heraclea, I cannot any longer stand being better off in respect to my security than my fellow-citizens, and if it please God, I shall sail by the spring. Now in

---

[10] For example, Cicero *Ep. ad Fam.* 2.1; Seneca *Ep. Mor.* 40.
[11] *Letters* 6 and 10 were probably influenced by the thirteenth letter attributed to Plato.

the middle of winter it is impossible. It would be absolutely absurd if I behaved like those who run away wherever they can, when something happens to their own city. On the contrary I definitely wish to be present when able men are needed. And even if perchance I cannot do anything useful, yet the voluntary sharing of your worry seems to me to come near virtue, even though it be a poor merit. I write this quite intrepidly since Lysis carries the letter to you.

Chion hears that Heraclea has fallen under the rule of Clearchus, and he plans to sail as soon as the winter storms abate; even if he can do nothing to change the government, he still wishes to share the fate of his countrymen. He expresses himself quite openly to his father, confident that the messenger will respect his confidence and not betray their cause to the tyrant. This letter indirectly predicts the end of the correspondence, but allows that several months still remain for writing.

As Chion waits for good weather, Clearchus, somehow getting news of his intentions, and regarding Chion's return to Heraclea as enough of a threat to wish to preempt it, sends an assassin to Athens. We find this out in *Letter* 13, where Chion describes vividly how he grabbed his assailant's knife and wrestled the man to the ground. This adventure parallels the military encounter in *Letter* 4, serving a similar purpose of retarding the main plot. Action narrative yields to reflection as Chion acknowledges that his return to Heraclea might be perilous: "living or dying, I shall be a good (ἀγαθός) man." He closes the letter by asking his father to persuade Clearchus that he is no political threat, but merely a quiet student of philosophy. This subterfuge (if it is one – it is unclear if he has already decided to kill the tyrant) contradicts his insistence on honesty in *Letter* 7, but seems reasonable considering the goal, euphemistically termed "performing a public service for my country."

Letter 14 is written at Byzantium, as Chion sets out on his journey home; it is an explanation of his principles, and a strong attack on tyranny in general. He uses illness as a metaphor to describe Clearchus' rule, but he himself feels invulnerable, because philosophy has taught him that as long as the soul remains free, even the threat of death is endurable. A virtuous man must protect his city, and Chion plans not to be killed until he can die for the right cause: the slaying of the tyrant (now explicitly stated). Chion incorporates direct questions in his letter, as if conducting a Socratic dialogue. He encourages his father to continue misleading Clearchus as to his intent, and to send any further information in letters to advance their cause.

Chion's next letter (*Letter* 15) congratulates his father on calming Clearchus' suspicions, and offers additional justification for devious means to a noble end:

> I congratulate my city that the tyrant allows himself to be lulled by what you said to him about me. I shall follow your advice and write myself too, leading him as far astray from the truth as possible. For if I wrote the truth, I should cheat my citizens and friends of the hope they have set in me, and that would be a treatment they have not deserved.

He elaborates on the evils of tyranny, arguing that a cruel despot paradoxically is better than a mild one, since his cruelty makes the citizens hate him. Chion has also written to Clearchus, purposefully "in an overwrought tone in order to make him despise me as a complete windbag." He includes a copy for his father, reproduced as *Letter* 16. *Letters* 15 and 16 thus resemble 7 and 8: the first of each pair presents guidelines for interpreting the second, warning that the subsequent letter is not entirely straightforward. *Letter* 15 turns out to be the last written communication between Chion and his father.

The letter to Clearchus (*Letter* 16) is indeed verbose and convoluted. To allay the tyrant's suspicions, Chion invents a reason for writing, that is, to defend himself against unjust accusations, and eulogizes a life of quiet study. He chronicles his early attraction to philosophy, depicting himself as wholly uninterested in politics, and mixes truth with deceit as he declares his code: "to honor a just man, to requite an unjust man with good deeds, or, if this is impossible, with silence." He turns again to Socratic dialogue, imagining a debate with the goddess Tranquillity on the value of self-control and the danger of worldly affairs. We may marvel at Clearchus' gullibility, but then he did not have the benefit, as we do, of reading this message in the context of the larger collection.

The final letter (*Letter* 17), addressed to Plato two days before the assassination of Clearchus, is written in a considerably more sober tone. Observing bad omens and visions, Chion suspects the end is near, and wishes Plato to know that he remains a worthy disciple. Eager to receive the posthumous glory (κλέος) his deed will bring, he now actively seeks death. He claims to be in good spirits, closing with a formal epistolary valediction: "Farewell (Χαῖρε), Plato, and be happy into a ripe old age; I think that I speak with you now for the last time." With a prediction of silence imposed by death, the letters, and the novel, end.

THE NOVEL IN LETTERS

It should be apparent from this summary of the epistolary collection that the letters form a coherent whole. Six letters from Byzantium (*Letters* 1–3, 14–16) frame the work, with descriptions of travel to and from Athens embedded within the frame (*Letters* 5, 12), thus providing a clearly delineated beginning, middle, and end of the (physical and spiritual) "journey." The novel is full of literary devices that unify the parts: repeated imagery (unfavorable winds in *Letters* 2, 3, 4, 12, 13), foreshadowing (violence in *Letters* 4, 13 anticipates a violent end), parallelism (recommendations in *Letters* 2, 7, 8; great men in *Letters* 4, 5), and a sustained focus (Chion's father as main addressee, Plato in *Letters* 6, 10). On the level of diction, many letters are written in a circular pattern, with word or phrase repetition at beginning and end (e.g. *Letters* 1, 2, 4, 8); elsewhere, one particular word (e.g. profit, *kerdos*) reappears in different letters. The letters are composed or edited to create a consistent and carefully structured story, quite different from, for example, the expansive and disorganized Phalaris collection.

Various philosophical themes connect individual letters, such as friendship, civic duty, and the value of a philosophical education. Much of the novel deals with the tension between a quiet life and a capacity for action. Chion's intellectual maturation in Athens entails contemplating what it is that makes a good citizen, while his return to Heraclea allows him to act on that knowledge. The letters may be read as entertainment, but they also challenge the reader to reconsider the relationship between personal lifestyle and obligations to a community. In this version, philosophy becomes the means by which the narrator learns best to fulfil his obligations.

So far the discussion could apply equally to other forms of ancient Greek fiction. Greek tragedy also pits personal duty and desires against public or political obligations (e.g. Sophocles' *Antigone*), and many of the Platonic dialogues address issues of the individual and the community. But what sets this work apart is its epistolary nature. Let us consider how epistolary form and convention make this novel unique.

Chion's letters closely resemble the epistolary styles defined by two ancient theorists who wrote handbooks of epistolary styles. Using the categories transmitted by Pseudo-Demetrius and Pseudo-Libanius,[12] the following types appear in Chion's collection: *Letter* 1 is consoling; 2 and 8 commendatory; 3, 4, 5, and 13 reporting; 6 thankful; 7 vituperative; 9 friendly; 11 accounting; 14 and 16 didactic; and 15 apologetic. Thus, in addition to being situated within a historical framework, the novel also seems to reflect certain stylistic conventions of letter writing. Ancient theorists agreed that letters should not be overly long ("Dem." *On Style* 228; Greg. Naz. *Ep.* 51.1–5; Julius Victor *Ars. Rhet.* 27; Ps.-Lib. *Epist. Styles* 50): accordingly, Chion cuts himself short in *Letters* 3, 4, 15. They believed that a letter is written conversation with one who is absent ("Dem." 223; Cic. *Ad Fam.* 12.30.1; 2.4.1; Sen. *Ep.* 75.1; Ps.-Lib. 2; Jul.Vict. *Ars. Rhet.* 27): Chion makes this view explicit in *Letter* 9 to Bion. They postulated that one should answer questions from previous letters (Jul. Vict. *Ars Rhet.* 27): Chion often refers to his father's letters when he responds. Finally, they used the image of a letter reflecting its writer's soul ("Dem." 227; Cic. *Ad Fam.* 16.16.2; Sen. *Ep.* 40.1): compare Chion "hiding" his soul behind the obfuscating verbosity of *Letter* 16. As we watch Chion develop intellectually, we also see his letters adapt themselves to the circumstances and moods of their addressees, another tenet of epistolary style.

As we have discussed in earlier chapters, all literary letters are self-conscious works of art and prone to rhetorical strategies, some specifically epistolary, others common to all fictional genres. What does epistolarity bring to this novel that other forms of narrative might not? In attempting to answer this question, we may consider the following evidence: references to the act of writing, sending, or receiving; clashes between the information required for the external and internal reader; and the absence of an external voice to verify or challenge the writer's single perspective.

In the epistolary novel, attention is drawn to the difficulties of sustaining communication. The author, aiming for verisimilitude, frequently explains practical aspects of writing and sending letters.

---

[12] The texts of all the epistolary theorists discussed here are found in Malherbe (1988).

The slave Lysis delivers *Letter* 1, later traveling back to Heraclea with *Letters* 7 and 12. In the last example, Chion fearlessly hints at tyrannicide, since, as he says, Lysis is wholly trustworthy. We are invited to imagine a specific situation of delivery, in which the identity of the messenger affects the contents of the letter: Chion can put the dangerous "truth" in writing because he trusts his messenger effectively with his life. In *Letter* 13, we again meet honest slaves, and are informed that Clearchus takes no interest in letters, an observation which could suggest censorship of the mail under different circumstances. When slaves are unavailable, Chion uses merchants en route to Heraclea: Thraso (*Letter* 2), Archepolis (*Letters* 7, 8), Simon (*Letter* 4). Chion admits that *Letter* 4 was written only upon discovering a ship about to sail; we are made to wonder how many adventures are left untold for lack of a messenger, causing gaps in the epistolary chronology.

In spite of these breaks, continuity is established whenever the writer becomes a reader by alluding to his father's letters. The epistolary experience, while predicated on an absent addressee, is inherently reciprocal and continuous. Chion answers his father's questions (*Letter* 11), records his views (*Letter* 15: "I will follow your advice ..."), recalls their conversations (*Letter* 3: "you must remember when ...") and quotes earlier letters (*Letter* 5: "you wrote to me that ..."). Allusions to other voices or texts are an important dimension of the genre. Unidirectional letters demand that we read through the prism of the recipient's voice, but preclude the balanced perspective produced by the presence of an external commentator (e.g. omniscient narrator) or several voices interacting (e.g. dramatic performance). The univocal collection which reproduces only one side of the correspondence forces the external reader to depend entirely on Chion's words.[13] Doubled letters (*Letters* 7–8, 15–16) let us test his honesty by comparing statements to the effect that he will write a "special" letter with the document itself. *Letter* 16 is particularly complicated because the author must explain how it found its way into the collection: Clearchus surely would not have returned the original. In the context of Richardson's *Clarissa*, T. Castle writes: "because it embodies a fictional history of its own production, the epistolary novel constantly re-

---

[13] An aspect noticed by ancient theorists: "A letter is one half of a dialogue" ("Demetrius" *On Style* 223 in Malherbe (1988) 12, 16, quoting Artemon.

minds the reader of the problems of origins."[14] This author's decision to include a copy of his letter for someone else's perusal is a perfect solution; the technique resembles that of embedded letters in other ancient novels.

The goal of verisimilitude in Chion's letters is nowhere more evident than in the tension between internal and external levels of narration. This takes the form of what the reader expects the narrator to know (in his role as Chion) and narrative omniscience, or, from another angle, what Chion's correspondents already know and what external readers must be told. In other novels, information is disseminated by embedded stories, oracular commandments, an omniscient narrator, or direct address to an ideal reader. The primary narrative complication of epistolary fiction, as we have been observing throughout this book, is that the author must make the narrator/letter writer speak to an addressee in order to communicate to us as readers. These multiple levels may provoke tension between the exigencies of fictive discourse (letter writer to addressee) and the necessity to clarify the plot for an external audience (author to reader).[15] Thus many details remain obscure in Chion's first letter, to be revealed only gradually by casual reference, because the author could not justify an explanation of what the internal reader (Chion's father, Plato) obviously already knew. For an epistolary novelist, the initial withholding of information from the external reader is a generic necessity.

The author, self-consciously aware of the epistemological limitations imposed by epistolarity, guides his character's voice accordingly. In *Letter* 3, for example, Chion acknowledges he cannot report Xenophon's exhortation of the troops because he was too far away to hear the exact words, but he could see the result, so it must have been a marvelous speech. In *Letter* 13, Chion describes an assault by Cotys, one of Clearchus' bodyguards, "as I learned later" he quickly adds, saving the narrative from contamination by hindsight or improbable omniscience. Epistolary writing exhibits an immediacy unknown to other modes, revealing its origins as the communication of "news." The assumption is that a letter is written during or immediately after a newsworthy event; the reality is that the item is "edited" as soon as it is written down, and already old by the time it reaches its recipient.

---

[14] Castle (1982) 154.   [15] On this fundamental problem, see Altman (1982) 185–215.

In our consideration of epistolary conventions, we must not ignore certain obviously literary characteristics of the novel. As stated at the beginning of this chapter, most of the letter headings read "to the same person" (τῷ αὐτῷ), which could be written only by an editor after the fact. In addition, we miss many mundane details such as those in Hellenistic private letters: gossip, news of family births and marriages, lawsuits. The collection has an earnestness about it which suggests that it was composed with a view to future reading, and that the pretense at "genuineness" went only so far. It also enters into the literary game of intertextual reference: thus, the Xenophon episode described in *Letter* 3 depends, for its impact, on the reader already knowing Xenophon's own account of the event. The author of *Chion* not only gives his own work credibility by tying it in with a real contemporary document, but also provides his readers with the thrill of encountering a familiar historical event from an unfamiliar viewpoint.

The final question I wish to ask of this letter collection is whether we are justified in calling it a novel. In N. Holzberg's terms, Chion exhibits all the significant characteristics of the genre of epistolary novel: gradual revelation of events, motif chains, an explanatory letter at the end of the collection (*Letter* 16), and even a sense of humor and self-irony.[16] In this chapter, we have identified the work as a historically inspired prose fiction composed solely of letters, arranged chronologically with a clear beginning, middle, and end, and containing a number of unifying themes and concepts. Chion as "hero" guides the plot, developing from shallow youth to dedicated good citizen, and we can spot villains, accomplices, and friends. If the traditional definition of a novel requires coherent structure, systematic development of plot and theme, and consistent characterization of the hero, the work certainly fulfils our expectations. History informs us that (unlike other ancient novels) the story concludes with the death of the protagonist, but only after he has accomplished the task he set for himself. Some would deny that the moral point of the tale survives, namely self-sacrifice for one's country, since we know that Chion's heroism was rewarded by the slaughter of his family and anointing of Clearchus' successor. But the novel itself ends before doom descends, on a note of hopeful martyrdom.

---

[16] Holzberg (1994) 32.

History draws the outlines of Chion's story, but epistolarity gives it form, encouraging the exposition of ideas as well as the description of events and the spiritual journey of the hero. Some of the letters explaining his views on tyranny approximate philosophical treatises, much against the grain of ancient epistolary theorists.[17] It is curious that although Chion puts great emphasis on being a man of deeds, he is represented using a mode more suited for communicating emotions and opinions than straight action narratives – just as we have already noted in the case of Alexander. It allows the novel more introspection and deeper character delineation than most ancient non-epistolary narratives achieve; instead of struggling only against external interference (e.g. pirates, robbers), the protagonist struggles also with his own opinions and decisions.

The epistolary novel progresses through personal communications, which we are invited to read over the internal reader's shoulder. As external interpreters, we partially relive the fiction of Chion's father's original reading, not knowing how the story will end. But on another level, the publication of the collection has modified our prerogative of reading through the single prism of the internal, private addressee. The collection becomes public property, written and edited with a view to *kleos*, posthumous glory for its purported author. What the epistolary narrator constructs in this novel is both true (historically accurate) and fictional (imaginatively elaborated upon), both private (ostensibly for Chion's father and friends) and public. The narrator invites us to share in a dialogue from the past, for which half the script is already written, and the other is left up to us to imagine. The epistolary form of the novel blends fact and fiction, private and public, and even past and present, as it invites the reader to imagine a response. It is this intimate involvement of the reader as respondent that sets the epistolary work apart from any other genre in antiquity.

In this chapter I have presented the *Chion of Heraclea* as a unique example of the epistolary novel: both fully epistolary and clearly novelistic. A young man writes letters home and in the process reveals his feelings and aspirations, the gradual development of his character: an epistolary "Bildungsroman" without an ounce of

---

[17] "Demetrius" *On Style* 230–31.

romance. But by focusing so strongly on the formal epistolary framework, and arguing for the uniqueness of the work itself, we have ignored other aspects that connect *Chion* with some of the other epistolary collections and (partially) epistolary novels in this section. I am thinking primarily here of the *Alexander Romance*.

If we had more evidence of the original epistolary core of the *Alexander Romance*, I suspect that the two works might look very similar. Both Chion and Alexander are historical characters from the mid-fourth century BCE, depicted in a work of historical fiction as writing letters back home to their family and friends. Chion writes primarily to his parents and to his teacher Plato, while Alexander writes to his mother and his teacher Aristotle. The young men are probably about the same age, that is, in the early years of adulthood. Chion is certainly more impressionable and less self-confident, but then he is not the son of a king. Both men live at first in the shadow of their fathers: we first meet Alexander as he sends away emissaries for Philip from Darius, refusing to write a return letter; Chion follows in his father's footsteps by seeking an education in Athens at the Academy. By starting in this way, the novels can emphasize the young men's own spiritual and intellectual development: Alexander becomes a greater conquerer than his father, while Chion finds his own path and insists on staying longer away from home than his father wishes. At the peak of their development, both men write a final letter in the face of death: Chion assumes the worst and expects to die the following day during his assassination attempt, while Alexander is fully aware that he lies on his deathbed and does not have much time left to live.

When we look more closely at the nature of Chion's and Alexander's letters, however, some telling differences appear. Chion's letters seem so much more intimate and affecting than Alexander's, whose letters have an imperial ring to them. Alexander seems trapped by his position as ruler, moving from conquest to conquest, so that even his letters to Olympias are boastful travelogues rather than personal messages between mother and son; only the final letter escapes his political, "public" mode and shows concern for his mother's feelings. Chion, a private citizen, by contrast, writes letters that are equally political in nature yet introspective and personal; instead of wandering into new territories, he explores the conflicting claims of his own mind, seeking to reconcile the study of philosophy and the pursuit of an active political life. Chion's final contribution to society, the liberation of Heraclea from a tyrant through violent means, may bring him closer to Alexander's usual routine of verbal intimidation and battle campaigns, but the two men are basically representative of opposite trends in epistolarity: the private citizen's personal letter-diary, and the public figure's epistolary chronicles.

The middle section of this book has dealt with a whole variety of novelistic prose letter forms with both private and "public" protagonists. The novels with embedded letters focused on private men and women, writing letters of love and intrigue that recalled the original paradigm of Homer's Bellerophon. The pseudonymous letter writers were closer to Alexander's type: famous men from history whose letters reflected their particular arena of action: philosophy, medicine, or politics. The similarities between the protagonists Alexander and Chion suggest a strong interest in this period in stories of personal development, whether of a "normal" young man from a small town in Pontus, or of the most famous man in his day, Alexander the Great.

We will now turn, in the final three chapters of the book, to epistolary works that were being written at about the same time as the novels, yet made no attempt to fit that generic category. The collections to be discussed below resemble the *pseudonymoi* in that their letters do not necessarily tell a complete and sustained story; they resemble the letters of Chion by including bits of gossip, news, and local color; they even recall the embedded letters of the ancient novel when they refer to erotic misadventure, or pirates and soldiers. But they are unlike anything we have come across yet in their total fabrication of authorial voice, unrelated for the most part to anything historical or literary. In this way, the letter writers of the Second Sophistic free themselves to write independently and wholly creatively. In the context of *ethopoieia*, we noted that the declaimer was meant to imagine what a famous character from history or literature might say in a given circumstance; but for Alciphron and Aelian, two of the authors to be discussed in this last section, the fun was in imagining precisely what that anonymous farmer might say upon finding mice in his flour bins.

IV

Epistolography in the Second Sophistic

CHAPTER 10

The Letters *of Alciphron*

> I resemble a messenger from antiquity, a bellboy, a runner, a courier of what we have given one another, barely an inheritor, a lame inheritor, incapable even of receiving, of measuring himself against whatever is his to maintain, and I run, I run to bring them news which must remain secret, and I fall all the time.
>
> J. Derrida, *The Post Card*[1]

The previous section focused on letter narratives that could claim some connection to the genre of the novel; this following section, while sharing the general cultural context of the Second Sophistic, presents collections of letters that are not necessarily related, that do not cohere in a "novelistic" whole the way Chion's letters do. Two of the authors to be discussed in detail, Alciphron and Aelian, compose diverse groups of letters organized according to fictional types: farmers, for example, in the case of Aelian. The third author, Philostratus, writes in his own voice to various addressees, mostly on the topic of love and seduction. All three authors use the letter form to sketch short scenes of emotional intensity, to invent predicaments in the personal lives of others. Missing in these collections is any sense of character development, sustained plot, or dramatic rhythm; these writers take advantage of the letter as a brief glimpse into the lives of (mostly) ordinary people dealing with momentary crises. The letters present one side of an issue and usually leave it unresolved, open to multiple resolutions in the minds of the readers.

The three writers I have chosen to discuss are rarely read even by classicists. Their status as epistolary collections, I suspect, limits

---

[1] J. Derrida, *The Post Card: from Socrates to Freud and Beyond*, trans. A. Bass (Chicago 1987) 8.

their appeal. We read embedded letters in the context of their larger genre: tragedy, history, the novel. We also eagerly read letter collections when their authors are famous for other things, as in the case of Seneca or Cicero, for example. But fictional letter collections are expected to have high literary merit on their own if they are to be worth reading at all; Ovid's *Heroides* has long suffered under this rule, and critics have been slow to attribute such merit to the three writers in question here. Aelian and Alciphron have been put to the service of authenticating Lucian or bits of Greek New Comedy, and an appreciation of Philostratus' epistolary work is mired in the debate over precisely which of several Philostrati might be responsible for this particular text. The lack of historical information about these epistolary authors has diminished our critical response to them, and contributed to their unpopularity. If this chapter on Alciphron is therefore longer than others in spite of its focus on one author and one group of texts, it reflects my attempt to show the merits of his work in the context of epistolary literature.

The *Cambridge History of Classical Literature* begins its short section on Alciphron with the unpromising statement "his personality is unknown and his date uncertain."[2] Yet this unknown personality has left behind a collection of 123 fictional prose letters in four books, organized under the headings of farmers, fishermen, parasites, and courtesans.[3] The occupations of the supposed letter writers point to connections with the wider comic tradition. Aristophanes' Dikaiopolis in the *Acharnians* is the archetypal farmer, and one can imagine a similar protagonist in Antiphanes' lost play *The Rustic*; fishermen appear in Menander's *The Fisherman* and Plautus' *Rudens*, while parasites and courtesans crowd the stages of Menander, Plautus, and Terence. Other parallels, including shared images of rustics, parasites, and courtesans, link Alciphron with Lucian, his fellow epistolographer Aelian, and Longus. This last literary grouping puts us generally in the period of the Second

---

[2] E. L. Bowie in P. E. Easterling and B. M. W. Knox, eds., *The Cambridge History of Classical Literature* vol. I, Greek Literature (Cambridge 1985b) 679–80.

[3] The most easily accessible text for the letters of Alciphron is the Loeb edition of Benner and Fobes (1949), which includes a summary of the manuscript tradition and its transmission. The translations that follow are mine, based on the text of Benner and Fobes.

Sophistic, and most scholars settle on an approximate date for Alciphron of 170–220 CE.[4] Not a lot to go on, but a start.

The two epithets associated with Alciphron in the tradition provide more information: he is called "rhetor" and "Atticist."[5] The designation "rhetor," originally meaning "orator," came to mean someone who trains other speakers in any and all forms of oratory, including epideictic rhetoric. The label "Atticist" implies that Alciphron was a follower of an archaizing prose style, imitating great Athenian authors of the fifth and fourth centuries BCE, especially historians and orators. The writers of the Second Sophistic were fascinated by old Attic words, phrases, and idioms, and used what was by then "archaic" syntax and diction to try to reproduce the charm and cultural impact of the literature of an earlier golden age.

E. L. Bowie states that "the archaism of language and style known as Atticism is only part of a wider tendency, a tendency that prevails in literature not only in style but also in choice of theme and treatment, and that equally affects other areas of cultural activity."[6] Alciphron's choice of topics and settings, as well as his choice of language and style, fit well into Bowie's scheme of multi-layered archaizing: the letters represent a fourth-century context, attempting to evoke both a rural (farmers, fishermen) and an urban (parasites, courtesans) environment. He chooses themes of New Comedy as illustrations for his works. While Menander was praised for showing scenes of "real life" to his audience, Alciphron creates for his readership a "reality" based on the literary representations of Menander, so at a second degree of distance.

---

[4] Much scholarly work has focused on literary relationships between Alciphron and other authors of the Second Sophistic. Benner and Fobes (1949) 32–36 offer the best general bibliography. See, in particular, C. Bonner, "On Certain Supposed Literary Relationships," *CP* 4 (1909) 32–44, 276–90; C. N. Jackson, "An Ancient Letter-Writer: Alciphron," *Harvard Essays on Classical Subjects* (Boston 1912) 67–96; A. Lesky, "Alkiphron und Aristainetos," *MVPW* 6 (1929) 47–59; D. A. Tsirimbas, *Sprichwörter und sprichwörtliche Redensarten bei den Epistolographen der zweiten Sophistik* (Speyer am Rhein 1936); J. J. Bungarten, *Menanders und Glykeras Briefe bei Alkiphron* (Bonn 1967); B. P. Reardon, *Courants littéraires grecs des IIe et IIIe siècles après J.-C.* (Paris 1971) 180–85; R. G. Ussher, "Love Letter, Novel, Alciphron and 'Chion'," *Hermathena* 143 (1987) 99–106; L. Santini, "Tra Filosofi e Parassiti: L'Epistola III. 19 di Alcifrone e I modelli Lucianei," *Atene e Roma* 40 (1995) 58–71.
[5] He is called ῥήτωρ by the surviving manuscripts and by Tzetzes' scholia to the *Chiliades* 8.895; Ἀττικιστής by Eustathius on *Iliad* 9.453. See Benner and Fobes (1949) 6, and on Atticism in general, S. Swain, *Hellenism and Empire* (Oxford 1996) 17–64.
[6] Bowie (1970) 3–41, esp. 3.

Part of the point of Alciphron's game is his readers' sophisticated awareness that his recreations of the past are precisely not "real." In his literary gamesmanship, Alciphron refers not just to Menander, but to a wide range of earlier authors, much in the vein of his sophistic contemporaries who prided themselves on their educated jokes and allusions: Homer, Hesiod, Demosthenes, and Aristophanes are just a few of his favorites.[7]

Alciphron and his fellow writers of the second and third centuries CE enjoyed a social and political climate that nurtured a strong sense of Hellenic identity and culture. While under Roman rule, individual cities were allowed a great deal of latitude, and from Hadrian to Marcus Aurelius, the emperors showed themselves for the most part willing to support Greek literature and the arts.[8] Pliny the Younger (*Ep.* 8.24) suggests in a letter that the Greeks should be allowed to keep their cultural dignity because all they had left was their "glorious past," a past that was invested with a patina of glory by its very antiquity. Of course, the "past" itself was a fluid and complex thing, its reconstruction loaded with ideological and political baggage; it was more than simple "nostalgia" that led sophistic writers to create their particular literary worlds. As C. P. Jones puts it, "the cult of antiquity does not imply disrespect for the present: rather, it validates the present with the stamp of culture"; and Greek culture, in this case epitomized by the culture of classical Athens, expressed the "cohesion of the educated elite of the empire."[9] The writers of this period appealed, as did their forebears, in different and individual ways to a set of canonical texts with which any educated person would have been familiar, and to a set of values that reflected what they viewed as the best of Greek *paideia*. For Lucian, perhaps the most familiar representative of his age, this consisted of combining a philosophical and a rhetorical heritage into a unique blend of wickedly intelligent satire and literary history. By imitating the old masters, he invited his readers to join in the "affirmation of a common heritage."[10] The result of Alciphron's exercise in imita-

---

[7] Most earlier scholarship on Alciphron has focused on his use of sources, but my goal here is to expore the epistolary nature of his work, not further *Quellenforschung*.

[8] See G. Anderson, *The Second Sophistic* (London 1993) 1–12; C. P. Jones, *Culture and Society in Lucian* (Cambridge MA 1986) 149–59.

[9] Jones (1986) 158–59.

[10] Jones (1986) 159.

tion and evocation of the past was a focus on a human tapestry of emotions and experiences organized according to the individual's role in society: his collection of fictional letters makes up a whole fourth-century world in miniature, but a world that explores precisely not the educated élite, but the uneducated underworld.

Other sophistic texts also fall under the rubric of miniaturism: G. Anderson considers the shorter dialogues of Lucian as part of the same literary phenomenon as the letter collections of Alciphron and Aelian; he points out that miniatures offer a natural opportunity for variation, as they can be worked into a series.[11] But I would argue that the "miniaturist" aspect of Alciphron's work is a direct result of his choice of epistolary form. Letters are by nature fragmentary glimpses into the lives of their writers, and are easily combined into collected correspondences. Although we are presented with only brief sketches of Alciphron's imagined past, his readers would have been familiar with its details from other literary sources, primed to fill in the gaps with their imaginations. B. P. Reardon rightly emphasizes the intentionally fragmentary nature of Alciphron's letters: he terms his art "du pointillisme littéraire," making its impact by suggestion rather than full exposition; but at the same time, the cumulative effect of all these sketches is one of a "grand tableau," evoking a society and culture long past.[12] The unity of the collection, the "tableau" of daily life, is balanced by the varied forms of individual letters: each letter reveals connections to other modes and genres, saving the whole from a potential flatness or structural conformity. In the fourth book alone, we see the flexibility of the epistolary text to present itself as funeral elegy (4.11: on the death of Bacchis), ecphrasis (4.13: pastoral scenes), narrative (4.14: beauty contest), drama (4.17: choosing between two lovers), and love story (4.18–19: Menander and Glycera's correspondence).[13]

As we have had occasion to observe more than once before, the form of the fictional letter itself can be seen as a product or development of the sophistic schools.[14] School exercises, or *progymnasmata*, were miniatures of sorts, as students tried their hands

---

[11] Anderson (1993) 190–96 speaks of "the art of the miniature."

[12] Reardon (1971) 182.

[13] See the discussion in Reardon (1971) 184.

[14] For an excellent introduction to the nature of sophistic school exercises, see Anderson (1993) 47–68.

at composition. The more advanced compositions were produced as entertainment for an adult audience, in which the challenge was to display the greatest amount of wit and learning in the smallest compass. The fictional letter may have evolved from rhetorical exercises in which a character is placed in a specific situation; the characters and the incidents could be fictitious or historical.[15] This kind of characterization (*ethopoieia*) often took the form of "what would so-and-so say if ...?" In the resulting rhetorical display, sometimes the speaker focused primarily on the character ("what did the farmer say on seeing his first ship?"), at other times on the emotions ("what did Achilles say over the corpse of Patroclus?").[16] Alciphron's version of the former is "what did the farmer say upon desiring to see the Big City?" (2.28 in full):[17]

I have never yet been to the city, and I don't even know what that thing is that men call a city, so I am eager to see this novel sight – men living together behind one wall – and to learn the other ways in which a city differs from country living. So if you find any excuse for a trip to the city, come now and take me along with you. And I really think it is time for me to learn more about it, since my upper lip is beginning to sprout with hair. So who indeed would be more appropriate to initiate me into the Mysteries there other than you, who spend most of your time roaming around inside the gates?

His version of the latter is "what did the fisherman's daughter in love say to her mother?" (1.11.1–4):

Dear mother, I am beside myself. I can't bear the thought of being married to that boy from Methymna, the captain's son to whom father recently engaged me; I have felt this way ever since I saw that young guardsman in the city at the Oschophoria ... and if I can't marry him, I will imitate Lesbian Sappho and ... throw myself into the surf.

But this last example also reveals how Alciphron's decision to adapt *ethopoieia* to letter form could develop the school exercise into literary art. The ability to continue the narrative in epistolary response and exchange throughout the collection means that the original single display, the moment of declamation linked to a specific occasion, may blossom into a sustained story, or a dialogue. So Alciphron has the girl's mother answer her letter, and make short shrift of her daughter's theatrical posturings (1.12):

---

[15] Jackson (1912) 72. For the general cultural background, see Russell (1983) 1–39.
[16] The examples are from Anderson (1993) 52.
[17] See also Virgil *Ec.* 1 on a similar theme.

My dear daughter, you have gone mad, and you are truly "beside your-self." You need a dose of hellebore ... you who, instead of being ashamed as a young girl should, have wiped all modesty from your face ... If your father should hear of any of this, he won't hesitate for a moment, but will throw you out as food for the fishes.

One of the great challenges of *ethopoieia* is to sustain the invented characterization without falling into either anachronisms (i.e. non-Attic linguistic forms and phrases), or language or actions inap-propriate to the situation. Sophistic authors take further risks by crossing class and gender lines in their characterizations. How can one author know how such different types think, speak, or act? The most obvious way is to take one's cues from the stereotypical characters of New Comedy. In the three examples above, Alci-phron succeeds in creating believable portraits by trying to see things through each character's eyes, yet each one is part of com-edy's stock in trade: the country bumpkin, the young person in love, the bourgeois parent. Thus the farmer, aptly named Phil-okomos ("Village-lover"), expresses discomfort even at uttering the name "city," since in his rustic naiveté he has no idea what "that thing is," and finds it hard to imagine many men living all to-gether behind one single wall. We are invited to picture the city as he sees it in his mind's eye: a version of an extended farmhouse, or a crowded stockyard.

With the girl in love, we turn to the comic world of erotic pas-sion and generational conflict. The girl's outpourings tie her to the world of her father and fiancé, almost in spite of herself, for as she tries to praise the beauty of her boyfriend from the city, her em-phatically marine terminology betrays her status as fresh off the boat: "his hair is curlier than seaweed, his smile more radiant than a calm sea, and the sparkle of his eyes is like the dark blue of the ocean ..." (1.11.2).[18] When our heroine Glaucippe ("Sea-Green") quotes Sappho and threatens a similar suicide for love, we might assume that she has been reading too much Menander.[19] Her mother's words are similarly waterlogged: her admonition to

---

[18] Her cultural limitations are directly reminiscent of Polyphemus' in Theoc. 13, where the Cyclops in love describes his sea-nymph Galatea in contrastingly land-locked terms.

[19] See the fragments of "Leukadia" ("The Girl from Lesbos"), in W. G. Arnott, ed. and trans., *Menander.* 2 vols. (Cambridge MA 1996) 230–31, where the story of Sappho's sui-cide leap off the rocks at Leukas for the sake of Phaon is related. Of course, the Sappho story was well known before Menander put it on stage.

"hold steady and whip on your own course" (1.12.2) hints at the actions of a ship's pilot, and her image of food for the fishes effectively deflates Glaucippe's romantic urban fantasies and reminds her of her place in the world.

The above letters testify to Alciphron's interest in pitting rural and urban personalities against each other; elsewhere (1.15), a fisherman takes a group of rich men and their courtesans on a pleasure cruise, and weighs the advantage of a good day's pay against the resentful glances of his fellow fishermen trying to make an honest living. The sheer number of variations of experience of Alciphron's *ethopoieiai* is astounding. These experiences range from the mundane (1.13: a fisherman tries to escape a moneylender) to the critical (4.18: Menander debates whether to leave Athens for Egypt), and from the practical (2.3: a farmer's request for a loan of wheat) to the practically pornographic (4.13 and 14: wild parties on a country estate). Most of the characters Alciphron introduces are purely fictitious, with wonderfully eloquent "speaking names": (1.21: the fisherman "Fair-sailing to Sea-love"; 3.25: the parasite "Garlic-sniffer to Crumb"). Only the last book, the letters of the courtesans, differs slightly from the rest of the corpus in that it exploits famous "historical" lovers such as Praxiteles and Phryne (4.1), Leontium and Epicurus (4.17), or Menander and Glycera (4.2, 18, 19).

Alciphron is not alone in this period in choosing lower class characters as the focus of his literary interest; Lucian writes his *Dialogues of the Courtesans*, Athenaeus offers an encyclopedic knowledge of courtesan lore (*Deipn.* 13), while Aelian devotes his epistolary collection to *Letters from Farmers*. Parasites and courtesans become the representatives of the great cultural heritage of classical Athens, and this is precisely the kind of witty paradox that the authors (and presumably readers) of the Second Sophistic must have enjoyed.[20] Parasites and courtesans boast of their own particular kind of *paideia*, as do their rustic counterparts. This leads to such contests of wisdom as Alciphron's debate between the advantages of a courtesan or a philosopher as a "teacher" (4.7.4–7), or Lucian's comparison between Odysseus and Plato in his paradoxical encomium *De Parasito*.

It is often tempting to compare Alciphron's fictional letters with

---

[20] Anderson (1993) 183–85; J. N. Davidson, *Courtesans and Fishcakes* (London 1997).

Lucian's short dialogues, and not just because the two authors are assumed to be contemporaries. Both share an interest in lively descriptions of characters and actions which are intrinsically interesting to their readership because of their great distance from late second-century urban intellectual life.[21] Of the two, Alciphron has suffered more from the charge of "artificiality," often simply because of his choice of epistolary form over, for example, dialogue or novel. The same scholar who called Alciphron's work "artificial" ends his critique with the statement "the game cannot sustain prolonged watching," suggesting that the letters are monotonous and trivial, hardly worth reading.[22]

There are several responses to this objection. First, the letter form implies a certain amount of conventionality which may be read as artificiality; the artificiality is specific to the genre, but not more intrusive than accepted conventions of other genres. Epistolary form is no more absurd or artificial than any other literary form, including novel or drama; it is just less usual and therefore unfamiliar.[23] Complicating this charge is the fact that these are not actual letters, but rather fictional letters presented in a literary package: epistolary *ethopoieia*, as it were. As such they also follow another set of conventions: those of rhetorical display. While we may never praise these texts as masterpieces of literature, we cannot fault them for following generic and performative guidelines built into their literary identity. They are *supposed* to be artificial: that is precisely the charm of the "game," and both Alciphron and Aelian go out of their way to acknowledge this fact. Aelian puts it best in his final letter (*Letter* 20), where a farmer tries to counter the prejudices of his addressee who is suspicious of his country origins:

If these letters sent to you are cleverer than you might expect the country to supply, don't be surprised; for we are not Libyan or Lydian farmers, but Athenian ones.

Letters by nature are conventional, clever, and written to have a particular effect on their readers. They persuade and manipulate just as an orator does, but in writing rather than in oral perfor-

---

[21] E. L. Bowie, "The Greek Novel," in Easterling and Knox, eds., *Cambridge History of Classical Literature*, vol. 1 (New York 1985) 680.

[22] Bowie (1985) 680.

[23] This is argued by Reardon (1971) 180–85.

mance, in "private" rather than public. But just how epistolary are these letters of Alciphron? Are there genre markers beyond the conventional epistolary opening and closing, which themselves appear in only a small fraction of the letters? How do the letters differ from short fictional essays, character sketches, or monologues? The rest of this chapter will discuss these questions at greater length, but let us pause briefly to consider some general points. There is no single answer for this varied collection. Some of the letters take great pains to emphasize their epistolary context, and refer self-consciously to their own engendering, sending, receiving, and reading; others assume the form of short essays or narrative descriptions with no acknowledgment of their epistolary framework. All, however, share their inclusion of an internal audience, a character directly addressed whose existence justifies the necessity of a written letter, whether or not that character remains a central figure or recedes into the background as the letter writer turns to his or her wider public, the external audience.

To consider the relationship of letter to dialogue, we can compare Alciphron's letters of courtesans in his fourth book with Lucian's *Dialogues of Courtesans*. Their literary goals are quite similar: to offer a glimpse into the fourth-century urban demi-monde, with tantalizing nods in the direction of famous lovers in infamous situations. Both offer the additional thrill of overhearing (or reading over the shoulder) what these women really talk about, especially, in the case of Alciphron, when men are not present. But on several levels, the dialogue form allows for a certain flexibility that the epistolary mode lacks.

First, Lucian's range of two to four speakers in any given dialogue allows for a number of unmediated different perspectives in the same dialogue. In *Dialogue* 2, the speakers include a courtesan, her lover, and her maid. The maid thinks she sees her mistress' lover celebrating his marriage to a citizen girl; in reality, she has been misled by a marriage taking place in the house next door. When the mistress scolds her lover for his behavior, he quickly explains the truth and comforts his beloved. The spoken context provides for vividness, simultaneous contrasting narratives, and revision. By contrast, Alciphron's letters introduce the intermediary (self-)editing of the letter writer him- or herself: the very act of writing takes us one step away from a vivid "colloquial" mode. Letter format discourages multiple voices in one text, and restricts

revisions to rewritings in an epistolary sequel. The fact of an op-
tional sequel, however, gives the collection a formal pattern that
the individual dialogue, in turn, cannot achieve.

Second, the fictional occasion of the dialogue allows things to
happen as the dialogue unfolds; action can invade and affect the
reported conversation. Thus, in *Dialogue* 13, a braggart soldier
straight out of New Comedy tries to impress a courtesan with his
courage but ends up scaring her so thoroughly that she runs away,
mid-dialogue. The soldier then asks his friend to chase after her
and tell her that it was all lies, that he cares more for her love than
his own reputation. All this is discussed as it happens. The letter,
by contrast, can report only what has happened in the past or
predict what might happen in the future; its present is lost in the
fiction of the act of writing, and no action other than writing can
occur within its boundaries. There are exceptions to this rule: a
reported knock at the door, or a break in the writing explained
later as an interruption of some sort. But attempts in Alciphron at
temporal vividness of the sort familiar from dialogue end up as
textual "problems": in 3.36, a parasite is brought to justice before
a certain Kleainetos who "at the present time (τὰ νῦν δή) holds
first place in the Council ...," but three lines later the same man
"was seized by a fever and died ... and now his household prepares for the funeral." Either we must assume that the first part of
the letter is meant to be written before the man's death (yet the
letter writer makes no mention of a temporal gap), or we are reduced to the sad comment of Benner and Fobes on this passage:
"perhaps Alciphron here ... had no clear idea of the situation he
was describing."[24]

Finally, dialogue form can expand to incorporate embedded
stories and even letters. In *Dialogue* 8, we read an embedded story
of advice from an older courtesan to a younger one. In *Dialogue* 10,
a courtesan, abandoned by her lover for philosophy, discusses with
her maid a letter from the neglectful lover: "the writing is not very
clear – obviously written in a hurry ... he doesn't even start by
wishing me well!" They plan their revenge, not by return letter,
but by a more public document: writing graffiti on the walls of the
Kerameikos accusing the philosopher in question of corrupting
her lover. The charm of the letter embedded in the dialogue is the

---

[24] Benner and Fobes (1949) 237 note b.

fiction of a fresh voice, a separate document, that appears as a visible artifact in the hands of the speaker. In a similar situation in Alciphron, during the letter exchange between Menander and Glycera (4.18–19), we learn that Menander has enclosed in his letter to Glycera a letter from King Ptolemy inviting him to Egypt. The courtesan tells us in her return letter to Menander that she waved the king's letters in the air and showed them off to her family, but she never quotes directly from them. She does not need to quote from Menander's letter, since we have it in its entirety. She cannot quote from Ptolemy's letter without breaking the illusion of her internal addressee: Menander knows full well what the king's letter said, since he sent her a copy in the first place. Ironically then, in the cases of Alciphron and Lucian, the dialogue form incorporates embedded letters more easily than the letter form itself does.

This list of comparisons is not meant to be exhaustive. It merely raises some of the generic questions surrounding Alciphron's choice of epistolary form. Now we can look in greater detail at the collection itself, continuing to ask questions about the impact of epistolarity on the contents of the four books. The fourth book will merit additional discussion at the end, since it differs from the previous three in two major ways: the inclusion of historical characters, and the more noticeable presence of women's voices.

JUST ORDINARY MEN (AND WOMEN)

One feature to note at the outset about Alciphron's first three books is the extreme ordinariness of their writers' lives. School exercises were based on famous examples from history and literature, yet when Alciphron expands *ethopoieia* into art, he chooses to record mundane, ordinary details of "regular" people's lives: their loves, their hates, their lunch menus, and their work woes. If one is going to invent fictional letters, or any sort of fictional narrative, one might be expected to invent something new, strange, or monumental: something like Ovid's larger-than-life heroines. While there is a clear appeal to the imagination in, for example, Lucian's "true" stories or letters from the dead, Alciphron does not ask his readers to stretch their imaginations that far. Daily lives in fourth-century Athens turn out to be not so different from daily lives in Alciphron's own day. The very ordinariness of the letters acts as a guarantee of their "authenticity." The appeal to the ancient audience must have been close to our modern interest in reading journals and fictionalized accounts of ordinary people: women pioneers in the early West, or foot soldiers in the Civil War. When it comes to the letters of the courtesans, however, ordinariness will be replaced by sensationalism and notoriety.

The bourgeois nature of Alciphron's letters and their obsession with socio-economic class are traits clearly borrowed from New Comedy, with its interest in impoverished young women, mercenary soldiers, and grumpy farmers. Alciphron's characters live in circumscribed conditions but write of breaking out of their assigned places: fishermen dream of becoming farmers, parasites want to be rich, country girls look to the city for salvation. Their dreams are more often than not thwarted at the start, or, if briefly fulfilled, then upset by disappointment or failure. In the entire collection, the only potentially successful move upward on the social and economic scale belongs to Menander, who is offered the chance to move to Egypt and consort with royalty; yet he hesitates to take it, reluctant to abandon his girlfriend. The letters thus uphold the stability of the social order, just as comedy does, while allowing the reader the temporary pleasure of grumbling along with the writers about the disappointments and complications of human life.

My analysis of the letters that follows will look closely at these themes: the litany of complaints, the desire to trade social places, and the consequences of falling in love in Alciphron's invented world. I will also explore the self-consciously epistolary aspects of the collection, including references to writing, reading, and sending letters, most of which are found in the fourth book, the letters of courtesans. Since many readers may not be familiar with Alciphron's work, I will go into some detail about individual letters, summarizing their contents. As an overview of the whole collection, let us consider the opening letter of each book, assuming that either author or editor placed it there for a reason, and that we can therefore read it as programmatic for the rest of the book.[25]

---

[25] Admittedly the textual tradition of the corpus is vexed. There are three main families of manuscripts, dated primarily to the 14th century, but ranging from 12th (B Vindobonensis phil. 342) to late 15th century (Φ Parisinus 3054). The manuscripts differ in their ordering of the individual letters. The earliest printed edition (Aldine 1499) included the first letter of only book 1, while Bergler's edition of 1715 added the first letters of books 2 and 3; Wagner's edition of 1798 included 4.1. Benner and Fobes' text is based on those of Schepers (1901, 1905), and I, in turn, am basing my discussion of epistolary organization on their reconstruction of the corpus.

Alciphron begins his collection with a book of letters from fishermen, and his opening letter dives *in medias res*. "Fair-weather" writes to "Love-boat" about his experiences in a storm, how the fishermen were forced to wait out the bad weather, but were rewarded in the end by a huge catch of fish. The letter virtually journalizes a week in the fisherman's life, and in good journalistic style, foregrounds temporal references: today the sea is calm, but three days ago the winds and waves were too rough for us to go out, so we sat around a fire on the beach to keep warm; today is the fourth day, the sky has finally cleared, and we were able to launch the boats and pull up bulging nets, selling some of the fish and taking the surplus home to our families. In addition to alerting us to this precise time frame, the writer manages to pack in a great deal of information in what appears to be a casual letter to (presumably) a fellow fisherman who was not present during the four-day event. He does this so matter-of-factly that we, the external readers, barely realize how much is there primarily for our benefit. Fair-weather's name declares his occupation; he provides a geographical location by alluding to the "fish sellers who ... hurried off from Phaleron to the city" (1.1.4). This much is internally consistent, since the existence of the letter implies that Love-boat is not at Phaleron, and may be interested in knowing where his friend sat out the storm. We discover that Fair-weather has a wife and children when he mentions carrying home the smaller, less valuable fish to his family. We even know what he does during his time off: sits around a fire inside a fishing shack on shore, trying to keep out the cold. All this could be "news" to Love-boat.

But Alciphron's eye for specifics pits the perspective of the internal addressee (i.e. what exactly is Love-boat to learn from this letter?) against the sophistic author's urge to document in the name of "historical realism." He does not just say that Fair-weather built a fire by the seashore to keep warm; rather, he transcribes every step of the man's actions, the location of the huts, the source of the fuel, the kind of tree the woodchips came from, and why they were conveniently lying about there in the first place (1.1.2):

We found shelter in the huts along the shore, after collecting a few woodchips that the carpenters had recently left behind after cutting down some oak trees, and we built a fire with them and fended off the bitterness of the cold weather.

The fish sellers and their baskets likewise receive close scrutiny, far beyond what a fellow fisherman might expect (1.1.4):

Now the fish sellers were immediately nearby, and they lifted their yokes to their shoulders, fitted into place the two fish baskets, one at each end, and put their money down for the fish...

The careful description of exactly how the catch was transported recalls Homer's elaborate justification as Odysseus transports a huge deer carcass back to his shipmates (*Od.* 10.156–73).[26] In both cases the information is there to convince the audience of the "realism" of the scene, not, in the case of Alciphron's fishermen, to share critical information between the writer and his addressee. The letter ends in neat ring composition, as Fair-weather announces that he had enough fish left over to feed his family "not for just one day, but for several days, in the case of bad weather" (1.1.5). We have been reading "a week in the life of a fisherman"; this four-day pattern of fair and foul weather, full and empty nets, can repeat itself endlessly, as the fishermen go about their predictable lives.

This opening letter works well as an introduction to the collection: it raises issues of epistolary verisimilitude (i.e. is the information primarily intended for an internal or external audience?), and pulls us abruptly into the rustic world of working men, glossing over the question of literacy among the uneducated. Alciphron offers his readers (presumably those "educated elites" again) a glimpse into the reality behind the fish they might find on their dinner tables. The letters of the fishermen that make up the rest of the book are similar in tone and content, emphasizing hard work, the vagaries of weather, and the difficulties of making a living from the sea. Those that differ look beyond the confines of the fisherman's life to other social roles: fishermen and money-lenders (1.13), for example, or fishermen as naval conscripts (1.14).

But the opening letter to book 2 does not function in a comparable programmatic manner, and reminds us how difficult it is to generalize about individual letters as opposed to the impact of the whole collection. *Letter* 2.1 is a short piece in the voice of a farmer, missing its title, about training puppies to chase hares.[27] The

---

[26] There are similar "effects of the real" in the accumulation of detail in Theocritus' literary accounts.

[27] Scholars point to connections with Xenophon's *Cynegeticus* 7.6–9, and possibly Aelian's *Letter* 11. See Benner and Fobes (1949) 85.

speaker reports an unexpected chase by the untrained dogs in which the keenest of the animals follows the prey into its hole, breaking its leg in the process. The farmer pulls out his limping puppy and a half-eaten hare, and closes with a moralizing tag: "I was hoping for a small gain, but carried home a great loss." There are no specifically epistolary traces in this short narrative, no sense of doubled audiences in the kind of information offered. But it does remind the reader of two other characteristics of these letters: a tendency to moralize or use clichés, and a predominantly complaining tone.[28] Other farmer's letters complain in a similar fashion about thieving animals, lazy slaves, bad crops, and unpredictable weather. *Letter* 2.1 also points to the bourgeois nature of the letters, so many of which obsess about money matters: the farmer's misfortune with his dogs is a matter of food on the table for his family, not a wasted day of sport or betting.

In some ways, *Letter* 2.2 represents its book better than 2.1. Much of the letter closely resembles Lucian's *Cock* (12), as the scene opens on a farmer rudely awakened from a pleasant dream by a rooster. The writer describes the dream to his friend (2.2.1–3):

> For it seemed to me, my dear neighbor, that I was someone magnificent and extremely rich; then I was attended by a huge crowd of slaves, and I thought they were my stewards and my overseers. I thought that rings loaded down my hands and I was wearing very precious stones; my fingers were soft and had completely forgotten the feel of tools. And flatterers appeared nearby ... and the citizens of Athens entered the theater and shouted that I should be elected general.

Here we encounter two of the main themes of the collection: complaints about the difficulties of one's lot, and a desire to trade places with another (apparently) more fortunate soul. The farmer dreams that he has become so rich that not only has he left the farm for the big city, and traded spade for rings and jewelry, but also he owns his own laborers now, slaves and overseers for the farm he previously worked with his own sweat and toil. The ultimate sign of success in the city is to be surrounded by parasites and flatterers, the implication being that the farmer now has more than enough to share with hangers-on. Throughout his collection, Alciphron invites different types to try on a new role, only to send them back where they belong: the farmer-turned-millionaire

---

[28] For a discussion of clichés in Alciphron, see Tsirimbas (1936).

encounters parasites in his dream in 2.2, but returns to being a farmer when he awakes; meanwhile, later in book 2, we shall see a parasite who tries on the clothes of a farmer for size, but quickly abandons the rustic life when his hands begin to blister.

Turning to book 3, the book of parasites' letters, the first letter begins with a complaint by one Trechedeipnos ("Dinner-chaser") to Lopadekthambos ("Dish-crazy") that the sundial is far from marking the dinner hour, yet starvation has already set in (3.1.1).

The pointer doesn't mark the sixth hour yet, and I run the risk of withering away, so pinched am I by hunger. So now, Lopadekthambos, it's high time for you to think of something, or even better, now's the time to hang ourselves with rope and crowbar.

He begs his friend to think of a scheme to find food, or if that fails, to provide the tools with which they can hang themselves. Perhaps by hanging themselves, he suggests brightly, they can topple the column that supports the hateful sundial, or bend the marker to mark the hours sooner: a scheme worthy of the great Palamedes.[29] His initial thought of suicide, raised in desperation, turns into a neat plan for turning the clock forward, therefore convincing his host to feed them. His young host is so well brought up by such a severe pedagogue that he eats strictly on schedule, and never snacks between meals (3.1.3):

So we need some plan like this that can trick and confuse Theochares' routine. Brought up by a strict and frowning pedagogue, he doesn't think at all like a young man, but like a Laches or an Apolexis, he is austere in his ways and doesn't turn to the filling of his stomach until the very hour of dinner.

This letter takes us from the farmlands into the back alleys of Athens, into a scene of childish schemes and mock suicide attempts, all in the name of outwitting one's host and getting a bite to eat. The personal names and the references to local topography bring us much closer to comedy than before; the names of the correspondents become more baroque and colorful each moment. The parasites of book 3 are constantly choosing between starvation and death, all grossly exaggerated (or so we think). They depend on their hosts yet complain bitterly about bad treatment at their hands, stuck in a hostile relationship of dependency and

---

[29] Consider the account of suicide in Plautus' *Stichus* 638–40.

laziness. The parasites' letters are the least epistolary of the entire collection, as they rarely even sustain the fiction of an addressee or a letter context. In fact, four of the letters ignore the purported addressee for a conventional address to the gods: *Letter* 3.11 opens with a prayer of thanks to Hermes, 3.13 with an invocation of a guardian angel, and 3.32 to "you blessed gods, may you be propitious and have mercy on me"; 3.37 veers away in the middle of the narrative from its initial addressee to speak instead to "you gods of Destiny." When the letters do share news with their addressees, it is often just to tell a friend about a particularly delightful (or more usually disastrous) party, or to extend an invitation either to share good luck or to sympathize in bad. These letters often end with a brief summary, a moral of sorts (e.g. 3.3; 3.21), and they all share frequent reference to place names in Athens and Attica. Their "Athenianness" leads them to write in educated and elegant ways, even if they are merely parasites, at the bottom of the social ladder: here is Alciphron's version (3.29.3) of a joke that we have already seen in Aelian:

Surely it is a good thing to speak in the manner of educated folk if one comes from Athens, where there is no one who hasn't had a taste of these things [i.e. literature, letters].

There are no real connections or cross-references between letters within this book, although a few appear well paired. This book also has the largest number of individual letters – forty-two – and most of the letters are shorter than average.

By contrast, the courtesans' book, consisting of nineteen letters of varying lengths, is more tightly constructed and organized, involving reappearing characters and connected story lines. This is clear from the first five letters alone: Phryne to Praxiteles (1); Glycera to Bacchis (2); Bacchis to Hypereides (3); Bacchis to Phryne (4); Bacchis to Myrrhina (5). This series of perspectives offered on basically the same event – Phryne's court appearance on a charge of impiety, ably defended by the lawyer Hypereides, and the ensuing lover-swapping among her fellow courtesans – invites us to read the sequence as a proto-epistolary novel. In the first (4.1), Phryne writes a letter of thanks and invitation to her lover, the artist Praxiteles. Next (4.2), Glycera writes to Bacchis about Menander, commending her lover to her friend Bacchis as he is about to visit her in Corinth. In *Letter* 4.3, Bacchis writes to

Hypereides, identified now as Phryne's lover, thanking him for his hard work on behalf on Phryne in court, indirectly benefitting all courtesans. Bacchis also writes 4.4 to Phryne on the subject of her court appearance, and worries that Phryne will abandon Hypereides for her old, abusive lover. Finally, in *Letter* 4.5, Bacchis scolds Myrrhina, who has taken up with Phryne's abusive lover now that Hypereides has left her for Phryne. The effect is dizzying but also intimate and gossipy, as the reader is invited into the inner circle of a group of courtesans.

After this tightly organized opening, the rest of book 4 is similarly interconnected: Thais writes both *Letters* 6 and 7; *Letters* 8 and 9 are a correspondence between lovers; *Letters* 13 and 14 are a pair of party descriptions; *Letters* 16 and 17 involve Lamia, Demetrius, and Epicurus' beloved Leontinum; and finally the most famous pair, *Letters* 18 and 19, are an exchange between Menander and Glycera, which brings us full circle back to *Letter* 2, in which Glycera sent Menander to visit a friend of hers (Bacchis) in Corinth. Bacchis reappears as the subject of a funeral elegy in *Letter* 11, and as the addressee of *Letter* 14, while Myrrhina laments yet another lost lover in *Letter* 10. The reader envisions a group of well-connected courtesans in Athens who knew one another and shared their lovers. It will be clear already just from the names of the writers that this book contains mostly female correspondents: sixteen of the nineteen letters are written by women: eight to a female addressee, and eight to a male addressee; only one (in the more usual format of the collection so far) is written by a man to another man, and two from a man to a woman.

The letters of book 4 reveal more allegiance to epistolary form than those in the other books: most contain at least the conventional epistolary farewell, ἔρρωσο, and many make self-conscious references to their writtenness. They are also composed under more probable circumstances than those of the preceding three books, considering that (fictional or historical) courtesans probably would have had the skill and often the occasion to write letters, in a way in which rustics and parasites would not.[30] Thus we read letters of invitation (4.1; 4.14), recommendation (4.2), thanks (4.3), warning (4.5), congratulations (4.19), and narrative description

---

[30] Note the nuanced and careful account of different classes of courtesans and their privileges in Davidson (1997) 73–136.

(4.13; 4.14: parties), all categories familiar from ancient epistolary theory, as well as more topical letters of jealousy (4.6; 4.10; 4.12), or protestations of passion (4.16). This inventive book even introduces us to an epistolary funeral lament (4.11) and a *paraclausithyron* in letter form (4.8). Its organization appears chronological, based on the sequence of letters surrounding Phryne's court trial at the start, but later we encounter an anomaly: *Letter* 11 is an elegy to the dead Bacchis, yet she reappears as the addressee of *Letter* 14, a party invitation from Megara.[31] One explanation for this incongruity may be found in a zeal for verisimilitude: *Letter* 14 may have been sent by a friend who had not yet heard of Bacchis' death, and the author/editor chose to place it there in order to highlight the temporal lag inherent in epistolary exchange. The letter was written when Bacchis was presumed alive and well, but arrived only after her sudden collapse. If we read it in this light, there is added pathos: Megara in *Letter* 14 accuses Bacchis of not coming to her party because she couldn't bear to leave her lover, while in truth, Bacchis did not appear because she had recently died.

The opening letter of book 4 is a fascinating text that invites many interpretations, and it is short enough to quote in full. In 4.1, the courtesan Phryne writes to her lover, the sculptor Praxiteles, congratulating him on a series of statues he has dedicated in a sanctuary of Eros at Thespiae. In between his Aphrodite and his Eros, a marble statue of Phryne herself stands in the place of honor, praised and admired by the local population (4.1):

... don't be afraid; for you have made a very beautiful work of art, such as nobody, in fact, has ever seen before among all things fashioned by men's hands: you have set up a statue of your own mistress in the sacred precinct. Yes, I stand in the middle of the precinct near your Aphrodite and your Eros too. And don't begrudge me this honor. For it is Praxiteles that people praise when they have gazed at us; and it is because I am a product of your skill that the Thespians don't count me unfit to be placed between gods. One thing is still lacking to your gift: that you come to us, so that we may lie together in the precinct. Surely we will bring no defilement on the gods that we ourselves have created. Farewell.

---

[31] Megara appears also in both letters: in 4.11.8, Bacchis' mourning lover complains that while his beloved is dead, Megara, "that dirty whore," lives on to cheat and torture men; Megara is the author of *Letter* 4.14, in which she teases Bacchis for her constancy to a single lover.

The text is printed as a fragment by the editors, one of only three fragmentary letters in the collection.[32] It is the opening that is suspected to be incomplete because of its abruptness; the ending, in contrast, is confirmed by the standard "farewell." The letter fits the mode of Pseudo-Libanius' "mixed letter" as described in his epistolary handbook (*Ep. Styles* 45, 92), including encouragement, praise, *ecphrasis*, and invitation.[33] Although the opening is somewhat abrupt – "don't be afraid" (of what? why should he?) – the information that follows clarifies the situation. The correspondents' historical roles also affect our reading of this letter; there is a tension between the fictionality of the letters and the documented historicity of Phryne and Praxiteles, just as we felt with the pseudonymous writers. We are in the somewhat oxymoronic territory of "historical fiction." No one would argue that Praxiteles did not exist, for he was one of the foremost sculptors of the fourth century, and his work survives to this day; while most agree that Phryne, a well-documented courtesan of that period, also existed, their actual historical relationship remains uncertain: was it purely professional, or also personal?[34] For the purposes of this letter, however, Alciphron leaves no room for doubt: Praxiteles and Phryne are lovers as well as artist and model.

At first glance, this appears to be a familiar tale: that of the male creation of an "ideal" female form, best known to us through Ovid's version of the Pygmalion story, in which a male artist molds a perfect beauty that remains silent and inactive. In this case, Praxiteles has sculpted a beautiful statue of Phryne that rivals Aphrodite in beauty. Yet here the model Phryne does not depend on her creator Praxiteles for animation, since another artist, Alciphron, permits her to speak. She, Phryne, is just as famous in antiquity as her renowned sculptor-lover, Praxiteles, although the body of the text gives only *his* name, either as a way to abide by epistolary conventions of verisimilitude, or perhaps enacting Phryne's own words of reassurance: "for it is Praxiteles that people praise when they have gazed at us." The female voice here may be unnamed –

---

[32] The others are 3.41, consisting of only seven words at the beginning of the letter, and 4.13.

[33] For the text of Pseudo-Libanius, see Malherbe (1988).

[34] For a recent discussion of this topic, see C. M. Havelock, *The Aphrodite of Knidos and Her Successors* (Ann Arbor 1995) 42–49, who argues that not only were Phryne and Praxiteles not romantically involved, but that Phryne herself was most probably fictitious.

we know it is Phryne only from circumstantial evidence – but it is far from powerless. Phryne controls what we hear and "see" in this letter, not Praxiteles.[35]

I have explored elsewhere how the female voice in this passage challenges traditional structures of hierarchy and power relations: of male and female, sculptor and model, viewer and viewed, even flesh and stone.[36] In this letter, Alciphron turns the Phryne who was an object of the sculptor's gaze (as well as of his love) into an art lover, gazing at the marble reproduction with a critic's eye. She reassures the artist that he shouldn't be afraid to have placed a mortal image where the divine should be, since her mortal beauty rivals that of the goddess of love herself (and, according to ancient sources, we know that Praxiteles modeled other statues of Aphrodite on Phryne, further confusing mortal and divine).[37] The artist, invited at the end of the letter to come to the sanctuary and embrace his beloved, is asked to imagine a choice between a living, breathing Phryne, and a marble statue begging to be brought to life at his touch. Phryne actually switches from her own voice to the voice of the statue halfway through the letter: "I am a product of your skill." Thus Phryne blurs the boundaries between herself as the artist's living inspiration and the artistic representation. In this inversion, the statue not only talks/writes back, but has the last word, and Praxiteles is the one cast in the marble silence of Galatea, frozen in his tracks at the moment of his choice. Yet this "last word," viewed from a slightly different angle (as if we are still walking around the statue to find its most beautiful part) is, of course, a male fantasy: Alciphron's ventriloquization. Alciphron is

---

[35] Cf., however, Y. L. Too, "Statues, Mirrors, Gods: Controlling Images in Apuleius," in J. Elsner, ed., *Art and Text in Roman Culture* (Cambridge 1996a) 133–52, who argues that being made into stone means allowing someone else control of your representation; it is a threat, a calcification, a negative experience and not a simple honor. While Phryne appears to approve of Praxiteles' work, and praises her own image, we can recover a sense of threat in her anxiety about her inscriptions (see below on Thebes) and perhaps even her wish to discover what Praxiteles viewed as his best work.

[36] P. A. Rosenmeyer, "(In)versions of Pygmalion: The Statue Talks Back," in L. McClure and A. Lardinois, eds., *Women's Voices in Ancient Greek Literature and Society* (Princeton, forthcoming 2000).

[37] Athenaeus (13.590f–591a) reports that Phryne was the model for a number of artists' renditions of the goddess of love: she inspired Apelles to paint his Aphrodite "rising from the sea" (Ἀναδυομένη), and Praxiteles' famous Knidian Aphrodite. Many of the anecdotes about Phryne and Praxiteles have been collected and translated in J. J. Pollitt, *The Art of Ancient Greece: Sources and Documents* (Cambridge 1990) 84–89.

as much in the business of representation as Praxiteles was, and Phryne may be interpreted as deprived of a specifically female "subjectivity" when he feeds her her lines.

Throughout his collection, Alciphron experiments with female perspectives interspersed among the male: we read letters from a young girl in love, an outraged mother, a misused wife, a confidante. In book 4, however, he focuses almost exclusively on the female voice, this time represented by a group of famous courtesans. This last book also, not surprisingly, is focused primarily on amatory themes. Love letters seem to have been connected in antiquity with female authorship: Ovid must have had this in mind when he had his heroines set pen to paper at crucial points in their affairs. But not a single letter written by Alciphron in the voice of a woman in his collection is actually a love letter in the strictest sense of the words, that is, letter written to her beloved to express her desire or seduce an unwilling partner. It is the men who write passionate pleas, while the women write offering advice, demanding money, spurning a lover, complaining, or insulting. Of course courtesans are not meant to plead for favors, and Alciphron, attempting to reflect the morals of Menander's day, would not have presented respectable girls sending secret letters to young men of their acquaintance. But he does occasionally find ways around his imaginary censor, as in the case of Glaucippe, a young girl but not a courtesan, whom we saw above detailing her beloved's charms in a letter to her mother (1.11).

I stated above that it should not surprise us that the courtesans' letters include amatory themes. But amatory themes percolate throughout the whole corpus, one of several themes that serve to unite the separate parts of the epistolary collection. Let us turn now to those themes individually: discontentment with one's lot in life, the related desire to trade social places, and the trials and tribulations of love.

EPISTOLARY TONE: COMPLAINTS AND ESCAPISM

Most of the letters of the fishermen, and many of the letters of the farmers, complain about their lot in life. The city folk, too, complain about the risks of their professions, but the reader tends to sympathize more with the inevitable poverty of the countryside than with the tricks of a motley bunch of parasites; our limited sympathy may result from Alciphron's greater familiarity with the urban classes, and his resulting idealization of country dwellers. By the sea and in the countryside, the poor man's enemy is usually the weather, the harvest, a misanthropic neighbor, or an intruder from the city. Thus the fishermen complain of their hard life, of harsh masters (1.2), bad weather, a disappointing haul (a dead camel! 1.20), and the humiliation of poverty so great that it makes a man look elsewhere for a livelihood: to farming, for instance (1.3), if one is a fisherman, or to a life of piracy (1.8). Farmers list their own occupational hazards: the threat of famine or drought (2.3; 2.33), wild animal attacks (2.18), theft (2.23), good-for-nothing slaves (2.21; 2.36), even rape (2.35). In *Letter* 2.2, discussed above, we saw a farmer rudely awakened from his dreams of wealth and power by the very symbol of his lowly status, "a vile and wretched rooster." Poverty is a consistent complaint throughout the first two books. It sends desperate men to moneylenders (1.13), who are usually defined as urban types; the phrase οἱ κατὰ τὴν πόλιν τοκογλύφοι, "those who carve out interest in the city," is translated in the Loeb as "shekel-grubbers who swarm the city" (2.5.1) – a wonderfully concise way of alluding to a modern stereotype of the userer.

If the primary tone of the rustic letters is bitter or discontented, there is one category of farmers' letters that evades such a negative impression, namely a handful of conventional idylls. In 2.9, the usual type of invented "speaking names" is traded for names of actual men well known for musical skills: "Pratinas" describes to "Epigonos" a suggestively Theocritean pastoral moment:

At high noon I chose a certain pine tree, airy and exposed to gentle breezes, and found shelter under it from the heat. While I was pleasantly cooling off, I thought I would put my hand to some music, and taking my syrinx, I ran my tongue along it; my breath sighed as my lips moved on the pipe, and the sweet pastoral song (νόμιον μέλος) reached my ears.

His goats, of course, are charmed by the music and gather around their "Orpheus" (2.9.2). But just in case we ourselves are wholly seduced into the green cabinet, "Pratinas" ends his description with pointed reference to his letter's status as "news," and the informational content of his friendly message (2.9.2):

Now I am announcing this good news to you because I wish my dear friend also to know that my herd of goats appreciates music.

And we thought it was just for the sake of an exercise in literary allusion!

Another pastoral moment crops up in a letter sent to accompany a honeycomb: the letter writer lovingly details the harvesting of new combs which are then divided between the country gods and the writer's friends (2.20.2: "I offer some now to you who are my friends").[38] The conventional connections between honey and poetry add a further level of sophistication to this cheerful message from "Twig" to "Little Pine Tree." The sweet abundance of honey should match the pleasant, plentiful pages of Alciphron's prose.

These two letters reflect a world of bucolic bliss and friendship, where complaints would seem incongruous, and where the personalities of the inhabitants match the innocence and good humor of the place. But two other examples challenge the fiction of a pastoral *locus amoenus*. They show the farmers trying hard to sustain the idea of a rustic paradise, but admitting reluctantly the fallibility of their construct. In 2.15, a farmer invites a neighboring household to celebrate the birthday of his son with a wild party of drinking and dancing. Even their dog is welcome:

And if you like, bring your dog too, for she is a good watchdog, and her deep barking frightens away those who have their eyes on our flocks. A dog such as that would not be considered unworthy to be a fellow guest.

This picture of harmony is undercut by the epistolary reply that immediately follows (2.16): the invited guest gratefully sends his family, but cannot come himself, since he and his watchdog are busy guarding a thief caught red-handed stealing farm tools. Instead of the expected predatory wolves here ("those who have their eyes on our flocks"), we discover that man is the enemy. In this flawed paradise, man is set against man instead of nature.

In 2.29, the writer sends a gift of a pair of piglets along with his letter. He gives two reasons for his largesse, one which fits with the complaining tone of the bulk of the rustic letters, and another

---

[38] See also the letter-poems in the *Greek Anthology* sent to accompany gifts, discussed in chapter 5 (e.g. *Anth. Pal.* 6.227 Crinagoras: a pen-nib as a birthday gift; 6.229 ibid.: a toothpick).

which points to the yearning for a state of (overly) romanticized pastoral bliss (2.29, in full):

The sow that I thought the other day was almost due has given birth, and I have an abundance of piglets. Their grunting is most unpleasant, but they are good to eat. I am giving two of them to you to keep. For I cannot feed them all because I have so little barley, and at the same time it is proper to the farmer's sense of fairness that those who have more than they need should give to their friends; we are like that, those whom the blessed earth has nurtured: simple, fond of others who are her nurslings.

The pig farmer is forced to give away part of his litter because he doesn't have enough food to feed them; the land has failed them, and his *locus amoenus* has turned bitter. On the other hand, he retains the humanity of a simpler, pastoral time. He defends his actions, motivated partly by survival, as the actions of a fair and well-nurtured human being: farmers are generous by nature because they have been nurtured by an equally generous Nature. They are "simple" (ἁπλοικοί), but good letter writers as well. We note that a seed of suspicion is sown by this literary farmer's self-depiction: he claims that the pigs' "grunting is quite unpleasant but they are good to eat." Would a "real" farmer be likely to find grunting unpleasant to his ears? This plays to the conceit of the genre, as the sophisticated reader, who surely would agree with the statement, pretends to "understand" this generous and sensitive letter writer.

Alciphron offers his readers the intellectual delight of pretending to be back in the *locus classicus* of Menander's Athens, encouraging them to think of their own potential epistolary responses to the unanswered letters. One could imagine the letter collection as an alternative to the old custom of skoliastic improvisation at an archaic or classical symposium: each reader would take up the challenge of an epistolary response in the voice of the internal addressee, in proper "archaizing" Attic Greek. In the last example, the reader would "become" the recipient of the two piglets, and compose a suitable thank-you letter. While readers might not be able to compose their imaginary return letters without grammatical errors and contextual anachronisms, they could sympathize with the timeless woes of Alciphron's characters, regardless of social class. I would argue that by including the flaws in his vision of the past, Alciphron is not emphasizing the nostalgic quality of his literary vision, but infusing it with contemporary sensibility, saying effectively "see, even in classical Athens, there were hardships." His call for cultural cohesion includes within it an acknowledgment of these hardships, the subject of his rustics' complaints.

The parasites of book 3 share with their country associates a tone of constant complaint, but their complaints are specific to their trade. The litany is familiar from fragments of New Comedy, or lines of Lucian. They never get enough to eat (3.3; 3.42); slaves as they are to their gluttonous bellies, they end up scavenging to survive (3.13.1):

For if there is a scarcity of invitations, I am forced to eat chervil and poor-man's oysters or to gather grass and fill my belly with plain water from the fountain of Callirhoe.

If they do manage to snatch a few crumbs, they inevitably end up with the worst bits of the dinner while other guests feast on dainties (3.37.1):

We have suffered terrible things. The others were served pork udders and innards and liver as delicate as dewdrops, but we had pea soup. They drank Chalybonian wine, while ours was sour and flat.

They constantly are abused by hosts and fellow guests (3.42), including being drenched with boiling water (3.2; 3.32) or sticky broth (3.25), or having a wine cup smashed in their faces (3.9; 3.12). Bad luck at gambling threatens ruin (3.6), but good luck at the same game leads to a broken skull and torn clothing after an assault by envious gaming companions (3.18). Stingy hosts (3.21; 3.38) and interfering pedagogues (3.1; 3.7) spell ruin of another kind. In despair, parasites turn to thoughts of suicide (3.1; 3.3; 3.13) or exile. But several adventures outside Athens (3.15; 3.24) are enough to teach them that luxuries in foreign lands are not comparable to those at home. One parasite, having been abused among the rich hosts of Corinth, concludes that it is better to be dead and buried in Athens than live high on the hog abroad (3.15.4):

Far better to lie stretched out as a corpse, buried in a tomb, in front of the Diomed gate or the gate of the Knights [i.e. at Athens] than to endure the so-called "good life" in the Peloponnese.

In all the letters describing dinner parties and feasts, only one parasite actually praises his host (3.29): the difference is that this

host is "imported," a newly arrived merchant from Istria, far sur-
passing the local Athenian men in his munificence. The man
sounds too good to be true (3.29.2):

He didn't invite just one parasite from the city, but all of us, and not
only us, but also the more expensive courtesans and the prettiest singing
girls and to put it broadly, all the people from the stage. And it's not
inherited money that he tosses around, but his own justly earned income.
He loves the harp and flute, his conversation is full of grace and charm,
and he is never insulting (ὑβρίζει οὐδέν).

This perfect party with its perfect host, as paradisiacal as the
farmers' pastoral bower, stands in the way, however, of a good
story. This is one of the few letters that describes a parasite's party
with no attention to food, only to intellectual and cultural entertainments (conversation, music). But it is precisely the insults and
the abuse, the physical *realia* of food and beatings that make for
entertaining reading on the subject of parasites; it is more effective
to vary the details of bad food and nasty tricks than those of epicurean bliss and good manners. The reader flips the page to
stories of stolen tablewares and narrow escapes (3.10; 3.11), disgust-
ing medical treatments for alcohol poisoning and overeating (3.4),
and humiliating barbershop encounters (3.30).

If the complaints of the parasites focus on the lack of good food
and the abundance of physical abuse, the complaints of the courtesans, true to convention, focus on their treatment at the hands of
lovers. An abandoned courtesan requests a love potion to seduce
her unfaithful beloved (4.10), while another jealous courtesan
whose former lover has married gets revenge by attacking his
bride's appearance in print (4.12).[39] Thais complains that her man
ignores her for the study of philosophy (4.7), while at the other
extreme, Leontium grumbles that her philosopher-lover Epicurus
is too possessive (4.17). Philosophers and sophists are common
whipping boys in this collection: the parasites' letters contain dis-
paraging remarks about hypocritical "wise men" (3.17; 3.19; 3.28),
and the courtesans are no more complimentary in their tone.
Thais puts it quite bluntly (4.7.4):

Do you think there is any difference between a courtesan and a sophist?
Perhaps so far in that they don't persuade through the same means, but
one end – profit – is the object of both.

---

[39] See similar tactics on the part of a jealous mistress in Lucian *Dialogues of the Courtesans* 2.1.

She acknowledges that sophists may be more intellectual, but courtesans are certainly more pious, and are in general better influences on men. She clinches her argument by asking her reader to judge between Aspasia the courtesan and Socrates the sophist in their value as teachers of virtue (4.7.7): one produced Pericles as pupil, the other Critias.[40] Leontium's complaints (4.17) about her philosopher-lover Epicurus are more mundane: some may say he is famous and powerful, but what she sees is a louse-ridden old man dressed in fleeces, bothering her with books and doctrines she doesn't understand, and insisting that she give up her younger boyfriend, which she is understandably reluctant to do.

Most of the courtesans' letters give only one side of the story; we will never know what reasonable complaints Epicurus might have offered about Leontium's behavior. However, one pair of letters does show both sides of an erotic complaint (4.8; 4.9). The lover Simalion writes begging to be let in and loved, chastising his beloved Petale for her hard heart (4.8). He depicts himself as an *exclusus amator*, coming again and again to her doorstep, watching her maids take messages to other lovers more fortunate than he, yet ignoring his laments. The conventional elegiac *paraclausithyron* evolves here into an epistolary exercise: the lovers communicate by letter, not by song. Alciphron also complicates the mode by presenting an answer: not the hoped-for epiphany of the beloved, but a return letter. So we realize that the maids must eventually have taken Simalion's letter inside to their mistress, and Petale did finally grant it a reading. Simalion now becomes one of the string of "more fortunate" lovers who receive a message back, but his message is not a happy one. Petale writes as follows (4.9.1–5):

I wish that the house of a courtesan were nourished by tears, for then I would be doing splendidly, since you provide me with a plentiful supply of those. But as it stands now, I need money, clothes, jewelry, maids. The whole arrangement of my life depends on this. I don't have an ancestral estate at Myrrhinus, or a share in the silver mines, but only my meager fees and some wretched offerings, much sighed over by my idiotic lovers; ... miserable me, I have a dirge singer, not a lover. He sends me wreaths and roses as if to the tomb of someone who died young, and he says he cries all night long. If you bring me a present, come without weeping; but if not, it won't be me, but yourself that you torture.

[40] See Xenophon's depiction of the encounter between Socrates and Theodote (*Mem.* 3.11), in S. Goldhill, "The Seduction of the Gaze: Socrates and his Girlfriends," in P. Cartledge, P. Millett, and S. von Reden, eds., *Kosmos* (Cambridge 1998) 105–24.

Alciphron's courtesans run the gamut of honest heart-of-gold types (Lamia to Demetrius, 4.16.5–7 "I will not play the courtesan and lie, as others do ... I couldn't bear, by the dear Muses, to deceive you; I am not so stony-hearted"), to the more pragmatic Petale quoted above. She accuses her lover of living a literary dream; she has no interest in being an elegiac mistress, the object of his weepy affection. He may think he lives in an elegiac poem, but she has a real life to lead. Let him forget roses, she answers, wreaths, poems and letters, and just plunder his parents' assets if he wants access to her charms (4.9.4: "don't you have any goblets in your house? ... raise some cash from your mother's gold jewelry or your father's bonds"). Later in the collection, Philoumena writes similarly to her Crito (4.15 in full):

Why do you torture yourself by writing so many letters? You don't need letters – what you need is fifty gold coins. So then, if you really love me, hand them over. But if you love your money more, don't bother me. Farewell.

In this book of courtesans' letters on the subject of love, the writers criticize their lovers' attempts at epistolary invention. A pile of love letters, they claim, is useless; what really counts in this world is money. The irony, of course, is that Alciphron's work is based precisely on the value of "writing so many letters" (πολλὰ γράφων).

In Simalion's mind, his girlfriend lives in an idealized world of erotic elegy, but Petale's response brings him back quickly to the reality of their erotic economy. This tension between an idealized world and an intrusive "reality" is perhaps best observed in the constant interplay between the different roles within the collection. Alciphron delights in portraying escapist fantasies and temporary role switches, and in the process constantly cross-references the types in his own collection. This is very much the game of *ethopoieia*, as the writer/speaker keeps trying on new hats, showing off his technical skill, flexibility in voice, and (in the case of oral presentation) improvisational talents. In the following paragraphs I consider the general attempts of fishermen and farmers to try out a new role (politician, pirate, urban playboy), and the problems that ensue when a "rustic" falls in love, usually, of course, with an inappropriate object of desire in the Big City. Then I turn to the parallel situations of parasites refashioning themselves as country folk in their eagerness to live an easier life away from urban ills. The courtesans of the fourth book do not participate in this game, somewhat surprisingly given the common plot in New Comedy of the inexperienced courtesan or slave girl revealed as a citizen. It may be that Alciphron's courtesans are too famous and experienced to allow for such shape-shifting.

EPISTOLARY ROLES: CROSSING THE PAGE

Let us begin with two letters depicting fishermen and farmers wishing to trade jobs. In *Letter* 1.3, a dispirited Glaucus writes to his wife Galateia that they should give up fishing and become farmers so that their children can have a chance to grow up in a safer environment, without fear of the dangers of the sea; one can only assume that they will also need to change their names. Ironically, Glaucus offers us a double justification for his change of heart: he knows the hardships of his life from personal experience, but also, and apparently with greater effect, from the overheard words of an unidentified Stoic philosopher, who lectured one day on the folly of men who make their living from the sea, quoting liberally from Aratus, while Glaucus happened to be selling his fish nearby.[41] This was the final push that Glaucus needed to reconsider his vocation. In a parallel letter in the second book (2.4), a farmer, one Eupetalos ("Greenleaf"), complains to Elation ("Pine-oar," presumably a fisherman) that the land no longer offers him a fair return for his hard work, and so he has decided to give himself over to the sea and the waves. He argues, almost in response to the farmer's letter above, that neither occupation is necessarily more secure: "before now some have been doomed to an early death (ὠκύμοροι) on land, and others have lived to a ripe old age on the sea." His Homeric tone and reasoned moralizing are undercut by the crude, almost Aristophanic opportunism of his final words: "It is better to return newly rich from the Bosporus or Propontis than to sit quietly on the fringes of Attica belching out famine and drought."

Images of wealth or power, attributed primarily to parasites and soldiers, consume the impoverished imaginations of humble

---

[41] In books 3 and 4 we see more frequent references to philosophers, who are more often reviled and ridiculed in the manner of Aristophanes' *Clouds* than respected as here; it may be a sign of Glaucus' naiveté that he so eagerly believes his Stoic enlightener.

countryfolk. In 1.9, a fisherman writes to a parasite for assistance; he asks his friend to arrange a permanent commission for him from the parasite's wealthy patrons, so that he can personally deliver his fish to the patron rather than selling in the open market for a smaller profit. The fisherman claims that "you parasites have a lot of influence with the young and the rich." In 2.2, discussed above, when a farmer dreams of great wealth and political power, he imagines himself surrounded by flatterers and parasites. The role of the parasite, to the inexperienced farmer, embodies all that is exotic, luxurious, and urban: to have one's own parasite is a mark of real success. Alciphron will upset this naive view when he gives his parasites their own voices later in the collection. But already in book 2, we are given a glimpse of what is to come. In 2.32, the parasite Gnathon invades the ranks of the farmers and writes a letter to one Kallikomides ("Pretty Village") about his former benefactor Timon, once a rich man surrounded by parasites and courtesans, who, having spent all his money, became a recluse and a misanthrope, living in poverty on a farm. Gnathon complains that he can't find another equally generous patron, and has decided to change his way of life and work for a living, so he asks Kallikomides to take him on as a hired farm hand, ready to do any work to fill his belly. The letter ends with his request for a job on the farm.[42]

In Alciphron's rogues' gallery, no one is content with his or her lot, but most would agree that the life of the soldier is a silly one. This attitude is clearly inherited from Menandrian and Plautine ridicule of the military life, or at least of certain thick-headed individuals in uniform. Thus the farmer in 2.34 describes a braggart soldier who was billeted in his house and simply would not stop talking about his exploits; he talked about killing Thracians by javelin, Armenians by pikes, and babbled on about catapults, phalanxes, and so forth.[43] He even dragged in prisoners and female captives, prizes of his prowess. The farmer tries to get him drunk to stop the verbiage, but wine only encourages the man. His worst offence seems to be that he is excruciatingly boring. Another farmer's son is in love with soldiery, going so far as to change his

---

[42] Later, in 3.34, we read of another parasite moving to the country, fully adopting the ways of a farmer, with the expected comic results.

[43] There are close parallels to this letter in Lucian *Dialogues of the Courtesans* 13, noted above.

name to Thrasonides (2.13). His mother Phyllis writes to him, begging him to come back to the farm, where he is needed by his parents, instead of glorying in his shield and triple-crested helmet, like a hired soldier from the wilder parts of Greece. She lures him with the bounty of the land: ivy, myrtles, wheat, wine, milk, and no ambushes or phalanxes. She even calls upon his filial duty to take care of them in their old age, and praises the security of farm life over the present precarious existence he has chosen. One can easily imagine the young man's return letter, if he bothered to write at all. As a final example of the small esteem of a life of violence, a fisherman writes to his wife (1.8) that he sees no way out of his financial misery other than joining a band of pirates; his mouth waters at the potential booty, but he can't endure the thought of staining his hands with blood. He asks his wife to make the decision for him, but we are not given her response. This fisherman would make an extremely reluctant pirate, in the best tradition of Gilbert and Sullivan.

Although some of Alciphron's rustics may be tempted by other lifestyles, a larger number is seduced not by a particular profession, but by the distractions of the Big City. We have already read *Letter* 2.28, in which a naive young man begs to be "initiated" into the rites of Athens by a more experienced friend. Both farming and fishing families are threatened with disaster when a member of the household wanders off and doesn't come back. Two country boys see the error of their ways in time. One curses a flute girl who has kept him overnight in the city by tricking him with strong drink and music; he tells her to use her wiles (θέλγε) on the local city boys, but he is going back to his country friends (2.14). Another is enchanted by theater shows, especially the magician playing the cup and shell game, but he is enough in control of his wits to say ruefully: "may no creature like that ever come to my farm. For no one would be able to catch him, and he would steal everything in the house and run away with all my farm belongings" (2.17). In another letter (2.37), a farm girl is more easily persuaded: Philometor ("Loves her mother") writes home to her mother in the country, telling her of the marvels of the city, and begging her to come and visit Athens before she dies. The entertainments she suggests are ceremonious occasions where a respectable woman might be seen in public: the daughter lists all the women's religious festivals by name, so we can assume that she has been in

Athens long enough to observe the whole annual cycle of holy days.[44] She ends her letter with the words "It would be boorish and uncivilized for you to leave this life without having tasted [the joys of] the city," and apologizes for her plain speaking. Since her mother's name is given as Epiphanium ("Epiphany"), we are probably meant to imagine that she answered her daughter's request not by letter, but by a personal appearance, joining her daughter to celebrate the sacrifices of the Kalligeneia.

Four similar letters conclude this section on the wicked ways of the city. In *Letter* 1.4, a fisherman complains to his wife that she has deserted her task of net repair on the shore and fled instead to the company of rich Athenian ladies, celebrating the Oschophoria and the Lenaia. He reminds her that her good father raised her to be initiated into the rites of marriage, not into other "insidious shows" (ἀπατηλῶν θεαμάτων) that they have in the city. He adds some moralizing: "for those who live by the sea, the land spells death just as surely for us as for the fish who are unable to breathe air." In the end, carefully choosing his words for full rhetorical effect, he offers divorce – "if it is the city you love (ἀσπάζη), farewell and go your way" (χαῖρε καὶ ἄπιθι) – but gives her the option of returning to him and being forgiven – "if you love (ἀγαπᾷς) your husband and things from the sea, make the better choice and come back (ἐπάνιθι)." The abandoned farmer of 2.8 is even more explicit in his letter to his errant wife, who has deserted him and the children for city ways and city gods. He mocks her new gods; instead of Pan and the Nymphs, she wants to build shrines to Kolian Aphrodite and fancy goddesses named Genetyllides. He claims she is mad, wanting to compete with fashionable ladies who are "dissolved in luxury"; his diatribe continues against the symbolically sophisticated use of cosmetics: their characters burst with vice underneath faces made up with rouge and white lead powder. His wife is told "if you have any sense, stay as you were before, when soap and water made you clean" (2.8.3). We are given no hints in either one of these letters about the ultimate decision of the wife in question, but the level tone of the fisherman's letter is certainly more encouraging than the paranoid posturings of the lonely farmer.

---

[44] She mentions the Haloa, Apatouria, Dionysia, and Thesmophoria, including specific references to each day (Anodos, Nesteia, Kalligeneia).

What is good for the goose is also always a possibility for the gander, and both fisherman and farmer are seduced by the city in their own ways. But while the country women are represented as fascinated by the colorful religious festivals and local city gods of Athens, their country menfolk are shown attracted to the city's red light districts. Again, the influence of comedy is not far off as older men are seduced by foreign courtesans. In *Letter* 1.6, a wife writes to her husband complaining of his behavior in deserting her and their grown children (with appropriately watery names Galene and Thalassion) to pay court to a girl from Hermione who now lives in the Piraeus. He is old enough to know better, yet he doesn't see how his beloved flirts with all the boys and consumes their gifts like a veritable Charybdis. It rankles her especially that her husband isn't content just to bring gifts of his trade (sprats and mullets), but rather delivers snoods from Miletus, gowns from Sicily, and gold jewelry to this common courtesan, objects of luxury that she herself can never enjoy. The wife counters that she was not born a nobody, and that she has fulfilled her marital duties to him, while he has abandoned himself to wanton pleasure; she demands that he come home to her, or she will ask her father to prosecute him for spousal abuse. In 2.21, a wife complains to her husband who has deserted her and her children at the farm to spend all his time at the Kerameikos, where she has heard that the worst scoundrels spend their lives in idleness and luxury. This husband of hers with his grizzled hair has turned into a "young man about town." The letter ends with the wayward farmer hanging about the alleyways in the city as his land lies idle at home.

The parasites in book 3 are no less shy about trying out new roles. Parasites become farmers or robbers (3.34), lovers (3.31), dock workers (3.4), and even actors (3.35). In its pivotal position following the dyad of rustic letters in books 1 and 2, but leading into the final book of courtesans' letters, the examples of role-shifting in book 3 point both backwards and forwards: backwards to the fishermen in the case of the dockworker, and forwards to the courtesans in the case of the parasite-turned-lover. Just as we met a farmer in book 2 who decided to try his hand at the life of a parasite, so here we meet his counterpart, a parasite who trades roles for a while with the "country mouse." In 3.34, Limopyktes ("Famine-fighter") writes that he got to know a certain farmer, romantically named Corydon, and decided to take advantage of their friendship to try out a new lifestyle. Ironically, Limopyktes is initially drawn to the farmer because of the man's insults (3.34.1): Corydon used to mock him frequently, and was more talkative and witty than most country folk, almost as if he were a "host" in disguise. As Limopyktes sets out his plan, the reader can already tell that this parasite is deceiving himself (3.34.1–2):

When I saw him, I thought it would be a godsend if I could get away from the business of town life and move into the country and live with a friend, a peaceful and hardworking farmer, who wasn't plotting an unjust income from lawsuits or blackmail in the marketplace, but one waiting to reap the fruits of the earth ... I dressed myself as a farmer, with a sheepskin around my shoulder and a hoe in hand, and seemed like a regular dirt digger.

For a while he delights in his transformation on Corydon's farm: he has escaped the insults and beatings, and the inequality of portions served at the houses of the rich. But soon reality sets in (3.34.3):

But when it became routine work day after day under orders, and I absolutely had to plough, or clear stony ground, or dig ditches, or set out plants in the ditches, then this occupation was no longer bearable, and I regretted my ridiculous behavior and yearned for the city.

Unfortunately, when the former parasite tries to take up his old trade, his hosts view him as a rustic, a rough and rude hillbilly who does not belong in the homes of rich urban patrons. What he viewed as temporary role-playing has become a permanent engagement, and he finds himself back at the beginning, no longer unwilling but now unable to make a living as a parasite. His final resort is a career as a robber with a band of Megarians on the coast, but he closes his letter with some reservations (3.34.5), wondering how long he can continue playing his latest, much riskier role.

Limopyktes' letter in book 3 asks us to reconsider some of the more idealized farmers' letters in book 2; it is a healthy corrective to the more "pastoral" versions of life in the country. But its main function is as a connector, an invitation to link the books of letters on rustic and urban subjects, to remind us that these letters are part of a larger whole. The same is true for the letters in book 3 that look forward to those in book 4, namely those that deal with issues of love, a topic we associate more readily with courtesans than parasites. Let us consider those letters, among others, in the next section.

LOVE LETTERS

The foolish old men of *Letters* 1.6 and 2.21 discussed above under the category of role-shifting find their counterparts in ten other "love letters" collected within books 1 and 2. Many of these love stories also include the same elements of tension between country and city ways, poor and rich families, or young and old, discussed above. So in 2.31, a wife of thirty years standing complains that her old husband, a grandfather already, has abandoned her for a harp girl, inappropriately named Parthenium ("Virgin"); he cares neither that he has bankrupted the farm on her behalf, nor that the young men laugh at his folly. In 1.16, we even meet a familiar face, as this fisherman is in love with what seems to be the same girl from Hermione whom we met in the Piraeus in letter 1.6. He describes his sad state in (again) appropriately marine terms, as if love were a storm at sea and his soul a wave-tossed ship (1.16.1–2):

Love, having fallen upon me, does not allow me to be steered by reason, but that part of me that is sober is constantly being swamped by passion.

Having once laughed at men in love, he acknowledges the irony of his own sad state, and marvels that he burns with a passion as hot as that of a rich young playboy. But this is the extent of his self-awareness; he still thinks he can marry the girl, proving himself a worthy fisherman to her father. His rusticity reveals itself in that he cannot even imagine a category other than marriage for his idealized beloved. The external reader knows from *Letter* 1.6, however, that she may not be as interested in monogamy as her suitor assumes. Here we see how the letter collection as a whole informs an individual letter, and how the two levels of audience, internal and external, read different meanings into the same situation.

The remaining eight examples of rustics in love are four paired letters, two pairs in each book (1.11, 12; 1.21, 22; 2.6, 7; 2.24, 25). The subject of love, it appears, inspired Alciphron to experiment with both sides of the epistolary exchange: in each case he presents an initial letter and its immediate response. While this epistolary technique takes something away from our imagination, as we are now told explicitly what the response was, it simultaneously makes for a more interesting and dramatic presentation, and anticipates the paired and polyphonic letters of the courtesans in his final book.

We have already looked at the first pair (1.11, 12), in which a young girl in love writes to her mother in despair over her father's choice of fiancé: who could think of a sea captain's son when such a handsome city guardsman stands available? Her mother scolds her harshly and reminds her of her duty to her father. In the second pair (1.21, 22), we meet a fisherman in love not unlike the passionate lover in 1.16; but this time we are introduced to him initially through a letter from his friend, who is concerned that this young suitor will lose his wits and his possessions while pursuing an unsuitable harp-girl. The friend, Euplous ("Good Sailing"), says he has heard from a neighbor all sorts of rumors about Thalasseros' ("Sea-lover's") behavior, and the neighbor's gossip is reported in the letter: Thalasseros sneaks off to deposit his daily catch at the girl's door, wastes all his money on her, and is suddenly well conversant with the complex musical terms used by his beloved – although these terms are probably puns suggesting varied positions and types of sexual intercourse.[45] Euplous tries to speak to Thalasseros in his own language: "Stop wasting your money on these things, in case the land instead of the sea shipwrecks you of all your possessions, and in case the harp-girl's bedroom proves to be your Calydonian Gulf or your Tyrrhenian Sea, and she herself, as she sings, another Skylla" (1.21.3).

Thalasseros responds not as a naive fisherman, but as one already initiated into the mysteries of Eros, and in the voice of a sophist. His letter, which ends the book of fishermen's letters, follows in full (1.22):

You warn me in vain, Euplous. For I would never think of abandoning this girl, since I am obeying the god who initiates us into the mysteries with his torch and bow. And anyway, it is natural for us fishermen to love, since the goddess of the sea gave birth to this boy [Eros]. On his maternal side, then, Eros is one of us, and struck by him to the heart, I keep my girl by the seashore, thinking that I am together with Panope or Galateia, the most beautiful of the Nereids.

---

[45] See Benner and Fobes (1949) 80–81. The neighbor reporting the gossip is a stock character from New Comedy, the fisherman-turned-cook Sosias, "who concocts a fine delicious anchovy sauce from the little fish that he catches in his nets."

Euplous speaks of Skylla and dangerous waters; Thalasseros in his lovestruck state changes her into Panope or Galateia.[46] Euplous mocks the young man's devotion to "music"; Thalasseros shows that love is the most natural thing for a fisherman, since Eros is the offspring of Aphrodite, born of the sea. Thalasseros' romanticizing answers to all Euplous' objections reflect the "madness" of love; he no longer perceives reality in the same way, nor speaks the same language as his sensible friend.[47] But even as Thalasseros claims he will keep his beloved with him by the seashore (ἔχω πρὸς θαλάττῃ τὴν κόρην), the image of that promiscuous girl in Piraeus undermines the certainty of his assertion. What he has now and what he will have tomorrow depend not on his constancy, but on the whims of a harp-girl.

The two pairs of love letters in the voices of fisherwomen and men share a sense of possibility, even if it is rudely quashed by one of the correspondents. The girl creates her own fantasy world of love which may survive in daydreams, and the young man sees only beauty and good in his mistress; on one level they can ignore the worldly reminders of sober citizens – at least for a while. But the rustics in love in book 2 belong to a much grittier and less fanciful world; these characters are more familiar from the smelly goats and coarse humor of sections of Theocritus. Theocritus' love-struck Polyphemos (*Id.* 11) comes to mind in *Letter* 2.6, as an old man indignantly lists the luxuries he has given the unfeeling object of his desire (2.6.1–2):

What of my belongings have you not taken and kept? Didn't you take figs? cheese from the baskets? a newborn kid? a pair of hens? Didn't all your other luxuries come from me? ... and you never give me a thought while I burn straight through with love. So farewell and go away. It will be hard for me, but I will bear my humiliation.

The answering letter shows us a different side of the story, although the girl pointedly ignores the list of gifts, which may or may not have been given. He had implied that he owned the farm; she tells us that he has lost his job as a farm hand by making a nuisance of himself with all the young girls. He leads us to believe that she has been ignoring him for some time; her version presents

---

[46] The name Galateia recalls Theocritus' misguided fisherman Polyphemus (*Id.* 11).
[47] This common erotic trope of misperception of reality is marvelously displayed in Lucretius *De Rerum Nat.* 4 in the passage on the dangers of passion and love.

a recent incident when the "old lecher" came up behind her and tried to kiss her, delaying her in her duties. She makes fun of his "melting looks and sighs," tells him to act his age, and threatens to "do something bad" to him unless he leaves her alone. The first letter invites us to sympathize with the disappointed lover; the second letter reveals a comic, bawdy context of an old man infatuated with a young girl who can give as good as she gets.

The final pair in book 2 follows a similar pattern (2.24–25). A farmer has brought a girl back from town to his farm, and now keeps her as if she were his fiancée. But she turns out to be ill-tempered, putting on airs and mocking him for his country ways, so he threatens to put her to work, to show her that her lover is her master too, to force her to perform manual labor with the rest of his crew. She fills out her side of the story in a return letter, opening with the bald statement: "I can stand anything except sleeping with you, master." She tells of running away from him and deciding to commit suicide rather than submitting, all because of his shaggy body, his smelly mouth, and his general wretchedness. Her objections bring us to the same conclusions as her master's, namely that he is too "country" for her. She closes her letter by sending him off to a proper partner, a "bleary-eyed country crone with only one tooth left in her mouth, who has perfumed her skin with pine oil"; we realize from this final volley that there is again an age difference adding further fuel to her disgust at his advances.

In presenting each paired set in sequence, I have tried to show how the inclusion of an epistolary response can force the reader to reread and reconsider the perspective or even the veracity of the first letter (not that the second, purely by its position, is automatically more privileged in its truth value). A response adds detail, answers questions, raises new unanswerable questions, and often redirects our thoughts on the initial epistolary situation. Since love affairs are particularly prone to miscommunication and false starts, Alciphron chooses to include both lovers' voices, or the voices of lover and confidant, offering a richer and more complex sketch of two characters.[48] It is more interesting to overhear an erotic exchange, to observe interaction, than to listen to a monologic

---

[48] But note that the only sequence of three connected letters (first letter, reply, counter-reply) charts an escalating argument between two fishermen over ownership of an old net (1.17, 18, 19): not exactly a promising narrative situation. On the other hand, this context of limited interest highlights the skill of the epistolographer in making it worth reading about.

fantasy. Letters can create dialogues in themselves, as the writer imagines and rehearses what the addressee might say; but the reality of a return letter adds a separate second voice to the dialogue, and that in turn provides vividness and "authority" to the words.

Erotic dialogue also plays a part in the letters of books 3 and 4: the parasites predictably act as go-betweens for their patrons, although we will meet one unusual parasite, himself the victim of Eros (3.31), and the courtesans, true to type, spend most of their letters discoursing on love.

Alciphron presents his parasites as hangers-on who know all the messy secrets of the household while the hosts live in blissful ignorance of their beloved's bad behavior. There are seven such letters with variations on the theme. In *Letter* 3.5, a parasite plots with his friend to kidnap a courtesan who has been coyly resisting their host's advances; they hope to be rewarded with money, clothes, and best of all open access to the rich man's house (3.5.3): "perhaps soon he will look upon us as friends rather than as parasites." Two other letters show a similar interest on the part of the parasite to act as a friend rather than as a flatterer: in 3.26 and 3.27, the parasite is insulted by the female slaves who want to keep their mistresses' behavior quiet, while he threatens to tell the master all. In 3.27, the master is particularly dense: he has yet to realize that his wife has given birth just five months after their wedding. Without his knowledge, the baby is quickly disposed of by exposure. The women abuse the parasite verbally, in spite of his awareness of their complicity in the deception. The nature of their insults is quite revealing of the parasite's sense (or mistaken sense) of his own importance to the host and the household (3.27.2):

Silence is the breeder of anger, and if they [the women] annoy me even a little bit, slandering me with the names "flatterer" or "parasite," and adding the other accustomed insults, then Phaedrias [the host] will know what has transpired.

The parasite in this letter is grossly insulted at being called ... a parasite. A great part of the insult lies in the fact that an equal would be addressed by name, not by social category, so that in calling him a parasite, the women deny him the special relationship with his master that he imagines he has.[49]

---

[49] On parasites in general, see E. I. Tylawsky, "Saturio's Inheritance: the Greek Ancestry of the Roman Comic Parasite" (Diss. Yale 1991), and C. Damon, *The Mask of the Parasite: a Pathology of Roman Patronage* (Ann Arbor 1997).

The knowledge that parasites obtain about the inner workings of a household brings them a sense of power. In one case, instead of wishing merely to be considered a friend, a parasite attempts to usurp the authority of the host himself. In 3.28, a young man has fallen in love with a courtesan who happens to be good friends with the household's parasite. The two social climbers work together to squeeze money and favors from the young man. The parasite plots for the future, when the young man will inevitably abandon his beloved to marry in his own class; then the parasite, made rich from the lover's gifts and bribes, will "ransom" the courtesan and marry her himself.

Other letters show the problems parasites encounter when they become involved in the love affairs of the household. In 3.33, a parasite informs on his host's wife, but the host believes her rather than him, and he begins to regret his hasty tongue. Even worse, in 3.36, the wife believes that her husband's parasite is actually a go-between for her husband and an Ionian juggling girl, so she kidnaps him and tries to have him murdered; he escapes, obviously, since we have his letter describing the ordeal. One final example offers deeper insight into the reasons a parasite might have to defend his host so firmly against erotic misadventure. In 3.14, a parasite speaks indignantly on behalf of his young host who is being mistreated by, in his words, "a low-down dirty whore" (ἱππόπορνος); the lover gives her everything she asks for, yet she still plays hard to get, scheming to take over his whole estate. The parasite is quite direct about his motives: while it pains him in general to see the young man lose his patrimony, since he remembers how hard the youth's parents worked to amass each obol, and while he feels sympathy even for the young man himself, what really bothers him is his own endangered status (3.14.4):

For if all the property of our good fellow is turned over to this woman, then fine feasting we will have in the future, fine indeed, by the gods!

If the lover gives all his money to the girl, there will be nothing left for the fancy dinners which he used to give so generously and kindly. When it comes right down to it, the courtesan and the parasite compete for the same economic resources, and both strive to elevate themselves from dependents to equals, to guarantee a more secure future for themselves. In this way, the household parasite is the male equivalent of a courtesan.

In only one case does a parasite put love in front of his other
appetites, and that is in the highly unusual *Letter* 3.31.[50] But even
here, the parasite is defined first and foremost by his status as
parasite; he cannot imagine a better way to describe his current
infatuation than to compare his taste for Nebris with his former
food cravings, much as the erotic vocabulary of the fisherman's
daughter (1.11) was limited to what she knew best, namely marine
imagery (3.31 in full):

> I saw Nebris carrying a basket in the procession, a girl with beautiful
> elbows and fingers, flashing glances from her eyes, tall and blooming,
> whose cheeks shine like marble. I was so inflamed with love that I ran up
> and wanted to kiss her mouth, forgetting who I was; but then I recovered
> my senses and kept close, wanting to kiss her footprints instead. Woe is
> me in my presumption, for now I don't crave lupines or beans or por-
> ridge, but I have been fed so well that I set my heart on things beyond
> my reach! Come here all of you and stone me to death before I am de-
> stroyed by my desires, and let the pile of stones be for me a lover's tomb.

The girl is described as a choice dish: untouched (virginal), well
presented, glossy, with good color and generous size.[51] She looks
so delicious that the parasite forgets his place and rushes up to
"taste" her, but quickly pulls himself back and adores her footsteps instead. He realizes that he has entered into a state of un-
requited passion that he cannot easily escape, and in good parasite
fashion, he would rather die than live in constant "hunger": the
parasite has become a lover, his appetites have grown beyond his
means. Instead of attempting suicide to end it all, he calls on his
compatriots to kill him, preferring a quick death to a long, linger-
ing decline, destroyed by his unfulfilled desires. His final resting
place will identify him in his new, unwillingly adopted role as a
lover scorned.

Here we have returned to the subject of role changes. Alciphron
is fascinated by the idea of an incongruous lover, whether that
person is a farmer, parasite, fisherman, or even a fisherwoman; in

[50] This passage resembles one in Longus' *Daphnis and Chloe*, where Gnathon the parasite
falls in love with Daphnis (4.17.3–7): "I who up till now once was in love with nothing but
your table ... now consider only one thing of beauty, and that is Daphnis." Gnathon
swears off all delicacies and says he will kill himself in front of Daphnis' door. See
Anderson (1993) 168. Alciphron's parasite, in kissing his beloved's footprints, looks
ahead to the complex foot fetishes exhibited in the love letters of Philostratus.

[51] A Nebris appears in Lucian *Dialogues of the Courtesans* 10, where she elicits feelings of passion in a fellow slave.

this way he points ahead to the love interests that dominate book 4. But on the whole these are the exceptions, and Alciphron creates them on a solid foundation of conventional, stereotypical behavior of certain classes of people. We still expect our parasites to live off their rich urban hosts, enduring all the ills that such a subservient status brings them.

The incongruity that Alciphron highlights in his letters is introduced in the context of a tightly bound social order. He explores the bathos of romantic feelings in "common" men and women, and the oddity of erotic language that is restricted by the lover's limited experience and low socio-economic status. He seems to be saying that you can always tell a person by their similes: if a boy has hair like curly seaweed, or a girl has cheeks like ripe apples, it is not difficult to guess the social rank of their admirers. The courtesans alone are unmarked by this kind of incongruity, presumably because, as women of the world, they, like Helen of Troy, can imitate the voices and tones of other people. But Alciphron associates them with an even more interesting trait than marked language, namely with writing: they are his letter writers *par excellence*.

EPISTOLARY SELF-CONSCIOUSNESS: CAUGHT IN THE ACT OF WRITING

Book 4, the letters of the courtesans, draws attention to its writtenness in a way the other three books do not. This may be because erotic exchange conveniently relies more heavily on writing (love letters, love poems, written oaths of faithfulness, etc.), and the characters involved in relationships with courtesans are usually aristocratic and therefore well educated, more likely to dabble in authorship.[52] The men write to seduce their beloveds – or so we assume from little evidence, since only three of the nineteen letters in this book are written in the voices of men. The women write for a variety of reasons which we will discuss below, but their constant references to the act of letter writing suggest the conventionality of the association between the worlds of erotic and epistolary exchange.

---

[52] See exceptions already discussed of farmers, fishermen – in love but out of their league.

It is instructive to compare specific references to written communication in books 3 and 4. The parasites acknowledge their acts of writing only three times in a total of forty-two letters. In *Letter* 3.23, the speaker is interested in finding someone to interpret his dream, but until he can find a skilled practitioner of the art, he finds no harm in communicating his odd vision to an old friend. This is letter as "news," as is 3.39, where a parasite is tortured by an excessively long wait for a mouth-watering dessert, and notes at the end of his letter "I write this to you, not so much delighted with the delicious food as exhausted by the long drawn out delay." The other reference to writing is internal to the story (3.26.2): a parasite writes of two-page love letters (γραμματίδια) going every day from his patron's wife to her lover, along with gifts of garlands and apples, through the services of complicit maids.

By contrast, book 4 contains ten references within the space of nineteen letters; more than half the letters allude to their own writing. Writers draw attention to their reasons for writing usually at the end of their letters: "I have revealed this to you so you won't blame me, for I will get even with them" (4.6.5); "I feel better having poured out my grief to you ... even to talk and write about her seems sweet to me" (4.11.9); "I am writing to you now to ask advice" (4.17.4). Another writer concludes her letter by telling a friend what she missed at a party the day before, offering the letter as a poor substitute for the event itself (4.13.19):

It was only proper that you should at least have the pleasure of hearing about the party ... even if you weren't able to participate. So I wanted to write to you a precise account of everything, and I was encouraged to do so.

The writers of book 4 look upon letters as integral to their affairs, but in different ways. Thus the scorned lover Simalion (4.8.4) writes to Petale that another man under the same circumstances would have written her an abusive and threatening letter, since she ignores and scorns him, but he writes with prayers and supplications, since he adores her. He hopes his pleading letter will win him more favor than an abusive one, but we know from her answer (4.9) that she remains unmoved. The tables are turned for another couple, when Myrrhine tries to win back her beloved from a rival who has caught his eye (4.10.2):

Love notes (γραμματίδια), maids as go-betweens, and all such things have been in vain, and no advantage comes from these things. In fact it seems to me that he has become more puffed up and scornful of me on account of these attempts.

Letters also define the interactions between Leontium and her jealous lover Epicurus. She complains to her friend Lamia that he tries to manage her every move, scolding her for everything, and "writing well-sealed letters" that presumably demand what he views as appropriate behavior from her (4.17.2). In her desperation to escape his prying and interfering, she claims that she will leave for some foreign destination rather than put up with his endless letters (4.17.3):

He wants to be a Socrates and to talk on and on and to pretend ignorance . . . and he counts on making me his Xanthippe. And the result will be that I will leave for some unknown destination and wander from country to country rather than endure his endless letters.

Epicurus uses letters to control, to pester, to express "ownership," but the result is that his beloved will do anything to escape his writings. This recalls the impatience of Petale in 4.15, discussed above, who complained of the uselessness of letters in the sphere of love. But there is added humor in the depiction of Epicurus in particular as a letter writer: he is famous in antiquity as the philosophical letter writer *par excellence*, but to the lover, his epistles are irritating at best, and at worst cause her to flee his presence.

In sharp contrast to Leontium's interpretation of letters as a kind of subjugation, or Petale's scorn of a useless piece of paper, Lamia writes to Demetrius of the honor she feels at being allowed, a mere courtesan, to write to such a powerful king. What's more, he even deigns to answer in turn; the letter opens with her words of gratitude (4.16.1):

You are responsible for giving me the freedom to address you, such a great king that you are, you who allow even a courtesan to write to you, and who think it not terrible to hold a conversation with my letters just as you do with my person.

For her, the act of writing a letter is an act of "freedom" (παρρή-σια), an act that puts her on par with the powerful king and conqueror. Her delight is intensified by the mutuality of the act, as Demetrius reads her words and writes back. The focus on letter writing gives way to fond memories of scenes together, and the text ends with an invitation to dinner: writing, for lovers, always remains secondary to an actual personal encounter, and Demetrius "holds conversation" with her letters only until they can meet again in the flesh.

It is a testament to the flexibility of the genre that a letter can be presented as doing so many contradictory things in the same collection. The writer can use a letter as a symbol of power and authority, to control or harass its reader, as in the case of Epicurus' monitory messages; letters can build a bridge between lovers who are apart, in a textual mutuality that remains second best to being in the beloved's presence, as with Lamia and Demetrius. Finally, letters can mean one thing to the writer and another to the reader, as when a man in love sends pages of passionate outpourings of the heart, only to be told that, in the eyes of his addressee, an ambitious courtesan, words are empty and meaningless. In his multiple references to the effect of letters, or the connection between letters and power, we should ask ourselves where we would place Alciphron's oeuvre along the spectrum: do we read it as convincing, powerful, and authoritative, or as a waste of paper?

Perhaps a step in answering this question comes in what is by far the best example of allusion to the act of writing and reading letters in book 4, namely the paired correspondence of Menander and Glycera (18, 19). Menander's letter already stands out in that it is written by not just a famous person but by a person famous specifically for his writing. Whether or not our expectations are justified, we somehow expect more from a letter "written" by the great comic dramatist, and we may even wish to associate Menander with the authorial figure of Alciphron, at least at some level.[53] Both Menander's and his beloved's letters are unusually long, and unique in that they owe their existence to a third letter, one from Ptolemy Soter, king of Egypt. At some time in the recent past, Menander had received a letter from Ptolemy inviting him to come to Egypt. Menander begins his letter to Glycera by swearing that, the apparent contents of his letter notwithstanding, he neither exalts himself nor wishes to be separated from her when he writes what will follow. The whole first paragraph is devoted to praising and affirming their till-death-do-us-part love, in exces-

---

[53] See also my associations of Alciphron as artist with Praxiteles/Phryne in 4.1.

sively melodramatic language: "let us be young together and let us grow old together, and by the gods let us even die together ..." (4.18.3). Then Menander turns to the specific business at hand (4.18.4–7):

The urgent reason for my present letter to you, as I lie ill in the Piraeus ... and you remain in the city for the Haloa in honor of the goddess, is as follows. I have received a letter from Ptolemy, King of Egypt, in which he begs a huge favor from me, and invites me, promising royally, as the saying goes, all good things on earth for me and for Philemon, too. For he says that Philemon also has received a letter. And Philemon himself has written, showing me his own invitation, which is in a lighter tone, and since not written to Menander, a little less elegant in style ... So now I am sending you the King's letter, in order that I may indeed bother you twice, making you read both my letter and the King's. And I want you to know what I have decided to write back to him.

A large amount of factual information is transmitted as Menander justifies his letter to the internal reader (for the sake of the external reader). This exposes the mechanics of Alciphron's fictional epistolary art: he needs to explain and justify in order to make this correspondence as "realistic" as possible. This "meta-writing" begins with the reason for the letter's existence: Menander lies ill in the Piraeus, subject to one of his frequent bouts of weakness, as he takes pains to tell us, and Glycera is detained in Athens in observance of a festival of Demeter, the Haloa. Otherwise this normally inseparable pair would not be reduced to sending messages in the first place. But it is clear that this information is included for our benefit, not Glycera's, who knows full well where her lover is and why.

Next Menander turns to the reason for his letter, namely another letter, this one recently arrived from Egypt, from King Ptolemy. The additional information that Ptolemy is "King of Egypt" is again most probably included for the sake of posterity; surely his name could stand on its own in Menander's time, but could it still among Alciphron's contemporaries? Alciphron may even be looking ahead to later readers. Thus far, Menander has mentioned his own letter and that of the king; now he adds that he has seen proof of the king's word in Philemon's letter. Philemon's letter included a copy of his own invitation from Egypt, which Menander dismisses as less well written: why should the king bother to write elegantly and correctly to Philemon, a lesser poet?

Menander here refers to the epistolary convention of writing with one's audience in mind: he cannot imagine the king taking as much care in the composition of Philemon's letter as he did with his own. Glycera is not given a copy of Philemon's letter or his royal invitation, so she will have to take Menander's word for its stylistic merits or flaws. But she does receive a copy of the king's letter to Menander, and he apologizes that she may be bored by reading both his letter, which describes what is in the king's letter, and the original document, the royal invitation to come to Egypt. Alciphron chooses not to "write" the king's letter into Menander's correspondence; we, the external audience, are tantalized by references to it by Menander and Glycera, but here the internal audience and internal consistency win out. Why does Menander feel it necessary to "include" the king's letter in his packet to Glycera? Surely she would have taken his word for it; there is not much to be misinterpreted in the invitation itself, or as much as we are told about it. Perhaps it is just the sheer enjoyment of layers of epistolarity, and the teasing effect of a letter hinted at but not given in full.

In Glycera's letter, we continue to be teased by this all-important but unreadable document, the king's letter. Glycera emphasizes its physical existence, saying that she waved it in the air in front of her relatives, excerpting parts that have to do with her own role as Menander's beloved. We are invited to imagine her opening Menander's letter and seeing the enclosed document, in unfamiliar handwriting; no wonder she tells us she read it first (4.19.1–4): "I immediately read the king's letter which you sent me." Her delight upon reading is so obvious that her companions wonder out loud at her reaction. She enlightens them at once, quoting herself in her letter back to Menander (4.19.2–4):

"Ptolemy, the King of Egypt," I said, "sends for my Menander, promising him half his kingdom, so to speak," speaking in a louder voice and more distinctly, so that all the women present might hear me. And saying these things, I waved and showed off in my hands the letter with its royal seal. "Are you glad to be left behind?" they said. But it wasn't that, Menander. No, by the goddesses, in no way could I ever be persuaded, not even if that proverbial ox were to speak, that Menander would ever wish or be able to leave his Glycera behind in Athens and reign alone in Egypt with all its wealth. Rather, this at least was clear from the King's letter, which I read: he had apparently heard about my relationship with

you, and wanted, with his Egyptian version of Attic wit, to tease you
gently with innuendo. I am delighted about this, that our love story has
sailed over the sea and reached him in Egypt. And he must be entirely
convinced by what he has heard, that he hopes for the impossible when
he wants Athens to come over to him. For what is Athens without
Menander, and what is Menander without his Glycera?

Glycera confirms Menander's words about the king's offer: it is
indeed a generous one, "half his kingdom, so to speak." But she
puts more emphasis on the physicality of the letter itself: she
waves it around, points to its royal seal guaranteeing its authenticity. For Menander, the letter was one in a series: Philemon had
received a similar invitation, although worded slightly differently.
For the direct recipients, a similar letter works to confirm the value
of their own: Philemon's invitation shows Menander that Ptolemy
is serious about patronizing the arts, not just an individual artist.
For Glycera, however, the eavesdropper on Menander's letter from
the king, its value lies in its uniqueness. Its seal, its handwriting, its
specific references to their situation all ratify its genuineness.

Glycera goes on in the letter to mirror what she reads as Menander's own vacillations between staying in Athens and going to
Egypt. Unable to make up her mind, she begs Menander to delay
his decision: "don't send the King any reply right now" (4.19.14).
She asks him to wait until they can talk it over with trusted
friends, or consult the oracle at Delphi, or best of all check with a
Phrygian diviner. She undermines the king's authority that she has
just been flaunting to her friends by saying "even if all the kings in
the world wrote to you, all of them are less royal in your eyes than
I am" (4.19.18). So now the king's letter is without value, unless
Menander's real "sovereign," his Glycera, should give it the stamp
of approval. As she plays with various scenarios of Menander in
Athens or Egypt, Glycera suggests that he can "take her with him"
in writing by exporting to Egypt a play that features her; but even
that is not enough for her, and she ends with a vision of her guiding Menander in a boat over the seas with her own hands, if he
decides that it is best to make the voyage (4.19.21).

While Menander may have vacillated in the body of the letter,
taking an armchair tour of Egypt as he contemplated its wonders
and riches, he ended it without a doubt that he would stay at
Athens (4.18.16–17):

King Ptolemy, may it be my fate always to be crowned with a wreath of Attic ivy, and to sing songs every year in honor of Dionysos of the Hearth, to participate in the rites of the Mysteries, and to stage a new play at the annual theatrical contests, laughing, rejoicing, competing, fearing defeat, and winning. Let Philemon go to Egypt and enjoy my blessings too; Philemon doesn't have a Glycera, and perhaps isn't worthy of such a treasure.

Glycera, however, reads between the lines and decides that he has not yet made up his mind. This kind of reading against the grain reveals her own sense of confusion about what is best for Athens, for herself, for Menander, and for them as a couple. Her reading of the king's letter confirms what appears to be a very "personal" style of interpretation: what fascinates her most is that their love story has reached even Egypt (4.19.4).[54] In her eyes, the best of Athenian culture comes down to her own self (4.19.3): "what indeed is Athens without Menander; and what is Menander without Glycera?" In reputation he is everywhere, but in reality "both night and day he is in my embrace" (4.19.6).

Most of Glycera's letter continues to waver between staunch refusals to go, and worried imaginings about the consequences of going. She is concerned about what people might think, and that she might be seen as an impediment to Menander's, and by implication Athens', ambition and fame. At times she says she will come to see him to discuss their decision, but then turns around and insists that he come to her in Athens. She finally insists on Athens, since, as she writes, if he does change his mind and decide to go to Egypt, he will have to prepare his plays to take with him (4.19.19). At the end of her letter, we are offered two scenarios: either Menander leaves Glycera behind but stages a play in which she is the main character, thus "bringing your own beloved in writing while you leave the reality behind in Athens" (4.19.20), a replay of the Stesichorean "Helen" story, as it were; or, they both set sail for Egypt. Her last words are telling, in their focus on her own fate and on the continued "confusion" between stage life and reality (4.19.21):

---

[54] She "corrects" herself in 4.19.6, saying that what made her happy was the information that Menander was loved not by Glycera alone but also by kings beyond the sea. On this letter in general, see Bungarten (1967).

I pray to all the gods that what seems good to you will profit both of us, and that the Phrygian woman will divine a better future than your *Theophoroumene* ("Woman Possessed by a Divinity") did. Farewell.

In spite of her constant indecisiveness, which actually makes for a vivid and entertaining letter, as she imagines a variety of future options, Glycera seems curiously more eager to travel to Egypt than Menander. Could Menander be stooping to a deceptive (male?) ploy of flattering his beloved and putting her in a position in which she feels obliged to try not to stand in the way of his reputation and fame? If Menander had announced in his letter that he had already made the decision to leave, Glycera would no doubt have complained and objected; this way, she is the one encouraging him to reconsider, to remember his public. Glycera's letter in turn may be interpreted as a stereotpyical "female" response, full of anxiety, indecision, self-doubt, and self-centeredness. I would compare it in style and content with many of Ovid's *Heroides*, as Glycera and the heroines try to resolve the conflict between their love for a man and their own sense of self-preservation in the affair. But it is really only Glycera's response, the last letter of book 4 and therefore of the entire epistolary collection, that would allow Menander (and Alciphron) to keep writing – both plays, since he needs his Glycera for inspiration and practical assistance, and letters. If Menander has his way, the couple will be happily reunited and have no further need of letters; he will stick to writing and producing drama in Athens. Only in Glycera's version are we offered an epistolary future.

With the letters between Menander and Glycera, Alciphron closes the entire collection. *Letters* 18 and 19 are certainly not typical of the rest of the work, which makes it all the more ironic that they are perhaps the best known and most appreciated of Alciphron's *Letters*. Here we meet two specific historical individuals, basically satisfied with their love and their lives, sharing thoughts on a crisis in Menander's life that is documented by other sources; the detailed contents of the letters are realistic and probably highly accurate. We have returned to the impulse of *ethopoieia*, as Alciphron imagines what this famous pair might have said after receiving King Ptolemy's invitation.

Let me conclude this chapter by returning to the label of "artificiality" often applied to the epistolary genre. This is a deeply self-conscious mode of writing, full of allusions to its own creation, sending, and receiving. Unlike drama or dialogue, epistolary fiction does not want its reading public to lose itself in the literary illusion to the point of losing sight of its medium. Even when Alciphron seems to "forget" that he is writing letters, ignoring epistolary opening and closing formulas, he still bases the content of his writing on epistolary form, confronting issues of epistolary verisimilitude and the sometimes conflicting demands of internal and external reader. He responds to the challenges of the genre in various ways: by having his character write to an uninvolved party, a confidant, who needs to be told the "whole" story (e.g. 4.17: Leontium writes to Lamia about her troubles with Epicurus); by leaving gaps in information for the external reader, thus satisfying the requirements of verisimilitude but often frustrating his audience (e.g. 3.36: temporal confusion); or by listing a litany of complaints directed by the writing character against the internal reader, summarizing their past interactions and indirectly also bringing the external reader up to date (e.g. 2.6: farmer to his beloved who rejects him). For the epistolary exercise to succeed, we the audience – both ancient and modern readers – need to feel included in the correspondence. We may feel included and implicated by the simple act of "reading over the shoulder," or peeking into someone else's letter files. But Alciphron's letters, I would argue, provide readers with an opportunity to write themselves into the correspondence, whether they are country or city folk, rich or poor, male or female, young or old. These letters, sometimes single and sometimes paired, invite a response, offer anyone with a minimum of education and culture the chance to try his or her hand at *ethopoieia*. Collected in book form, they remind us of the volume and variety of rhetorical display in both Menander's and Alciphron's Athens.

CHAPTER II

Aelian's Rustic Letters

> If these letters sent to you are cleverer than you might expect
> the country to supply, don't be surprised; for we are not Lib-
> yan or Lydian farmers, but Athenian ones.
>
> Aelian *Letter* 20

Just as Alciphron has endured constant comparison with Lucian,
so Aelian has long lived in the shadow of Alciphron. The letters
preserved under his name are believed to be the work of Claudius
Aelianus, a Roman writing in Greek in the late second and early
third centuries, who also wrote two works of paradoxography, the
De Natura Animalium, and the *Varia Historia*.[1] All three of his extant
works reveal his taste for miscellanies, consistent with his contemporaries' comparable fascination with miniaturism and collections. It is tempting to think of Aelian as the poor cousin simply
because he reduced Alciphron's lengthy and lively quartet of urban
and rustic authors into a single volume of twenty letters written in
the voices of farmers. Thus Benner and Fobes suggest that Aelian
was a younger contemporary of Alciphron, influenced by his work,
but not as talented an epistolographer: "in substance, the *Letters*
are comparable to the poorest letters of Alciphron."[2] They criticize Aelian for his frequent use of clichés, his vulgarity, and his
numerous echoes of classical authors (especially Homer, Hesiod,
Eupolis, Aristophanes, and Menander) – all elements that we have
accepted in Alciphron as integral to his specific literary undertak-
ing. Earlier in the twentieth century, C. Bonner argued convincingly that Aelian did not plagiarize Alciphron's work, but that
both authors drew heavily on earlier sources, particularly comedy;
yet his final words reveal an intense dislike of the very author he

[1] Easterling and Knox (1989b) 120; Benner and Fobes (1949) 344.
[2] Benner and Fobes (1949) 345.

champions: "these letters of Aelian are throughout little more than a stupid patchwork of material derived chiefly from the comedy."[3] A more positive assessment is that of E. L. Bowie, who retains Alciphron as the *comparandum*, but finds merit in the brevity, wit, and formal construction of Aelian's work: "it is more important that Aelian's letters are entertaining than that they are derivative."[4]

The twenty letters are preserved in two manuscripts under the heading ἐκ τῶν Αἰλιανοῦ ἀγροικικῶν ἐπιστολῶν, which leaves open the possibility that the collection is not complete as it stands.[5] This heading reminds the reader of the arbitrary nature of any letter collection. In the spirit of the fiction, we could ask ourselves who collected these letters, how they came into Aelian's hands, and why they are ordered the way they are. Also, are we meant to view the collection as "complete?" E. L. Bowie argues that the letters form a carefully constructed whole: "their vignettes of rural life, starting with a roll in the hay and skillfully rehandling this theme from various viewpoints in alternation with complaints, quarrels and enkomia of rustic simplicity, build up a harmonious cycle."[6] Each of the letters takes on the perspective of its supposed writer and reports a particular event or a general scene, ranging from an accident on the farm (*Letter* 2) to the mundane details of a farmer's life (*Letter* 4). Aelian constructs his collection around two pairs of letters (*Letters* 7–8, 11–12) and one group of four (*Letters* 13–16), while the rest of the individual letters offer variations on country themes.

Bowie assumes that the letter collection forms an artistic whole, which is not necessarily the same thing as an epistolary whole. An epistolary whole would assume a correspondence between two persons, or at most a small group of people, over a given time, collected later by some unnamed editor who reassembled the letters chronologically to reveal both sides of the correspondence to a wider public. The editor would either invent some fiction explaining how the letters arrived in his hands, or ignore the issue altogether, assuming that the reader would not question the provenance of his edition. Aelian as author and editor plays with two

---

[3] Bonner (1909) 32–33, arguing against the thesis of H. Reich, *De Alciphronis Longique Aetate* (Königsberg 1894).
[4] Easterling and Knox (1989b) 122.
[5] See E. L. De Stefani, "Per il testo delle epistole di Eliano," *SIFC* 9 (1901) 479–88, esp. 480.
[6] Easterling and Knox (1989b) 121.

levels of epistolary organization in his collection: he offers three sets of grouped, answered letters to satisfy the reader's interest in sustained dialogue, and presents the rest of his examples as single, unanswered letters from writers who appear only once in the collection. The first level of organization reminds us of Alciphron's subset of courtesans' letters in book 4 (*Letters* 4.1–5), while the latter functions as a miscellany, an apparently arbitrary mélange of country letters presented in the name of literary entertainment. Aelian's work gains additional coherence through brief reappearances of characters: thus the name Mania appears in *Letters* 1 and 2 and the farmer Anthemion who writes *Letter* 4 becomes the addressee of *Letter* 5.

In the absence of an editorial preface, the reader turns to the opening letter for orientation, but in this case, Aelian postpones his most programmatic piece until the end of the book (*Letter* 20). *Letter* 1 opens instead *in medias res*, and turns out to be a narrative of rape.[7] Euthycomides writes to Blepaios (*Letter* 1, in full):

While I was drying my grapes in the hot sun, Mania came near, playing coy, and began to insult me with much jeering. But actually for some time now I had been infatuated with her, and I was thinking I might do something wild. So, approaching her, I grabbed her in my eagerness – and she was eager, too – and I let go of my grapes and crept over to her, and with great eagerness harvested her fruits. But let these things be as secret as the Great Mysteries, I ask you in the name of Pan.

The letter begins with a reference to the writer ("while I was drying ...") and continues with a first-person recitation of the event. Mania is presented as "playing coy" but really just as eager for sex as the writer. The addressee and the external audience are informed that the two of them have a past: "for some time" (παλαιόν) Euthycomides has had his eye on Mania, and this encounter is meant as a culmination of their flirtation. But this letter between two men, one boasting of his sexual adventure in the fields, is not, perhaps, the best place to look for insight into the woman's emotions: how does Euthycomides know that Mania is only "playing" coy? In his own eagerness to do something wild (θερμόν), can he really judge her own eagerness? Aelian juxtaposes the two ad-

---

[7] For similar subject matter, see Alciphron *Letter* 2.35. Note that Alciphron's collection also began *in medias res*, suggesting that this might be the rule rather than the exception for such epistolary collections.

jectives to suggest their common purpose: "I, eager, grabbed her, eager" (ἄσμενος ἀσμένης ἐλαβόμην); but on second glance, the critical apparatus reveals an editorial hand. The manuscripts read simply ἄσμενος. Meineke reads ἄσμενος ἀσμένης, while Hercher offers simply ἀσμένης. There is much at stake in this reading, and not just the epistolographer's reliability as a source. The letter shows the supposed writer's view of the events; the internal and external readers are left to worry about his objectivity.

The internal reader emerges only at the end of the letter in the single word "you" (σοι), a dative of reference: "Let these things be secret, I ask you ..." Blepaios is drawn into the lurid secrets of the letter and then ordered to keep silent about them. We are not told why this apparently casual act of sex is unspeakable, as secret as the Great Mysteries: we are told only that this is so, and the letter writer both trusts his friend to enjoy the story and to keep it to himself. As external readers, our pleasure in eavesdropping is, of course, intensified upon reading this warning: yet the writer's words are undermined by the very fact of our reading them – obviously his warning has failed. Blepaios is meant to keep the story to himself, but the letter we have just read lets us in on the secret, invites us into the inner circle of Euthycomides' friendship, and assumes that we will share his "great eagerness" and satisfaction in the deed. We can imagine this letter never reaching Blepaios, but falling by the wayside, where it is picked up by Aelian and added to his collection. Or we can imagine Blepaios betraying his friend for the sake of a good laugh. All of this still sustains the fiction of "real" farmers' letters.

That fiction is carried further by *Letter* 2, where the situation of Mania is unexpectedly elucidated. Comarchides writes to Dropides that an acquaintance of his has fallen and hurt his leg.[8] After passing on this information, the writer closes with a conventional farewell (*Letter* 2):

Give my regards to the ewe, the one with the soft wool, whose praises I sing to you, and give my greetings (χαίρειν κέλευε) to the two heifers and the dog and to Mania herself.

The conventions of epistolary closure are somewhat disturbed as Comarchides lists a ewe, two heifers, and a dog in front of his ad-

---

[8] The first part of this letter is taken from Menander's *Georgos* 46–52.

dressee's presumed wife, Mania, and we suspect either a parody of the traditional formula, or a pointed suggestion that animals on the farm are more valuable than a working woman.[9] But we can read backwards to a better understanding of Euthycomides' reluctance for his deeds to be made public, for Mania appears to be the wife, or at least the property, of Dropides. All four men must be acquainted, and Euthycomides is fearful of the outcome of any gossip.

These first two letters of the collection thus remind us of the impact of the letter form on the reader. The opening *in medias res* mimics the assumption behind any letter: there is a prior connection between the sender and addressee, and we, the external readers, are privileged to glimpse only a fragment of their relationship through the letter in question. We are invited to invent fuller scenarios, but if we are given too much information, we mistrust the nature of the letter. If it is written with the internal reader in mind, it retains its charm as a private, secret document that has somehow come under scrutiny by a third party; when the information it contains is clearly intended for an external reader, the act of reading is no longer transgressive, and therefore not as exciting or pleasurable. In this pair of letters we experience the additional thrill of being left in doubt as to some of the details – who is Mania? what is her relationship to Euthycomides? what will happen next? – but then being informed fully in the next letter, which at first appears to have nothing to do with the other. Having given up on fully understanding the need for secrecy in the first letter, we are pleasantly surprised by the explanation suggested by the second. The delayed explanation keeps us guessing and, more importantly, keeps us reading.

The first two letters propel the reader forward; the last letter functions as an explanation for the letters that precede it, tying the collection together as a whole. *Letter* 20, from Phaedrias to Sthenon, opens innocently enough with a comment on the value of the countryside: "It is in the countryside that all beautiful things grow." Phaedrias appears to be talking about crops and fruits, the earth's nourishment for mankind. But his letter then takes a more metaphysical turn:

---

[9] See Alciphron *Letter* 2.15.1 for a similarly highly valued dog who is invited to a party along with the rest of the family.

And justice and self-control also grow in the countryside, the most beautiful of trees and the most useful of fruits. So, then, do not scorn farmers; for there is a certain kind of wisdom in them too, not expressed by an elegance of tongue or enhanced with the power of words, but strong in its silence and expressing its goodness through its own lifestyle. If these letters sent to you are cleverer than you might expect the country to supply, do not be surprised; for we are not Libyan or Lydian farmers, but Athenian ones.

The letter begins as a eulogy on the countryside, the joy of a farmer's life in self-sufficiency on his farm. But the references to justice (δικαιοσύνη) and self-control (σωφροσύνη) as the most valuable crops of the land alert the reader that this letter is really on the subject of letters, in other words a commentary on the farmers' letters that have come before, a postponed programme. With the admonition that Sthenon should not scorn farmers, we also realize that this addressee, unlike the others preceding it, is no farmer, and what's more, he is disdainful of the apparent lack of intellectual refinement in the whole breed. From the next sentence, it becomes clear that Sthenon values only wisdom that expresses itself in elegant language and sophistic argumentation, and we assume that he himself either is or wishes to be considered a cultured and educated man, in his eyes the very opposite of a stereotypically boorish farmer. Aelian's letter writer alludes to the topical issue of *paideia* that dominated the Second Sophistic, as we have seen in the previous chapter: whoever could lay claim to true "culture" also had power over his peers. But here, interestingly, eloquence is presented as antithetical to goodness, since eloquence often relies on deception and dishonesty; thus the farmers are "strong in [their] silence."

Phaedrias defines the competition over culture here as "the power of words" against the "strength of silence;" we can also read this as the city, represented by the doubting Sthenon, against the country, ably defended by Phaedrias. Phaedrias glorifies deeds (lifestyle) over words, even if his argument falters when he is then forced to define his farmers by their silence; after all, these are the same rather voluble farmers whose letters we have just been reading. And Phaedrias himself is one of them, as he includes himself in the final phrase: "we are Athenian farmers." The final sentence betrays the writer's own brand of cultural snobbery. He separates Athenian farmers from non-Athenian, putting them into a subcategory in which their Athenianness elevates their silent, simple country ways. Thus they have the best of both worlds, the innate justice and self-control of farmers, and the *paideia* and cleverness of Athenian citizens. Here are farmers, still honest and good, who can read and write and argue with the best of them. Now the reader can accept the fiction of rustic epistolographers without undue amazement or concern about verisimilitude. Phaedrias' clever twist at the end of his letter applies both to *Letter* 20 and to the entire collection: the letters are full of rather clever things (σοφώτερα).

With that assessment by an internal character, we turn back to the collection to (re)read it sophistically, to hunt for "wisdom" lurking in its lines. Aelian's farmers stand united against the world in their hatred of injustice and violence, personified by thieves, bad neighbors, devious courtesans, insolent soldiers, and court-room orators. Orators use deception as a tool of their trade, while farmers prove their honesty in simple ways. *Letter* 17 praises the good nature and generosity of farmers, and prays that jealousy and envy never enter their hearts: "may that curse fall upon wild goats and courtroom orators" (τοὺς ἐν δικαστηρίοις ῥήτορας). But in his attempt to write convincingly, Aelian turns to none other than the orators as models for those letters that proclaim precisely the evils of legal prosecution. *Letter* 3 complains of a slave who is stealing from her master's friend, and threatens legal action: it is based on an oration of Isaios.[10] The letter already presents itself as a legal document as the writer includes his name and deme affiliation, a reference to his ancestors, and the monetary value of the slave in question (3):

For indeed the graves of my ancestors would justifiably complain if I, Eupeithides of the deme Korydallos, allowed myself to be abused, especially by a slave worth about two minae.

This sounds more like an official deposition than a neighborly warning. In another example, *Letter* 6 turns to Demosthenes 55 (Against Kallikles) as its model to narrate an argument between two men about ownership of land; Aelian borrows even the names of the characters, Kallaros and Kallikles, from the orator.[11] This

---

[10] Isaios fr. 10 (43) Thalheim; see E. L. De Stefani, "La fonte delle epistole III e VI di Eliano," *SIFC* 19 (1912) 8–10.

[11] De Stefani (1912) 8–10: Demosthenes 55 (Against Kallikles).

letter also contains a proverb from Hesiod that sums up the dispute: "it is an ancient saying that 'a bad neighbor is a bad thing'" (*W&D* 346). Letter 6 closes with a surprise:

> But there is nothing to be gained by violence on your part. For we will not sell the farm to you; before that happens our master (ὁ δεσπότης) will take you to court over this matter, if he has good sense.

At the end of the letter we discover that, while Kallikles may be the neighboring landowner, the writer of this letter is a slave, writing on behalf of his master. We may find ourselves wondering where a slave could learn to read Hesiod and Demosthenes, and to write a letter with such easy allusiveness.

The bad neighbor returns in the group of four letters 13–16. In *Letter* 13, Kallipides writes to Knemon, whom he labels a "wild man" (ἄγριος), a threat to the neighborhood, that he should learn to control his temper. He lists a series of wild acts by Knemon that stirred him to write and advise the man. The three letters to follow include replies and counter-replies, as Knemon's temper flares. Aelian intensifies the language of abuse as his Knemon doggedly writes back to defend himself against his neighbor, not hesitating for a moment to reveal his *ethos* as that of the quintessential misanthrope.

The sources for their encounter are obvious: comedy (Antiphanes' *Timon*, Menander's *Dyskolos*), perhaps Lucian's *Timon*, and certainly both Alciphron's letter on Timon (2.32) and his triad of *Letters* 1.17–19, which deals with an escalating argument between two fishermen over the ownership of an abandoned net.[12] In the case of both Alciphron and Aelian, the triviality of the subject (a broken fishing net, polite manners) is counterbalanced by the elaboration of the correspondence. One letter on such a subject is certainly readable, but three or four letters, which lead to *aporia* as neither side wins the argument, are more difficult to appreciate. Perhaps the challenge for Aelian was to (pretend to) extemporize repeatedly on a theme that on the surface had little appeal or interest. This type of variation on the theme reveals the direct influence of sophistic *ethopoieia*, yet seems to find perverse pleasure in choosing a theme of utmost triviality. But, of course, it is precisely *other* people's triviality that can be so fascinating to read about.

[12] See O. Ribbeck, "Agroikos: eine ethologische Studie," *ASG* 9 (1884) 3–113, esp. 11–15; C. Graux, "Chorikios: Apologie des Mimes," *RPh* 1 (1877) 209–47, esp. 228 note 5.

Aelian's quartet of letters shows itself quite aware of its epistolary nature in direct references, even at the height of passion, to the act of writing. Kallipides offers his first letter (13) as a kindly reminder, addressed to a good man (ὦ βέλτιστε Κνήμων), who will surely see the error of his ways: "take this as friendly advice (φίλα παραγγέλματα) from a friend, medicine for your manners." But Knemon's first response is to say that although he should have answered the letter with silence, he feels forced to discuss the matter with his detractor, to give his own side of the issue:

There was really no need for me to reply at all, but since you are interfering, and force me to discuss things with you against my will, at least I have this advantage, that I can chat with you by messengers (δι' ἀγγέλλων σοι λαλεῖν) and not in your actual presence. So let this be now what they call a Scythian reply to you.

We have noted before that to answer a letter at all may say more about the relationship of the sender and addressee than the contents of the return letter. Knemon could have ignored the letter and gone about his business; instead he is tempted into correspondence and has thus already given up part of his much prized independence and solitude. He claims he is forced to answer, but this could also be seen as his own doing: his grumpy nature pushes him to snap back at his would-be benefactor. At any rate, he sustains the image of a misanthrope by appreciating the mediating role of the letter: at least he does not have to face another human being in person. His reply is not particularly short, nor is it encoded: presumably the meaning he assigns to "Scythian" is "terrible" or "rough," both compliments in his mind.[13] He uses the same verb (λαλεῖν) to describe the action of "casual talking" through a letter that appears in the epistolary theorists ("Dem." 232; Greg. Naz. *Epistle* 51.4: τὸ λαλικόν). But his "chatting" promises to be harsh and nasty, not what we would expect given the connotations of the term.

Kallipides' reply (*Letter* 15) is another attempt to placate: he invites Knemon to a party, hoping he will mellow with drink, music, and flute-girls. He terms his letter again "the advice of a friend," and imagines his neighbor's face in front of him as he reads the

---

[13] Herodotus 4.127 offers as an example the reply of the Scythian king Idanthyrsus to Darius: a succint κλαίειν λέγω, the ancient equivalent of "go to hell."

letter: "stop scowling and replace that dark and sullen look with cheerfulness." Knemon rises to the bait, again making explicit his reasons for answering at all (*Letter* 16):

I am writing back so that I can rebuke you and at the same time to vent my anger on you. What I would like most is for you to be present, so that I could kill you with my very own hands ... I could even eat you raw.

Knemon wants to make it clear that he replies not out of courtesy, nor to answer Kallipides' invitation, but rather to insult him further and to express his own anger. He then offers a humorous variation on the standard epistolary (postcard) formula of "having a great time – wish you were here." Knemon's version is "I wish you were here ... so that I could kill you." The wish to eat his enemy raw, familiar from Homer, is his logical extension of the "Scythian" theme: he acts as a barbarian, an uncivilized monster, while his correspondent attempts to speak to him as a true Greek, a proper and civilized gentleman. This back-and-forth between conciliatory Kallipides and furious Knemon could go on forever, or at least as long as Knemon chooses to reply. But Aelian had made his point, and further variation might have proven tiresome. He extended Alciphron's trio into a quartet, but stopped without real resolution at the end of Knemon's second reply. We assume that Kallipides did not write back, and that Knemon continued in his wild and unfriendly ways. In this instance, the "friendly letter" failed to do its work. Either that, or Kallipides took a hint from the treatment of Menander's *dyskolos*, and went personally to drag the misanthropic farmer to his party, abandoning epistolary for bodily intervention.

An interest in epistolary exchange also fuels Aelian's two letter pairs, both reminiscent of letters in Alciphron. In one set, Lamprias writes to Tryphe about his success at a rabbit chase (*Letter* 11), and Tryphe writes back in mock praise (*Letter* 12).[14] The bantering tone of both is appropriate to the occasion: this particular rabbit is so skinny that Lamprias could barely see it. Lamprias writes in his letter as if he were in dialogue with Tryphe, who may be either sister or wife (*Letter* 11):

[14] J.-R. Vieillefond, "La lettre II.1 d'Alciphron et la *Chasse* de Xénophon", *RPh* 55 (1929) 354–57, esp. 357 connects this letter with Alciphron *Letter* 2.1.

For when he was flayed and the skin removed, only then did he become visible, or rather, for I am not speaking (λέγω) correctly, then he was even more invisible than before. But you, Tryphe, stop giggling at me ...

Lamprias writes of "speaking" in his letter, and corrects himself as he writes. He acts as if he can see Tryphe in front of him when he scolds her for laughing, but we must be meant to assume that Lamprias sent the letter along with the skin as a gift; if he were in her presence, there would obviously be no need for a letter. These details work against epistolary verisimilitude. Tryphe's letter in return matches Lamprias' humorous tone, but sustains the epistolary illusion; she promises to hang up the rabbit's skin as a monument to his hunting skills, but chides him for being too involved in his sport to pay her any attention. When she claims she will also record his success in writing (ἔσται ... ἀνάγραπτον), we are not sure if she means to set up an inscription, or that this very letter, acknowledging his deed, will serve as written praise and testimony.

The second pair shifts the male–female discourse from what appears to be a respectable household (Lamprias respectfully mentions Tryphe's father as a disciplinarian) to a more sordid scene. In *Letters* 7 and 8, Derkyllos and his beloved Opora exchange words about their love affair.[15] Derkyllos' letter accompanies a gift, just as Lamprias' did: in this case, the man sends figs, grapes, and wine to his girlfriend, and promises to send roses in the spring. He claims to love her not for her beauty, which other men admire, but for her unusual name: Opora, or "Harvesttime." His letter is in praise of her name, which well suits her occupation (*Letter* 7):

I praise you as I praise our mother earth, and I admire the brilliance of the man who gave you your name, for no doubt he wanted the passionate crowd of your lovers to be not just those from the city, but the country folk as well.

He says her name alone would be enough of a lure for farmers, and it is for the sake of her name that he sends the earth's bounty. But Opora's response is predictable, with the added joke that sending fruit to Opora is as bad as the proverbial "coals to Newcastle" (*Letter* 8):

---

15 This pair may be based on Alexis' *Opora*; see B. Warnecke, "De Alexidis ΟΠΩΡΑ," *Hermes* 41 (1906) 158–59. See also Aristaenetus *Letter* 2.1.

Your gifts are indeed wonderful, fruit worth two obols and wine so young that it is insulting. [My slave] Phrygia may drink it up, but I drink Lesbian and Thasian wine, and I want money. To send ripe fruit to Opora is the same thing as adding fire to the fire.

Opora writes back the standard sophisticated courtesan's response: don't send useless gifts, send money! We encountered her spiritual sisters in Alciphron *Letters* 4.9 and 4.15. She puts him in his place by insulting his gifts, and simultaneously informs the external reader that Derkyllos has totally misread the situation: this is not about love, but about an investment. She redefines the *aition* of the name that Derkyllos is so passionate about. Her name, she writes, teaches her that the beauty of the human body is like that of fruit: but whereas trees can bloom again, a courtesan has only one harvest time, and so she needs to put aside money for her old age when her body will have withered. Her name to Derkyllos may define abundance and sweetness, but to Opora herself it defines her reason for wanting to make money now while she still can. It is worth reminding ourselves here that Aelian has just slipped the letter of a courtesan into his collection of farmers. As Opora shifts from addressee to writer, her own voice intrudes directly into the farming scenes. But having read Alciphron's collection, this "intrusion" seems less abrupt than it would otherwise seem; with this single courtesan's letter, Aelian seems to acknowledge Alciphron's inspiration for his work.

While the portrayal of Opora in *Letter* 8 is not as damning as it could be, Aelian juxtaposes it with *Letter* 9 from Chremes to Parmenon, in which the former acknowledges the good advice of the latter (sent in a previous letter?) which he ignored to his own peril. Parmenon apparently warned his friend to stay away from courtesans, and Chremes gives his reasons at some length (*Letter* 8): they all want only money; they pretend to be in love with you but lock you out of their homes, acting coy and refusing sex until they get what they want; they are gluttonous and badly behaved when dining privately – they eat like farm workers when unobserved, licking the plates and gulping down their food – but in your presence they pretend to be high class. These are all the stock insults of New Comedy, as is Chremes' closing complaint about a soldier, one Thrasyleon, who gets in the way of his encounter with the courtesan Thebais. There is humor in the slight attempt at epistolary verisimilitude at the end of the letter, when Chremes identifies the unwelcome solider as "Thrasyleon, I think, or something like that," as if reminding Parmenon that he had not been formally introduced to the man.

Aelian may not include the actual voice of any courtesan other than Opora (*Letter* 8), but he does have more to say on the subject. In *Letter* 19, an old man complains to a friend that his son has deceived him by bringing home a wife who turns out to be a "reformed" courtesan. At first she is modest and well behaved, but soon her clever artifices and luxurious ways reveal themselves, and her father-in-law threatens to sell her as a slave unless she accepts her share of the farmwork. This scenario recalls Alciphron's *Letter* 2.24, where another city girl misbehaves on the farm and is threatened with severe punishment unless she mends her ways.

The letters on the subject of courtesans introduce an urban theme into Aelian's rustic setting without changing the general impact of the collection. In *Letter* 18, Aelian also finds a way to introduce a fisherman, recalling Alciphron's whole book on the subject. This fisherman is actually a farmer who has left the land to go seafaring, hoping to make a better living than on the farm.[16] Its writer is one Demylus, who writes to his friend Blepsias that his neighbor Laches has abandoned agriculture in favor of sailing, "or so they say" (φασί). This last word is crucial: Demylus denies full knowledge of his neighbor's plans, but reports what he has heard from others. This becomes more interesting as Demylus proceeds to attribute all sorts of actions, emotions, and motivations to Laches, waxing poetic in his letter (*Letter* 18):

He measures other seas now and rides their waves and lives the life of a seagull, fighting with the winds that blow contrariwise. From cliff to cliff he sails on; with an eye to profit and his mind set on making a quick fortune, he said a long goodbye (χαίρειν) to his little goats and his former pastoral life ... in his imagination he see Egyptians and Syrians, and gazes at their wares ...

After more in this vein, Demylus concludes that "as for us, although we work hard and make little profit, the land is much more stable than the sea." But the conventionality of the conclusion does not mask the oddity of the bulk of the letter. Demylus imagines here what he could not possibly know. From the simple fact of Laches' departure, he invents a whole scenario of long farewells,

---

[16] Again, this *topos* is familiar from Alciphron's *Letters* 1.3 and 2.4.

fortune seeking, imaginary bazaars, shifting shorescapes, and dangerous weather. Demylus uses Laches' reported trip as an excuse for his own armchair travels. It is Demylus' imagination that leads him to Syrian bazaars and the "life of a seagull," not Laches'. When the letter closes with "since the land is more to be trusted than the sea, it offers us safer hopes," we feel as if Demylus has a hard time convincing himself not to abandon this safe lifestyle and follow Laches in the steps of the fisherman. The letter, instead of passing on interesting news to Blepsias, reveals the hidden adventurer in sensible Demylus.

It is curious that Aelian should limit himself to the letters of farmers, but then unobtrusively include a letter from a courtesan and (indirectly) a fisherman as well. In this way, he seems to beg for comparison with his fellow epistolographer Alciphron. He gains the advantage of the unity of an epistolary collection based on one theme – the voices of farmers – but incorporates thematic variation through the courtesan's reply (*Letter* 8) and Demylus' daydreams of sailing (*Letter* 18). He gains the trust of his audience by inventing plain-speaking honest rustic characters, but admits in *Letter* 20 that all we have read is indeed decked out in rhetoric, elaborately expressed in speech. In his final letter (*Letter* 20), he comes closer to identifying himself with the writer than anything in Alciphron ever does: "we are Athenian farmers," he says, and includes himself. The ultimate irony, of course, is that Aelian came from Rome and claimed never to have left Italy.[17]

---

[17] Easterling and Knox (1989b) 122.

CHAPTER 12

The Erotic Epistles *of Philostratus*

> The erotic epistolary style is one in which we offer words of
> love to a beloved.
>
> Pseudo-Libanius, *Epistolary Styles* 44[1]

We have already remarked on the lack of historical information
on Aelian and Alciphron; the identity of the last author of epistolary fiction from the Second Sophistic that we will discuss is
equally shadowy, although his name may be more recognizable
because of other, more canonical works attributed to him. A collection of seventy-three prose "erotic letters" (ἐπιστολαὶ ἐρωτικαί)
has come down to us from antiquity, transmitted under the name
of Philostratus of Lemnos.[2] Unfortunately, we know of four different family members with that name. Most scholars identify this
particular one as Flavius Philostratus II, born *ca.* 170 CE, who
studied in Athens and later belonged to the philosophical circle in
Rome patronized by Septimius Severus and his wife, Julia Domna.
Flavius Philostratus is best known for his *Lives of the Sophists*, a biographical work that sheds light on the habits and personalities of
the Second Sophistic, and his *Life of Apollonius of Tyana*, a biography of the mystical philosopher of the first century CE. The erotic
letters, however, are of a different nature altogether: they are for

---

[1] Malherbe (1988) 72–73.

[2] See K. Münscher, "Die Philostrate," *Philologus* Suppl. 10 (1907) 467–557, esp. 524–36; F.
Solmsen, "Some Works of Philostratus the Elder," *TAPA* 71 (1940) 556–72, esp. 566; G.
Anderson, *Philostratus* (London 1986) 274–75; G. W. Bowersock, "Philostratus and the
Second Sophistic," in Easterling and Knox, eds., *CHCL* 1.4 (1989) 95–98. The two surviv-
ing families of manuscripts order the letters quite differently, complicating our under-
standing of Philostratus' editorial intent in this epistolary collection. The Teubner text of
C. L. Kayser, *Flavii Philostrati opera II* (Leipzig 1871) differs in its organization from the
Loeb text of Benner and Fobes (1949). See also P. Hansmann, *Des älteren Philostratos erotische
Briefe, nebst den Hetärenbriefen des Alkiphron* (Frankfurt 1989). I use the Greek text of Benner
and Fobes (1949) but write my own translations.

the most part unhistorical, lacking in social context, and written to unnamed objects of affection who are differentiated only by sex ("to a boy," "to a woman"). The Loeb editors offer the following observation on the "spirit" of the epistolary collection:[3]

Many of the love letters are written in a strange, brooding spirit which almost cloaks the occasional grotesqueries – so long as one reads to oneself and sympathetically – but utterly fails to cloak the grotesqueries when one reads to someone else; e.g. *Letter* 18, to the boy whose sandal made his foot sore, and *Letter* 25, to the woman who was not pretty when she was angry. That such grotesqueries can be cloaked at all is an indication of the author's skill in putting his reveries into words.

Almost all the assumptions of this assessment may be challenged. The classification of "love letters" may not do justice to Philostratus' skill in stylistic variation on an erotic theme: what appears on the surface to be a love letter may include a variety of other literary foci: mythological allusions, catalogues and lists, paradoxical encomia, and so on. The grotesque, they claim, is "cloaked" by the author's skill. Perhaps a more enlightened response would be that Philostratus' skill lies precisely in evoking the grotesque to challenge our basic notion of love and the love letter. He brings to light the often bizarre nature of erotic feeling and expression with his explorations of fetish and obsession. Finally, the editors assume that one would want to read these love letters aloud to one's beloved, that the letters may function as conventional tools of erotic persuasion or seduction. But it is more likely, to my mind, that Philostratus' collection functions as a sophistic exercise in *variatio*, a group of letters meant to be read only to oneself, "sympathetically," with an eye to literary craftsmanship rather than practical application. In this, the letters of Philostratus follow in the literary footsteps of Aelian and Alciphron.

Following the reconstruction of Benner and Fobes, the collection consists of two main groups arranged according to subject (erotic and miscellaneous), all written in Philostratus' own voice but addressed to different recipients. These two main groups provide some useful statistics: of the fifty-three erotic letters in the first group, twenty-three are addressed to unnamed boys (1, 3–5, 7–11, 13–19, 24–27, 46, 56–58, 64), and thirty to unnamed women (2, 6, 12, 20–23, 28–39, 47, 50, 54–55, 59–63). This section in-

[3] Benner and Fobes (1949) 393.

cludes many letters on the same subject to a man and to a woman, although the pairs are not always directly juxtaposed. The second group is a miscellany of twenty letters: two are erotic (48, 53, both "to a certain friend"), and the remaining eighteen deal with a number of different subjects and are all addressed to named persons (40–45, 49, 51–52, 65–73). The collection ends with a letter addressed to Julia Domna, wife of Septimius Severus and a patron of the arts in her own right, that discusses contemporary cultural trends and advises the queen on matters of literary taste, a kind of epistolary *ars scribendi*, in which the fifth-century sophist Gorgias appears as the hero of the day (73).

Philostratus' self-presentation as a letter writer unmediated by other assumed voices represents a radical departure from the structure of other epistolary collections we have studied thus far, where both writer and addressee were fictional. Alciphron's persona hid behind imaginary urban and rustic types, while Aelian borrowed the voices of Athenian farmers for his letters. Here we are invited to imagine the author Philostratus himself in love, not hiding behind an invented persona, but ostensibly sharing his own experiences with us in the letters. The focus on the author is further intensified by the mostly anonymous identities of his addressees. The expectation of a love letter is that it will have a specific, named addressee: someone made famous by the author, such as Alciphron's Menander and Glycera, or an invented name, such as his Glaucippe. But Philostratus challenges that assumption not only by the large number of individual letters – we may be dealing with as many as fifty-two different "beloveds" in his circle – but also by the anonymity.[4] Is Philostratus telling us that the identity of his addressees is so unimportant that he will not bother to assign a name to them, or that conversely it is so important that only he will know the true identity of each particular beloved? Either way, we are left with only the author's identity as a guide to reading this epistolary collection.

While the letters themselves reveal few explicit epistolary conventions (e.g. formal openings or closings), the fictional situation of writing is quite probable. Instead of the dubious motivations of Aelian's farmers, we encounter a wide variety of situations in which writing a letter is expected: letters of persuasion, love,

---

[4] Philostratus uses the title "to the same" only for *Letters* 32, 33, 37.

praise, and blame; letters of advice (65–69), recommendation (71), or business (70); even letters accompanying gifts (35: love gifts; 45: pomegranates; 49: figs), the latter two reminiscent of Chion's thank-you letter to his father for gifts of fish, honey, and wine (*Letter* 6).

In two examples, Philostratus plays with the rules of letter writing, referring to the act of writing itself. In *Letter* 14, he takes advantage of epistolary convention to characterize his beloved's hard heart:

My greetings to you (χαῖρε), even though you do not wish them; my greetings (χαῖρε) to you, even though you don't write, you who are loving to others but contemptuous of me.

The repetition of χαῖρε puns on the goodwill inherent in the word – "hello, be well, fare well" – while contrasting the boy's cruel behavior: he will return neither love nor letter to his desperate lover. In a letter to a woman, Philostratus equates writing love letters with the most natural of acts, but she denies him that pleasure (*Letter* 39):

Will you not allow an exile even to write? Then don't allow lovers to breathe, or to cry, or to do all the other things that come naturally.

He begs not to be sent away, since he is already an exile in a foreign land. We may imagine that he has sent many letters already, and now sits outside her door awaiting a response. Her answer, presumably after tearing up his many pages, is to forbid him to write again. He tries another tack: a lover must write letters just as he breathes and weeps; it is the natural state of a man in love, and the cruelest thing to take away from him.

Here Philostratus paints a picture of letter writing as a natural reaction of a lover. But he frequently writes with such rhetorical flourishes and elaborate mythical or literary allusions that it is difficult to suspend disbelief and accept these letters as effective communications, "sincere" love letters rather than poetic showpieces. This is true particularly in the letters of erotic persuasion, where Philostratus takes one theme and varies it in half a dozen letters to different boys; elsewhere in the collection, he argues one definition of virtue to pursue a courtesan, and then promptly argues the opposite to seduce a respectable woman. He adjusts his opinions from letter to letter in order best to further his own immediate erotic interests. His letters reflect sophistic training more overtly and unabashedly than those of Aelian and Alciphron, again perhaps because he presents his unmediated voice as writer, rather than trying to reproduce the perspective of other, less-educated classes. The voice he presents us with is also highly idiosyncratic and almost obsessive about sexual matters; there is a streak of cruelty and masochism running through the collection that stamps it as uniquely Philostratean. The author is a victim of *eros*, and his letters deal with this victimhood in a variety of ways, alternately begging, threatening, persuading, praising, scolding, and commanding. Below, we will investigate more closely the different voices Philostratus adopts to argue his case(s).

RHETORICAL POSTURES

Letters 1, 2, and 4 show how Philostratus manipulates one particular image or theme in sophistic argumentation. *Letter* 1 accompanies a gift of roses to a boy; the flowers compete with the message to arrive first in the presence of the beloved. In *Letter* 4, the lover will reject roses for the same reason that he glorifies them in *Letter* 1: their wounding (or "coloring") of Aphrodite. Here is *Letter* 1 in full:

> The roses, carried on their leaves as if on wings, have hastened to come to you. Receive them kindly, either as souvenirs of Adonis, or as the coloring of Aphrodite, or as the eyes of the earth. For just as a wild-olive wreath suits an athlete, an upright tiara the Great King, and the crest of a helmet a soldier, so roses are appropriate for a beautiful boy, because of their similarity of fragrance and the particular nature of their color. You will not wear the roses; they will wear you.

This is juxtaposed with the much more concise *Letter* 2, addressed to a woman:

> I have sent you a crown of roses, not in order to honor you, even though I would like to do this too, but to do a favor to the roses themselves, so that they might not wither.[5]

But turning to *Letter* 4, the rose takes on a very different character. Philostratus had apparently sent something earlier, whether a

---

[5] Or, in Ben Jonson's version, "To Celia:" I sent thee late a rosy wreath, / Not so much honouring thee / As giving it a hope that there / It could not wither'd be. See I. Donaldson, ed., *Ben Jonson* (Oxford 1985) 293.

letter or a gift, and his beloved responds with blame and complaint. *Letter* 4, which follows in full, is a defense of his actions:

You blame me because I didn't send you roses. But I didn't do this negligently or on account of not loving, but rather I was considering that, since you are red-haired and thus crowned with your own "roses," you don't need flowers from others. Homer didn't put a garland on red-haired Meleager, since this would have been adding fire to fire, and a double torch to that other torch, nor did he do this for Achilles or Menelaus, or any other of his long-haired heroes. The flower is terribly grudging, short-lived, and swift to die, and it is said that its first origins are very sad. For the thorn of the rose pricked Aphrodite as she passed, as the Cyprians and Phoenicians tell the story. Let us not crown ourselves with blood, but flee the flower that spares not even Aphrodite.

In *Letter* 1, Aphrodite's pricking herself on the rose was part of a grand and noble erotic genealogy, but in *Letter* 4 it becomes a reason to shun the rose as a love-gift. Philostratus argues that the rose is not even allowed a place in epic, so horrible are its origins and habits. The negative points are recounted as evidenced by others: "it is said...," "the Cyprians and Phoenicians say ..." But the positive decision to keep roses away from Philostratus' beloved is supported by Homer himself, the ultimate authority. *Letter* 4 concludes with an invitation that places his beloved firmly by his side in the epistolary fiction: the "you" and "I" of the opening, reported in the context of reproach, are merged in agreement in the "let us ..." of the final line. Even the external reader is included in the exhortation. In the space of one short letter, Philostratus' rhetorical skills have persuaded both us and his beloved not just to forget and forgive the missing gift of roses, but to reject completely the whole flower species.

In the examples above, either we are meant to enjoy the (self-) contradiction, as we read Philostratus' collection as a whole, or we may choose to imagine the fictional situation of each individual addressee: the addressee of one letter has no idea that the addressee in the next is being seduced by exactly the opposite argument. Some of Philostratus' most rhetorical letters function also as paradoxical encomia, praise of things that are instrinsically unpraiseworthy.[6] In *Letter* 15, which will be discussed below, the

---

[6] See Anderson (1993) 190; H. Harwood, "Sirens and Silenoi: The Paradoxical Encomium from Antiquity to the Renaissance" (Diss. Yale 1996).

praise of a beloved boy's new beard is obviously paradoxical: beard growth on a young *eromenos* conventionally heralds the beginning of the end of an affair, as the boy moves into a new social and sexual role, namely that of an active lover. Elsewhere, the narrator tries to convince his beloved that a poor foreigner of good character (such as himself, he implies) is a better lover than a rich citizen (7, 8, 23, 28).[7] He lists mythological examples of famous foreign lovers, highlights the humility and loyalty of a poor man in love, and paints a devastating picture of the insensitivity of a wealthy lover.

Philostratus makes these encomia serve a specific purpose: they are presented as methods of erotic persuasion, cleverly sustaining the epistolary illusion. He asks us to believe that he writes not to show off his skill at arguing both sides, but to convince a particular person to accept his love. For the encomium to be persuasive, again we must read only one letter at a time, mirroring the fictional situation of the single addressee. Thus Philostratus argues in four letters that prostitution and promiscuity are evils (22, 23, 27, 40), but turns around paradoxically in two other letters (19, 38) to claim that he loves a boy or a woman specifically because of that status. In *Letter* 22, Aristagora and Lais are paraded as negative examples for their use of cosmetics to snare men; in *Letter* 38, in praise of a female prostitute (πόρνη), they reappear as positive role models "in whose footsteps you also walk." Philostratus sums it up thus (*Letter* 38):

That which to others seems infamous and worth reproaching, namely that you are without shame, bold, and well satisfied, is exactly what I love the most about you.

Selections from his parallel *Letter* 19, to a male prostitute, show the lengths to which Philostratus will go to "win" his case:

You sell yourself, but then so do mercenary soldiers. You go with anyone who pays, but then so do ship's pilots ... Please don't be ashamed of your eagerness to satisfy, but be proud of your readiness: for water is also available to all, fire doesn't belong to just one person, stars are public property, and the sun is a shared god.

---

[7] This may be modeled on Socrates' similar arguments for the "best" lover in Plato's *Phaedrus*.

All this is couched in a "love letter," including praise for the beloved and an implicit request that the beloved share himself with Philostratus, who does not mind being one of a crowd.

Philostratus acknowledges and even defends the other side of the argument in separate letters; but the external reader is obliged to read the letters separately – not consecutively – in order to sustain the image of a unified collection. In the collection of Alciphron, the artistic unity came from a fourfold variation in voice, a division into four different perspectives on similar topics: fishermen, farmers, parasites, and courtesans in love. But in Philostratus, we must face the possiblity that such artistic unity is not his goal; rather, he writes in his own voice without regard for linear consistency or sustained self-characterization. The letters are openly rhetorical, full of tricky arguments and surprises, like a good court case. The beloved will be persuaded not by tired epistolary ploys ("wish you were here," "I read your letter and imagine your presence"), but by verbal agility. At stake in Philostratus' collection is not "sincerity" or unity of purpose, but the exact opposite: particularity, artistic skill, variety, and enjoyment of words. Like his prostitute above, Philostratus is indeed "without shame, bold, and well satisfied" in his treatment of epistolary form; he is as promiscuous with his imagery as he is with the multiple objects of his affection. His collection of both erotic and miscellaneous letters most nearly approximates a real jumble from a lost mailbag, not an epistolary diary of self-revelation.[8]

This kind of arguing both sides is, of course, one of the hallmarks of the sophistic movement. Philostratus proves that he can take any argument and turn it on its head. But what works well in the context of epideictic rhetoric, in the public sphere of declaiming and competing, may at times threaten the epistolary illusion, as I will discuss below.

---

[8] There is, of course, a good deal of careful organization in this jumble: thus, Philostratus matches letters, either within the gendered series (e.g. *Letters* 30 and 31 to a married woman considering a lover, or 32 and 33 on eyes as drinking cups), or to boys and women on the same topic. *Letters* 7 (to a boy) and 23 (to a woman) discuss the advantages of an impoverished lover; *Letters* 8, 28, and 47 a foreign one; *Letters* 16 and 61 complain about the beloved's hair being cut off; *Letters* 19 and 38 praise a life of prostitution; *Letter* 18 (to a boy) and the pair 36 and 37 (to a woman) are eulogies on naked feet.

DIALOGUE AND LETTER: EPISTOLARITY UNDERMINED

Philostratus argues first one side of an issue and then the other in order to show his skill at rhetoric, but it is precisely this skill that tempts him away from a believable epistolary framework and into the related mode of dialogue. In another sophistic sequence, Philostratus juxtaposes three letters on the ugliness of new beard growth on the face of an *eromenos* (13, 14, 58) with one perversely stating just the opposite (15). The letter in praise of facial hair opens with a direct question to his beloved which both brings immediacy to the situation and challenges the epistolary fiction (*Letter* 15): "Why do you point to your beard, my boy?" This explicit address, while it conveniently introduces the addressee, asks us to imagine a momentary gesture as the inspiration for Philostratus' written response. It is highly unlikely that Philostratus would observe his beloved point to his beard and not answer in person, but rush home to write down his answer. There is no distance, no obvious block to communication, no clear motivation for a letter here. The opening line leads us to assume a reported dialogue, with the respondent's words suppressed, rather than a letter.

In *Letter* 15 scholarly expertise is combined with dialogue-like immediacy. Philostratus turns yet again to Homer for support for his own opinions: "even the poet Homer calls the boy with new down on his chin the loveliest."[9] He speculates that the epic poet must have experienced this himself in order to write about it, touching and kissing the beard of the boy he loved. Thus Homer, too, is drawn willy-nilly into the real-life event unfolding on the page, made to seem present in flesh and blood. Next it is the beloved's turn again to be invoked. Philostratus argues sophistically that his beloved used to be somewhat womanish with his smooth, soft cheeks; now that he shows his first down, he is more manly and therefore more perfect. At this point Philostratus again, as in the opening lines, reacts to his beloved's movements behind the scenes: "but what [do you mean]? Did you want to be no different from a eunuch?" The letter ends with criticism of that "disfigured breed." In attempting to make his epistolary situation vivid, incorporating interjected voices and reactions, Philostratus effectively

---

[9] *Il.* 24.348; *Od.* 10.279.

destroys the epistolary illusion, and turns his letter into a dialogue. A letter is meant to make those absent present, but this letter takes that task to an extreme, and deconstructs the genre in the process.

Two other letters follow the pattern just described, approximating dialogue rather than written text. In *Letter* 25, Philostratus writes to a woman whose beauty is obscured when she becomes angry.[10] He starts by telling her that yesterday he found her in a rage and thought he was looking at another woman. He urges her to be calm (*Letter* 25):

Don't be harsh or furious, and don't steal away your beauty or take away your own roses, the ones that bloom in the eyes of you beautiful women. And if you don't believe what I say, take your mirror and look how your face has changed. Well done, you have listened to my advice.[11]

With that final sentence, we are meant to imagine the unnamed woman, holding the letter in one hand, using the other hand to take up her mirror; as she acknowledges to herself that her angry face is indeed unbecoming, she takes Philostratus' advice and relaxes her scowl. But in the context of letter writing, we must not imagine an instantaneous reaction from the writer, who is meant to be waiting to hear from his beloved at some distance, even if it is just outside her front door. Either Philostratus is merely imagining that she has taken his advice, and congratulates her on that assumption, or he has once more broken the epistolary illusion in his eagerness to move the action forward.

In *Letter* 28, Philostratus again writes to seduce a beloved woman, this time begging her not to spurn his petition in spite of his low social status. Halfway through the letter, he suggests a course of action (*Letter* 28):

Come now, if this seems like a good idea to you, let's settle the matter with an agreement: either let's both stay here or let's go away from here together. You don't agree to this . . .

Philostratus makes a suggestion in his letter and imagines an immediate reaction from his beloved; this, of course, could happen only if the two were face-to-face, not exchanging letters regulated

---

[10] For a similar sentiment, see Philostratus *Letter* 53; Aristaenetus *Letter* 1.17: "if you are furious, you become less beautiful;" also Ovid *Ars Am.* 3.507–8.

[11] Some of the manuscripts finish with, "For you hated yourself, or feared yourself, or didn't recognize yourself, or changed your mind."

by the "real" time of composition, delivery, and reception. By including an immediate reaction on the part of his internal reader, Philostratus has the opportunity to consider the issue from yet another angle, to invent a new line of persuasion. The strong temptation of rhetorical and logical display pulls him away from epistolary verisimilitude and into the sphere of dialogue.

THE "GROTESQUE"

Philostratus' attempts to add vividness to his letters lead him into the realm of dialogue, but also push him in the direction of emotional outbursts in his letters that strike the reader as odd in a written context. This, combined with the peculiar elements of masochism and fetishism in Philostratus' work, sets him apart again from his contemporaries Aelian and Alciphron. In *Letter* 18, he suggests that a boy whose sandal pinches him would be better off walking barefoot, and to convince him, Philostratus turns to a listing motif. He brings in a battery of barefoot heroes: Diogenes, Crates, Ajax, Achilles, and of course Jason with his one sandal. The letter recommends that nothing should come between the boy's naked feet and the earth, that the very dust will welcome his steps, and that "we" shall all kiss his footprints. The last lines take the letter out of its mode of advice and so far into ecstatic praise that we seem to be reading a hymn or ode (*Letter* 18):

Oh perfect pattern of most dearly beloved feet! Oh strange new flowers! Oh plants of the earth! Oh kiss left lying on the ground!

The women in *Letters* 36 and 37 are treated similarly. Ideally, says Philostratus, they would be wholly naked all the time, but barring that, he prefers them to reject shoes, socks, and foot rings. They are encouraged by their own catalogue of barefoot heroines: Thetis of the silver feet, naked Aphrodite, the daughters of Leucippus. They are to keep their feet naked and ready for those who might want to kiss them, walking softly and leaving a true footprint on the ground behind them, thus pleasing also the earth with their "kisses." *Letter* 37 ends again ecstatically, but this time with an added twist (*Letter* 37):

Oh unchained feet! Oh liberated beauty! Oh three times happy me and blessed too, if only you should tread on me!

The lover begs to be stepped on by the naked and beautiful foot of his beloved.[12] Elsewhere he asks his beloved to torture, maim, and even kill him, all in the name of love. A boy who scorns him is invited to pick up a sword and stab him (5): "I yearn (ἐπιθυμῶ) even for a wound." He offers to take an arrow in battle for one (7) and to hang himself for another if it will prove his love (57): "I am ready to die if that is your command." To a woman he writes that he is prepared to suffer beatings, to run through fire, to commit suicide for her love (23), and again begs to be touched, even if it is with a sword (47). He sums it up in *Letter* 48: "I am very happy in my misery" (καὶ πάνυ χαίρω τῇ κακοπραγίᾳ). This is an angle of erotic persuasion unexplored in any other love letter collections we have encountered thus far, and one difficult to analyze. Philostratus appears to present himself overcome by love, turning to any method to get a reaction from his beloved. His letters are pleas for attention, whether positive or negative. In this way, the letters hope to sustain the relationship, and, indirectly, the correspondence. The beloved is invited to respond, even if it is just with a command to die. Philostratus' erotic desperation is echoed by his eagerness to continue to write, to debate, to argue, and to persuade.

"FOR I HAVE USED THE APPLE AS A LETTER, TOO"

Philostratus equates the freedom to write to his beloved with the freedom to love, as we saw in *Letter* 39, and hopes that his beloved will either allow him to continue to write, or allow him to be in her presence, even if she wishes only to harm him. One last example from Philostratus' collection, which we have encountered before in chapter 5, takes the bold step of asking the beloved to write back; it also self-consciously includes within its lines references to two further letters. Here is *Letter* 62 in full:[13]

But when Alexander was judging the goddesses, the woman from Sparta was not yet present; for if she had been, he would have voted her alone beautiful, the one he himself desired. So since then he made an error in judgment, now I will set it straight. Do not fight or quarrel with one another, goddesses! For look here, I have the apple. Take it, fair one, con-

---

[12] See *Anacreontic* 22: "I wish I were a sandal, if only you would step on me."
[13] I have also discussed this letter in Rosenmeyer (1996) 9–31.

quer the goddesses, and read the inscription. For I have used the apple as a letter, too. The other was an apple of Eris ("Discord"), this one of Eros; the other was silent, but this one speaks. Don't throw it away, don't eat it! For not even in war is an ambassador thus abused. What, then, have I written on it? It will speak for itself: "Euippe, I love you." Read it and write underneath: "and I you." The apple has room to receive those letters too.

Philostratus opens his letter in the mythological past, referring to the judgment of Paris. He introduces himself as the new "Paris," and addresses the goddesses in his letter. This immediately challenges the epistolary situation in which his beloved is meant to read these words and act as the central addressee. But the letter goes on to return to his "fair one" as the focus. Yet before his encouragement of his beloved, he draws attention to himself with an ἰδού. "Look!" he says, "I am holding the apple." This word is borrowed from the sphere of immediacy. If the woman reads the letter, surely she cannot see him in the action he describes unless he stands in her presence, and if he stands in her presence, he has no excuse to write a letter. Again, he could be inviting her to imagine him in this position, but the deictic term is jarring in an epistolary context.

Next Philostratus hands the apple to his beloved, explicitly calling it a letter. One could ask whether Philostratus is deliberately straining the category "letter," as did Callimachus and Heliodorus, or just insouciantly treating it as a mode which allows him to show off his skill in scene-sketching in miniature, without caring too much about epistolary plausibility. In the convention of letters accompanying gifts, we could imagine that Philostratus sends the written letter and the apple-letter at the same time, and that his written letter functions as an explanation of the enclosed gift. The way *Letter* 62 unfolds, we see the series of imperatives – "take it ... conquer ... and read the letters on it" – as referring to two separate and parallel items, letter and apple. But the written letter is then usurped by the apple-letter. Philostratus tries to control his beloved's reading of the apple by his explanatory and directing letter, but he directs her attention solely to the apple.

We are warned that this is no ordinary apple; rather, it is a letter with a voice of its own: "it speaks" (φθέγγεται). But its speech is indirect, reported by Philostratus in the explanatory letter. "What, then, have I written on it?," he asks his beloved, interrupt-

ing the presentation. "It will speak for itself" (αὐτὸ ἐρεῖ). Philostratus claims that the apple-letter will speak for itself, but of
course the apple is able to communicate only through a reader,
and since the letter writer has not yet sent his letter, the only
reader available here is the writer himself. The double level of
quoting – "my letter says that my other letter says the following
..." – appears to add authority, but really shows how Philostratus
tries to manipulate his reader by not just one letter, but by two
interwoven epistolary sources.

What the apple says is necessarily (given the physical restraints
of the surface) brief and to the point: "Euippe, I love you." This is
the only instance where we are given the name of an "unnamed"
beloved, in this letter within a letter. The personal name anchors
the letter, particularizes the situation, while the unnamed *ego* keeps
the epistolary illusion of intimacy. The apple begs for an immediate response to this declaration. Euippe is invited to write two
words in response, on a "tablet" already provided: the apple itself.
We can assume that she can "throw away" the written letter as
long as she sends back the apple, filled up with the words Philostratus provides her. Euippe should write underneath his words
"and I you" (κἀγὼ σέ). Her words depend entirely on his: he has
supplied the name (Euippe) and the verb, the all-important "I
love" (φιλῶ). Her response requires the minimum of effort, just a
completion of the formula. Philostratus tries to place one inscription close to the other so that his declaration can control hers. But
how do we know to whom the "you" (σέ) in question really refers?
Why doesn't Philostratus ask her to use his name in the response?
Perhaps in trying to minimize his beloved's effort at writing, he
reflects her own hesitation; writing "and I you" may be the written
equivalent of Euippe's holding her fingers crossed behind her back:
she commits to love, but the formula may be interpreted differently by different readers, and she can easily undo the promise.

I pointed out above that *Letter* 62 is the only erotic letter in
Philostratus' collection that names the beloved. Let me conclude
this chapter with some brief comments on the identity of the letter
writer, not in an attempt to solve the notoriously complex issue of
the "real" Philostratus, but rather to observe his method of con-
structing a self within the epistolary collection. We have observed
how willing the narrator is to argue either side of a case, to adapt
his arguments to suit the situation. This verbal flexibility, or rhe-

torical promiscuity, combined with his stated allegiance in *Letter* 73 to the sophist Gorgias, places him firmly in the mainstream of the Second Sophistic authors. But within the erotic letters, Philostratus several times emphasizes his status as an outsider, a foreigner in exile (e.g. 8, 28, 39). What could have been a reasonable excuse for writing – "I am a foreigner and therefore write from afar" – turns into an attitude – "I am a foreigner in exile in your town." In *Letter* 8 (to a boy), he begins:

Do not be amazed if I, a foreigner, love you, for eyes may not be convicted of being foreign ... no, both to foreigner and to citizens they are the messengers of the soul.

In *Letter* 28 (to a woman), he again emphasizes the irrelevance of a person's birth status:

A beautiful woman should draw up a catalogue of lovers on the basis of their character, not of birth status, since even a stranger may prove to be a decent person, while a legitimate citizen may turn out to be evil ... If the fact that I am a foreigner does not keep me from being in love, please do not let it stop you from having a love affair.

Both letters turn to catalogues to prove their point, listing names of happy matches between local and foreign individuals: Hyllus and Herakles, Polycrates and Smerdies, Helen and Paris, Andromeda and Perseus, and so forth. But *Letter* 28 takes the issue beyond that of love's boundaries to political borders. Why should love allow legislators to impose limits, when Eros is stronger than any mortal force?

For what indeed are the countries other than worthless measurements done by narrow-minded legislators who circumscribe their own holdings with borders and gates, in order that we may be crowded together in goodwill, hesitating to transgress the rule book of love of one's own country?

This outburst, quickly abandoned for more conventional lover's talk, may imply that Philostratus views himself in this collection as a citizen of the world, that his writing is his passport, and that *eros* should be the social leveler in the circles in which he moves. Elsewhere he argues that poverty, much like foreign birth, should not stand in the way of love (7, 23). Philostratus never reveals his national origins or present location. *Letter* 8 speaks of foreign gods: "Foreign is Asclepius to the Athenians and Zeus to us;" the tantalizing "us" in this context tells us only that the narrator refers to himself as a non-Athenian, perhaps (at this point) a Roman. Philostratus' letters are much less "Athenian" than those of Alciphron or even Aelian, with his "Athenian farmers." Rather his love letters are disassociated from place and time. His literary examples support this, plucked from the storehouse of myth and the pages of Homer, as opposed to Alciphron's clear identification with the literature and society of fourth-century Athens.

It is difficult to say why Philostratus chose to portray himself as an impoverished foreigner in his erotic letters. Such a posture appears not to facilitate his erotic endeavors, and, since he is exiled, it serves no purpose in setting up a physical distance between writer and addressee that would add both to the tension and to the realism of the fictional epistolary situation. But it is remarkable, in the Second Sophistic culture of literary and oratorical display, that the author presents himself in this collection as unassisted by political connections, accident of birth, or financial status. He is defined only by his skill at writing, and works that much harder to prove himself the cleverest writer in (presumably) an adopted language. The success of his letter writing will win him not only true love but lasting artistic fame. But the letter, that most intimate of genres, gives us no real insight into the historical identity of this Philostratus.

Throughout this chapter we have witnessed a new development in epistolarity, as the genre begins to be fractured by other modes of writing. Philostratus seems torn between the demands of epistolarity and his own instinct for the rhetoric of dialogue, drama, and encomium. His sophism leads him to abandon the unified collection of letters of Alciphron and Aelian, where the adopted voices function as organizational motifs, for a series of individual messages that say whatever it takes to seduce the beloved; yet unlike the collection of Alciphron, we never see any evidence of mutual love or an exchange of letters. Philostratus' own voice does not act as a unifying force, mostly because of the flexibility of his views, his opportunism in the face of *eros*. If we recall the trope that a letter should reflect a man's soul, we will reasonably conclude that Philostratus has the soul of a sophist, and is very much a product of his society. If this is autobiography in letters, it shows a fragmented life and a chameleon-like character. Philostratus' choice of erotic letters provides him with an excellent medium for the constant reinvention of himself. But his decision to write all the letters in his own voice, unlike Aelian's and Alciphron's attribution of different opinions to different speakers, challenges our own flexibility as readers: we enjoy each erotic letter as a miniature masterpiece of persuasion, yet stumble over our ability to read what appear to be self-contradictory letters in a sequence as part of a collection. We have come a long way, and not just in time, from the role of the letter in Homer and Euripides, where a single letter could have the power of life or death over a person; when Philostratus speaks of torture and death in his letters, it is the metaphorical torture of a person in love, and the lover's own death-wish.

Afterword

The epistolographers of the Second Sophistic whom we have studied in the last two sections of the book by no means mark the end of the tradition of imaginative letter writing that we have traced since Homer. In fact, the tradition survives and flourishes for another five hundred years, first in the hands of Aristaenetus, writing in the fifth century CE, and then of Theophylactus of Simocatta, writing in the seventh century CE.

The first letter in Aristaenetus' collection of two books is sent from Ἀρισταίνετος to Φιλόκαλος.[1] Most scholars suspect that the writer of *Letter* 1, whose name means "Worthy of the Best Praise," is as fictional as his addressee, "Lovebeautiful." Fortunately, enough details emerge in the letters to assign this epistolographer to the fifth century CE, as classical paganism begins to give way to Byzantine Christianity.[2]

Aristaenetus is not as much obsessed with an Attic past as was his predecessor Alciphron, and is less specific about place and time; but he is still defined by a kind of vague Atticizing.[3] His *Letter* 1.5 purports to be a message from Alciphron to Lucian; elsewhere he imitates passages in Achilles Tatius, Menander, Philostratus, Plato, and Homer. Aristaenetus seeks to represent the general ambience of a world still devoted to *eros* and the pursuit of *hetairai*: thus his main themes are jealousy, disappointment, joy, and all the emotional highs and lows of love affairs. In Aristaene-

---

[1] W. G. Arnott, "Pastiche, Pleasantry, Prudish Eroticism: the Letters of 'Aristaenetus'," *YCS* 27 (1982) 291–320, esp. 291. The letters are transmitted in a single manuscript that dates from *ca.* 1200.

[2] The evidence is discussed in Arnott (1982) 294–96, and includes references in *Letter* 1.26 to a celebrated mime Caramallus, and to two Romes, a younger (Byzantium) and an older one, as well as linguistic and rhythmical characteristics.

[3] Arnott (1982) 303 points to three rare examples of specific Attic features: Alcibiades' beauty (1.11); the eleven police commissioners (2.22); and the deme Alopeke (1.4).

tus' *Letter* 1.14, when "Lovemoney" tries to convince her musical lover that "no flute will tempt a *hetaira*, no lyre persuade her, in the absence of money," we hear an echo of Alciphron's Petale (*Letter* 4.9), who rejected tears and love poems, and insisted on cash in hand. In Aristaenetus' *Letter* 1.6, a seduced girl writes about a conversation she has with her nurse, which closely resembles Euripides' scene between Phaedra and her nurse in the *Hippolytus*. We have already discussed Aristaenetus' version of Acontius and Cydippe (*Letter* 1.10), in which an apple becomes a love letter; an apple sends a similar message in his *Letter* 1.25, although instead of inscribing it, the lover takes a bite out of it before tossing it to his beloved, who quickly hides it in the folds of her dress.

If many of the letters of Aristaenetus remind us of Alciphron's fourth book, the collection of Theophylactus combines Alciphron's courtesans with Aelian's scribbling farmers, and for good measure adds philosophical letters in the best Cynic and Socratic traditions. We have only scraps of biographical information about Theophylactus. He was apparently born in Egypt, and became a prominent Byzantine scholar, writing eight books of *Histories* dealing with the years 582–602 CE (coinciding with the reign of the Byantine emperor Mauricius) about the relationship between Byzantium and the Turks; he is also said to have written a work on curiosities from the natural world. His eighty-five prose *Letters* are considered a work of his youth.[4] His work is divided into three kinds of letters: philosophical musings on how to live one's life and how to solve ethical problems; letters from farmers reflecting daily life on the farm; and erotic letters of the demi-monde. The sequences are strictly ordered around an alternation of each kind: first a philosophical letter, then a rustic, then an erotic one, the pattern repeating twenty-eight times.[5]

I mention these later authors in passing in order to point to the quantity of material that remains for discussion on the subject of fictional letter writing, material just outside the confines of the "classical world," but very much part of the same literary tradition. At the same time, the Christian letter writers were active,

---

[4] L. J. Engels and H. Hofmann, *Neues Handbuch der Litteraturwissenschaft, vol. 4: Spätantike* (Wiesbaden 1997) 647.
[5] See Kytzler (1967) 299.

many of whose letters, while not fictional in the same way that a letter by Alciphron may be termed "fictional," use identical epistolary tropes. Thus St. Ambrose dictates part of his letter to a scribe, but then turns to his own handwriting for the last section, which is meant for Emperor Theodosius' eyes only. St. Jerome complains that a rushed messenger forces him to cut his letter short. Sidonius describes a country party to his friend Donidius, complete with banquets, entertainments, and baths, that rivals Alciphron's rustic orgy (*Letter* 4.13), and finishes as follows:

> You would have a great story if I turned the page and continued on the other side; but I am always ashamed to disfigure the back of a letter with an inky pen. Besides, I am on the point of leaving here, and hope, by Christ's grace, that we shall meet very shortly.[6]

Sidonius' teasing closure reminds the reader of several themes we have discussed throughout the book. He refers to the physical constraints of the page as an excuse to stop writing: he claims not to have enough paper, to hesitate to "disfigure" the back of the page with his inky pen. He also hopes to replace written words with oral communication, to meet up with his addressee so that he can finish the story in Donidius' presence. The letter is a fine medium *in absentia*, but Sidonius is about to visit his friend in person. Thus, to reverse Ovid's phrasing, just as letters used to carry back and forth their silent voices, soon their tongues will perform the task of paper and hands (*Trist.* 5.13.27–30).

Each stage in the history of letter writing in the ancient world reveals the tension between the utter conventionality of epistolography and the specific characteristics of any given cultural and historical context. I have tried to show how certain aspects of fictional letters remain constant: the allegiance to "real" epistolary convention including a concern with sustaining epistolary verisimilitude, the awareness of multiple audiences, and the knowledge that one can reinvent oneself with each new page, for example. At the same time, as the letter form reappears in a multitude of genres throughout literary history, each new manifestation explores different angles of the letter's flexibility.

In the classical period, Herodotus used letters to enliven his narrative, Thucydides to support his historical arguments; both

---

[6] These examples are taken from D. Brooke, *Private Letters, Pagan and Christian* (London 1929) 151–52, 154–55, 175–77.

included letters as external reassurance, to persuade their readers of the authority and integrity of their work. Euripides turned to the letter as a way to bring on stage a mechanism for change or surprise in an entirely believable and visually effective way, one which bypasses the usual directness of dramatic dialogue. The letter itself, when carried on stage, stands in for an actor coming forth to divulge a new wrinkle in the plot, whether a short-cut or a complication. Kinetic letters further the plot by misdirection or by providing true information unknown up to that point. The letter is read out loud for the sake of the external audience, but the implication is always that its contents are private and possibly dangerous. Accordingly, letters on stage are more often than not in the hands of women, because the entire arena of intrigue, for which letters provide the best means of communication, is one associated in tragedy most often with female characters.

In the postclassical periods, including the Hellenistic and imperial ages, letters appeared in fictional narratives sometimes still as dangerous messages with the power to change a person's life, and at other times simply as bits of useful information. The novelists most closely imitated Euripides in their incorporation of letters into their texts; in this case, instead of bypassing dialogue, the letters function as intermediaries in love affairs between young people often separated by great distances. Here we shamelessly read over the shoulder of the addressee, not waiting for the letter to be read aloud to an internal character. The adventures of the lovers in the novels also frequently involved one partner assuming the other had been killed; in that case, a letter could announce the survival of the beloved while playing with an ever-present anxiety about epistolary authenticity: calling attention to familiar handwriting, summarizing experiences that only they had shared. This last aspect also allows the author to vary a first- or third-person narrative and the narrative pace: the letter could cover a great deal of ground in a few paragraphs.

The novel's enjoyment of the letter is connected with its general interest in intertextuality and allusiveness. Other prose fictions of the same era shared those interests and used letters in a similar fashion. The most varied use of epistolary material is found in the *Alexander Romance*, where letters appear as the containers for Alexander's military commands, challenges to his enemies or demands for tribute, diary-like travelogues, and even a last will. Alexander is depicted as a master letter writer, but one trapped by his own dependence on epistolarity; thus, when his enemies write back, he is forced to argue paradoxically against the power of words, scorning their letters as empty and powerless. We also confront here the familiar conundrum of the letter as an impediment to action: as long as Alexander writes, he cannot engage his enemies in action; and conversely, when he enters into the presence of his correspondent, all letters cease. The same is true, of course, for the heroic Chion, but for a slightly different reason: his letters home stop when he decides to forgo epistolary plotting for action, and is killed in the act of tyrannicide.

In all the works mentioned thus far except the last, letters appeared primarily embedded in other narratives and genres: historiography, tragedy, the novel, the romance. With Chion, we encountered a true epistolary novel with a complete and sustained story told entirely in letter form. But all the epistolary collections, including the *pseudonymoi*, share an assumption of historicity and accuracy, either by choosing historical figures to work with, or by setting their stories in familiar historical milieus. The letter was imagined as a document, an artifact that guaranteed some sense of authenticity.

The last section of this study turned to a totally different kind of epistolary experiment, one in which the authorial voice and the addressee were a complete fabrication, unrelated for the most part to any historical or previous literary reality. The imperial epistolographers thus freed themselves to write wholly creatively, although still based on the society and customs of their literary ancestors in fourth-century Athens. Alciphron, Aelian, and Philostratus turned to letter collections as an exercise in "miniaturism," a game of endless variation on a theme. Many of their letters stood alone as glimpses into urban or rustic lower-class life; others were paired responses, or used *topoi* that reappeared throughout the series. These letters were masterpieces of rhetorical display, paeans to classicism; their wickedly inventive and meaningful addressees' names are tributes to the human imagination. Finally, Philostratus capped the development of the epistolary tradition in this period by introducing his own persona as letter writer, unmediated by other assumed voices or identities. His focus on himself was even more clearly defined by the almost total anonymity of his fictional addressees.

In the beginning of this study, I suggested that the letter Proetus gives to Bellerophon could be seen as introducing three major themes of epistolary writing: the connection between letter writing and treachery; the association of women with erotic letters; and the category of letters as casual conversation – the letter of recommendation or friendship that Bellerophon assumed Proetus' letter to be. These themes reappear in all the epistolary authors we have discussed. Thus, Euripidean letters combined the first two elements, as deception, murder, and sex were translated into written documents read aloud on stage. The historians focused mainly on the first element of epistolary deception, probably because women played a less important role in military and political spheres. The novel, too, embedded letters full of trickery, death-threats, and a full range of eroticism, from love letters between separated couples to invitations for illicit affairs.

We have read so many stories of the dangerous and wicked uses to which letters may be put that it is worth pointing out that there are instances in antiquity of forged letters being used sympathetically. In Plutarch's *Life of Theseus*, we are told that Ariadne was so disconsolate at losing her beloved that the women of Naxos invented messages from Theseus to comfort her as she lay dying in childbirth:

The women of the island then took care of Ariadne, trying to comfort her since she was miserable in her loneliness, and brought her forged letters (γράμματα πλαστά), pretending they had been written to her by Theseus...

The novel, too, could use a letter somewhat dishonestly to comfort and calm: at the end of Chariton's story, Callirhoe wrote to Dionysius a message that explained her choice to return to her husband, but also carefully worded her letter in such a way as to allow Dionysius to believe that she still loved him, and would remember him forever. Dionysius keeps the letter as small comfort, but Chariton keeps his wife.

In classical Greek authors, then, and in the ancient Greek novelists, the first and second elements of Proetus' letter are imitated and developed. These authors share an interest in the potential of any letter to deceive, and the related scope for use and misuse of writing in an erotic context, in which lover and beloved may be separated and turn to letters for communication. The third and

missing element of Proetus' letter, namely the letter as casual conversation, is developed first by the epigrammatists of the Hellenistic period, when the more frequent use of letters in daily life may
have begun to "normalize" the nature of the written text. This
trend continues in the letters of Alexander, the pseudonymous
letter writers, and Chion, who all treat letters as relatively
straightforward pieces of information: items of news, letters home
to the family, requests for gifts, and so forth. Alexander varies his
epistolary styles between civil epistolary form and bombastic military threats, but remains within the framework of the letter as
"conversation." Even Chion, who refers jokingly to Bellerophon in
the context of a letter he writes on behalf of a man who seeks an
introduction to his father back home in Heraclea, admits no real
echoes of the Homeric passage. His letter may deceive, since it is a
false letter of recommendation, but there is no sense of mystery or
supernatural power in the letter, and this is no matter of life and
death, especially since he alerts both his father and the external
reader to the game being played: the false friend is publically
shamed, not murdered.

The shift that begins in the Hellenistic period continues in the
authors of the Second Sophistic, who place their fictional letters in
the hands of the non-élite: farmers, fishermen, parasites. We have
come far from Euripides' dramatic representation of an illiterate
herdsman trying to read the name on the sail of Theseus' ship, who
describes the alphabetic letters one by one as if they were living
creatures.[7] Letters now are put to mundane uses, the equivalent
of conversation, τὸ λαλεῖν, as the rustics complain about their
poverty and the parasites about their empty bellies. Not even the
courtesans' letters reflect any serious trace of treachery or sexual
danger. By this time, fictitious letters appear as literary entertainment for an audience that may have grown up practicing the letter
form in school exercises; the challenge for these authors and readers is one of thematic variation and archaizing wit.

But I do not mean to imply that the development of the letter as
literary device is either unidirectional or totally consistent. Much
like the complicated ordering of the letters of Phalaris, the history
of imaginative letters in ancient Greek literature is not a straight
line from mystification to "normalization." The genre of fictional

---

[7] Eur. *Theseus* 382 Nauck 2nd edn.

letters always contains within itself at least one and often all three elements of Proetus' letter, and it is merely a question of degree as to which element is emphasized at any given moment. As stated above, Aristaenetus' *Letter* 1.6 recalls a scene from Euripides' *Hippolytus*, complete with dangerous sexuality and the threat of broken confidences; yet these authors write separated by some eight centuries. In between these two, and composing in Latin rather than Greek, Ovid takes to new heights the connection between women, *eros*, and letters in his *Heroides*. In what I have argued above, finally, I hope to have shown that Ovid was not alone in "inventing" the imaginative letter in ancient literature.

Bibliography

Aalders, G. J. D. (1971) "Political Thought and Political Programs in the Platonic Epistles." *Pseudepigrapha* 1 (Entretiens sur l'antiquité classique, Fondation Hardt 18). Geneva, 147–75.

Albert, P. (1896) *Le Genre épistolaire chez les anciens*. Paris.

Altman, J. G. (1977) "The 'Triple Register': Introduction to Temporal Complexity in the Letter-Novel." *L'Esprit créateur* 17: 302–10.

(1982) *Epistolarity: Approaches to a Form*. Columbus, OH.

Anderson, G. (1982) *Eros Sophistes: Ancient Novelists at Play*. Chico, CA.

(1984) *Ancient Fiction: The Novel in the Greco-Roman World*. London.

(1986) *Philostratos*. London.

(1993) *The Second Sophistic*. London.

Anderson, W. S. (1973) "The *Heroides*," in J. W. Binns, ed., *Ovid*. London and Boston, 49–83.

Arndt, C. (1994) "Antiker und neuzeitlicher Briefroman", in N. Holzberg, *Der griechische Briefroman: Gattungstypologie und Textanalyse*. Tübingen, 53–84.

Arnott, W. G. (1973) "Imitation, Variation, Exploitation: A Study in Aristaenetus." *GRBS* 14: 197–211.

(1982) "Pastiche, Pleasantry, Prudish Eroticism: The Letters of 'Aristaenetus'." *YCS* 27: 291–320.

(1996) ed. and tr., *Menander*, 2 vols. Cambridge, MA.

Austin, J. L. (1962) *How To Do Things With Words*. Oxford.

Babbitt, F. C. (1931) tr., *Plutarch's Moralia*, vol. III. Cambridge, MA.

Baca, A. R. (1969) "Ovid's Claim to Originality and *Heroides* 1." *TAPA* 100: 1–10.

Bakhtin, M. (1981) *The Dialogic Imagination: Four Essays*. Austin, TX.

Barchiesi, A. (1993) "Future Reflexive: Two Modes of Allusion and Ovid's *Heroides*." *HSCP* 95: 333–65.

Barnett, R. D. (1948) "Early Greek and Oriental Ivories." *JHS* 68: 1–25.

Barreno, M. I. *et al.* (1975) *The Three Marias: New Portuguese Letters*. trans. H. R. Lane. New York.

Barrett, W. S. (1964) *Euripides Hippolytos*. Oxford.

Barthes, R. (1977) *Fragments d'un discours amoureux*. Paris, trans. R. Howard, *A Lover's Discourse: Fragments*. New York, 1978.

Bartsch, S. (1989) *Decoding the Ancient Novel: The Reader and the Role of Description in Heliodorus and Achilles Tatius.* Princeton.

Baxter, J. H. (1980) *St. Augustine: Select Letters.* Cambridge, MA and London.

Bellamy, R. (1989) "Bellerophon's Tablet." *CJ* 84: 289–307.

Benner, A. R. and E. H. Fobes (1949) *The Letters of Alciphron, Aelian, and Philostratus.* Cambridge, MA.

Benstock, S. (1991) *Textualizing the Feminine.* Norman, OK.

Bentley, R. (1697) *A Dissertation upon the Epistles of Phalaris, Themistocles, Socrates, Euripides and Others. Reflections upon Ancient and Modern Learning,* 2nd edn. London.

Benveniste, E. (1948) "L'Expression du serment dans la Grèce ancienne." *RHR* 134: 81–94.

Berger, J. (1972) *Ways of Seeing.* London.

Beschorner, A. and S. Merkle (1994) "Der Tyrann und der Dichter," in N. Holzberg, *Der griechische Briefroman.* Tübingen, 116–68.

Bianchetti, S. (1987) *Falaride e Pseudofalaride: Storia e leggenda.* Florence.

Billault, A. (1977) "Les Lettres de Chion d'Heraclée." *REG* 90: 29–37.

Bing, P. (1988) *The Well-Read Muse.* Göttingen.

Blakemore Evans, G. (1974) ed., *The Riverside Shakespeare.* Boston.

Bonner, C. (1909) "On Certain Supposed Literary Relationships." *CP* 4: 32–44, 276–90.

Bowersock, G. W. (1969) *Greek Sophists in the Roman Empire.* Oxford.

and E. L. Bowie (1985) "Philostratus and the Second Sophistic," and "Between Philosophy and Rhetoric," in P. Easterling and B. M. W. Knox, eds., *Cambridge History of Classical Literature,* vol. 1. New York, 655–58, 679–82.

Bowie, E. L. (1970) "Greeks and their Past in the Second Sophistic." *Past and Present* 46: 3–41.

(1978) "Apollonius of Tyana: Tradition and Reality." *ANRW* II xvi 2: 1652–99.

(1985) "The Greek Novel," in P. Easterling and B. M. W. Knox, eds., *Cambridge History of Classical Literature,* vol. 1. New York, 683–99.

(1994) "The Readership of Greek Novels in the Ancient World," in J. Tatum, ed., *The Search for the Ancient Novel.* Baltimore, 435–59.

and S. J. Harrison (1993) "The Romance of the Novel." *JRS* 83: 159–78.

Bowman, A. K. and G. Woolf (1994) eds., *Literacy and Power in the Ancient World.* Cambridge.

Brinkman, A. (1909) "Der älteste Briefsteller." *RhM* 64: 310–17.

Brooke, D. (1929) *Private Letters, Pagan and Christian.* London.

Brownlee, M. S. (1990) *The Severed Word.* Princeton.

Bruno, O. (1967) "L'epistola 92 dello Pseudo-Falaride e i Nostoi di Stesicoro." *Helikon* 7: 323–56.

Bungarten, J. J. (1967) *Menanders und Glykeras Briefe bei Alkiphron.* Bern.

Burian, P. (1985) ed., *Directions in Euripidean Criticism.* Durham, NC.

Burnett, A. P. (1971) *Catastrophe Survived*. Oxford.

Burstein, S. (1989) "*SEG* 33.802 and the Alexander Romance." *ZPE* 77: 275–76.

Cairns, F. (1969) "Propertius 1.18 and Callimachus, *Acontius and Cydippe*." *CR* 19: 131–34.

Calame, C. (1983) "Entre oralité et écriture." *Semiotica* 43: 245–73.

 (1993) "Rythme, voix et mémoire de l'écriture en Grèce classique," in R. Pretagostini, ed., *Tradizione e Innovazione nella cultura greca da Omero all' età ellenistica: Scritti in onore di Bruno Gentili*. Rome, 785–99.

Cameron, A. (1995) *Callimachus and His Critics*. Princeton.

Campbell, D. A. (1967) *Greek Lyric Poetry*. London.

Carradine, D. and S. Price (1987) eds., *Rituals of Royalty: Power and Ceremonial in Traditional Societies*. Cambridge.

Carson, A. (1986) *Eros the Bittersweet*. Princeton.

Cartledge, P. A., P. Millett, and S. von Reden (1998) eds., *Kosmos*. Cambridge.

Castle, T. (1982) *Clarissa's Ciphers: Meaning and Disruption in Richardson's "Clarissa."* Ithaca.

Chadwick, J. (1973) "The Berezan Lead Letter." *PCPS* 199: 35–37.

Clark, K. (1956) *The Nude: A Study in Ideal Form*. Princeton.

Clay, D. (1989) "A Lost Epicurean Community." *GRBS* 30: 313–35.

Cole, S. G. (1981) "Could Greek Women Read and Write?" *Women's Studies* 8: 129–55; repr. in H. Foley, ed., *Reflections of Women in Antiquity*. London, 219–45.

Coletti, M. L. (1962) "Aconzio e Cidippe in Callimaco e in Ovidio." *RCCM* 4: 294–303.

Cotton, H. (1984) "Greek and Latin Epistolary Formulae: Some Light on Cicero's Letter Writing." *AJP* 105: 409–25.

Courtney, E. (1965) "Ovidian and non-Ovidian *Heroides*." *BICS* 12: 63–66.

Criscuolo, U. (1970) "Cratete di Tebe e la tradizione cinica." *Maia* 22: 360–67.

Cugusi, P. (1970) ed., *Epistolographi Latini Minores*, 2 vols. Turin.

 (1983) *Evoluzione e forme dell' epistolografia latina nella tarda repubblica nei primi due secoli dell' impero*. Rome.

Cunningham, I. C. (1971) *Herodae Mimiambi*. Oxford.

Daly, L. W. (1952) "Callimachus and Catullus." *CP* 47: 97–99.

Damon, C. (1997) *The Mask of the Parasite: a Pathology of Roman Patronage*. Ann Arbor.

Davidson, J. N. (1997) *Courtesans and Fishcakes*. New York.

Day, A. A. (1938) *The Origins of Latin Love Elegy*. Oxford.

Day, G. (1987) *From Fiction to the Novel*. London.

Day, R. A. (1966) *Told in Letters: Epistolary Fiction Before Richardson*. Ann Arbor.

Deferrari, R. J. (1926–39) trans., *St. Basil: the Letters*, 4 vols. London and New York.

Deissmann, A. (1923) *Licht vom Osten*, 4th edn. Tübingen, trans. L. Strachan, and repr. as *Light from the Ancient East*, 1927, NY.

Derrida, J. (1975) "The Purveyor of Truth." tr. W. Domingo *et al.*, *YFS* 52: 31–113.

(1987) *The Post Card: from Socrates to Freud and Beyond.* trans. A. Bass. Chicago.

De Staël, A.-L.-G. (1894) *De L'Allemagne*, 5 vols. Paris.

De Stefani, E. L. (1901) "Per il testo delle epistole di Eliano." *SIFC* 9: 479–88.

(1912) "La Fonte delle epistole III e VI di Eliano." *SIFC* 19: 8–10.

Detienne, M. (1992) ed., *Les Savoirs de l'écriture en Grèce ancienne.* Lille.

Dietzler, A. (1933) *Die Akontios-Elegie des Kallimachos.* Griefswald.

Dihle, A. (1991) *Griechische Literaturgeschichte*, 2nd edn. Munich.

(1994) *Greek and Latin Literature of the Roman Empire.* trans. M. Malzahn. London.

Dilthey, C. (1863) *De Callimachi Cydippa.* Leipzig.

(1884) *Observationum in epistulas heroidum Ovidianas.* Göttingen.

Doenges, N. A. (1981) *The Letters of Themistocles.* New York.

Dörrie, H. (1967) "Die dichterische Absicht Ovids in den *Epistulae Heroidum*." *A&A* 13: 41–55.

(1969) "Krates." *Der Kleine Pauly* 3: 327–28.

(1971) ed., *Epistulae Heroidum.* Berlin.

(1975) "Sokratiker-Briefe." *Der Kleine Pauly* 5: 257–58.

Doty, W. G. (1969) "The Classification of Epistolary Literature." *Catholic Biblical Quarterly* 31: 183–99.

Dowden, K. (1989) tr., *The Alexander Romance*, in B. P. Reardon, *Collected Ancient Greek Novels.* Berkeley, 650–735.

duBois, P. (1988) *Sowing the Body.* Chicago.

DuQuesnay, I. M. Le M. (1979) "From Polyphemus to Corydon," in D. West and T. Woodman, eds., *Creative Imitation and Latin Literature.* Cambridge.

Düring, I. (1951) ed. and tr., *Chion of Heraclea: A Novel in Letters.* Acta Universitatis Gotoburgensis, vol. 57.5.1–123.

Eagleton, T. (1982) *The Rape of Clarissa: Writing, Sexuality, and Class Struggle in Samuel Richardson.* Minneapolis.

Easterling, P. E. (1985a) "Alciphron." *Cambridge History of Classical Literature*, vol. 1. Cambridge, 679–80.

(1985b) "Anachronism in Greek Tragedy." *JHS* 105: 1–10.

and B. M. W. Knox (1985a) "Books and Readers in the Greek World." *Cambridge History of Classical Literature*, vol. 1. Cambridge, 1–41.

and B. M. W. Knox (1985b) eds., *Cambridge History of Classical Literature*, vol. 1. Cambridge.

Egger, B. (1988) "Zu den Frauenrollen im griechischen Roman. Die Frau als Heldin und Leserin," in H. Hofmann, ed. *Groningen Colloquia on the Novel*, vol. 1. Groningen, 33–66.

(1994) "Women and Marriage in the Greek Novels," in J. Tatum, ed., *The Search for the Ancient Greek Novel.* Baltimore, 260–80.

Ehringer, E. (1629) *Themistoclis epistolae Graeco-Latinae a Bibliteca Ehringeriana.* Frankfurt.

Ellendt, F. (1872) *Lexicon Sophocleum.* Berlin.

Elsner, J. (1996a) ed., *Art and Text in Roman Culture.* Cambridge.

(1996b) "Naturalism and the Erotics of the Gaze," in N. B. Kampen, ed., *Sexuality in Ancient Art.* Cambridge, 247–61.

and A. Sharrock (1991) "Re-viewing Pygmalion." *Ramus* 20: 149–82.

Emeljanow, V. E. (1967) "The Letters of Diogenes." Dissertation, Stanford University.

Engels, L. J. and H. Hofmann (1997) eds., *Neues Handbuch der Literaturwissenschaft, vol. 4: Spätantike.* Wiesbaden.

England, E. B. (1886) *The Iphigeneia Among the Tauri of Euripides.* London.

L'Esprit créateur (1977) 17 no. 4 (Winter).

Exler, F. X. (1923) "The Form of the Ancient Greek Letter: A Study in Greek Epistolography." Dissertation, Catholic University of America.

Francklin, T. (1749) *The Epistles of Phalaris.* London.

Friedländer, P. (1948) *Epigrammata: Greek Inscriptions in Verse from the Beginnings to the Persian Wars.* Berkeley.

Frontisi-Ducroux, F. (1996) "Eros, Desire, and the Gaze," in N. B. Kampen, ed., *Sexuality in Ancient Art.* Cambridge, 81–100.

Funaioli, G. (1948) "L'epistola in Grecia e in Roma," in G. Funaioli, ed., *Studi di letteratura antica,* vol. 1. Bologna.

Fusillo, M. (1988) "Textual Patterns and Narrative Situations in the Greek Novel," in H. Hofmann, ed., *Groningen Colloquium on the Novel,* vol. 1. Groningen, 17–31.

(1991) *La Naissance du Roman.* Paris.

Gärtner, H. (1984) ed., *Beiträge zum griechischen Liebesroman.* Hildesheim and New York.

Garrison, E. (1989) "Suicide Notes in Euripides' Hippolytus," in K. Hartigen, ed., *Text and Presentation,* vol. IX. Landham, MD, 73–85.

Gaselee, S. (1947) ed., *Achilles Tacitus.* Cambridge, MA.

Gaudon, S. (1986) "On Editing Victor Hugo's Correspondence." *YFS* 71: 177–98.

Genette, G. (1980) *Narrative Discourse: An Essay in Method,* trans. J. E. Lewin. Ithaca.

(1988) *Narrative Discourse Revisited.* Ithaca.

Gerhard, G. A. (1905) "Untersuchungen zur Geschichte des griechischen Briefes I. Die Anfangsformel." *Philologus* 64: 27–65.

Gigon, O. (1965) "Kynikerbriefe." *Lexicon der Alten Welt.* Zurich.

Gill, C. and T. P. Wiseman (1993) eds., *Lies and Fiction in the Ancient World.* Austin, TX.

Gillis, C. M. (1984) *The Paradox of Privacy: Epistolary Form in "Clarissa."* Gainesville, FL.

Gleason, M. (1995) *Making Men*. Princeton.

Godman, P. and O. Murray (1990) eds., *Latin Poetry and the Classical Tradition*. Oxford.

Goff, B. E. (1990) *The Noose of Words*. Cambridge.

Goldhill, S. (1995) *Foucault's Virginity*. Cambridge.

(1998) "The Seduction of the Gaze: Socrates and his Girlfriends," in P. Cartledge, P. Millett, and S. von Reden, eds., *Kosmos*. Cambridge, 105–24.

Goldsmith, E. (1989) ed., *Writing the Female Voice: Essays on Epistolary Literature*. Boston.

Goldstein, J. A. (1968) *The Letters of Demosthenes*. New York.

Goold, G. P. (1995) *Chariton: Callirhoe*. Cambridge, MA.

Gow, A. S. F. (1965) ed., *Theocritus*, 2 vols. Cambridge.

and D. L. Page (1968) *The Greek Anthology: the Garland of Philip*, 2 vols. Cambridge.

Gratwick, A. S. (1979) "Sundials, Parasites, and Girls from Boeotia." *CQ* 29: 308–23.

Graux, C. (1877) "Chorikios: Apologie des Mimes." *RPh* 1: 209–47.

Grenfell, B. P. and A. S. Hunt (1898) eds., *The Oxyrhynchus Papyri*, vol. 1. London.

Griffin, M. (1989) "Philosophy, Politics, and Politicians at Rome," in M. Griffin and J. Barnes, eds., *Philosophia Togata: Essays on Philosophy and Roman Society*. Oxford, 1–37.

Grube, G. M. A. (1941) *The Drama of Euripides*. London.

(1961) *A Greek Critic: Demetrius on Style*. Phoenix suppl. 4. Toronto.

Gudeman, A. (1894) "Literary Frauds Among the Greeks," in *Classical Studies in Honour of Henry Drisler*. New York, 53–74.

Gulley, N. (1971) "On the Authenticity of the Platonic Epistles." *Pseudepigrapha* 1 (Entretiens sur l'antiquité classique, Fondation Hardt 18). Geneva, 105–30.

Gunderson, E. (1997) "Catullus, Pliny, and Love-Letters." *TAPA* 27: 201–31.

Gunderson, L. L. (1980) *Alexander's Letter to Aristotle about India*. Meisenheim am Glan.

Gutzwiller, K. J. (1998) *Poetic Garlands*. Berkeley.

Hägg, T. (1971) *Narrative Technique in Ancient Greek Romances*. Stockholm.

(1983) *The Novel in Antiquity*. Oxford.

Haight, E. (1955) tr. and ed., *The Life of Alexander of Macedon*. New York.

Hansmann, P. (1989) *Des älteren Philostratos erotische Briefe, nebst den Hetärenbriefen des Alkiphron*. Frankfurt am Main.

Harris, W. V. (1989) *Ancient Literacy*. Cambridge, MA.

Hartog, F. (1980) *Le Miroir d'Hérodote*. Paris.

Harvey, E. D. (1989) "Ventriloquizing Sappho: Ovid, Donne, and the Erotics of the Feminine Voice." *Criticism* 31: 115–38.

Harvey, F. D. (1966) "Literacy in the Athenian Democracy." *REG* 79: 585–635.

Harward, J. (1932) *The Platonic Epistles*. Cambridge.

Harwood, H. (1996) "Sirens and Silenoi: The Paradoxical Encomium from Antiquity to the Renaissance." Dissertation, Yale University.

Havelock, C. M. (1995) *The Aphrodite of Knidos and Her Successors*. Ann Arbor.

Havelock, E. A. (1982) *The Literate Revolution in Greece and its Cultural Consequences*. Princeton.

Heinemann, M. (1910) *Epistulae Amatoriae Quomodo Cohaerent cum Elegiis Alexandrinis*. Strasburg.

Heiserman, A. R. (1977) *The Novel before the Novel*. Chicago.

Hercher, R. (1858–59) ed., *Erotici Scriptores Graeci*, 2 vols. Leipzig.

(1870) "Zu den griechischen Epistolographen." *Hermes* 4: 427–30.

(1873) *Epistolographi Graeci*. Paris, repr. Amsterdam 1965.

Herman, G. (1987) *Ritualised Friendship and the Greek City*. Cambridge.

Herzog, R. (1930) "Griechische Königsbriefe." *Hermes* 65: 455–71.

Heubeck, A. (1979) *Schrift*. Göttingen.

Higbie, C. (1999) "Craterus and the Use of Inscriptions in Ancient Scholarship." *TAPA* 129: 43–83.

Hinck, H. (1869) "Die ἐπιστολιμαῖοι χαρακτῆρες des pseudo-Libanios." *Neue Jahrbücher für Philologie und Pädogogik* 99: 537–62.

Hofman, M. (1935) *Antike Briefe*. Munich.

Holzberg, N. (1986) *Der antike Roman*. Munich.

(1994) *Der griechische Briefroman: Gattungstypologie und Textanalyse*. Tübingen.

(1995) *The Ancient Novel: An Introduction*, trans. C. Jackson-Holzberg. London.

Hooper, F. and M. Schwarz. (1991) *Roman Letters: History from a Personal Point of View*. Detroit.

Hopkinson, N. (1988) *A Hellenistic Anthology*. Cambridge.

Horowitz, L. K. (1981) "The Correspondence of Madame de Sévigné: Letters or Belles-Lettres?" *French Forum* 6: 13–27.

Hout, M. van den (1949) "Studies in Early Greek Letter-Writing." *Mnemosyne* 4th series, vol. 2: 18–41, 138–53.

Howald, Ernst. (1923) *Die Briefe Platons*. Zurich.

Huet, P.-D. (1670) *Traité de l'origine des romans*. Paris.

Huit, C. (1889) "Les Epistolographes grecs." *REG* 2: 149–63.

Hunt, A. S. and C. C. Edgar (1932) trans., *Select Papyri*, vol. 1. Cambridge, MA.

Hunter, R. (1993) "Callimachean Echoes in Catullus 65." *ZPE* 96: 179–82.

Hurwit, J. M. (1990) "The Words in the Image: Orality, Literacy, and Early Greek Art." *Word and Image* 6: 180–97.

Hutchinson, G. O. (1998) *Cicero's Correspondence, A Literary Study*. Oxford.

Isbell, H. (1990) trans., *Ovid: Heroides*. London.

Jackel, S. (1964) *Menandrii Sententiae*. Leipzig.

Jackson, C. N. (1912) "An Ancient Letter-Writer: Alciphron." *Harvard Essays on Classical Subjects*, 69–96.

Jacobson, H. (1971) "Ovid's Briseis: A Study of *Heroides* 3." *Phoenix* 25: 351–56.

(1974) *Ovid's Heroides*. Princeton.

Jacoby, F. (1940–58) ed., *Die Fragmente der griechischen Historiker*. Leipzig.

Jakobson, R. (1960) "Closing Statement: Linguistics and Poetics," in T. A. Sebeok, ed., *Style in Language*. Cambridge, MA, 350–77.

Jameson, F. (1972) *The Prison House of Language*. Princeton.

Jebb, R. (1907) *Essays and Addresses*. Cambridge.

Jedd, S. (1989) *The Violence of Representation*. London.

Jeffery, L. H. (1962) "Writing," in A. J. B. Wace and F. H. Stubbings, eds., *A Companion to Homer*. London, 545–59.

Jensen, K. A. (1989) "Male Models of Feminine Epistolarity; or, How to Write like a Woman in Seventeenth-Century France," in E. C. Goldsmith, ed., *Writing the Female Voice: Essays on Epistolary Literature*. Boston, 25–45.

Johnson, B. (1977) "The Frame of Reference: Poe, Lacan, Derrida." *YFS* 55/56: 457–505.

Johnson, R. (1968) "Anatomy of a Literary Device: the Included Letter." Dissertation, Illinois University.

Johnston, P. A. (1983) "An Echo of Sappho in Catullus 65." *Latomus* 42: 388–94.

Jones, C. P. (1986) *Culture and Society in Lucian*. Cambridge, MA.

Jost, F. (1966) "Le Roman épistolaire et la technique narrative au XVIIIᵉ siècle." *Comparative Literature Studies* 3: 397–427.

(1968) "L'Evolution d'un genre: le roman épistolaire dans les lettres occidentales." *Essais de littérature comparée* 2. Freiburg, 88–179, 380–402.

Kampen, N. B. (1996) ed., *Sexuality in Ancient Art*. Cambridge.

Kamuf, P. (1980) "Writing Like a Woman." in S. McConnell-Ginet, *et al.*, *Women and Language in Literature and Society*. New York, 284–99.

(1982) *Fictions of Feminine Desire: Discourse of Heloise*. Lincoln, NE.

Kany, C. E. (1937) *The Beginnings of the Epistolary Novel in France, Italy, and Spain*. Berkeley.

Kaster, R. A. (1983) "Notes on 'Primary' and 'Secondary' Schools in Late Antiquity." *TAPA* 113: 323–46.

Kauffman, L. S. (1986) *Discourses of Desire: Gender, Genre, and Epistolary Fictions*. Ithaca.

(1992) *Special Delivery: Epistolary Modes in Modern Fiction*. Chicago.

Kaufman, V. (1990) *L'Equivoque épistolaire*. Paris.

Kayser, C. L. (1871) ed., *Flavii Philostrati opera II*. Leipzig.

Kennedy, D. F. (1984) "The Epistolary Mode and the First of Ovid's *Heroides*." *CQ* 34: 413–22.

Kennedy, G. A. (1963) *The Art of Persuasion in Greece*. Princeton.

(1972) *The Art of Rhetoric in the Roman World, 300 BC–AD 300*. Princeton.

(1983) *Greek Rhetoric under Christian Emperors*. Princeton.

Kenney, E. J. (1967) "Liebe als juristisches Problem." *Philologus* 111: 212–32.

(1970) "Love and Legalism: Ovid, *Heroides* 20 and 21." *Arion* 9: 388–414.

(1983) "Virgil and the Elegiac Sensibility." *ICS* 8: 44–59.

Kenyon, F. G. (1931) *Books and Readers in Ancient Greece and Rome*. Oxford.

Keyes, C. W. (1935) "The Greek Letter of Introduction." *AJP* 56: 28–44.

Kim, C.-H. (1972) *Form and Structures of the Familiar Greek Letter of Recommendation*. Missoula, Montana (SBL Diss. Series #4).

Kindstrand, J. F. (1981) *Anacharsis*. Uppsala.

Knox, B. M. W. (1968) "Silent Reading in Antiquity." *GRBS* 9: 421–35.

(1979) *Word and Action: Essays on the Ancient Theater*. Baltimore.

Köhler, L. (1928) "Briefe des Sokrates und der Sokratiker." *Philologus Suppl.* 20.2. Leipzig.

Konstan, D. (1994) *Sexual Symmetry: Love in the Ancient Novel and Related Genres*. Princeton.

(1997) *Friendship in the Classical World*. Cambridge.

Konstan, D. and P. Mitsis (1990) "Chion of Heraclea: A Philosophical Novel in Letters." *Apeiron* 23: 257–79.

Körte, A. and A. Thierfelder (1959) eds., *Menandrii quae supersunt*, 2 vols. Leipzig.

Koskenniemi, H. (1954) "Cicero über die Briefarten (*genera epistularum*)." *Arctos* 1: 97–102.

(1956) *Studien zur Idee und Phraseologie des griechischen Briefes bis 400 n.Chr.* Helsinki.

Kris, E. and O. Kurz (1979) *Legend, Myth, and Magic in the Image of the Artist*. New Haven and London.

Kristeva, J. (1980) *Desire in Language: A Semiotic Approach to Literature and Art*, trans. T. Gora, *et al.* New York.

Kroll, W. (1923) *Catull*. Stuttgart.

Krumbacher, K. (1897) *Geschichte der byzantinischen Litterature*, 2 vols. Munich, repr. New York, 1958.

Kuch, H. (1989) ed., *Der antike Roman*. Berlin.

Kytzler, B. (1967) ed. and tr., *Erotische Briefe der griechischen Antike*. Munich.

Lacan, J. (1972) "Seminar on the Purloined Letter," trans. J. Mehlman. *YFS* 48: 38–72.

La Penna, A. (1963) "La seconda Ecloga e la poesia bucolica di Virgilio." *Maia* 15: 484–92.

Lenardon, R. J. (1961) "Charon, Thucydides, and 'Themistokles." *Phoenix* 15: 28–40.

(1978) *The Saga of Themistocles*. London.

Lentz, T. M. (1989) *Orality and Literacy in Hellenic Greece*. Carbondale, IL.

Lesky, A. (1929) "Alkiphron und Aristainetos." *MVPW* 6: 47–59.

(1966) "Prose Romance and Epistolography," in *A History of Greek Literature*. New York, 857–70.

(1967) tr., *Aristaenetos: Erotische Briefe der griechischen Antike*. Munich.

Lipking, L. I. (1988) *Abandoned Women and the Poetic Tradition*. Chicago.

Littlewood, A. R. (1967) "The Symbolism of the Apple in Greek and Roman Literature." *HSCP* 72: 147–81.

Longo, O. (1977) "Techniche della communicazione e ideologie sociali nella Grecia antica." *QUCC* 27: 63–92.

(1981) *Techniche della communicazione nella Grecia antica*. Naples.

Luck, G. (1961) "Brief und Epistel in der Antike." *Das Altertum* 7: 77–84.

Macleod, M. D. (1872–87) ed., *Luciani Opera*. Oxford.

Malherbe, A. J. (1977) *The Cynic Epistles*. Missoula, MT.

(1988) *Ancient Epistolary Theorists*. (SBL 19) Atlanta, GA.

(1991) "Seneca on Paul as a Letter Writer," in B. A. Pearson, ed., *The Future of Early Christianity: Essays in Honor of Helmut Köster*. Minneapolis.

Marcks, J. F. (1883) *Symbola critica ad epistolographos graecos*. Bonn.

Martin, H.-J. (1994) *The History and Power of Writing*. Chicago.

Mazal, O. (1971) ed., *Aristaenetus: Epistularum libri duo*. Stuttgart.

McConnell-Ginet, S. (1980) *et al.* eds., *Women and Language in Literature and Society*. New York.

McKeon, M. (1994) *The Origins of the English Novel, 1600–1740*. Baltimore.

Meltzer, F. (1982) "Laclos' Purloined Letters." *Critical Inquiry* 8: 515–29.

Merkelbach, R. (1954) "Die Quellen des griechischen Alexanderromans." *Zetemeta* 9. 2nd edn., 1977.

(1989) "Der Brief des Dareios im Getty-Museum und Alexanders Wortwechsel mit Parmenion." *ZPE* 77: 277–80.

Merkle, S. (1996) "The Truth and Nothing But the Truth: Dictys and Dares," in G. Schmeling, ed., *The Novel in the Ancient World*. Leiden, 564–80.

Meyer, C. (1955) *Die Urkunden in Geschichtswerk des Thukydides*. Munich.

Momigliano, A. (1966) *Studies in Historiography*. London.

Monaco, G. (1965) "L'epistola nel theatro antico." *Dioniso* 39: 334–51.

Montevecchi, O. (1953) ed., *Papyri Bononiensis*, vol. 1. Milan.

Morgan, J. R. (1993) "Make-Believe and Make Believe," in C. Gill and T. P. Wiseman, eds., *Lies and Fiction in the Ancient World*. Austin, TX, 175–229.

Morgan, J. R. and R. Stoneman (1994) eds., *Greek Fiction: The Greek Novel in Context*. London.

Morgan, T. (1998) *Literate Education in the Hellenistic and Roman Worlds*. Cambridge.

Müller, W. G. (1980) "Der Brief als Spiegel der Seele: Zur Geschichte eines Topos der Epistolartheorie von der antike bis zu Samuel Richardson." *A&A* 26: 138–57.

Münscher, K. (1907) "Die Philostrate." *Philologus Suppl.* 10: 467–557.

Murray, O. (1990) "The Idea of the Shepherd King from Cyrus to Charlemagne," in P. Godman and O. Murray eds., *Latin Poetry and the Classical Tradition*. Oxford.

Nauck, A. (1889) ed., *Tragicorum Graecorum Fragmenta*, 2nd edn. Leipzig.

Niessing, W. (1929) *De Themistoclis epistulis*. Freiburg.

Novakovic, D. (1982) "L'Invention dans la littérature épistolaire antique." *L&G* 20: 69–121.

Nylander, C. (1968) "Assuria Grammata: Remarks on the 21st 'Letter of Themistokles'." *Opuscula Atheniensia* 8: 119–36.

Olsson, B. (1925) *Papyrusbriefe aus der frühesten Römerzeit*. Uppsala.

Ong, W. J. (1982) *Orality and Literacy*. London.

Oppel, E. (1968) *Ovids Heroides: Studien zur inneren Form und zur Motivation*. Erlangen-Nürenburg.

Osborne, R. (1994) "On Looking – Greek Style. Does the Sculpted Girl Speak to Women Too?" in I. Morris, ed., *Classical Greece: Ancient Histories and Modern Archaeologies*. Cambridge, 81–96.

Page, D. L. (1934) *Actors' Interpolations in Greek Tragedy*. Oxford.

(1978) *The Epigrams of Rufinus*. Cambridge.

(1981) ed., *Further Greek Epigrams*. Cambridge.

Paoli, U. E. (1923) "Sulla corrispondenza amorosa degli antiche." *Studi Italiani di Filologia Classica*. 3: 251–57.

Parker, R. (1983) *Miasma*. Oxford.

Paton, W. R. (1916) *The Greek Anthology, Books 1–6*. Loeb Classical Library, repr. 1993. Cambridge, MA.

Penella, R. J. (1979) *The Letters of Apollonius of Tyana: A Critical Text with Prolegomena, Translation, and Commentary*. Leiden.

Penwill, J. L. (1978) "The *Letters* of Themistocles: An Epistolary Novel?" *Antichthon* 12: 83–103.

Perrin, B. (1920) *Plutarch's Lives*. London.

Perry, B. E. (1955) "Literature in the Second Century." *CJ* 50: 295–98.

(1967) *The Ancient Romances*. Berkeley.

Perry, R. (1980) *Women, Letters, and the Novel*. New York.

Peter, H. (1965) *Der Brief in der römischen Literatur*. Hildesheim (repr. of Leipzig, 1901).

Petrucci, A. (1993) *Public Lettering*. Chicago.

Pfeiffer, R. (1949) *Callimachus*, 2 vols. Oxford.

(1968) *A History of Classical Scholarship I*. Oxford.

Philippson, R. (1928) "Verfasser und Abfassungszeit der sogenannten Hippokratesbriefe." *RhM* 77: 293–328.

Platnauer, M. (1938) *Euripides' Iphigenia in Tauris*. Oxford.

Plepelits, K. (1976) *Chariton von Aphrodisias: Kallirhoe*. Stuttgart.

Podlecki, A. J. (1975) *The Life of Themistocles*. Montreal.

Pollitt, J. J. (1990) *The Art of Ancient Greece: Sources and Documents*. Cambridge.

Preston, J. (1970) *The Created Self: The Reader's Role in Eighteenth-Century Fiction.* New York.

Rabe, H. (1909) "Aus Rhetoren-Handschriften: Griechische Briefsteller." *RhM* 64: 284–309.

Rattenbury, R. M., T. W. Lumb, and J. Maillon (1943) eds. and trans., *Héliodore: Les Ethiopiques,* 3 vols. Paris, 2nd edn. 1960.

Reardon, B. P. (1969) "The Greek Novel." *Phoenix* 23: 291–309.

(1971) *Courants littéraires grecs des IIe et IIIe siècles après J.-C.* Paris.

(1974) "The Second Sophistic and the Novel," in G. Bowersock, ed., *Approaches to the Second Sophistic.* University Park, PA, 23–39.

(1976) "Aspects of the Greek Novel." *Greece and Rome* 23: 118–31.

(1982) "Theme, Structure, and Narrative in Chariton." *YCS* 27: 1–27.

(1989) *Collected Ancient Greek Novels.* Berkeley.

(1991) *The Form of Greek Romance.* Princeton.

Reich, H. (1894) *De Alciphronis Longique aetate.* Königsberg.

Reuters, F. H. (1963) *Die Briefe des Anacharsis.* Berlin.

Ribbeck, O. (1884) "Agroikos: eine ethologische Studie." *ASG* 9: 3–113.

Richardson, S. (1985) ed. A. Ross, *Clarissa.* London.

Richlin, A. (1992) ed., *Pornography and Representation in Ancient Greece and Rome.* New York.

Rimmon-Kenan, S. (1983) *Narrative Fiction.* London and New York.

Roberts, W. (1843) *History of Letter Writing from the Earliest Period to the 5th Century.* London.

Roberts, W. J. (1902) *Demetrius on Style.* Cambridge.

Rohde, E. (1960) *Der Griechische Roman und seine Vorläufer,* 4th edn. Hildesheim.

Romberg, B. (1962) *Studies in the Narrative Technique of the First-Person Novel.* Stockholm.

Romm, J. S. (1992) *The Edges of the Earth in Ancient Thought.* Princeton.

Rosbottom, R. C. (1977) "Motifs in Epistolary Fiction: Analysis of a Narrative Subgenre." *L'Esprit créateur* 17: 279–301.

(1978) *Choderlos de Laclos.* Boston.

Rosen, R. and J. Farrell. (1986) "Acontius, Milanion, and Gallus: Vergil *Ecl.* 10.52–61." *TAPA* 116: 241–54.

Rosenmeyer, P. A. (1992) *The Poetics of Imitation: Anacreon and the Anacreontic Tradition.* Cambridge.

(1994) "The Epistolary Novel," in J. R. Morgan and R. Stoneman, eds., *Greek Fiction: The Greek Novel in Context.* London and New York, 146–65.

(1996) "Love Letters in Callimachus, Ovid, and Aristaenetus, or, The Sad Fate of a Mail-order Bride." *MD* 36: 9–31.

(1997) "Ovid's *Heroides* and *Tristia*: Voices from Exile." *Ramus* 26: 29–56.

(1998) "Her Master's Voice: Sappho's Dialogue with Homer." *MD* 39: 123–49.

(2000) "(In)versions of Pygmalion: The Statue Talks Back," in L. McClure and A. Lardinois, eds., *Women's Voices in Ancient Greek Literature and Society*. Princeton.

Rösler, W. (1980) "Die Entdeckung der Fiktionalität in der Antike." *Poetica* 12: 283–319.

Ross, D. O. (1975) *Backgrounds to Augustan Poetry: Gallus, Elegy, and Rome*. Cambridge.

Rousset, J. (1962) *Forme et Signification*. Paris.

    (1964) "Le Roman par lettres." *Forme et signification. Essais sur les structures littéraires de Corneille à Claudel*. Paris, 65–108.

    (1973) "La Monodie épistolaire: Crébillon fils," in *Narcisse romancier: Essai sur la première personne dans le roman*. Paris, 114–26.

Russell, D. A. (1983) *Greek Declamation*. Cambridge.

    (1988) "The Ass in the Lion's Skin: Thoughts on the Letters of Phalaris." *JHS* 180: 94–106.

Russell, D. A. and M. Winterbottom (1972) eds., *Ancient Literary Criticism*. Oxford.

Rütten, T. (1992) *Demokrit: lachender Philosoph und sanguinischer Melancholiker. Mnemosyne*, Supplements. Leiden.

Sakalis, D. T. (1989) ed., *Hippokratous Epistolai*. Joannina.

Santini, L. (1995) "Tra Filosofi e Parassiti: L'Epistola III. 19 di Alcifrone e i modelli Lucianei." *Atene e Roma* 40: 58–71.

Schenkeveld, D. M. (1964) *Studies in Demetrius On Style*. Amsterdam.

    (1992) "Prose Usages of AKOUEIN 'To Read'." *CQ* 42: 129–41.

Schepers, M. A. (1969) ed., *Alciphron*, reprint of 1905 edn. Stuttgart.

Schmeling, G. (1996) ed., *The Novel in the Ancient World*. Leiden.

Schneider, J. (1954) "Brief." *Reallexicon für Antike und Christentum*, vol. II. Stuttgart, 564–85.

Scobie, A. (1969) *Aspects of the Ancient Romance and its Heritage*. Meisenheim am Glan, rev. 1973.

Sebeok, T. A. (1960) ed., *Style in Language*. Cambridge, MA.

Segal, C. (1981) *Tragedy and Civilization*. Cambridge, MA.

    (1982) "Tragédie, oralité, écriture." *Poétique* 50: 131–54.

    (1986) *Interpreting Greek Tragedy; Myth, Poetry, Text*. Ithaca.

    (1987) *La Musique du Sphinx: poésie et structure dans la tragédie grecque*. Paris.

    (1992) "Signs, Magic, and Letters in Euripides' *Hippolytus*," in R. Hexter and D. Selden, eds., *Innovations in Antiquity*. New York, 420–56.

Selden, D. L. (1994) "Genre of Genre," in J. Tatum, ed., *The Search for the Ancient Novel*. Baltimore, 39–64.

Seylaz, J.-L. (1958) *Les "Liaisons dangereuses" et la création romanesque chez Laclos*. Geneva.

Sharrock, A. (1991) "Womanufacture." *JRS* 81: 36–49.

Showalter, E. (1985) ed., *The New Feminist Criticism*. New York.

Showalter, E., Jr. (1986) "Authorial Self-consciousness and the Familiar Letter: The Case of Madame de Graffigny." *YFS* 71: 113–30.

Showerman, G. (1977) *Ovid: Heroides and Amores*, vol. 1. 2nd edn. rev. G. Goold. Cambridge, MA.

Singer, G. F. (1963) *The Epistolary Novel.* New York.

Smith, R. A. (1994) "Fantasy, Myth, and Love Letters: Text and Tale in Ovid's *Heroides.*" *Arethusa* 27: 247–73.

Smith, W. D. (1990) ed. and tr., *Hippocrates: Pseudepigraphic Writings.* Leiden.

Snowdon, K. (1970) *Blacks in Antiquity.* Cambridge, MA.

Solmsen, F. (1940) "Some Works of Philostratus the Elder." *TAPA* 71: 566–72.

Solodow, J. B. (1988) *The World of Ovid's Metamorphoses.* Chapel Hill.

Speyer, W. (1971) *Die literarische Fälschung im heidnischen und christlichen Altertum.* Munich.

   (1974) "Zum Bild des Apollonios von Tyana bei Heiden un Christen." *Jahrbuch für Antike und Christentum* 17: 47–63.

Stählin, O. (1960) tr., *Clemens Alexandrinus Stromata Buch I–VI*, vol. II, 3rd edn. Berlin.

Steen, H. A. (1938) "Les Clichés épistolaires dans les lettres sur papyrus grecques." *Classica et Mediaevalia* 1: 119–76.

Stehle, E. and A. Day. (1996) "Women Looking at Women: Women's Ritual and Temple Sculpture," in N. B. Kampen, ed., *Sexuality in Ancient Art.* Cambridge, 101–16.

Steiner, D. T. (1994) *The Tyrant's Writ.* Princeton.

Stephens, S. A. (1994) "Who Read Ancient Novels?", in J. Tatum, ed., *The Search for the Ancient Novel.* Baltimore, 405–18.

   and J. J. Winkler (1995) eds., *Ancient Greek Novels: The Fragments.* Princeton.

Stewart, A. (1997) *Art, Desire and the Body in Ancient Greece.* Cambridge.

Stirewalt, M. L., Jr. (1993) *Studies in Ancient Greek Epistolography.* Atlanta.

Stoneman, R. (1991) tr., *The Greek Alexander Romance.* London.

   (1994) "The Alexander Romance," in J. R. Morgan and R. Stoneman, eds., *Greek Fiction: The Greek Novel in Context.* London, 117–29.

   (1996) "The Metamorphoses of the *Alexander Romance*," in Schmeling, ed., *The Novel in the Ancient World.* Leiden, 601–12.

Stowers, S. K. (1986) *Letter Writing in Greco-Roman Antiquity.* Philadelphia, PA.

Susemihl, F. (1891–92) *Geschichte der griechischen Litteratur in der Alexandrinerzeit*, 2 vols. Leipzig.

Sutton, R. F. (1992) "Pornography and Persuasion on Attic Pottery," in A. Richlin, ed., *Pornography and Representation in Ancient Greece and Rome.* New York, 3–35.

Svenbro, J. (1988) *Phrasikleia.* Paris.

   (1990) "The 'Interior' Voice: On the Invention of Silent Reading." in F. I. Zeitlin and J. J. Winkler, eds., *Nothing to Do with Dionysos?* Princeton, 366–84.

Swain, S. (1996) *Hellenism and Empire.* Oxford.

Sykutris, J. (1928–29) "Proklos Peri epistolimaiou characteros." *Byzantinisch-Neugriechische Jahrbücher* 7: 108–18.

(1931) "Epistolographie." *RE suppl.* 5: 185–220.

(1933) *Die Briefe des Sokrates und die Sokrater.* Studien zur Geschichte und Kultur des Altertums 18. Paderborn.

Syme, R. (1972) "Fraud and Imposture." *Pseudepigrapha* 1 (Entretiens sur l'antiquité classique, Fondation Hardt 18). Geneva, 3–17.

Taplin, O. (1978) *Greek Tragedy in Action.* Berkeley.

Tatum, J. (1994) ed., *The Search for the Ancient Novel.* Baltimore.

Taylor, A. R. (1981) *Male Novelists and their Female Voices: Literary Masquerades.* Troy, New York.

Testud, P. (1966) "Les Lettres persanes, roman épistolaire." *RHLF* 66: 642–56.

Thomas, R. (1989) *Oral Tradition and Written Record in Classical Athens.* Cambridge and New York.

(1992) *Literacy and Orality in Ancient Greece.* Cambridge and New York.

Thraede, K. (1970) *Grundzüge griechisch-römischer Brieftopik.* (*Zetemata* 48) Munich.

Todorov, T. (1966a) "Catégories du récit littéraire." *Communications* 8: 125–51.

(1966b) "Choderlos de Laclos et la théorie du récit." *Tel Quel* 27: 17–28.

(1967) *Littérature et signification.* Paris, 39–49.

(1970) "The Discovery of Language: *Les Liaisons dangereuses* and *Adolphe.*" *Yale French Studies* 45: 113–26.

(1977) *The Poetics of Prose,* tr. Richard Howard. Ithaca.

Too, Y. L. (1966) "Statues, Mirrors, Gods: Controlling Images in Apuleius," in J. Elsner, ed., *Art and Text in Roman Culture.* Cambridge, 133–52.

Tracy, V. (1971) "The Authenticity of *Heroides* 16–21." *CJ* 66: 328–30.

Trumpf, J. (1960) "Kydonische Äpfel." *Hermes* 88: 14–22.

Tsirimbas, D. A. (1936) *Sprichwörter und sprichwörtliche Redensarten bei den Epistolographen den zweiten Sophistik.* Speyer am Rhein.

Tudeer, L. O. T. (1931) *The Epistles of Phalaris: Preliminary Investigation of the Manuscripts.* Helsinki.

Tylawsky, E. I. (1991) "Saturio's Inheritance: the Greek Ancestry of the Roman Comic Parasite." Dissertation, Yale University.

Ussher, R. G. (1987) "Love Letter, Novel, Alciphron, and 'Chion'." *Hermathena* 143: 99–106.

(1988) "Letter-Writing," in M. Grant and R. Kitzinger, eds., *Civilization of the Ancient Mediterranean,* vol. III. New York, 1573–82.

Verducci, F. (1985) *Ovid's Toyshop of the Heart.* Princeton.

Versini, L. (1979) *Le Roman épistolaire.* Paris.

Vieillefond, J.-R. (1929) "La Lettre II.1 d'Alciphron et la *Chasse* de Xénophon." *RPh* 55: 354–57.

Vinogradov, Y. G. (1971) "Drevneisheye grecheskoye pismo s ostrova Berezan." *VDI* 118: 74–100.

Walker, A. (1992) "Eros and the Eye in the Love-Letters of Philostratus." *PCPS* 38: 132–48.

Warnecke, B. (1906) "De Alexidis ΟΠΩΡΑ." *Hermes* 41: 158–59.

Warner, W. B. (1979) *Reading Clarissa: The Struggle of Interpretation.* New Haven.

Watt, I. P. (1957) *The Rise of the Novel.* Berkeley, CA.

Weichert, V. (1910) ed., *Demetrii et Libanii qui feruntur "Typoi epistolikoi" et "Epistolimaioi characteres."* Leipzig.

Weinreich, O. (1962) *Der griechische Liebesroman.* Zurich.

Welles, C. B. (1934) *Royal Correspondence in the Hellenistic Period.* London.

Wesseling, B. (1988) "The Audience of the Ancient Novels," in H. Hofmann, ed., *Groningen Colloquia on the Novel,* vol. 1. Groningen, 67–79.

West, S. (1985) "Herodotus' Epigraphical Interests." *CQ* 35: 278–305.

White, J. L. (1986) *Light from Ancient Letters.* Philadelphia, PA.

Whitehead, D. (1990) tr., *Aineias the Tactician: How to Survive under Siege.* Oxford.

Whitman, C. (1974) *Euripides and the Full Circle of Myth.* Cambridge, MA.

Wilamowitz-Moellendorff, U. von (1889) "Unechte Briefe." *Hermes* 33: 492–98.

(1893) *Aristoteles und Athen,* vol. 1. Berlin.

Wilkinson, L. P. (1955) *Ovid Recalled.* Cambridge.

Wilson, N. G. (1983) *Scholars of Byzantium.* Baltimore.

Winkler, J. J. (1982) "The Mendacity of Kalasiris and the Narrative Strategy of Heliodorus' *Aithiopika.*" *YCS* 27: 93–158.

(1985) *Auctor et Actor: A Narratological Reading of Apuleius' Golden Ass.* Berkeley.

Winkler, J. J. and F. I. Zeitlin (1990) eds., *Nothing to Do with Dionysos?* Princeton.

Wissowa, G. (1894–1959) ed., *Paulys Real-Encyclopädie der classischen Altertumswissenschaft: neue Bearbeitung.* Stuttgart.

Witowski, S. (1906) *Epistulae privatae Graecae.* Leipzig.

Wohl, V. (1998) "Plato avant la lettre: Authenticity in Plato's Epistles." *Ramus* 27: 60–93.

Wright, F. A. (1932) *A History of Later Greek Literature.* London.

Yale French Studies 71 (1986) on "Men and Women of Letters."

Zeitlin, F. I. (1985) "The Power of Aphrodite: Eros and Boundaries of the Self in *Hippolytus,*" in P. Burian, ed., *Directions in Euripidean Criticism.* Durham, NC, 52–111.

(1996) "Playing the Other: Theater, Theatricality and the Feminine in Greek Drama," in F. I. Zeitlin, ed., *Playing the Other.* Chicago, 341–74.

Zilliacus, H. (1949) *Untersuchungen zu den abstrakten Anredeformen und Höflichkeitstiteln im Griechischen.* Helsingfors.

Zweig, B. (1992) "The Mute Nude Female Characters in Aristophanes' Plays," in A. Richlin, ed., *Pornography and Representation in Ancient Greece and Rome.* New York, 73–89.

Index

Achaeus
  Omphale fr.33   63 n.9
Achilles Tatius
  Leucippe and
    Clitophon
    1.1–3   147–48
    2.31   148
    4.11   149 n.23
    5.7   148
    5.10–12   148–49
    5.18–20   150–52
    5.24–25   152–53
Aelian   308–21, 343
  De Natura   308
    Animalium
  Varia Historia   308
  Letters from Farmers   262
    1, 2   309–11
    3   314
    4, 5   309–10
    6   314–15
    7   309, 318
    8, 9   309, 318–21
    11   269 n.27, 309, 317–18
    12, 13, 14, 15, 16   309, 315–17
    17   314
    18, 19   320–21
    20   263, 308, 310, 312–14, 321
Aeneas Tacticus
  31.17   48 n.9
Aeschylus
  fr. 293   62 n.7
  Eumenides
    275   62 n.6, 117 n.39
  Libation Bearers
    450   62 n.6, 117 n.39
  Prometheus Bound
    460–61   26, 61
    789   62 n.6, 117 n.39

  Seven against Thebes
    103   92 n.67
  Suppliants
    178–79, 991–92   62 n.6, 117 n.39
    946–49   62 n.5, 71
Alcaeus,
  fr.332   236
Alciphron
  Letters, general   255–307, 319–20, 324, 340, 343
  Letters, individual
    1.1   267 n.25, 268–69
    1.2   278
    1.3   278, 285, 320 n.16
    1.4   288
    1.6   289, 291
    1.8   278, 287
    1.9   286
    1.11, 12   260–61, 277, 291–92, 297
    1.13, 14, 15   262, 269, 278
    1.16   291–92
    1.17, 18, 19   294 n.48, 315
    1.20   278
    1.21, 22   262, 291–93
    2.1   267 n.25, 269–70
    2.2   270, 278, 286
    2.3   262, 278
    2.4   285, 320 n.16
    2.5   278
    2.6, 7   291, 293, 307
    2.8   288
    2.9   278–79
    2.13, 14   287
    2.15, 16   279, 312 n.9
    2.17   287
    2.18, 20   278–79
    2.21, 22, 23   278, 289, 291
    2.24, 25   291, 294, 320
    2.28   260, 287
    2.29   279–80

Alciphron (*cont.*)
2.31   291
2.32   286, 315
2.33   278
2.34   286
2.35, 36   278, 310 n.7
2.37   287–88
3.1   267 n.25, 271, 281
3.2   281
3.3   272, 281
3.4   282, 289
3.5   295
3.6, 7, 9, 10   281–82
3.11, 12, 13   272, 281–82
3.14   296
3.15, 17, 18, 19   281–82
3.21   272, 281
3.23   299
3.24   281
3.25   262, 281
3.26   295, 299
3.27   295
3.28   282, 296
3.29, 30   272, 281–82
3.31   289, 295, 297
3.32   272, 281
3.33   296
3.34   286 n.42, 289–90
3.35   289
3.36   265, 307
3.37   272, 281
3.38   281
3.39   299
3.41   275 n.32
3.42   281
4.1   262, 267 n.25, 272–
                74ff., 301 n.53, 310
4.2, 3, 4, 5   262, 272–73, 310
4.6   273–74, 299
4.7   262, 273, 282–83
4.8, 9, 10   273–74, 282–84,
                299–300, 319, 340
4.11   259, 274, 299
4.12   274, 282
4.13, 14   259, 262, 273–74,
                275 n.32, 299, 341
4.15   284, 300, 319
4.16   273–74, 284, 300
4.17   259, 262, 273, 282–
                83, 299–300, 307
4.18, 19   259, 262, 266, 273,
                301–02, 303–06
Alexander Romance   190–91, 169–92,
                251–52, 342
1.23   175, 177

1.35–36   172, 175, 177
1.37–38   178–179, 187 n.27
1.39–42   180–82
2.8   181
2.11–12   182
2.13–15   186 n.26
2.16   183
2.19   182 n.22
2.20–22   172, 183–84
2.23–41   173, 190
2.26   188
3.2–5   172–73, 184 n.23
3.18   173, 185
3.19–22   185–86
3.25–29   173, 187–88
3.27   189–90
3.27–30   173 n.14
3.30–33   181, 190–91
Alexis
    Opora   318 n.15
Altman, J.   69, 75
Anacharsis
    Letters   209–17
    1–10   209 n.40, 212
    1   210, 212
    2   211
    3–4, 8   213
    5, 6   214
    7   211–13
    9, 10   214
Anacreontic 22 333 n.12
Anderson, G.   259
Anthologia Palatina
    5.9   105 n.14, 107
    5.80   108
    5.90–91   102–03
    6.227, 229, 261   102–05, 109, 279
                n.38
    7.77, 516   102 n.8
    9.341   127 n.62
    9.401   19
    11.44   105–06
    12.130   127 n.62
    12.150   115 n.34
    12.208   67 n.20
Antiphanes
    Sappho fr.194   96
    The Rustic 256
    Timon   315
Antiphon
    5.53–56   31
Antonius Diogenes
    The Incredible   156, 200
    Things Beyond
    Thule

Apollonius King of
  Tyre, Story of
  20–21   155–56
  26   161 n.38
Aristaenetus   112–16, 121–23,
                         126–30, 339–40,
                         346
  Erotic Letters
  1.1, 1.5   339
  1.6   340, 346
  1.10   113–16, 121–23, 127–
                         29, 340
  1.14   340
  1.17   331 n.10
  1.25   340
  2.1   318 n.15
Aristophanes
  Acharnians   256
  Clouds   285 n.41
  Frogs 1043ff.   90 n.63
  Thesmo. 768–84   64
Aristotle
  Poetics   72–73
Athenaeus
  Deipnosophistae
  10.450e–451b   96
  13   262
  13.590f–591a   276 n.37
Atossa   25–28, 49, 186
Augustine
  Letters 15.1   22
Ausonius
  Ep. 14.74   96 n.77

Barthes, R.   127
Basil
  Letter 9   4
Bellerophon   25, 28, 40–44, 49,
                         55, 60, 133, 154,
                         181, 240–41, 252,
                         344–45
Bentley, R.   195
Berezan, letter from   29–30, 77
Bonner, C.   308–09
Bowie, E. L.   257, 309

Callimachus   110–15, 121–22, 126–
                         30, 340
  Aetia
  46–47   225 n.69
  67   111–15
  72, 73   126
  75   112–13, 128
  Ep. 46   115 n.34
Castle, T.   247–48

Catullus
  13   106 n.16
Chariton   137–47, 154, 235, 344
  Chaereas and
    Callirhoe
  1.1   137
  4.4–7   139, 141–42
  5.1   150
  5.2, 5.4, 5.6   142–43
  6.2   143
  8.4–5   78 n.39, 144–46
  12.131   150
Charondas   26
Chiliades
  11.45   257 n.5
Chion of Heraclea
  Letters, general   194, 202, 216, 234–
                         52, 325, 343–45
  Letters, individual
  1   237–38, 245–47
  2   238, 242, 245–47
  3   235, 238, 245–47,
                         248–49
  4   238, 243, 245–47
  5   239, 245–47
  6   239, 240, 242, 245–
                         46
  7   239–40, 242–47
  8   239–42, 244–47
  9   239, 241–42, 246
  10   226, 239, 245
  11   239, 242, 246–47
  12   239, 242–43, 245,
                         247
  13   239, 243, 245–48
  14   243, 245–46
  15   244–47
  16   244, 245–47, 249
  17   191, 239, 244–45
Cicero
  Ad Att.
  9.4   236
  11.4   152 n.28
  Ad Fam.
  2.4.1   206 n.34, 246
  3.11.2   153 n.29
  12.30.1   246
  16.16.2   74 n.28, 246
  Tusc. Disp.
  5.32.90   210
Clement of
  Alexandria
  Stromateis
  1.16.76   24–25
  1.16.77   210 n.42

Crates   221–24
Letters
1   222, 224
8   222
28–33   222–24
Cratinus
fr. 316   64
fr. 128   71
Deissmann, A.   5–7
ps.-Demetrius
Epistolary Types   203 n.31, 206 n.33, 241 n.9
"Demetrius"
On Style
223   246, 247 n.13
223–35   102 n.10
227   4, 74 n.28, 198, 246
228   59, 220, 246
230–31   250 n.17
232   316
234   164 n.43
292   226
Democritus (and   217–21
Hippocrates)
Letters
3, 5, 7   205
10–14, 16, 17   218–20
18–21, 24, 26, 27   219–20
1–21   220 n.62
Demosthenes
Against Phormio   51 n.15
Against Kallikles   314, 314 n.11
Diodorus Siculus
1.95   52 n.16
3.3   159 n.36
12.13.2   26
Diogenes Laertius
1.105   210 n.42
6.80   221
6.98   221
Diogenes   206, 221–24
Letters
3   222, 223
17   223
22   205
40, 49   206
Dionysius of
Halicarnassus
On Thuc. 42   59
Doty, W. G.   8–9
Dowden, K.   170
Epic, letters in   39–44
Epictetus
4.1.29–31, 156   221

Epistolae Senecae et   217 n.55
Pauli
ethopoieia   197, 235, 252, 260–63, 266, 284, 306–07, 315
Euripides   61–97, 342–45
Alcestis 304ff.   89 n.57
Hippolytus
856–65   72, 88–89
866–75   91
877–86   72, 91–92
944   93 n.71
958–61, 971ff.   93
985   62 n.6
1022–77   93
1253ff.   93
1320–23, 1336ff.   93 n.73
Iphigenia at Aulis
34–40   80
97–123   72, 81–83
119, 128   84
124–26   81
138   83 n.50
153–56   83 n.50, 84
164–302   85
308, 318ff.   85
358–64   86
Iphigenia at Tauris
582–90   73
641–42   72
760–93   72, 76–79, 105 n.14
Palamedes
fr. 578.3–5   26, 61, 64
Theseus
fr. 382   63, 345 n.7
Trojan Women
fr. 506.2–3, 661   62 n.6
Gildon, Charles
Post Boy Rob'd of   200 n.24
His Mail
Glycera   301–06
Gorgias
82B 11a30   26
Helen 17   62 n.6
Gregory of
Nazianzus
Epistles
51.4   316
51.1–5   246
Gudeman, A.   199
Gurney, A.   66
Hecataeus
FGrH 1F20   26

Heliodorus 157–68
  Aithiopika
  1.10–11 157
  2.6, 10–11, 23, 33 157–59
  4.5–8, 12 159–61
  5.9 162
  7.24 162 n.41
  8.3, 15; 9.1 163
  9.24, 10.4 165
  10.1–22 163–64, 166–67
  10.34, 36 167
  10.41 138
Hellenistic period
  poetic letters in 98–130
  practical letters in 98–100
Heraclitus
  Letters 6, 9 206
Herodas
  Mimes
  1 31, 99
  3 99
Herodotus 47–54, 138, 341
  Histories
  1.8–12 53
  1.99 25 n.14
  1.123–25 47–48
  2.36 159 n.36
  2.53 45
  3.40–45 29, 50 n.13, 51–52, 54, 78 n.39
  3.126–28 50
  4.76 210
  4.127 316 n.13
  4.131 177 n.18
  5.14 51 n.14, 54
  5.35 48
  5.55, 57–61 26, 236
  6.4 51
  6.109, 123 236
  7.239 22, 48–49
  8.19–22 52, 59
  8.128 50 n.12
Hesiod
  Works and Days
  60–105 49
  346 315
Hipparchia 221–24
Hippocrates 205, 217–21
Historiography, 45–60
  letters in
Holzberg, N. 196–97, 215–17, 220, 230–33, 240
Homer
  Iliad
  2.876, 6.167–70, 40
  6.177

6.168–70 22, 28
7.183–89 41
9.453 257 n.5
13.5–6 214 n.49
24.348 330 n.9
  Odyssey
  10.156–73 269
  10.279 330 n.9
Horace
  Odes 1.20.1–2 106 n.16
Hughes, T. 2

Iamblichus
  Babyloniaka 154 n.31
Isaios
  fr. 10 (43) 314 n.10

Jones, C. P. 258
Julian
  7.212D 221
Julius Victor
  Ars Rhet. 27 241 n.9, 246

Kenney, E. J. 128
Kindstrand, J. F. 210
Koskenniemi, H. 8

Laclos, Choderlos de 65, 67
Lesbonax 26
letters
  apple as 108–30, 161, 333–35
  Christian 340–41
  conventions of 13, 29–30, 33–34, 58, 77–78, 83–84, 103–05, 107, 149–50, 175–77, 182–84, 192, 206–08, 211, 216–17, 237–38, 249, 263–64, 273–75, 311, 324–25
  courtroom use of 30–31, 142–43
  deathbed 190–91
  decorum and 2–3
  definition of 5–12, 19–24, 57–60, 62–63, 109–10, 221
  delivery systems of 23–24, 47–50
  dialogue vs. 262–66, 330–32
  friendship and 44, 51–52, 241–42
  gifts and 100–05, 240, 318, 325–27, 334
  immediacy in 3–4, 74
  invention of 24–27
  invitations 105–06
  kinetic vs. static 65–66, 88, 137, 172–73, 188, 342

letters (*cont.*)
love and ... 69, 106–30, 154–56, 277, 284, 291–300, 322–38, 344
materiality of ... 22–23
physical marks on ... 139–40
pseudonymous ... 193–233, 343–45
schools and ... 32–34, 197–99, 235, 252, 259–60, 345
temporality in ... 70, 74–76, 118, 122–23, 205, 239, 265, 274
treachery and ... 27–28, 43–44, 45–60, 71, 110–30, 133, 168, 181, 186
unity and order of ... 215–17, 220–31, 245, 259, 272–73, 309–10, 321, 329, 337
verisimilitude in ... 35, 85, 102 n.8, 104, 108, 137, 168, 200, 204, 211–12, 219, 225, 237, 246, 248, 269, 274–75, 307, 314, 318–19, 332, 341
women and ... 25–27, 43–44, 49, 74 n.28, 87–88, 91 n.64, 95–97, 184–89, 266, 273, 276–77, 342
ps.-Libanius
Epistolary Styles ... 203 n.31, 206 n.33, 241 n.9, 246, 275, 322
Livy
Ab urbe condita
40.29.3–14 ... 201 n.26
Longus
Daphnis and Chloe
1.8.1 ... 136 n.8
4.17.3–7 ... 297 n.50
Lucian ... 118–19, 133–34, 171, 256, 258–59, 263–66, 281, 308
Amor. 16 ... 127 n.62
Anacharsis ... 210
Cock ... 270
De Parasito ... 262
Dialogues of the Courtesans
2 ... 262, 264, 282 n.39
8 ... 265
10 ... 265, 297 n.51
13 ... 265, 286 n.43
Dialogues of the Sea Gods

7 ... 118–19
How to Write History ... 135 n.4
Nigrinus ... 135 n.4
Passing of Peregrinus ... 135 n.4
Phalaris 1, 2 ... 225 n.69
Timon ... 315
Verae Historiae ... 225, n.69
2.29 ... 133
2.35 ... 78 n.39, 134
Lucretius
De Rerum Natura 4 ... 293 n.47
Menander ... 301–07, 317
Dyskolos ... 315
Epitrepontes ... 64
The Fisherman ... 256
Georgos ... 311 n.8
Leukadia ... 261 n.19
Misoumenos ... 64
Sententiae ... 27
Sikyonios ... 64
New Comedy ... 267, 271, 281, 285–86, 292 n.45, 308, 315, 319
novels, letters in ... 68–69, 133–68, 272, 342–45
Nylander, C. ... 232
Ovid ... 12, 14–15, 44, 74–75, 113–14, 116, 123–26, 128–30, 256, 266, 277, 306, 341, 346
Ars Amatoria
1. 457–58 ... 113 n.30
3.507–08 ... 331 n.10
3.625ff. ... 48 n.9
Heroides
4 ... 91 n.66
15 ... 150 n.25
20, 21 ... 113, 116, 124–26, 129
Remedia Amoris
381–82 ... 113 n.30
Tristia
1.1 ... 105 n.14
3.11 ... 225 n.69
5.13 ... 98, 107 n.19, 341
Palamedes ... 26, 43, 64
paraclausithyron ... 274, 283
Parthenius
Erotika Pathemata ... 113
pastoral ... 278–80, 290
Penwill, J. L. ... 232

Phalaris | 224–31, 345
  Letters
  2, 3, 8, 13, 14, 18– | 226
    20, 23, 24, 30,
    40, 59, 67–69,
    78–80, 89, 103,
    119, 128, 131,
    135, 142–46
  25 | 227 n.73
  55 | 205
  59 | 227–28
  80 | 227–28
  88, 92, 93, 108– | 226 n.71
    09, 121, 147
  117 | 205
  131 | 227
  135 | 227 n.73, 228
  142–43 | 226, 227 n.73, 228–
      29
Philostratus | 119–20, 207, 322–38,
     343
  Apollonius of Tyana,
    Letters of
  11 | 206
  19, 49 | 207
  62 | 205
  83, 86, 100 | 213
  Apollonius of Tyana,
    Life of
  4.27, 7.35 | 207, 322
  Erotic Epistles
  1–2 | 323, 326–27
  3–39, 46, 50, 54– | 323
    64
  4 | 326–27
  5, 23, 39, 48, 57 | 333
  6, 14, 35, 45, 65– | 325
    69, 70–71
  7, 8 | 328, 329 n.8, 336
  13–15, 58 | 327, 330
  16, 30–33, 36, 47 | 329 n.8
  18 | 329 n.8, 332
  19, 38 | 328, 329 n.8
  22, 27, 40 | 328
  23, 28 | 328, 329 n.8, 336
  25, 28 | 331
  32–33, 36–37 | 324 n.4, 329 n.8,
     332
  39 | 333, 336
  40–45, 48, 51–53, | 324
    65–73
  47, 49 | 323–25, 333, 329
     n.8
  53 | 331 n.10
  62 | 119–20, 333–35
  Lives of the Sophists | 322

Pindar
  Olympian
  9.35 | 121 n.51
  10.1–3 | 62 n.6
  Pythian
  1.95–96 | 225
Plato | 236, 239, 242–44,
    251
  Epistles | 202, 227
  Phaedrus | 328 n.7
  274d–277a | 120
  274e–275e | 96 n.77
  275d–276a | 62 n.6
  Phil. 38e–39a | 62 n.6
  Resp. 1 | 213 n.46
  Symposium 203d7 | 115 n.34
Plautus
  Curculio | 22
  Rudens | 256
  Stichus | 271 n.29
Pliny the Elder
  Naturalis Historia
  13.27 | 43
  13.84–87 | 201 n.26
Pliny the Younger
  Epistles 8.24 | 258
Plutarch
  Life of Alexander | 175 n.15
  Life of Demetrius | 1
  Life of Numa | 201 n.26
  Life of Theseus | 344
  Moralia
  252a | 99
  254d | 99–100
  367a | 121 n.51
  790a–b | 98
  801c | 121 n.51
Poe, E. A. | 66
Polybius
  5.43, 50, 57, 61 | 99
Polycrates of Samos | 29, 51–52
progymnasmata | 259–60
Propertius
  1.18.22 | 127 n.62
  2.25.11 | 225 n.69
  3.23.3 | 22

Reardon, B. P. | 170, 259
Richardson, S.
  Clarissa | 4, 65, 74, 199, 233,
    247–48
Romm, J. | 170
Russell, D. A. | 225–26

Samuel
  2.11.14–17 | 40

Seneca
  Epistles
    40.1 — 74 n.28, 78, 151 n.27, 246
    75.1 — 246
Second Sophistic — 135–36, 194, 252, 256–59, 261, 266, 313, 322, 329, 336–37, 345
Sidonius
  Letter 4.13 — 341
skutale — 23, 55
Socratic Epistles — 201–02, 206–08
Sophocles
  Ajax — 62 n.7
  Antigone — 62 n.6
  Oedipus Coloneus — 62 n.7
  Philoctetes — 62 n.6
  Trachiniae — 62
Steiner, D. — 27–28, 41–42, 202–03
Stesichorus
  PMG 213 — 26
Stirewalt, L. — 9–10
Stoneman, R. — 170–71
Sykutris, J. — 8, 11–12
Syme, R. — 195–96
Synesius
  Letter 138c — 26–27

Tertullian
  De Corona 8.2 — 26
Themistocles
  Letters
    1–21 — 215, 231–33
    3 — 204
    6, 7, 14, 20 — 208–09
    8, 16 — 205
Theocritus
  Idylls
    7 — 108 n.22
    11 — 115 n.34, 293
    13 — 261 n.18

    18 — 127 n.62
    28 — 100–01
Theon — 33–34
Theophrastus
  Characters 24 — 31
Theophylactus — 340
Thucydides
  History of the Peloponnesian War
    1.20 — 236
    1.128–34 — 55–56
    1.136–37 — 56, 193, 231
    4.50 — 56
    6.53–59 — 236
    7.8–16 — 57–60
    8.33, 38–39, 50–51 — 56–57
Todorov, T. — 66–67
Tragedy
  letters in — 61–97
  epistolary devices in — 63–72
  tyrannicide — 23–37, 242–45, 247, 343

Virgil
  Eclogues
    1 — 260 n.17
    10 — 127 nn.62 and 63

Xenophon — 201, 235–38, 248–49
  Anabasis 1.6.3–5 — 51
  Cynegeticus 7.6–9 — 269 n.27
  Cyropaedia
    2.2.9; 4.5.26–34 — 46
  Memorabilia
    1.2.32ff. — 213 n.46
    6.3 283 n.40
Xenophon of Ephesus
  Ephesian Tale 2.3–6, 10 — 155, 235